Utamakura, Allusion, and Intertextuality in Traditional Japanese Poetry

Edward Kamens

Yale University Press

New Haven and London

Published with assistance from the Frederick W. Hilles Publication Fund of Yale University.

Printed in the United States of America by BookCrafters, Inc., Chelsea, Michigan.

Library of Congress Cataloging-in-Publication data

Kamens, Edward, 1952-
Utamakura, allusion, and intertextuality in traditional Japanese poetry / Edward Kamens.
   p.   cm.
Includes bibliographical references and index.
ISBN 0-300-06808-5 (cloth)
1. Waka—History and criticism. 2. Japanese poetry—History and criticism. 3. Allusions in literature. 4. Metaphor in literature. 5. Intertextuality. 6. Names, Geographical, in literature. 7. Literary landmarks—Japan. I. Title.
PL728
895.3'1009—dc21   96-44433 CIP

A catalogue record for this book is available from the British Library.

The paper in this book meets the guidelines for permanence and durability of the Committee on Production Guidelines for Book Longevity of the Council on Library Resources.

10 9 8 7 6 5 4 3 2 1

To the memory of Elizabeth Kamenetzky
and Beatrice Rosenberg

If it should be true that reality exists
In the mind: the tin plate, the loaf of bread on it,
The long-bladed knife, the little to drink and her
Misericordia, it follows that
Real and unreal are two in one: New Haven
Before and after one arrives, or, say,
Bergamo on a postcard, Rome after dark,
Sweden described, Salzburg with shaded eyes
Or Paris in conversation at a café.
This endlessly elaborating poem
Displays the theory of poetry,
As the life of poetry. A more severe,
More harassing master would extemporize
Subtler, more urgent proof that the theory
Of Poetry is the theory of life,
As it is, in the intricate evasions of as,
In things seen and unseen, created from nothingness,
The heavens, the hells, the worlds, the longed-for lands.
—Wallace Stevens, from "An Ordinary Evening in New Haven"

Contents

Illustrations

Tables

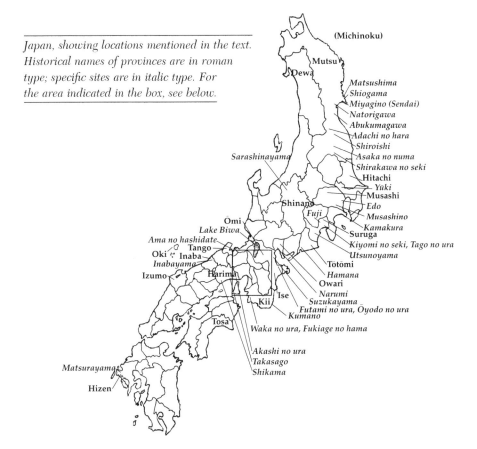

Japan, showing locations mentioned in the text.
Historical names of provinces are in roman
type; specific sites are in italic type. For
the area indicated in the box, see below.

(Michinoku)

Mutsu

Dewa

Matsushima
Shiogama
Miyagino (Sendai)
Natorigawa
Abukumagawa
Adachi no hara
Shiroishi
Asaka no numa
Shirakawa no seki
Hitachi
Yūki
Musashi
Edo
Musashino
Kamakura
Suruga
Kiyomi no seki, Tago no ura
Utsunoyama

Sarashinayama

Shinano

Fuji

Ōmi
Lake Biwa
Ama no hashidate
Tango
Oki Inaba
Inabayama
Izumo
Harima

Totōmi
Hamana
Owari
Narumi
Suzukayama
Ise
Kii
Futami no ura, Ōyodo no ura
Kumano

Tosa

Waka no ura, Fukiage no hama

Akashi no ura
Takasago
Shikama

Matsurayama

Hizen

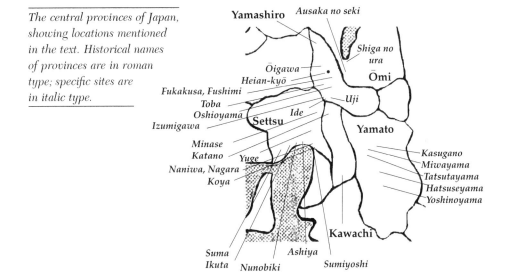

The central provinces of Japan,
showing locations mentioned
in the text. Historical names
of provinces are in roman
type; specific sites are
in italic type.

Yamashiro

Ausaka no seki

*Shiga no
ura*

Ōigawa
Heian-kyō

Ōmi

Fukakusa, Fushimi
Toba
Oshioyama
Settsu
Ide
Uji

Izumigawa

Yamato

Minase
Katano
Yuge
Naniwa, Nagara
Koya

Kasugano
Miwayama
Tatsutayama
Hatsuseyama
Yoshinoyama

Kawachi

Suma
Ikuta
Nunobiki
Ashiya
Sumiyoshi

Acknowledgments

Work on this book has been supported by a Morse Fellowship and by a Mellon Fellowship at the Whitney Humanities Center, Yale University. Research travel to Japan was supported by grants from the Sumitomo Fund, Council on East Asian Studies, Yale University. Many colleagues, friends, students, and others have commented on parts of the manuscript at various stages and have provided invaluable advice and many suggestions: among them I would particularly like to thank Matsuno Yōichi, Chino Kaori, Mimi Yiengpruksawan, John Treat, Norma Field, Mack Horton, Kang-i Sun Chang, Edwin McClellan, John Morris, Dan O'Neill, Miryam Sas, Mark Silver, and my wife, Mary Miller. And for their gracious assistance I offer my special gratitude to Hamada Naotsugu, Horino Sōshun, and Koikawa Yuriko.

Prologue: The Buried Tree

In 1692, the philologist Keichū (1640-1701) began the preface to one of his several studies of the place-names used in traditional Japanese poetry by observing that, "When there is a place-name [*meisho*] in a Japanese poem, it does for that poem what a pillow does for us in sleep. When we rest on a pillow, we have lavish dreams. When we refer to famous places, we make fine poems. Is this not why we call them '*utamakura*' [poem-pillows]?"[1] Writing in scholarly Chinese, Keichū invokes the spirit of play in his Japanese subject: just as a Japanese poem (*Yamato uta*) might, he manipulates the associations that cluster around the terms he is examining while he elaborates on the rhetorical figure with which he has begun. There are no poems in this preface, but, like many commentators before him, Keichū mimics the rhetoric of Japanese poetry as he writes about it in another medium.

The subject of his study, the names of "famous places" (*meisho*) used in poetry, had for centuries also been called *utamakura*—"pillows for poems"—though not necessarily for the reason Keichū suggests. He probably knew better, yet he wanted nonetheless to make this point: that just as pillows support the body in sleep and give us comfort so as to enrich our dreams, so do certain place-names serve as supportive and enriching implements in the making of fine poems. In addition to this play with these names, Keichū's opening statement is further enriched by an ambiguity of the kind that often characterizes the language of Japanese verse as well: the verb *yoru,* which he uses in parallel in the phrases translated above as "when we *rest* on a pillow" and "when we *refer* to famous places," is inscribed in the printed text with a character typically used in causal expressions to mean something like "because of" or "thanks to." Its sound, however, is identical to that of another verb that means "lean upon," "rely upon," "rest upon," and, in some contexts, "refer to [something]." In other words, just as he might have done were he writing a Japanese poem rather than a Sino-Japanese essay, Keichū puns on this verb in order to make it function simultaneously in multiple, juxtaposed, and overlapping semantic contexts: he thus represents the idea that both the pillow and the place-name are facilitating agents, loci of contact through which rich potentialities may be realized, while also reminding the reader of what the head does on a pillow ("rest," "nestle") and what the poet does with place-names in a poem ("refer," "rely"). This underlying ambiguity, which comes into play as soon as the script on the surface of the text is interpreted as representing sound, augments the elegance and the authority of Keichū's semi-serious offering of a plausible explanation of the origin of the term *utamakura.*

One might say that Keichū is asking his readers to believe that the term *utamakura* is both accurately descriptive of the function of place-names in poetry and, at the same time, a figure or metaphor for that function. He is also inviting us, I believe, to think of the phenomenon of dreaming as somehow analogous to the act of making poems—that is, as something that takes place when the psyche is allowed or allows itself to listen to those myriad voices of others that lie within its own voice and to explore the myriad images of people, things, places—real and imagined—that it has stored within itself, and then reproduces these stored voices and images, albeit in altered configurations, as dream. For the poets whose work of poem-making was the subject of Keichū's study, the voices heard at such times of creative psychic activity were invariably the voices of their predecessor poets, and the people and things and, especially, the places that were named or described in poems were almost always those that had previously been inscribed in other poems. And to a great extent, the work of the poet in this tradition, it was understood, was the ingenious rearrangement of materials into new poems that transparently displayed their points of contact with, as well as departures from, earlier poems.

About four hundred years before Keichū, the poet and essayist Kamo no Chōmei (1155?-1216?) also employed the rhetoric of metaphor—or reference to one thing in order to reveal the characteristics it shares with some very different thing—to explain his own view of the function of place-names in Japanese poetry, in the midst of various observations about poetic lore and practice in a text that has come to be known as *Mumyōshō* (A Treatise Without a Name). The deployment of a place-name in a poem, Chōmei writes, should be governed by precedent and by other features in the poem under construction. He offers this analogy: "To make a water garden, we place rocks close to the spot where we plan to plant pines, and where we plan to dig a pond and set water running in streams we construct an artificial 'mountain' which can further beautify the view. In the same way, we improve the configuration of a poem through our use of the names of famous places. Knowledge of how to use them constitutes one of the most important of the elements of our poetic heritage."[2]

Here, the poem-making act is treated as if analogous to the act of making a garden—a controlled, ideal space for refreshment, repose, contemplation—and the proper use of *utamakura* (once again treated as identical with "place-names"—*meisho,* or *tokoro no na*) is a design technique that can be compared to those that a well-trained and ingenious garden architect might employ. This scheme acknowledges, of course, that both the water garden and the poem are artificial creations, simulacra (of nature, of speech) carefully planned so that their various elements may combine to produce an aesthetically pleasing effect of partial sameness with and partial difference from their models. Just as the garden's architect lays the ground for certain features of the man-made landscape (which is prepared so that an observer may both view it as outsider and move through it as if part thereof) by first installing and preparing still other features, so does the architect of the poem (which, upon its completion, the reader may read as outsider, as an identity other than that of the poem's maker or speaker, or as insider, imagining that his or her identity temporarily overlaps or joins with that of the poem's maker or speaker) lay the groundwork for its total impact through strategic placement of key elements. And, just as the features built into the garden are conventional elements of garden design—transplanted pines and stones, artificial streams, ponds, and peaks—so are the key elements of the poem, such as place-names, elements of a predetermined lexicon, items to be selected, as it were, from a catalog of likely candidates, and then carefully arranged within the space of the poem.

"And if the configuration (*sugata*) of the poem and a particular famous place's name (*meisho*) are not well suited to one another," warns Chōmei, "things will be very much amiss, and even if there is considerable elegance in the poem, it will sound disjointed."[3] Here, like most medieval poets and critics, Chōmei uses the term *sugata* to refer to the final configuration or total effect produced by the various elements of a poem as they come together in conveyance of the poet's idea of the poem.[4] According to traditional Japanese poetics, the various consituent elements (words, *kotoba*) of a poem are "configured" so as to express and project the sensations and sentiments (*kokoro*) held by the poet at the time of composition. *Sugata*, which literally means "physical form," is thus a figure for the contours of that stratum of text that is thought of as lying on a visible (or otherwise perceptible) surface, underneath, behind, or within which lie the feelings that led to the making of that stratum of text, a reading of which lays bare those feelings once again. Accurate perception of these feelings through the medium of the text is held to be tantamount to understanding the meaning of the poem, also traditionally termed its *kokoro*.

Sugata, then, is the visible result of the poet's efforts to fuse "idea" and "word" as poem, just as the garden is the visible result of the architect's efforts to fuse his conception with the materials at hand or those brought to the scene from elsewhere, so as to create a new landscape. Chōmei's point is that if a place-name is to be used as an element of design, it must be the *right* place-name for the totality of that design, as tastefully chosen, installed and displayed within its contours as might be a decorative stone or a transplanted tree within the contours of a garden. And this point is further amplified when Chōmei, in the manner of most poet-critics of his day, offers several well-known poems as examples. One of these examples is one of the most widely admired (and frequently discussed) of all medieval Japanese poems, a work by Fujiwara Shunzei (or Toshiyori, 1114-1204) best known through its appearance in an Imperially sponsored anthology, the *Senzai wakashū,* which Shunzei himself edited.

> yū sareba nobe no akikaze mi ni shimite
>   uzura nakunari Fukakusa no sato
> As night falls, the autumn wind from the fields
>   pierces to the body's core
> and the quail's cry is heard in Fukakusa,
>   the village of deep grass.

Chōmei claims that this poem's configuration (*sugata*) itself is "very desolate," (*monosabishiki*), and that it is a configuration into which the place-name "Fukakusa no sato" carries extraordinarily apt associations (*tayori*). It is clearly this matching of this *sugata* with these associations that Chōmei deems so exemplary—so much so, in fact, that Chōmei says that there is simply no need for any further explanation of the poem's excellence: it can and will speak for itself.[5]

The identification of such place-names as Fukakusa no sato as *uta-makura*—that is, as elements upon which the structure of a poem rests—seen in both Keichū's and Chōmei's statements on the subject—points to their highly utilitarian, if highly aestheticized, role in poem design. This function may perhaps be understood even better when we note that in its earliest appearances (toward the end of the tenth century), the term *uta-makura* did not refer to place-names but rather to booklets—sheaves of bound paper (also called *makura,* because, it is believed, they sometimes did serve as pillows)—which contained lists of such place-names as well as many other words and phrases of special importance to practitioners of the art of making poems.[6] These handbooks, like the special lexical items listed in them, were also "foundations for poetry" and focal points of "reference" and "reliance," and so, in retrospect, the descriptive name *utamakura* seems to suit them very well.

Though it is apparently not the first handbook believed to have been so named, the earliest surviving *utamakura* handbook was compiled by the poet Nōin (988-?)—some of whose best-known poems feature particularly adroit use of place-names and other kinds of words such as might be found in an *utamakura*—and many similar guidebooks (some called *utamakura,* others not) were made for several centuries thereafter.[7] But well before the time of Chōmei (the late eleventh and early twelfth centuries), *utamakura* had come to mean, in most of its usages, place-name(s) frequently used in poetry to invoke specific associations and sentiments. And, indeed, as Chōmei said, knowledge of the proper use of *utamakura* had long been, and would long continue to be, "one of the most important elements" of the traditional poet's heritage. To be sure, because this tradition still survives—for Japanese poem-makers still make poems in these same forms, using these same lexi-cons—*utamakura* are still important as tools of the poetic craft.

My interest in pursuing the study of *utamakura* here has much to do with their utility in processes of poem design. But I myself am a reader, not a maker, of poems; and so my greater objective is to reach and share some understanding of how *utamakura*—that is, poetic place-names *and* the names of other things and other special kinds of poetic language also termed *utamakura*—came to be what they are, and to share an understanding of what they contribute to the work of poem texts as we read them.[8] This work often has much to do with the weaving of webs of associations among and between poems—a process that is often carried out through gestures of allusion, from one poem to another or others. According to our inclinations as readers, we may think of these webs of association either as the poem-maker's own design or as constructs that we perceive as we read the poem—or, perhaps, as both. The corpus of *waka*—the many thousands of Japanese poems composed, for the most part, in the orthodox thirty-one-syllable form—lies at the core of a canonical tradition in which we can learn much by plotting the signifying patterns of both allusion (overt gestures made by the maker of one poem to another poem or poems or other texts) and of inter-textuality (the radical interrelatedness or interdependence of all texts) in its larger sense. Allusiveness is extremely conspicuous in this tradition, and many specific instances of allusion, as well as the nature of allusion itself in this tradition, are major concerns of this book. But I would maintain that even when a poem of this tradition makes no explicit allusion through ges-ture, playful or otherwise, to another particular poem, it nonetheless rather transparently relates itself intertextually to virtually all other poems in the tradition, by replicating familiar formal structures and enacting familiar atti-tudes; and even when these structures and attitudes are overthrown by something unfamiliar or unorthodox, that seemingly antagonistic relation-ship is also one that attains significance through intertextuality. Also, when-ever a commonality of textual materials is celebrated through the gesture of allusion, and whenever a disjuncture of materials or treatments disrupts the illusion of harmonious textual continuity, significations are produced. That is to say, the act of making or of recognizing an allusion, as well as the act of participating in an intertextuality by positioning a text in some relationship of similarity to or difference from any or all other texts, are acts that in themselves have significance. In traditional Japanese poetry, such gestures and acts carry as much weight and call for as much attention as do the more readily perceived (though no less significant) constituents of poems—their words—from which they are inseparable. This is why I have undertaken to discuss *utamakura* (a special class of words) *and* allusion *and* intertextuality together in this book.

The terms *allusion* and *intertextuality* often appear in contemporary lit-erary criticism as if in opposition to one another, but their definitions and uses have also begun to overlap. In her essay "The Poetics of Literary Allusion," for example, Ziva Ben-Porat writes: "The literary allusion is a device for the simultaneous activation of two texts. The activation is achieved through the manipulation of a special signal: a sign (simple or complex) in a given text characterized by an additional larger 'referent.' This referent is always an independent text. The simultaneous activation of the two texts thus connected results in the formation of intertextual patterns whose nature cannot be predetermined."[9] Here, the contribution that allusion can make to what the reader eventually may experience as intertextuality is eminently clear. One may note, however, that if allusion is a device, it must be deployed or utilized by someone, which is to say that an author's role, and an author's intentions, must be in play; and if one of the outcomes of such deployment is "the formation of intertextual patterns," then that author must have some role in the process that inevitably leads to that formation—even though, as most exponents of the term would argue, intertextuality is something that exists or emerges in texts independently of authorial intentions or other agents of purposeful design.

Similarly, we find, in *The New Princeton Encyclopedia of Poetry and Poetics*, Earl Miner's definition of allusion as "a poet's deliberate incorporation of identifiable elements from other sources, preceding or contemporaneous, textual or extratextual"—in which the poet, and one who is "deliberate," maintains a high profile—alongside Helen Regueiro Elam's definition of intertextuality as a term that "refers to those conditions of textuality which affect and describe the relations between texts, and in most respects is synonymous with textuality"—in which no author, intender, or designer is involved. Miner also states that allusion is "distinguishable" from intertextuality in that "intertextuality is involuntary: in some sense, by using any given real language, one draws on the intertexts from which one has learned the words, and neither the poet nor the reader is aware of the connections."[10] Involuntary, perhaps, yet this statement still involves a person—a speaker, writer, perhaps even a poet—who uses language and may or may not be aware of where it is coming from and what it may or may not be connected to.

In the field of Japanese poetry, some contributions have already been made toward the reconciliation of these terms, in recognition, I believe, of their respective and joint utility in this discipline. In one study, for example, Haruo Shirane begins with a straightforward definition of intertextuality as "the dependence of every text on other texts" and then clearly poses the term in contradistinction to allusion: "The classical concept of allusion is founded on, or at least appeals to, the notion of authorial experience and intention, as is evident in the attempts by scholars to establish which texts or sources a given author may have read or otherwise come in contact with. Intertextuality dispenses with the classical criteria of authorial consciousness or contact and replaces it with an approach which takes into account not only the literary tradition but the role of a collective unconscious."[11] Eventually, however, Shirane maintains that poets at the end of the Heian period (the late eleventh century)—among whom he justifiably treats Shunzei as paradigm—had an "awareness of the intertextual nature and function of literary texts"; that Shunzei in fact was a "pioneer in the development of what may be called an intertextual poetics"; and that, although Shunzei of course "does not use terms like intertextuality" in his own writings about poetic praxis, he nevertheless "has a profound awareness of poetry both as a highly codified object and as an intertextual construct."[12] Here, again, intertextuality is something that poets are said to have been "aware" of, that it is something in the development of which they could be "pioneers"— something they could sense in the existing corpus of poetry, something they could prolong or extend, something they could participate in through their own efforts. In other words, intertextuality, in this context, is not wholly beyond the reach of agency, but rather something toward which poets, among others, may strive, perhaps even through such obvious gestures as allusion, as well as through yet subtler means—in addition to the fact that it may also exist regardless of what poets do. This may or may not be what Shirane means to imply as a characterization of the role of the poet in the Japanese tradition, but it does come close to what I would offer as my own view.[13]

Accordingly, I offer here some results of my contemplation of what I have come to see as three particularly conspicuous and interrelated features of the *waka* tradition—that is, the structural role of *utamakura* (especially place-names, as well as other kinds of words used in special ways), the operations of allusion, and the intertextuality of this poetry. I seek, among other things, to elucidate the function of place-names as foundations for poem designs, or as loci of reference and reliance in the elaborative associative schemes which poets forge among poems—or in which poems appear to be engaged as we read, here and there, through and across the canon. I also seek to show how these allusive and intertextual constructs energized and preserved the tradition of *waka* across the many centuries of its long history, creating multidimensional discourses between and across texts that mirror the multidimensional discourses of disparate times. I tend to treat these features of this poetry not only as features that readers can observe, but as features that exist largely through the efforts, or designs, of the poets who made those texts. I admit that we can learn only so much, if anything, about *why* they wrote poems as they did; but we can see, quite clearly, *what* they did, and can learn a great deal through that examination.

The *waka* tradition to which I refer here is a long-lived one: its earliest poems date from well before the eighth century, when they were first permanently recorded; and poems are still composed today in the classical molds formulated in the ninth, tenth, eleventh, and twelfth centuries. It is also a tradition that has almost always had close ties, through patronage, practice, and protection, to the Japanese Imperial institution, viewed both in the past and today (though on rather different bases) as the embodiment of the continuity of Japanese culture. For these and other reasons, *waka* has long been held in high esteem, as a central, prestigious literary genre that embodies much of what Japanese culture has been supposed to be. Despite this privileged status, there have been periods when the *waka* tradition lay fallow, periods of stagnation, periods of overshadowing by other, often closely related genres. Though these periods were seen by some as moments of peril, both by poets of these times and in hindsight, the tradition survived—even when the Imperial institution, its long-time protector, was no longer so central or powerful as it had been. And that survival was due, at least in part, to the tradition's alliance with other traditions. For the *waka* canon—this vast collection of hundreds of thousands of poems, the aggregate product of at least a dozen centuries, if not more—also serves as a foundation for virtually all other traditional Japanese literary genres, including other forms of poetry (which, in many cases, descend directly from *waka*), for elements of narrative fiction and other prose writings, for drama, and for many other forms of expression, including the visual arts (painting, calligraphy, and other media); and, in turn, these other traditions have often provided venues for and material for *waka*. Thus, *waka*'s place in the intertextual matrix that is Japanese textuality is both prominent and secure; and within this vast fabric, the intertextuality that is woven around and through the poetics of places and place-names—which figure so prominently in *waka* poetics and in the poetics of other genres and arts—may be singled out, as it is in this book, as a kind of cross-section, examination of which may, in turn, help us understand more about the poetics of the whole.

The central figure for this study, the buried tree, is *not* a place-name but an *utamakura* nonetheless—a word that has long served in multiple and rich ways in the *waka* lexicon, often in close association with one or another *utamakura* that *is* a place-name. The word translated here as "the buried tree" is *umoregi,* and in the following pages I will show how this word has served for centuries as a multi-purpose figure for entities that are at once "dead" and "alive," for entities that are survivors across long spans of time, for entities that change in some (but not all) aspects of their form and character as time passes, for entities that are at times hidden from and at other times exposed to view—entities, one might say, that are much like the *waka* tradition itself. This figure of "a buried tree"—that is, a once living tree that has metamorphosed over time, while hidden beneath the surface of a body of flowing water, into a new, stonelike substance—surfaces quite early in the history of *waka*; it eventually takes its place in the expanding but self-limiting *waka* lexicon as a truly potent, pivotal, and association-rich poetic nominal (i.e., an *utamakura* in the broad sense—that is, a word of special significance and special utility in the making of poems); it is linked, at times, to particular places where buried trees are in fact found, and the name of one, Natorigawa, the Natori River, becomes, in part through this linkage, a typically potent and durable *utamakura* in the narrow sense—that is, a place-name of special significance and utility in poem design. It continues to surface repeatedly, and conspicuously, across and through the long history of *waka*, undergoing further metamorphosis along the way.

Like many another *utamakura*, including those that are place-names and those that are not, the word *umoregi* enters Japanese verse as a referent to a physical object, but it does so, it seems, so that it may be used, for the most part, in reference to other things—that is, as metaphor—or at least as something very much like what we call metaphor. Thereafter, throughout *waka* history, this figure, like many others, maintains its multivalence: the makers of poems continue to show interest in its utility as *figure* but also in its utility as *thing*—and, if anything, their interest in the thing increases as does their interest in and recognition of the value of the figure. *Umoregi* itself continues to be a rare, prized commodity, valued for its utility in the manufacture of other things (fine household furnishings or potent incense, for example); likewise, practitioners of the art of poetry prize *utamakura* like *umoregi* for their utility in the manufacture of poems. Thus, words for things themselves become *things*, commodities that must be recognized as such and then collected, assayed, displayed, transmitted, and preserved, in a process which only increases their value, and power. One aim of this book is to follow this process of the commodification of poetic language, largely by following the vicissitudes of a single "commodity," the word *umoregi*, or, "the buried tree"; and also by examining other related processes of collection, recollection, display, and transmission of such "goods."

Umoregi is only one word/thing (thing/word) among thousands treated in this way in the *waka* tradition, no more conspicuous than many others. But it surfaces repeatedly in particularly intriguing ways as one reads across the corpus of *waka* and on into other texts in related genres: for example, at a point that may be considered relatively late in the span of *waka* history (though by no means an end point), within a memoir that the famous poet and painter Yosa Buson (1716-83) appended to a collection of *hokku* (seventeen-syllable) verses he composed in 1777. The poems and the memoir were published shortly after Buson's death, under the title *Shin hanatsumi*

(A new flower gathering), with illustrations by his executor, Matsumura Gekkei (figure 1).[14] In the passage in question, Buson is remembering something that happened to him some three decades previously, during an extended sojourn in the northeastern provinces of Japan, an area rich in *utamakura* (*meisho*) sites. As Buson meanders through his memories, he remembers that it was while visiting one such site, the scenic lagoon called Matsushima, that he unexpectedly came into possession of an apparently genuine piece of a buried tree found previously at yet another nearby *utamakura* site, in the Natori River valley. The story he tells about this event places Buson not only amidst the rich resonances of these sites but also within a close-knit if far-flung community of fellow artists for whom such sites, and the objects found therein, hold various degrees of special antiquarian value. Here is the story as Buson tells it:

Tenrin'in in Matsushima is an awesome Zen monastery that stands beside the Zuiganji temple. When I was a visitor there, the abbot gave me an old piece of wood about a foot long. "The Daimyō of Sendai, Lord Captain So-and-So, was a poet of extraordinary accomplishment," he told me. "He had the bottom of the Natori River dredged by a large crew of laborers, and at last they dug up a piece of a buried tree [*umoregi*] that was made into a box to hold writing paper and an inkstone. He presented it to the Nijō House, along with a brush with a stem of lespedeza [*hagi*] from Miyagi Plain. This is a bit of that same buried tree, and I can assure you that it is a thing not to be taken lightly."

The grain of the wood had much of the marked clarity of zelkova [*tsuki*]. Having been under water for so many hundreds of years, it had turned black, and it made a clanging sound when struck, as does tempered steel. I think it must have weighed about fourteen pounds. I wrapped it in a kerchief and managed to get as far as the post-station of Shiroishi with it slung over my shoulder. But I was not sure that I could bear the fatigue of carrying it on such a long journey, so I stuck it under the veranda of the inn where I stayed that night and left it there when I set off again the next day.

Some time later, while on a visit to [the poet Isaoka] Gantō in Yūki, I mentioned it to [the poet] Tanpoku, and he flew into a rage. "You're such a stupid old priest," he scolded. "To have thrown away a treasure [*kibutsu*] like that! I want it, even if you don't. Let's see—there must be someone who can help me get it right away!" He sent word to [the poet] Shinryū in Sukagawa, and Shinryū sent a messenger with a letter to the inn at Shiroishi, which said, "When priest Buson stayed here some time ago, he left behind a certain item. We have come in search of it." Fortunately, the innkeeper found it and gave it to the messenger, who brought it back with him. Eventually, it came into Gantō's hands [from Tanpoku], and he made it into an inkstone-lid inscribed with the name "*Gyokaku*" ("Fish and Crane"). It is more than seventy leagues from Yūki to Shiroishi, and quite

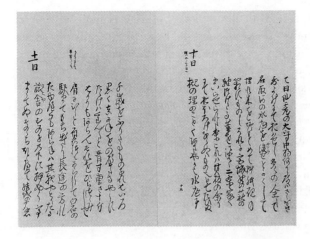

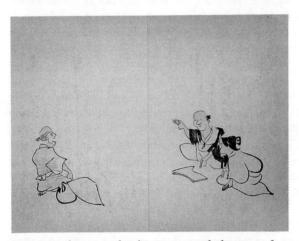

1. Section of Buson's Shin hanatsumi, *including text of episode describing Buson's acquisition of a piece of Natorigawa* umoregi *at Tenrin'in and illustration of scene at Shiroishi inn (Shinryū's messenger asks the inn-*

some time had passed [since I left it there], so it was quite something to have recovered it.[15]

Tenrin'in, where this story takes place, is one of two subsidiary temples adjacent to Zuiganji, the central institution in the religious complex in Matsushima favored by several generations of the Date family, long the most important and powerful house in the Sendai region. Tenrin'in itself was a relatively late addition to the Matsushima religious compound when it was

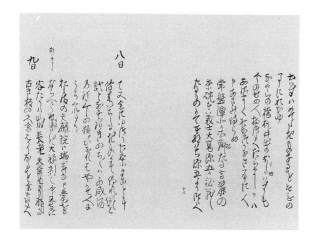

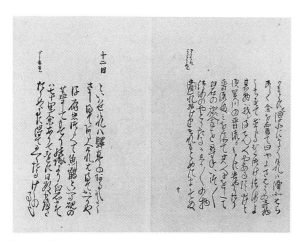

keeper about the piece of umoregi *left behind by Buson.)*
Woodblock print illustration by Matsumura Gekkei.
From a 1921 reprint, courtesy Harvard-Yenching
Library.

founded, in 1663, as a memorial for a daughter of one of the greatest scions of the Date and the first Sendai Daimyō, Masamune (1567-1636).[16] At the time of Buson's visit (1742-43?), Tenrin'in would have been under the administration of its sixth abbot (*chōrō*), Gensui, who died (two years after Buson) in 1775, so it may well have been Gensui who gave Buson this "old piece of wood about one foot long" (*furuki ita no shaku amari bakari*).[17] The gift was a local *meibutsu*, a famous local product of the sort that might be proffered with pride by any denizen of the region. Such a commodity would surely have seemed a very appropriate parting gift, a commemoration of Buson's stay in the temple, a memento of such time as these two men—a priest (perhaps one who particularly liked poetry, or paintings) and a poet-painter (who is travelling in the area as a quasi-priest)—may have spent together. But the particular "old piece of wood" that the abbot gave Buson bore a very special pedigree: its peculiar value must have been heightened not only through its capacity to embody the hallowed literary lore of the vicinity but also by its specific provenance in an archaeological project carried out by a Date lord, a hereditary patron of the Tenrin'in itself. So giving away this "piece of wood" may well have been tantamount to giving away one of the temple's greater or lesser treasures, or a bit thereof, as fragments of holy relics, made into powerful talismans, were (and still are) given or sold to temple visitors.

In presenting this particular object to Buson, the abbot may have used the name "the Sendai Daimyō," to whom its discovery was to be traced, but, for whatever reasons, Buson leaves the names out of his account: instead, he refers obliquely to a "Lord Captain So-and-so," as if the exact name has been forgotten (which it may well have been, after more than thirty years), or as if recalling it hardly matters. Other details of the exchange seem to have been more easily retained in Buson's memory, which may suggest that Buson is deliberately omitting the Daimyō's name, out of deference. In any case, he does remember this: a Sendai Daimyō of some former time, much given to poetry and poetic pursuits, went so far as to search for the residue of *waka*'s past in the bottom of a river in his own domain, and was fortunate to find exactly what he was looking for, just where he thought it would be.

Commentators agree that this astute Sendai Daimyō, described here as "a poet of extraordinary accomplishment" (*sōnaki utayomi*), is probably Date Yoshimura (1680-1751), the fifth Date lord of the Sendai domain. Thoroughly schooled in the traditions of the past and in the lore of his own domain, he no doubt knew just what he was looking for when he dredged the bed of the Natori River, which flowed through his territories in the northeastern province of Mutsu and into Sendai Bay.[18] *Umoregi* had been found in its waters from time to time since antiquity, and so the name of the river and its prized product had long been linked to one another in the literal realm of that commerce. And, through this linkage, in part, both *umoregi* and the name of the river had also long since achieved the status of *uta-makura,* and their linkage to one another, as such, had also been conspicuous for several centuries, owing to their joint appearance in such poems as the following anonymous one, best known through its inclusion in the *Kokin wakashū* (Love Poems III, 650).

> Natorigawa seze no umoregi arawareba
>   ika ni semu to ka aimisomekemu[19]
> When we first met, did we consider what would happen
>   should our love be as exposed as are the buried trees
>   that come into view in the shoals of the Natori River?

This poem takes ample advantage of the fact that the name of this river, Natorigawa, can suggest an alternative or contingent signification—"the taking (or getting) of a name" (*na-tori*)—that is probably in no way related to the origin of this toponym but is nonetheless quite useful in the design of a poem about love. The discourse of love in *waka* often finds its way to a transitional focus on lovers' concerns about reputation, their "name" (*na*), and when it does so the place-name Natorigawa has often suggested a place for itself—as it did here, in *Kokin wakashū* #650—in a poem that reads as a lover's utterance to his or her beloved. But there is more to be said about its role in this particular setting. The nominal clause that opens the poem, "the fossilized trees in the rapids of the Natori River," also introduces the verb *arawaru*, "to become visible," which in this context can be linked to the lovers' desire to protect their privacy. So *arawareba* serves doubly, as "the fossilized trees *are* easily *seen* in the shallow waters of the rapids" *and*, with the lovers as implicit subject, as "should our love *become known* to others." (Such clauses in *waka* are called *jo*, prefaces or guide phrases: they often contain or lead the way to *utamakura* place-names.) (Figure 2.)

The anonymous poet may well have deployed these elements as he or she did here in order to compose a variation on a familiar love theme, perhaps with the conventionalized topic of illicit love (rather than a "real" illicit love in which he or she was a participant) in mind. But, on the other hand, the whole exercise may have been set in motion simply through the associations that link the poem's discrete elements—things that are hidden, things that emerge into view, names and reputations, the torrents of the river and the torrents of passion—and that so powerfully suggest the context of illicit love. In any case, when the *Kokin wakashū* compilers came across the poem early in the tenth century, they classed it as a love poem, on the basis of its message and theme as they perceived them, in one of five chapters containing poems that they deemed to be similarly exemplary instances of the use of language specifically associated with the topic of love by generations of poets. In the carefully crafted *Kokin wakashū* sequence this poem is both preceded and succeeded by other poems about the desire to avoid unwarranted ill repute

名取川

をとめ乃望木

ゆくられえ

いのて

せんとの

そめ

2. *Natorigawa scene, with inscription of* Kokin wakashū #650, *("Natorigawa/seze no mumoregi/arawareba/ika ni sen to ka/aimisomekemu.") From "Twelve Scenes of Miyagi," prints by Baikan published ca. 1887, Sendai. Courtesy Sendai-shi Hakubutsukan.*

for involvement in illicit love: the Natori River and the buried trees revealed in its rapids are only one set of possible embellishments of, or means of addressing, that theme. They distinguish this poem from others on the same or related topics, but they also link it to others in the *waka* canon that use the same language in other ways.

Knowledge of the poetic lore that embraced the places and things named in such poems (that is, these elements of *kotoba*) mattered as much as, and was really inseparable from, understanding the passion of the poetic utterance (that is, its *kokoro*) for accomplished latter-day poets like Yoshimura;

and it was certainly that kind of knowledge that prompted him to put his men to work in the river bottom. In his mind, it would seem, the poem's description of *umoregi* "in every rapid of the river" was historical fact, begging to be proven once again. Perhaps what moved him was a desire to possess some tangible evidence of a direct relationship between *waka* rhetoric and the physical world. There, in a river flowing through his own domain, was a piece of *waka* history waiting for someone to lay claim to it. And, it seems, Yoshimura got what he went looking for.

What the Tenrin'in abbot eventually gave Buson, then, was literally a fragment of yet another fragment, sought out and treasured as a material link to a long-lived and time-hallowed tradition, still viable and potent in Yoshimura's and Buson's own time. In *Shin hanatsumi,* this story is one among several that Buson tells about collectors of rare antique treasures (*kibutsu*): alongside it stand stories of the proud owner of an ornamental nail-head cover said to come from the palace of the first Qin Emperor, of a Korean tea bowl handed down through a line of poets, and of a master poet's manuscripts handed down through his associates and disciples—Buson himself among them. Inter alia, Buson also refers to other stories of eccentric medieval collectors of the invaluable material detritus of *waka* and its history—men who took inordinate pride and pleasure in their possession of a tiny fragment of a famous bridge often named in poems, or in ownership of the dried carcass of a "singing frog" from a place often praised in poetry as their special habitat.[20] Buson's concern in these passages is with the difficulty of proving the authenticity of such treasures, but he suggests that it is the value that has been attached to them in their passage from owner to owner, the pedigree of sentiment, that matters—not the verity of provenance. In retrospect, Buson understands why his friend Tanpoku—an inveterate collector of *kibutsu*—was so angry with him when he learned what Buson had done with the abbot's gift, and why he then went to such lengths to retrieve the bit of fossilized wood.[21] "One should do whatever one can to take possession of things that one seeks to possess," Buson observes at a later point in the memoir, "and one should make haste to see things that one wishes to see. Do not casually assume that there will be other opportunities to see or possess such things. It is very unlikely that another chance of obtaining such satisfaction will come along."[22] Buson had allowed a fragment of the tangible *waka* past to slip from his hands; his friends, perhaps more interested than he in the possession of such properties, made haste to correct the error.

Then, to preserve the treasure, Gantō, the eventual owner of what Buson so freely threw away, emulated Yoshimura.[23] The Sendai Daimyō had made his treasure into an offering to the preeminent house of hereditary *waka* authority, the Nijō, descendants of Fujiwara Teika (1162-1241), a pillar of late medieval poetic professionalism and examplar of both orthodoxy and innovation. The offering itself was an instrument for the making of new poems, fashioned like those poems themselves from materials retrieved from poetry's distant but living past; and it was accompanied by yet another such instrument, a brush whose stem was made from lespedeza (*hagi*) grown on Miyagi Plain, another *utamakura* site in the Sendai domain known especially for its association with that shrub, which is itself a hallowed *waka* fixture. Gantō was an amateur poet, and a part-time one at that, compared to the Nijō masters; still, just like them, each time he sat down to write a poem and lifted the ink-stone lid that he had had made from Buson's erstwhile *umoregi* fragment, it may have seemed to him that it was as if he were laying his hand upon the whole of a vast, reusable poetic past, that the force of that past might flow into him as he laid his hand on the lid's polished grain, eventually to take shape again in the words he would write on the paper that lay before him.

It was reverence for the past—nostalgia in its own particular dimension—that prompted Yoshimura's dredging and his offering to the Nijō house; and it was a similar kind of reverence, transferred like Yoshimura's to a physical thing, that made Buson's friends more eager than he to recover and keep the antique bit of wood that had come to him by chance and which he had so blithely cast away. The effect of any poem that might be made with the instruments fashioned from these fossilized bits would also entail a profoundly nostalgic recognition of these instruments as embodiments of the vast and complex poetic past. Like these bits of petrified wood made into useful new tools, each bit of *waka* language dredged and re-dredged from the poetic past carried its own store of sentiment and accrued invested power. That sentiment remained viable precisely because it had been felt and understood so many times through the ages, and that power remained desirable because it had enabled poet after poet to be a maker of poems and a transmitter of that power. At first, it seems, Buson scarcely realized or cared what this thing that the abbot had placed in his hands might be. He describes its tactility, but seems indifferent to its symbolic weight. Later, hearing about it in casual talk, his friends recognized its value instantly. Perhaps they needed the object more than he, while for him it was enough to know what it was: there was no need to possess it, especially if its weight should prove insupportable. But, in the end, Buson seems to have been glad to know that the object had indeed been retrieved and could be put to such appropriate use.

As I have come to understand it, the power of *utamakura*—of *utamakura* words like *umoregi,* and of *utamakura* place-names like Natorigawa—is very much like the power invested in the bit of wood that Buson possessed so briefly and which he then allowed to pass into the hands and on to the uses of others. Like buried trees that lie below the surface of the waters that conceal them, each such word in the *waka* lexicon, each phrase of prior linkage of those words, lies just below the surface of the mind of the composing poet (as do voices and images in the psyche of the dreamer), and that poet has only to search through his or her memories of other poems in order to retrieve that word or phrase for use in a new instrumentation. Once inscribed in a new poem, the retrieved and reset language gleams with the patina of its past usage (as does a polished stone interpolated into the design of the water-garden); its presence decrees that the poem within which it is encountered is indeed a poem, like thousands written before it and like other thousands that may be written hence. The power invested in such language may threaten to make it an insupportable, crippling burden, but if properly understood and properly used to ignite the reader's recognition and summon recollection, that power may give life to the poems of the present, illuminating them in the light of the poems of the past and offering assurance that the creation of poems may continue in the future.

In the following chapters, I pursue this characterization of these aspects of the *waka* tradition in further detail. In chapter 1, I explore the tripartite nexus of *utamakura* (in its several senses, and most particularly that of place-name) with the operations of allusion and intertextuality. In chapter 2, I pursue the two linked *utamakura, umoregi* and Natorigawa, across time as poets of several generations repeatedly refer to or "rest" their poems upon them. In chapter 3 I examine a variety of instances of the antiquarian assembling, hoarding, re-fashioning, and displaying of the matériel of *waka*'s past—activities which carry the commodification of *waka* language, and of the objects to which it refers, into new dimensions. And in chapter 4 I examine a desperate early-thirteenth-century political ritual exercise in the revival of the power of *utamakura* in a mixed-media royal poem-and-painting program. This chapter will serve as a reminder that such poem-making as is examined here rarely, if ever, takes place in politically neutral environments; indeed, the story of *utamakura*, like the story of *waka* itself, is charged at many points through its intersections with the story of the vicissitudes of Imperial power, and it can be seen, like much else in the history of Japanese civilization, as yet another feature of an account of the ongoing struggles of centers versus peripheries. Some scholars see the appropriation of the names of places into the language of an authorized and protected discourse—*waka*—as yet another form of colonization, a neutralization of regional identity that leads inevitably toward its subsumption into a relatively homogenized and anonymous "national" conglomerate. Scholars whose roots are in the Northeast, which is but one of many areas of Japan in which regional identity still remains quite strong, express this view most sharply. The fact that such resentment against the encroachments of "the center" is still so keen is evidence, I think, that though the lamented acts of subsumption took place long ago, regional cultures and and their traditions nonetheless can and will be maintained; and, if nothing else, such views remind us that it is also important to look at such central or centralized traditions as *waka* from more than one perspective—that is, not only from the inside out, or from the center toward its borders, but, if possible, from the other way around.

Throughout this book, I treat poems as I believe their makers knew them, as texts that might be both seen and heard, and as texts that interact with and share key characteristics of other kinds of languages, both verbal (for example, song or prayer) and visual (for example, painting or calligraphy). I have also striven to make a point of reading and discussing poems from a variety of textual sites within the *waka* canon—that is, not only from the context of the selective, exclusive Imperial anthologies. Because these royally commissioned anthologies (*chokusenshū*, of which there are twenty-one) were made in circumstances of intense selectivity and exalted purpose that automatically lent them immense prestige, they and the poems in them are invariably treated as the very paradigms of *waka* art—as indeed they are, in many ways. They represent the values of the times in which they were made and of the men who made them; and many of them are, in their own right, brilliant textual tapestries of *ex post facto* design, the structure and texture of which are themselves remarkable and admirable for their own sake. This is why poems from these anthologies so often occupy the foreground in studies of *waka,* both in Japan and elsewhere.

But explorations of the nature of the complex history and character of *waka* are automatically skewed if they confine themselves to or rely too extensively on these anthologies as the source for poems, or if poems are read only as they are treated in these anthologies, because doing so limits the reader to reading only those poems that the *chokusenshū* editors have pre-selected (for all their various reasons) and to reading them as they are read, or presented, by those editors. If the purpose of a given study is to come to an understanding of the structural principles that govern the composition of a given anthology, or to try to get a sense of the dominant stylistics of a particular period by treating an anthology produced in that period as paradigm (which one can do with some, but not all, of the *chokusenshū*), then there is good reason to confine one's purview to one or another of these

texts, or to several of them as a coherent, historically significant group. But
if one is interested in an aspect of the *waka* tradition that is evinced across
its history and in all sorts of compositional situations and moments that
precede any subsequent selection for and re-contextualization in anthologized resettings (when and if they occur), and if one is interested in the
factors that may have shaped the making of particular poems in the very
moment they were made, by particular makers (insofar as this can be known
or surmised), rather than in the values and agendas that motivated the
selection process and shaped the given anthology that was its result (a line
of inquiry which is equally interesting and historically important, but which
is a different kettle of fish), then a selection of poems from *chokusenshū*
alone simply will not suffice.

For these reasons, I have looked at poems from throughout the *waka*
canon, which is selective and confined enough as it is, but which includes
thousands and thousands more poems than just those that are found in the
chokusenshū. I have also made a point of selecting for discussion here a
range of poems from a wide range of sources, and of treating them, wherever
possible, in the context of their primary settings.[24] That is, poems are read
here, wherever possible, in the textual settings that are those of the particular
literary-social gathering, or the more private compositional exercise, in
which, so far as we can tell, they were first made, rather than in the context
of any anthologized setting into which they may subsequently have also been
placed. Re-placement in anthologized settings often produces some distortion or a significant alteration of the dynamics of reading: when, for example,
poems are arranged in a *chokusenshū* so as to display their generic or
thematic or figural commonalities, or so as to produce the impression of an
unfolding quasi-narrative (the progress of a season and the changes it brings
to the landscape, or the progress of a love affair), the autonomy (such as it
is) of the poems so re-placed is automatically effaced, and the reader's sense
of the poem's relationship to its maker (insofar as it can be sensed) must give
way to or coexist with a sense of the poem's place and role in the textual
enterprise of the anthology itself. These dynamics are, of course, of interest
in themselves, and the tactic of reading poems as other readers (i.e., editors)
have previously read them does have the merit of assuring subsequent
readers that they are at least proceeding by means that others have adopted
before—in ways that are historically significant and that still wield great
authority.

But an approach taken wherever possible to poems in their prior contexts
frees us to read them in still other ways, *and* gives us a much wider range
in which to roam in search of poetry that illustrates and gives evidence of

features that transcend any particular anthology, text, or occasion. Because the poetics of *utamakura*, the poetics of places and place-names, the operations of allusiveness, and the operations of intertextuality are all features that transcend any particular text, period, or genre, it seems best to frame this inquiry as broadly as possible, at least in terms of its purview across the canon.

In many, perhaps most, of the poems in which it appears, the figure of the buried tree refers, in its most literal guise, to secreted, precious lodes that come into view here and there, from time to time, in shoals—in places where flowing waters part and lay those shoals, and their deposits, open to inspection, collection, and use. The figure may be a fitting one for the experience of reading across the *waka* canon as well: for hundreds of figures like this one make their appearances on its textual surfaces, then recede, then rise again, and again; the ripples and the resonances they produce also repeatedly return to make themselves seen or heard across vast spans of textual space and time. Any single moment of such appearance, or resonance, is simply part of a continuum, reaching back to prior moments of usage and laying the way open for future moments of re-use. And, like the river's shoals, each poem is a space, and a moment, in which the deposits of time and memory lie exposed to view. Re-use of the past is this tradition's way of making the old ever new: matériel that seems as ancient as Natori-gawa's buried trees is repeatedly dredged, refashioned, and displayed in new artifacts that reveal, and revel in, their pedigrees. The products of this process, recapitulated for centuries, are *waka* poems.

1

Utamakura, Allusion, and Intertextuality

Among the love poems composed on various occasions and brought together by the great Japanese poet Fujiwara Teika (1162-1241) in *Shūi gusō*, his own collection of his lifetime's work, are several pairs of poems ostensibly exchanged in the midst of love affairs. For the most part, the poems reproduced in this section of *Shūi gusō* appear to be taken from communications (letters and the like) that passed between Teika and several unnamed women at various stages of courtship. But one cannot help wondering if these women existed, whether these affairs indeed took place: it may be that, in many instances, Teika was the author on both sides of the exchange, that he invented these exchanges as an exercise in the art of such corresponsive verse, imitating the structures and mannerisms and reconstructing the scenarios of those vast numbers of pairs of verses exchanged (also ostensibly) by lovers and other correspondents and then classified in the earliest comprehensive collection of Japanese poetry (the encyclopedic *Man'yōshū*, a late eighth-century anthology) as *sōmonka* (songs that are personal exchanges) and replicated in equally countless pairings of poems in subsequent anthologies, in prose narratives (*monogatari*) that incorporate poetry into stories of love (and of other human affairs), and in many other kinds of texts.[1]

Embedded as they are, then, in this tradition of corresponsive verse, these pairs of poems in *Shūi gusō* effectively create a series of plausible tableaux; whether they arise from "real" amours or are largely fiction matters less than the understanding—the tacit bargain between Teika and his reader (whether a woman whose love he sought, or a more detached reader)—that they are to be viewed against the rich background of analogous pairs of poems from similar situations, both real and fictive. And that such an understanding must be in force is further signaled by the language of the poems themselves, as in the following pair, where the very words of other love poems (well-known to poets like Teika) resound:

> seki wabinu ima hata onaji
> > Natorigawa arawarehatene seze no umoregi
> Natorigawa yukute no nami ni arawarete
> > asasa zo mien seze no umoregi[2]

These poems are so deeply enmeshed in, and engaged with, a traditional poetic language of love that translation alone cannot begin to do justice to them; paraphrase may serve them (and our purposes) better, but further explication is also required if we are even to begin to read these poems as a reader in Teika's own time might have read them. That hypothetical reader may not have needed such explication, but we do if we are to enter into and understand a text such as this. The reason for this is, of course, that the text is designed in such a way as to be both opaque and transparent; what it says is rather simple, but the way it is said is not. Teika expected his reader(s) to appreciate both the opacity and the transparency—the form and the content, inseparable and interactive—and we should try to do likewise.

So, the first poem of the pair says, "I have grown weary of holding them back (*seki wabinu*), and now it can make little difference (*ima hata onaji*) if the waters of Natorigawa, 'The River of Scandal,' are allowed to flow; so let the buried trees in its many shoals (*seze no umoregi*) be revealed (*araware-hatene*)!" And the reply: "As those waters of the Natorigawa flow, their shallowness shall be easily seen, as shall the buried trees in all those shoals." It will be readily apparent that this is a quasi-conversation couched in figures, an extraordinary discourse conducted in a special, obviously literary idiom. The "speaker" of the first verse (who we may assume to be male, either because we identify the voice as Teika's, or for thematic and contextual reasons explained below) uses a practice-hallowed poetic code to say that he is tired of worrying about rumor, tired of concealing his love for the girl he addresses: he will "let the waters flow," and if the affair is revealed as a result he will not care. But his beloved has little faith in him or in this show of brash courage: she uses the same code but readjusts its elements to say that she suspects he will not be able to withstand the effects of gossip about their love, and that what will really be revealed is the "shallowness" of his feeling for her.

The matter of this exchange might seem to be reducible to a rather mundane give-and-take—the tendering of a fervent avowal devolving into a coy mini-spat between two lovers, real or imagined, at a difficult stage of their affair—if its constituent language did not further complicate the text as much as it does, and if this textual moment did not bear such strong resemblance to countless other similar moments of exchange in the canons of earlier verse. In fact this exchange re-stages an archaic (or at any rate antique) scenario that has its roots in the earliest so-called *sōmonka* (eighth century and earlier) where, again and again, a man (or sometimes a woman) frets about the consequences of detection of a secret love, and a paramour chides him (or her) for such qualms. And Teika carries out this restaging through words that are intentionally borrowed from other specific texts to produce a kind of *déjà lu* (or *déjà entendu*) effect (for the supposed corre- spondents and for subsequent readers). The primary *locus classicus* for both verses in Teika's exchange text is the anonymous Natorigawa love poem from the *Kokin wakashū*—a poem which, as we have already seen, bears some relationship to the facts about that river, and which, as we shall see, would be treated throughout *waka* history (as it is here, by Teika) in much the same way as were the deposits of fossilized wood found in its waters, as a rich lode, available for repeated acts of reclamation and refashioning.

> Natorigawa seze no umoregi arawareba
>   ika ni semu to ka aimisomekemu[3]
> When we first met, did we consider what would happen
>   should our love be as exposed as are the buried trees
> that come into view in the shoals of the Natori River?

In this poem, the template for what I shall here refer to as Natorigawa poesy, the role of the place-name might be described (as might be the place-names in many other poems) as peripheral, as something attached to and involved with but not necessarily essential for the conveyance of the poem's message, which is, in this case, something like this: "Now our love affair has been exposed, though when we began it we gave little thought to such conse- quences."[4] But, on the other hand, this toponym (like others used in many poems) might well be described as an essential element of the poem's figural scheme, an indispensable, though not necessarily irreplaceable, part of the language that makes the poem "poetic." The message might have been

3. The Natorigawa (near Akiu Spa, Miyagi Prefecture.) Photo by the author.

conveyed in any number of ways, and the figural scheme might have been composed of many other elements. We cannot possibly tell why the person who made this poem chose to do so in this way, with these words. But what matters most is that he or she did so; and we *can* come to some understanding of what these words may mean, or what they may signify in such a poem, or what it is that they contribute to the performance of its textual work.

Like most (though certainly not all) of the toponyms used in this and other ways in traditional Japanese poetry, the Natorigawa named in this poem is a real river, in northern Honshū, the largest island of the Japanese archipelago, and, as we know, it is indeed a river in which buried trees (*umoregi* or *mumoregi*, whole trees or parts thereof transformed over time into stone-like texture) are (or were) found.[5] Such trees were (and are) also found in many other rivers, and they appear in many other poems (as they do here) to suggest or represent objects or entities or conditions that remain hidden from view for long periods but which can and do come to light (as do hidden love affairs). Thus, though their appearances in poems are invariably figural, there is also some real or at least plausible basis—in this case, a geographical or topographical basis—to most such instances of figural scheming, as there is in the genesis and elaboration of much poetic figuration, and of most symbol systems (see figure 3).

Yet, as I have also noted, it is also the very sound of this river's name, Natori, that prompts its appearance (rather than that of some other river, or some other place, or something else altogether), along with its topographically justified and figurally potent buried trees (rather than some other object or entity) in this verse, as a kind of pun: for this word *Natori* not only names the river and gives the poem's figural "action" (of anticipated discovery) a specific setting, but it also signifies "getting a [bad] reputation," unjustly or otherwise, through the revelation of one's private affairs (*na-tori*: *na* is "name, reputation"; *tori* is "getting, taking").[6]

Formally, the whole clause that opens this poem, "Natorigawa seze no umoregi" (the buried trees in the many shoals of the Natori River), which includes this place-name, may be thought of as being there to "lead" the reader (as if unaware) to or prepare for or embellish (meaningfully) the verb *arawaru*, "to become visible," and that verb serves doubly, in two overlapping syntactic schemes, as "the trees do [inevitably] become visible in the river's shoals" *and*, with two lovers (the poem-speaker and his or her paramour) as implicit subject, as "should our love become known to others." Such flexibility of syntax, and the plasticity of many other words and of juxtapositions of words, are manipulated in similar ways in many other instances in Japanese versification: the manipulations seen here are by no means unusual, and analogous structures (with differing constituent elements) can be found in countless other poems, in the *Kokin wakashū* and elsewhere. But the words *Natorigawa* and *umoregi* are brought together into this poem—like so many others in its general structure, yet unlike them in the particulars of its makeup—through a fixed association (based on topographical fact) and are then made to (or are allowed to) work together there as the focal nodes of its figural scheme.

In their own way, these elements of the poem demand as much of the reader's attention as does its message, from which they are, finally, inseparable. For the real message here may be not only that which one lover supposedly has to say to another, but also something to the effect that what is being said (or made) here is a poem. Without these particular words, the poem would have to do what it does in some other way; with them, it does what it does in a way that is meant to be recognizably poetic in that it is complex, indirect, encoded, but not impenetrable if the hearer or reader has the tools—knowledge and understanding acquired one way or another—to gain access to it. And one such tool (also essential for understanding Teika's much later pair of Natorigawa poems and the nature of their relationship to the template) is a recognition of the special poetic status of the words *Natorigawa* and *umoregi* (the buried tree) as they occur in these and in a large number of other poems.

Natorigawa is a fine example of that category of words within the *waka* lexicon that has come to be known as *utamakura*; and, although common modern usage of this term might not lead one to do so, the word *umoregi* may be described as an *utamakura*, too, as it often appears, together with Natorigawa or the names of other rivers, *or* independently, as one of those richly signifying kernels or nodes within a poem through which the maker of that poem reaches out to make contact with other poems (or poetic moments) and thereby to complicate or enrich the signifying process of that poem as a whole. With Natorigawa, as with most of those toponyms that would come to be called *utamakura*, such complication or enrichment of the signifying process is usually brought about in one of two ways. One is an evocation of the physical features (real or putative) of the named place, or of any or all of the agglutinated associations (derived from history, lore, or prior literary usage) adhering to the place, by means of the straightforward reiteration of its name and/or by means of mention or description of some of those physical features (such as Natorigawa's shoals or its buried trees); and the other is an aural-based and usually figurative (and hence *not* straightforward) play with aspects of that name itself (such as the punning on the unpacked syllables *na-tori*). Most poems that so name, dilate upon, or otherwise play with Natorigawa and its features do perform one or the other of these most typical *utamakura* operations, but many perform both, often in consecutive or even in overlapping configurations. This is yet another reason why it is a particularly good, if by no means extraordinary, example of the category.[7]

But, as I have noted, the term *utamakura* originally referred not to toponyms alone, nor only to "*words* of frequent *reference*" in general, but rather to texts *of* and *for* reference—specifically, handbooks for poets in which these and other words used frequently in poetry (or words used in special ways) were listed and sometimes explained or illustrated through examples of their use in actual poems. To some extent, the slippage in the referentiality of the word *utamakura*—between reference to these hand-books and reference to the place-names and other lexical items therein—remains unresolved throughout much of *waka* history. At times, the distinction is scrupulously maintained: for example, in the written compendium of his personal store of *waka* lore and expertise, the influential poet and critic Minamoto Toshiyori (or Shunrai, 1055-1129) defines *utamakura* as "books in which the names of places are written," and proceeds to a discussion of the proper use of place-names in which they are consistently referred to as *tokoro no na* (simply, "the names of places"), and never as *utamakura*.[8] Still, there seems to have been a tendency to confound the terms from rather early on, as we can see in still other collections of *waka* lore—for example, in an episode in *Kojidan* (an early thirteenth-century collection of miscellaneous tales) concerning the poet Fujiwara Sanekata (d. 998): for several years he was one of the most dashing and favored gentlemen at the Imperial court, but by 995 he had fallen into such disgrace (for various reasons that remain somewhat obscure, but which may have had to do with scandalous love affairs, breaches of decorum, and the envy of rivals) that the Emperor Ichijō felt compelled to send him off to the undesirable and hence punitive post of governor of Michinoku, the most remote province in the far northeast of Japan. The emperor's words of appointment and farewell, we are told, were something to the effect of a dismissal as well as of a charge to Sanekata to take private advantage of his mission, to "go off and have a look for yourself at all those *utamakura*" (*utamakura mite maire*).[9]

In this case, Ichijō most certainly did not mean that Sanekata should go somewhere and immerse himself in the study of *waka* handbooks, but that he should think of his tour of duty in Michinoku as a chance to tour its famous poetic sites (which are numerous, and which include Natorigawa) in person, rather than to imagine them and write about them at a distance. If these were the emperor's words (and they may well be apocryphal), they may have been meant to display both his irritation as well as just a bit of envy of Sanekata's opportunity. Perhaps the emperor also knew, or guessed, that Sanekata might not come back. Sanekata died in Michinoku three years later—after a fall from his horse, it is said, near the shrine of a Natori-area deity, Kasajima dōsojin. The putative site of his burial lies within that shrine's modern precincts as well. Thus, Sanekata and his story became part of the lore of this place, and also part of the web of associations linked to it: the tale of his presence and his death thereabouts made the *utamakura* of the northeast and especially those of the Natori area collectively even more famous and more deeply embedded in poetic tradition than they were beforehand. One result was that still later poets, such as Saigyō (1118-1190) and, much later, Bashō (1644-94), who literally followed in Sanekata's footsteps—by choice, rather than in exile—would make a point of seeking out Sanekata's vestiges, and of memorializing his presence and death in these environs with their own poems, composed on the spot.[10]

So, even though the most correct (if rather pedantic) way to use the word *utamakura* today would still be in reference to handbook texts, or to the category of potent poetic nominals one might find listed in such handbooks, the term is, in light of such precedent as that demonstrated in the Sanekata story, most likely to refer to place-names like Natorigawa—that is, to the names of places of the kind to which the emperor directed Sanekata's attention, and of the kind whose importance in *waka* poetics has been recognized by generations of poem-makers and poem-readers with the appellation, tantamount to accolade, of *utamakura.* In such usage, the distinction between a place-name and the place it names is often also obscured: thus, places whose names have earned the status of *utamakura* are often themselves termed *utamakura.* In addition, the hybrid (and seemingly redundant) terms *meisho utamakura* and *utamakura meisho* are often used today in identification of famous-place *utamakura,* that is, of a subcategory of *utamakura*-in-the-broader-sense that consists of those toponyms made famous through their repeated, significant use in poetry. But *meisho* (or *nadokoro*) is, in turn, a much larger category of places that are famous for all kinds of reasons: so *meisho utamakura* and *utamakura meisho* may also be thought of as subcategories of these, as they are places that are famous precisely because of their roles in poetry, rather than as the sites of historical events, or because of their beautiful scenery, or because they have some other kind of cultural significance. At the same time, however, a particular *meisho utamakura* may also be a historically important site, or may be much visited because of its scenic beauty, as well as because of its associations with poetry, for these are by no means exclusive categories.

I will trace, hereafter, the process that made Natorigawa (for example) a *meisho utamakura,* as well as the process that made *umoregi* (its buried trees and those of other sites as well) an *utamakura* in the broader sense of a specially potent poetic nominal such as may be found not only in at least dozens (and perhaps hundreds) of poems but also in an *utamakura* text— that is, a poetic handbook, a practical guide to the working poetic lexicon. What we need to understand now, however, is that both the place-name Natorigawa and the word *umoregi* so closely associated with it were lexemes (that is, important items in a specific lexicon) with very special powers, and had been so for a very long time, when Teika used them as he did in the poems with which we have begun, and that he (or, he and his correspondent) used them precisely because they were possessed of those powers, and had been possessed of them for so long.[11] Through the placement of these special words and the deployment of their powers within his poems, Teika shaped his discourse in a special way: one might say that it was through such means as this—the calculated, meaningful use of language made significant in particular ways by its use in another poem (or poems)—that he made his poems poetic and significant in *their* own "new" way, through their alliance and interaction with other, earlier, "old" poems.

But the allusive and intertextual texture of Teika's *seki wabinu* discourse is not limited to its engagement with the *Kokin wakashū* Natorigawa verse: its threads are also intertwined with those from a poem that appears in the *Gosen wakashū* (the second in the series of Imperial anthologies initiated with the *Kokin wakashū*) with a short prose preface (*kotobagaki*) explaining that the poem was sent by Prince Motoyoshi (Motoyoshi no miko, or Moto-yoshi Shinnō, 890-943, the Emperor Yōzei's son) to the lady known as the Kyōgoku Consort (Fujiwara Hōshi, daughter of the politically important Fujiwara Tokihira and one of the wives of Emperor Uda) "after their affair became known" (*koto idekite nochi ni Kyōgoku no miyasundokoro ni tsuka-washikeru*):

> wabinureba ima hata onaji
> Naniwa naru mi o tsukushite mo awan to zo omou[12]

A rough paraphrase of this poem would be, "I care about nothing else but being with you, my love, and I will be, even if it is the end of me," but, again, how this is said, or why it is said *as* it is said, must be further explained and is, in a sense, what the poem is *about*. Yet even before the poem is elucidated in any detail, the link between it and the first in Teika's amorous exchange must be apparent. The later invocation of the slightly altered but readily recognizable language of the earlier poem's first words alone amply forges that link, in what might be described as an aural dimension (if both poems are read so as to be heard) and/or a visual dimension (if the two linked poems are simply seen, as written, or, for that matter, printed texts). But there is also a thematic link, supported by the roughly analogous situations in which the two poems (Motoyoshi's and Teika's) were ostensibly made: in both cases, male speakers say that they are casting all caution aside and giving them-selves up to love affairs that are (for unspecified reasons) difficult or even dangerous for them to pursue. Notably, Motoyoshi conveys this through a "code" that also features a place-name, Naniwa (the ancient name for part of the region now occupied by the city of Osaka), as well as a scenic attribute of that place, its *miotsukushi* (channel buoys). Both the place name and the word for this feature of the place are deployed (in much the same manner as are Natorigawa and its buried trees in the *Kokin wakashū* poem encoun-tered above) for the purposes of significant, meaning-full word play. In this case, the significance (in and for the poem) of the scenic feature associated with Naniwa is transformed, as soon as it is named, by the gravitational pull of the poem's unfolding syntax: the lexeme *miotsukushi,* literally "stakes in the water" (*mio tsu kushi*) that mark shallow channels, immediately dissolves into the contingently homophonous clause *mi o tsukushite,* meaning "even if my body (*mi*) perishes" (literally, "even if I use up (*tsukus[u]*) my body (*mi*)—even if I die), to form a key part of the poem-speaker's vow to pursue his love, come what may.[13]

Thus, while it is only the first clause of Motoyoshi's *wabinureba* that echoes explicitly in Teika's *seki wabinu,* Motoyoshi's "old" poem and Teika's "new" one are also akin in attitude and especially in their figural procedures; for that matter, figural language holds the same status in the *Kokin wakashū* Natorigawa poem as well, and that poem also bequeaths its legacy on Teika's not only in the actual words that are carried from one poem to the other but also in the understanding of the poetic function of such words. Put another way, all three poems are intertextually related, in a narrow sense (their literally allusive relationships) and in a larger sense as well: for they all make use of specific elements of a poetic language of figuration in analogous ways. Such use of language is a genre-wide, perhaps even genre-defining charac-teristic; and such use certainly appears to be intentional on the part of *waka* poets, when they consciously and purposefully produce such generically and canonically correct compositional exercises as these. To be "correct," a *waka* poem must transparently display its points of sameness and difference vis à vis all other poems of its kind. It cannot do this without some effort, design, or intention on the part of the poet. One end result of all this effort, design, and intention is the reader's strong impression of generic similarity and interconnectedness in the ultimate aggregate of canonical texts. I call this an impression of *waka*'s "intertextuality," but it is not an intertextuality that occurs by accident—not, that is, without the intercession of working, designing poets, who, in turn, look to their readers in anticipation that their designs will be understood and appreciated for the manner in which they display these very features of recognizable sameness and difference—that is, the features that determine the texture of the resultant intertextuality.

One additional example of similar interplay among poems may serve to illustrate how these intertextual dynamics form and gather their cross-ca-nonical momentum—invariably, though not always, achieving certain antic-ipated effects. This example also consists of an exchange of poems in the *sōmon* pattern: and this one happens to occur amidst the collected works of the aforementioned Motoyoshi. As in many collections of the works of indi-vidual poets (*shikashū*), the sequence of prose prefaces in much of his personal anthology (*Motoyoshi Shinnō shū*) joins with the poems therein to form a skeletal quasi-narrative of the events and circumstances in which the Prince (supposedly) wrote those poems, and most of those circumstances have to do with love. Thus the reader follows the Prince through several secretive and apparently rather dangerous affairs like the one that produced his *wabinureba* poem, and it is in the midst of one of these that the Prince is portrayed as having cause to send the following verse to the Third Princess from the Kan'in Palace (*Kan'in no sannomiya*):

> mumoregi no shita ni nageku to Natorigawa
>   koishiki se ni wa arawarenubeshi,

which the lady was to understand to mean: "If you sigh (or bemoan your frustrations, *nageku*) there beneath the buried tree in Natorigawa (in that 'space' where our love is carried on in secret), you may be certain that our love will become readily apparent in that river's churning, passionate shoals" (*koishiki se*). That is, "If you complain about the course of our secret affair, it will soon be a secret no more." But the lady countered,

> wa ga kata ni nagarete ka yuku
>   mizuguki no yoru se amata ni kikoyureba ushi[14]

which meant, "How can I be sure that those waters will carry your love to me? I am distressed to hear how many are the shoals (*se*) in which your inkbrush (*mizuguki*) finds a place to rest"—that is, "You write to me about 'the shoals of love,' but why should I care? You write such things to lots of women; you flourish your brush at all of them in just the same way!"

There need be no mistake about the double significance of this "brush:" the suspicious lady deliberately equates the tool with which the Prince produces words with that with which he dabbles in the lives of other women as well. He invoked Natorigawa and its poesy (based in *Kokin wakashū* poem #650) to try to deflect her demands on him; she, in turn, deftly deflected and altered the riverine/aquatic imagery of his poem, sidestepping into another figural scheme in which the brush her lover dips into watery ink is treated (perhaps deservedly) with distrust. The force of his Natorigawa rhetoric is to no avail: Motoyoshi drew upon it with confidence, or perhaps he did so cynically, but in any case the lady saw right through him, and told him that his jive would not work on her. In other words, his consciousness, in the circumstances described as those in which he made this poem, included, and drew him to, the language of an older, well-known verse ("Natorigawa seze no umoregi arawareba"); but in this case the charm of those words failed.

The sequence of poems in the Motoyoshi collection continues with similarly testy exchanges between these two, and then their affair seems to dissipate without resolution; this lady is replaced by another, and by still others, and the rhetoric continues to pour forth, similarly burdened with all the allure and pain of love. Seductive as this rhetoric and its power may be, it becomes clear here—as elsewhere—that such rhetoric does not always work, either to smooth the course of love affairs or to other ends; yet *waka* poets depended upon it and strove for centuries to keep it "working." They labored at length—for about a millennium and a half—by writing poems, or collecting them, or analyzing and criticizing them, to prolong the genre's life and to ensure its survival against and in spite of the forces of change, displacement, and destruction. Their collective product, viewed from today's perspective, is a massive canon of several thousand *waka* poems, many of which look and sound startlingly alike: and it is precisely on those points of likeness, as well as the points of difference, that the reader's attention often most readily falls, and which contribute so much toward forming for the reader what I would describe as the impression of an (at least) canon-wide intertextuality. And it is my belief that the reader forms such an impression in large part because the poets who were the makers of the poems in that canon were also readers who had formed, or had inherited, a similar impression and who wished that others might share it, and who therefore sought to gain access to the powers of that canon and its intertextuality, both for themselves and for other readers, through the addition of their own works to the ever-expanding network of its constituent texts.

It is possible to describe a relationship between or among texts as inter-textual—where there is, as Julia Kristeva has said, a "transposition of one (or several) sign system(s) into another"—on the seemingly pure level of text alone, or, at least, in that dimension of consciousness where, through the act of reading, a reader and a text make contact with one another.[15] In such a description it will be those inherent aspects of those texts that are understood by the reader (through whatever means) as intertextual—that is, interrelated to multiple texts—that will come under scrutiny. The author, whose status for so many readers today is so dubious, is, of course, left out of this picture. But what if we choose to keep him or her there? One will do so if one is inclined to think of and respond to texts as things made and which have makers about whom there are also some things to be known and understood (if possible). In the Japanese tradition, as elsewhere, there are some texts that are understood as having been made by *other than human* hands or minds, and which therefore must be approached and understood in their own way; but such texts are not necessarily held to be wholly beyond understanding by virtue of their divine or magical origin; and, ultimately, they too are read, as are those texts that are unequivocally presented as the work of human minds, in terms of documented and narrated (or potentially documentable or narratable) experiences and circumstances—those real conditions that, it is claimed and believed, gave and give rise to the making of verse. What one is then concerned with is not only what comes through to the reader from the text to form that reader's conscious understanding of it, but also what was (or was not) active in the consciousness of the maker of the text at the time that he or she made it, according to the documentation or narrative of its making. But if the reader is skeptical of such traditional accounts of and theories of poetry's rise from supposedly documentable or narratable circumstances, what then, if anything, is left as a means of access to that consciousness? Can the text itself serve this purpose? I would say, with some caution, yes; *waka* texts, with their dual transparencies and opacities of design (such as those we have seen in Teika's *Shūi gusō* Natorigawa exchange), may so serve: for example, if we see a particular deployment of an *utamakura* place-name, or a particular gesture of allusion, as a trace left in the poem from the operations of the poem-maker's hand or mind as he or she consciously and deliberately went about preparing it to "work" within its genre, its lineage. And I would say, again, that the intertextuality which we then, ultimately, perceive when we read across the canons of that genre is, in large part, also a product or end result of that consciousness—or, at least, as much a product thereof as it is a result of the content and contours of our own readerly consciousnesses.

It goes without saying that one must use caution in making and then trying to support any such critical speculations about writerly or readerly consciousness, and that the zeal to do so should not blind one to the weaknesses of certain kinds of evidence or arguments. This means that one must choose one's evidence for argument carefully, and use it honestly, and not ahistorically or distortedly. When contemplating the relationship between Teika's *seki wabinu* poem and Motoyoshi's *wabinureba* poem, for example, it is indeed tempting to point out that Teika used Motoyoshi's *wabinureba* to represent that poet when he compiled his famous anthology, the *Ogura hyakunin isshu* (One hundred poems by one hundred poets, first devised sometime in the 1230s), and to argue that this poem, therefore, must surely have held some special place in Teika's creative consciousness at the time that he made the (undated) pair of poems with which we began. It is even more tempting to argue something similar on the basis of the fact that Teika included *both* Motoyoshi's poem and the *Kokinshū* Natorigawa poem—both of the poems from which elements are woven into the *Shūi gusō* love exchange—among the model verses listed in the treatise he wrote in 1209 for the youthful shogun (and aspiring poet) Minamoto Sanetomo (i.e., in *Kindai shūka*), and that he did so again in a still later treatise (*Eiga no taigai*, ca. 1221).[16] But to argue in this way might be to go too far; if nothing else, we must recognize that the historical sequence of these events, and all the attendant circumstances, are impossible to reconstruct, even if it seems desirable or useful to do so. It is better, therefore, to argue on the basis of the evidence that Teika's *Shūi gusō* poems themselves provide—that is, the language they so explicitly share with others—that Motoyoshi's "old" *wabi-nureba* poem and the even "older" *Kokin* Natorigawa poem were somehow jointly active in the creative process when Teika made his "new" *seki wabinu* poem, whenever that was—and that Teika expected this interplay to be recognized, or recognizable, in some dimension or stratum of the perception or consciousness of the hearer or reader of his text, whenever he might hear or see it. The complexity of the resultant texture of interwoven texts, in any case, is certainly due to more than one or two gestures of allusion per se: for it is, beyond that, also a recapitulatory exercise performed in what is already a profoundly intertextual ambience. The performer knows and values that ambience, and his or her goal is to make an incremental contribution to it. But he or she cannot do so without wishing to do so, without willing his or her poem to conform to both writerly and readerly expectations. The intertextual increment, therefore, cannot be achieved without the exercise of intention.

In *The Pleasure of Reading*, Robert Alter has expressed strong reservations about the use of the term *intertextuality* by Kristeva and others influenced by her work, largely on the grounds of these critics' apparent disregard for, or denial of, intention. He is much more comfortable with descriptions of most interrelations between texts as "allusions," which he defines, with Ziva Ben-Porat's phrase, as "simultaneous activation[s] of two texts' in patterns of interrelations that are usually quite unpredictable."[17] Indeed, intention maintains a strong presence throughout Alter's argument, as here, where he offers his own means of distinguishing between the competing terms: "Whereas allusion implies a writer's active, purposeful use of antecedent texts, intertextuality is something that can be talked about when two or more texts are set side by side, and in recent critical practice such juxtaposition has often been the willful or whimsical act of the critic, without regard to authorial intention."[18] I shall not venture here to judge this "recent critical practice," but I will argue that, in the Japanese texts under scrutiny here, allusion certainly occurs, and that it certainly does "simultaneously activate multiple texts," but that the effect thereof may fairly be termed an intertextuality, and that *both* allusion and intertextuality are produced through the will—or perhaps even the whim—of the author, in anticipation of the comprehending response of the reader.

I risk this tandem use of both these terms in the belief that both are appropriate to the description of the tradition under scrutiny here, and that the two terms may be used (in this discussion, at least) complementarily— that is, that they need not be so opposed as Alter sees them. I would suggest, furthermore, that much of the language that has long been used in studies of allusion in the work of such English poets as Dryden and Pope may still be applicable to studies of allusion *and* intertextuality in other traditions. Take, for example, Reuben Arthur Brower's assertions that, "For Dryden and for Pope allusion, especially in ironic contexts, is a resource equivalent to symbolic metaphor and elaborate imagery in other poets. Through allusion, often in combination with subdued metaphors and exquisite images, Pope gets his purchase on larger meanings and evokes the finer resonances by which poetry (in Johnson's phrase) 'penetrates the recesses of the mind.'" In addition, "Like Dryden, [Pope] was catholic in his tastes and he enjoyed an easy commerce with the poetry of the past and present . . . [and a] direct and lively contact with Homer and the greater Roman and English poets and with many lesser English and French poets of his own generation and of the century before him. Feeling no nineteenth-century compulsion to be merely original, he took pleasure in imitating the poets he read and admired, one and all."[19]

Transferred, if they may be, across time and cultural space to the present discussion of *waka,* the implications that arise here from Brower's language —from his idea of "getting a purchase on" things and of conducting "commerce" with and among texts—as well as his indication that there was and is "pleasure" to be had in performing or in witnessing the act of imitation, will, I think, prove worthy of our contemplation. And perhaps even more worthy of our consideration, at this point, are the perspectives and insights offered by Thomas M. Greene in *The Light in Troy,* his study of intertextual strategies in an earlier stage of the tradition of imitation, in the poetry of the Renaissance. There, inter alia, on the power that lexemes acquire as they age, Greene writes:

> Time may be the element in which words are eroded but it is also the element in which, for each of us, they acquire accumulatively their being and their wealth. We understand any usage of a word as the last in a series which possesses coherence; the word's relative stability *now* derives from the stability of that series, just as our feeling of its gathering potency grows out of that series' provocative complexity. The origin of the series, our first encounter with the word, is likely to be lost to us. But the word contains its problematic power because it derives from

a flexible but continuous chain of concrete occasions that we organize automatically as we speak and listen.[20]

For this reader, this general description of "the word" is a startlingly apt one for the word, and particularly for such words as may be called *utamakura*, as it operates in and forms and reforms itself in *waka*. Again, elsewhere, having said that, "The word carries with it a story of its development, its evolution," and that he will "refer to this process of creating signifying constructs as 'etiology' and instances of the process as 'etiologies,'" Greene goes on to claim that "an etiological allusion fabricates a context that is itself of course subject to alteration, distortion, anachronism; it provides only a semblance of rootedness, an artifice of eternity. Still, I submit that it represents a limited means, a human means, for dealing with the force of rupture." And then, once more on the dynamics of language's movement through time, he writes: "The poetic word achieves its brilliance against the background of a past which it needs in order to signify but which its own emergence is tendentiously and riskily shaping."[21]

It will become clear in the course of this discussion, I hope, that *utamakura* place-names and the related elements of *waka* language that are used and reused in similar ways are indeed words that carry particularly rich "stories of their development and evolution," and that they figure very prominently, and repeatedly, in "etiological allusions" that are very much "subject to alteration, distortion, anachronism," but are nevertheless seized upon, again and again, for the creation of "semblances of rootedness" and "artifices of eternity." For we will indeed find, in many instances of *utamakura* poesy, written at various times in a variety of circumstances, some rather desperate expressions of the desire to defy time and change, efforts to ignore history, or to rewrite it, by emphasizing *sameness*—improbable samenesses, or unities, of vision or of experience, spanning disparate times. The means for producing this impression are often the deliberate reuse of the same means of expression (words) used in other times, in other places—that is, in other poems. Try as it may, a poetry so designed cannot really bring about such erasures of time's passing; if anything, the attempt reveals most plainly just how much change time does bring about, how impossible it is to dull its force, how deeply we feel that force. Through allusions and other gestures to other moments in its own history, this long-lived tradition of Japanese poetry *does* successfully represent its own continuity, creating an impression that, though all else may be subject to time's exigencies, poetry resists and overcomes. But this, too, is a false self-representation, or a fiction: the traditions of poetry are as subject to change as everything else in Japanese culture, or in any culture. Nonetheless, here, in *waka,* is the voice of a culture, or at least the voice of its elite, representing its relationship to its cosmos as what it is not and perhaps never was—but as that which it collectively seems to wish that relationship to have been: again, and again, this collective voice augments its rather desperate attempt to create a lasting illusion of having stemmed the flow of time, and it does so through the willed (and sometimes rather loving) reuse, in a present time, of words from another (often nostalgically longed-for) former time, the image of which is invariably deeply distorted by the imperfection of memory or by the imposition of an ideological lens. Once such an illusion becomes part of ideology, as it does in the *waka* tradition, its adherents cling ever more tenaciously to it and to its affects. The *waka* canon may be seen as the collective "affect" of just such an illusion: over time, it generates a vast textual infrastructure that manages to overarch the span of time and even gives the sense of having brought about time's collapse, so that the past seems to merge indistinguishably with the present. And it is, in particular, through allusions to other moments in its textual history that the practitioners of and participants in this long tradition of Japanese poetry collectively contrive to represent its seeming continuity.

To this reader, this rather desperate effort—to alter the world through texts projected into or inscribed upon it—seems especially poignant, and it seems ironic, too, that this attitude, while inherently doomed, should also have contributed as much as it did to the shaping of traditional Japanese poetics and to ensuring their long-term survival and pre-eminence across and through time—and to propelling their influence, as well, into virtually every genre of Japanese literature. It also seems remarkable that such a great part of the task, or burden, of enabling or abetting the inculcation of an ideology of cultural continuity—a tool for survival, but also a rationale for withholding acknowledgment of change—should have fallen (or been placed) on something so seemingly fragile (though durable) as this literary language of poetic figuration—a code in which things are so often represented by other things, where one word is so often not only substituted for another but also made to *be* another (at least contingently) even while it is still itself. It seems equally remarkable that this task should have been carried out, for the most part, through the development and long-term extension of an art of figuration, and of allusion to previous and other figurations, by a tradition (or, by its participants) constantly and repeatedly turning inward upon itself in search of sustenance. But then, one wonders, where else was such a burden to fall, and how else might such a tradition have taken shape?

For one answer, one might look to Jacques Lacan's writings on metonymy and metaphor (or "condensation" and "displacement") and find therein another language that could be of use in describing the prominence of figuration in Japanese poetry and its capacity to perform so much hard work: there is, for example, his image of a powerfully "signifying chain," "rings of a necklace that is a ring in another necklace made of rings," by means of which texts acquire their strength, from and through one another.[22] Some readers may already have associated my use of the figure of the buried tree with Lacan's exploration of the particular signifier *tree*, the "trans-subjective wealth" of which permits him "precisely in so far as I have this language in common with other subjects, that is to say, in so far as it exists as a language, to use it in order to signify *something quite other* than what it says." Alongside this must also be placed Lacan's bare and challenging characterization of metaphor as the substitution of one word for another: "That is the formula for the metaphor," he says, "and if you are a poet you will produce for your own delight a continuous stream, a dazzling tissue of metaphors."[23] I would say here that this is just what generations of Japanese poets do appear to have produced—though perhaps not only "for their own delight."

Now, given what has been written previously in English about Japanese poetry, it is not unreasonable to expect that a reader who does not know Japanese or Japanese literary scholarship will nonetheless be able to read many of the poems discussed herein and understand something of what is "poetic" about them, and something of how figural language works in them. Up to now, most modern British and American studies of Japanese poetry have emphasized the dominance of natural phenomena and seasonal cycles in its topoi and in its imagistic schemes, the overwhelming concern for mutability that shapes it thematically, and the affective lyricism that is identified both in theory and in practice as the primary impulse for composition. Many of the poems discussed here might readily be analyzed in these terms by anyone who has read the works of Robert Brower, Earl Miner, or Helen McCullough.[24] And many of the figural schemes adopted by generation after generation of poets are also well-known, though their full complexity is often hard to convey in translation. For example, the frequent transferences and transpositions of identity between a poet or his or her subject and another object in nature that represents him or her, or the subject, are perhaps less complete or final than many translators find it possible to suggest. For example, this poem—"haru ya kuru hana ya saku to mo shirazariki / tani no soko naru umoregi nareba,"[25] which is by the late tenth-/early eleventh-century poet Izumi Shikibu, and which we will encounter again in our discussion (in the following chapter) of the development of the figure of the buried tree (*umoregi*) in independence from association with particular places or place-names—is simultaneously readable as description of a fossilized tree to which humanlike sentiments are attributable and as a metaphor for the poet herself, bemoaning her own obscurity. One might suggest this by offering two parallel translations:

A. *It* did not know that spring had arrived
   or that the blossoms had come forth,
for *it* is a tree that lies buried in the valley's depths.

B. *I* did not know that spring had arrived,
   that the blossoms had come forth,
for *I* am a tree that lies buried in the valley's depths.

or through a typographically clumsy hybrid of the two:

C. *I*[*it*] did not know that spring had arrived,
   that the blossoms had come forth,
for *it* is[*I am*] a tree that lies buried in the valley's depths.

The indecisiveness represented in version C at least has the virtue (if no other) of indicating that it is impossible, and even misleading, to judge one reading "primary" and the other "secondary," as it was certainly the poet's plan to present them as concurrent and inseparable, by means of her language's own structural ambiguity. It should perhaps be explained here that the poem—like most, though by no means all, in the *waka* canon—has no pronouns (neither "I" nor "it"): the only subject of the verb *shiru*, "to know" (*shirazariki*, "did not know") in the poem is *umoregi*, the buried tree. But the poet knows that she can count on the reader to recognize the figure as one which may very well represent something other than or besides itself in this or any poem in which it appears.

This planned or "willed" complexity is surely the most striking thing about the poem, and any discussion of the poem should try to explicate just that. But that is not all that is poetic about the poem. What must also be understood is the way that the poem (or the poet making it) deliberately engages with an existing figural scheme, which focuses on the natural phenomenon of the buried tree and its physiology and then does things with it that are both like and unlike the things done with that figure in other poems (or by other poets). In other words, this poem, like so many others, is purposefully designed so as to resonate with a somewhat familiar and yet somewhat unfamiliar ring. There is no explicit allusion to any other specific buried tree poem here, but there is an intentional, knowing, and calculated intertextuality that is at work here, enriching the poem and the reader's experience of

it: through its constituent language, the poem itself displays its interconnectedness with others, and thus places itself (or, is placed, by its author—
who knows just what she is doing) within the canon, in genealogical
apposition to innumerable other poems—both those that share the buried
tree figure and others that use other figures in similar (metaphorical) ways.

Explicitly allusive operations among pairs and groups of poems, achieved
through the compositional practice usually termed *honkadori* (allusive variation), are fairly well-known to Western readers of *waka* and Western studies
thereof.[26] Through our studies in this and other cultures, scholars have
acquired an understanding of the poetic power of allusion (and of other
referential interactions) in general: and we have recognized the impulse to
use that power, especially in poetry and in poetic drama, and have become
familiar with some of the consequences of doing so. But exactly how does
allusion work in and across the *waka* corpus, where the relatively narrow
range of figures, diction, and rhetorical schemes available to (or used by)
poets working with and within the tradition would seem to make almost
every poem allude or intertextually relate itself in some way to others? How
well prepared are we to explain the impression that a Japanese poem that
gestures explicitly, or more generally, toward another (or to many) makes on
the reader, or to describe *how* it makes that impression?[27]

Upon encountering these operations in a specific poem or groups of
poems, many traditional and contemporary Japanese commentators are
likely to focus immediately on those elements in them that are most readily
read as being pre-determined, as to their function in a given poem, by
previous usage; or, in some cases, the commentator may read later usage, or
analogous usage in another roughly contemporaneous context, back onto or
across to the poem at hand in order to arrive at an understanding of the
function of individual words and phrases as well as an approximation of the
totality of the target poem—sometimes termed its *daii*, "the greater meaning
of the complex whole." This approach—which amounts to taking a poem as
the sum of its parts—has its roots in the most ubiquitous and deeply ingrained principle or tenet of *waka* exegesis, the assumption, or belief, that
the poem's real "work" is nothing other than the expression of sentiment
(*kokoro*) through the manipulation of words (*kotoba*) and the particular
associations that accrue to them. One can read in many places about this
kokoro/kotoba (sentiment/language) relationship, which is the fundamental
and most familiar schema of Japanese poetics.[28] But, for the most part,
English-speaking scholars have not sufficiently explored the implications of,
or the limitations of, or the possible alternatives to this schema. We do have
ample representations of the tradition, in anthologies of translations and a

small but growing number of critical studies,[29] but we have said too little and can read too little in English that analyzes precisely how the language (*kotoba*) of Japanese poetry operates through these means that are so strikingly repetitive, reproductive, and cross-referential; and we have also said too little about what these operations, in themselves, may signify.

An important corollary of the central *kokoro/kotoba* tenet of Japanese poetics is the principle, repeatedly made manifest in praxis, that certain sentiments can be expressed again and again and thus be reencountered as familiars from the past, given new life in new castings, through the manipulation of a limited lexicon composed of sets of words and figures associable with them that are the avatars of a similarly limited repertory of sentiments. What appears to be a unified aesthetic based on this principle and the practices it engendered and that was engendered by it remained potent for many hundreds of years—from long before the seventh and eighth centuries, when songs and poems were first recorded in a script reproducing the sounds of the Japanese language, up to and through the nineteenth century—and they are still operative for contemporary readers and writers of *waka*. But ample attention to the words used in the production of the artifacts of this aesthetic (that is, in poems) will show that, in many and perhaps even in most instances of poem production, a reversal of the *kokoro/kotoba* tenet is a more accurate model of what actually took place: for word (discourse, oral and written) existed in a state conditioned by prior usage and then was put to use in poems which, to a greater or lesser extent, reflected something that their makers felt when they made them. And often, what was felt more than anything else was *the consciousness that a poem was being made*.

Yet even if, as I believe, this was most often the case, it is still important to see this procedure (*kotoba/kokoro*) as a result of and as a vehicle that sustains a profoundly nostalgic impetus. The drive to retrieve, recreate, and revivify past experience (especially poem-making) through the recycling of the language used in that past generated and shaped poetic composition (and other literary production) through generation after generation, as poets in each age reverted to the same circumscribed lexicons and the special grammars linked to them by their acknowledged forebears.

Such nostalgic (one might also say conservative) inclinations or impulses are not unique to Japanese literature or Japanese culture, but their presence and effects are particularly marked there, and have therefore received and will continue to receive considerable attention, and have been and will continue to be analyzed in various ways, by both Japanese and non-Japanese critics. The history of *waka* has been portrayed as a rise from primitive origins toward a point of high sophistication and a subsequent but inevitable decline. And that decline has often been attributed, in part, to the strangulation of *waka* by the severe circumscription of its lexicon, its reliance on the recycling of its rhetorical elements, and, the suppression, by and large, of liberating expansion and experimentation. That *waka*'s pre-eminence as genre and as cultural institution deteriorated over time is an indisputable fact. Because the prosperity of the genre was so closely linked to that of the Imperial court and and its institutions, it necessarily followed them in their general decline from the late twelfth century onward. Beginning also at about that time, other genres of poetry—especially *renga,* "linked verse"— which were not so exclusively claimed by elite practitioners as *waka* was, eclipsed the older genre in intensity of production and as the favored object of patronage, even while remaining structurally and aesthetically rooted in *waka.* For these reasons, critics often use language that emphasizes *waka*'s institutional decline in their treatments of certain phases of its history, and seem to be comfortable using such phrases as "the end of the tradition" when discussing this stage of *waka*'s history.[30] But it is also possible to portray *waka* as a continuously self-revitalizing tradition—at least across a millennium, and more—and to claim that the tendency to repetition, or the penchant for recycling, and the limiting of emotional and rhetorical range did not gradually kill *waka*; rather, these essential characteristics may be, in great part, what kept *waka* alive, even when it was displaced or overshadowed by other genres and forms which were, nonetheless, descendant from or dependent on it. The sentiments (*kokoro*) represented in and accessible through *waka* were highly prized; but even more prized, and even more essential to the durability of the genre, was *waka* language (*kotoba*) itself. The prolonged survival and protection of that language became, for many patrons and practitioners, an end in itself, and one toward which they labored with great emotional intensity and deep personal investment.

This is particularly evident in the works—not only poems but also the treatises, diaries, and other records—of Fujiwara Shunzei, his son Teika, and many other poets (male and female) in the circle of Emperor Gotoba—that is, the poets associated with and active in the era of the *Shin kokin wakashū* (or, more briefly, the *Shin kokinshū*), the eighth of the Imperially commissioned *waka* anthologies (*chokusenshū*), which was compiled by these same men in the first decade of the thirteenth century; and this is one of the reasons why so much attention is devoted to their works in this study (as in many others). The compilation of the *Shin kokinshū* took place at a time of transition and crisis, both political and cultural: civil turmoil and violent warfare had shaken the country for several decades and continued to do so,

and institutions that had long seemed impregnable and immune to change
were threatened, and some were transformed. Amid these conditions, Fujiwara Shunzei, Teika, and their patrons, colleagues, and competitors were all
very much aware of and were deeply drawn into the literary culture that had
survived into these times, and they sought to preserve it even as they sought
to make it new. This is, in part, why allusive variation (*honkadori*) is such a
conspicuous feature of their poetic works, and it goes a long way toward
explaining the grounding, and the force, of Shunzei's and Teika's joint rec-
ommendation—proffered by implication by the former in judgments between competitors in formal poetry contests (*utaawase*), and more explicitly
by the latter in his treatises—that poets of their age would do best to keep
the words of their poems "old" while striving, at the same time, to convey
sentiments that would seem "new" (*kotoba furuki . . . kokoro atarashi*).[31]

   This was, in effect, a manifesto for experimentation in the balancing of
kotoba and *kokoro* but also, perforce, in the arts of allusion and intertextuality—and such experimentation was, of course, to be controlled through its
confinement within the perimeters of the known, old lexicon, the established
repertoire of poetic words.[32] Needless to say, not every poem made in the
Shin kokin era is a *honkadori* poem—but a great many are, and for this
reason this age, and its works, are looked to as a high-water mark in the
development of allusiveness as a component of *waka* art. This was also, for
many of the same reasons, an era in which place-name poetry—which was
by this time inherently allusive, and was recognized as such—saw a kind of
revival on the basis of a strong awareness of its own precedents and history.
The Saishōshitennōin program of 1207, for example, was an exercise in text
and image manipulation of famous places—of their names and of their visual
properties—carried out in the context of remembrance of earlier such manipulations in poetry's past: it may be seen as a highly charged attempt to
revivify antique practices and relationships and to achieve anew an idealized
ancient equilibrium or harmony in a troubled world that might then be
rewritten or redrawn by the participating poets and painters in a more
perfect form. They failed in this attempt, of course, but much can be learned
by contemplating what was at stake—politically, emotionally, symbolically—
in this endeavor.[33]

   Before proceeding to this and other matters, however, some further orientation may be useful to those readers who have limited familiarity with
the contours of the tradition under examination here. No Japanese text of
any kind was written down before the early fifth century, when the Chinese
writing system was introduced from the Asian mainland; and the earliest
texts of any kind of Japanese literature that survive are from the early eighth

century. There was, of course, a rich oral tradition prior to that, but our picture of it is deeply colored by the fact that it was first preserved in writing carried out under the auspices of a central governing elite seeking to create its own self-justifying cultural "history," and doing so with a strong consciousness of how this had been done in China. The poem often cited as the originating text for the whole *waka* canon is dated to this vast, preliterate span of time, and, in particular, from that legendary period that is termed the "age of the gods" (*kami no yo*): it is attributed in the earliest national histories (the *Kojiki* and the *Nihon shoki,* completed in 712 and 720, respectively), in the preface to the *Kokin wakashū* (905), and elsewhere to the rather unruly deity Susa no o no mikoto, the brother of the sun-goddess Amaterasu no ōmikami, who is the putative progenitor of the Imperial clan. Susa no o's geographical base was the once-powerful region of Izumo (in the west, facing Korea), a region thoroughly marginalized by dominant and geographically central Yamato by the eighth century; so there is some irony in the fact that what is celebrated as the first *Yamato uta,* the first Japanese poem, is actually a poem that celebrates the landscape, and the very name, of this suppressed Izumo.[34] It is also Susa no o's wedding song:

> yakumo tatsu
> Izumo yaegaki
> tsumagome ni
> yaegaki tsukuru
> sono yaegaki o[35]
> In Izumo, land of covering clouds,
> I build a covering fence around my wife,
> and oh, that covering fence!

The *waka* tradition takes this as a model poem for several reasons, among them the seemingly simple fact that it is a song of thirty-one syllables, with clusters (*ku*) of five, seven, five, seven, and seven syllables.[36] Though mischievous and unruly (he is best known for his misdeeds, which brought about his estrangement from his divine sister and his exile to the domains of mortals), Susa no o is thus traditionally acknowledged as the first being on (the Japanese) earth to have sung or composed in this so-called regulated pattern, which throughout the long history of the *waka* tradition has been the standard, dominant form.

The first great anthology of Japanese poetry, the *Man'yōshū,* compiled by the end of the eighth century, is the major repository of longer poems, or *chōka,* which are of variant length but which also adhere to the alternating five-seven syllable format; one or more shorter thirty-one-syllable poems (called *tanka,* short poem), which elsewhere and most commonly stand alone, also often follow these longer poems as codas (or envoys, *hanka*), as does this example by an early eighth-century poet, Yamabe Akahito:

Waka no ura ni shio michikureba kata o nami
  ashibe o sashite tazu nakiwataru[37]
At Waka Bay, when the tide is high, there is no beach,
  and so the cranes are crying as they make their way toward beds of reeds.

The place described here, Waka Bay, lends itself to many later poems that are not "about" that place so much as they are about *waka* (Japanese poetry) itself; and it is able to do so because of the same aural (as well as scriptorial and hence visual) plasticity that is to be found in many other place-names and that is, therefore, a fundamental aspect of their poetic utility and usage. Waka no ura probably had its name long before the invention of the Sino-Japanese word *waka*, which is usually written with two Chinese characters that mean "Japanese" and "song/poem." Written in another way, the word *waka* could also mean "young." And perhaps more important, if the word *waka* is simply heard, or if it is written (as it well might be) with phonetic letters (*kana*) rather than with any of the graphs (*kanji*) suggested above, its meaning, or specific semantic significance, remains flexible, multivalent, and ambiguous.

But, if Akahito intended any overt play with the possible double meanings of this place-name, to be perceived either aurally, when the poem was sung, or visually, when it was seen in script (one way or another), it would certainly have been the play between this meaning of *waka* as young and the association of the cranes with great age (they are symbols of eternity in both China and Japan) that he had in mind. And even if he did not, we may, as readers, see this play in the poem, and consider how it works for us: it may, among other things, appear to involve the poem, at least in part, with a dialectic between all that which appears to be young, fresh, and situated in the now, and that which is aged, wizened, and situated in the past. As a result, one might say, the poem itself is simultaneously in these dual realms, or in some vague temporal territory in between. Likewise, *waka* in general, as well as this poem, may be said to be situated in both past and present, or at least to appear to do so from our perspective when we, as its readers, try to stand where poets stand and see what they see, hear what they hear, and remember what they remember, which is what they so often invite us to do. But, in order to do so, we must enter into their past through words that reach us only now across the immensity of elapsed time, as does the light of distant stars.

But, as it happens, this poem by Akahito is quite firmly grounded in its own distinct (though distant) time, and its setting in an anthology (the

Man'yōshū) is specifically designed so as to guide us to that time and to the place where the poem was made. The prose preface that precedes the *chōka* to which Akahito's Waka no ura poem is attached (as one of two codas) indicates that all were written on the occasion of a royal visit by the Emperor Shōmu to the province of Kii (where Waka no ura is located) in the early winter of 725. Akahito was there, too, apparently as a kind of court scribe, and these poems are presented (in the *Man'yōshū*) as having been composed on the spot, as a contribution to and commemoration of this moment of contact between a ruler and this specific place in his realm. In both the *chōka* (*Man'yōshū* #917) and in its envoys, Akahito reproduces the sheer pleasure of viewing the seaside scene in which this contact takes place, but he also reminds us of the significance of his sovereign's having established a temporary residence in this locale at a vantage point from which he can admire and lay claim to a site where time seems to stand still: the Emperor sees just what was seen in the age of the gods, his ancestors, and is reminded that this aged, ageless land is his, as it was theirs. In this sense, too, the coda-poem's overt involvement in the Waka no ura landscape and with that which is eternal and ancient, as well as that which is fresh and new, may be in harmony with the whole enterprise of which it and the *chōka* are now the only lasting marks—in harmony, that is, with the ideology that lay behind this particular Emperor's visit to a place that had been visited more than once by his own royal predecessors.[38]

Almost nine hundred years after this event, in the year 1600, in a time of civil warfare, when the samurai-poet Hosokawa Yūsai consigned to the safe-keeping of a younger colleague (Karasumaru Mitsuhiro) a collection of irreplaceable literary documents which represented the continuity of the *waka* tradition itself, responsibility for which he shared with the then-reigning and much-beleaguered Emperor (Goyōzei), Yūsai conveyed this poem as well:

> moshiogusa kakiatsumetaru ato tomete
> mukashi ni kaese Waka no ura nami[39]

This was a transparently encoded exhortation to the newest guardian of the physical remains of a great literary tradition, and it may be paraphrased as follows:

> Deposit these traces of sea grasses gathered over time
> and then return them to the past, oh waves on the shores of Poetry Bay.

To convey his message and the prized goods that it accompanied, Yūsai used the conventional figure of strands of seaweed (*moshiogusa*), gathered for the process of extracting salt from seawater at such marine locales as Waka no ura, as a trope for script, or text, and thus as a representation of the many strands of poetic tradition gathered over time and passed down (by "wave after wave," or generation after generation of poets) in the precious documents that had been in his care. His verb *kakiatsumetaru* doubles as "raked and gathered" (as seaweed is raked and gathered on the shore) and as "written and gathered" (as are texts); and, in the place-name itself, *ura* (most literally "bay") may also mean "the hidden aspect" of *waka*, as might be revealed in the secret content of the documents. So this is a largely figurative or abstract Waka no ura, in contrast to Akahito's more literal beachscape, yet among all the strands of grasses culled over the centuries to which Yūsai refers, the traces of Akahito's poem are prominent: though not explicitly heard or seen, Akahito's thirty-one syllables lie behind and within and contribute to the making of and the impact of Yūsai's. Furthermore, in both poems, though in different ways, the central figure of Waka no ura stands for something other than itself alone. Such differences as there may be in what it stands for are differences wrought by the differences in time and circumstance—yet the link between the two poems that is forged through the presence in both of this place-name also has the effect of diminishing those differences, or of mitigating—even while evincing—their effects.

Over the course of the very long interval between Akahito and Yūsai, Waka no ura had become one of poetry's (*waka*'s) most special sites, but it had been transformed from a real site of royal and bardic visitation to a more abstract and ideal place inhabited by poetry itself; its name now stood for the protected dwelling place of the *waka* tradition and its texts, a haven where they might reside undisturbed through time, awaiting innumerable future visitations. Yūsai's "visit" took place when it seemed that the tradition itself was under siege, and so it was particularly fitting that even this textual gesture of return—this act of symbolic rescue—was also a recapitulation of the allusive gestures which, long before his time, had come to characterize that tradition and its own complicated negotiations with and across time. Here, at least, this instance of intertextual work coincided with some real success: the tradition, embodied in Yūsai's precious documents as well as in this poem, survived to be raked and gathered yet again from this and still other shores.

It is intertextuality of the kind that can be seen here—a simultaneous engagement of disparate texts across time, not only through explicit allusion but also through a network of associations that collide and congeal in the reader's consciousness—that is often less than readily apparent to Western readers of Japanese poetry (though perhaps all too apparent to their Japanese counterparts) and that therefore warrants special explication and discussion. For what may be most significant about this particular poetics of allusion and the literary tradition to which it gives shape is this great gap— this man-made chasm—between the continuities and contiguities that allusion suggests and even celebrates, on the one hand, and, on the other, the disruptions and transformations that nevertheless go forward in the social, phenomenal world into which such poems are flung, or on which they are inscribed, as if the one (the illusion of continuity) might obliterate or at least neutralize the other (the inevitability of change).

In *The Past Is a Foreign Country,* David Lowenthal reminds us that the word *nostalgia* was coined relatively recently, in the late seventeenth century, to describe an acute physiological condition caused by morbid longing for the home place.[40] I have already suggested that *nostalgia*—which one encounters in Japanese most often as a loan-word from English (*nosutarujia*) but which is occasionally translated with a modern Sino-Japanese word for homesickness (*kyōshū*)—may be of use in describing some aspects of the conditions that generate the relationships among *waka* poems. Indeed, some of the works we will examine here betray the signs or effects of what we may be inclined to think of as an almost morbid or pathological yearning for other times and their conditions, or for other places, in the form of texts. We should remember, however, that for most of these poets the past, if distant, was never really foreign: they believed, or acted as though they believed, that, through contact made through texts, its terrains remained familiar and accessible and could be traversed again and again in search of resources for the making of new texts.

I frequently find myself pressed by my American students, or by Japanese colleagues, to explain my own understanding of *mono no aware,* that elusive but ubiquitous key concept in traditional Japanese aesthetics.One might translate it as "that which there is in and about things or entities or states (*mono*) that has the power to move us emotionally," and which may be understood, at least provisionally, as an identification of the source of such emotional impact of phenomena or experience as may be perceived by the sentient observer of or participant therein. Certainly, *mono no aware* embraces and is deeply involved with a particular kind of nostalgic sentiment: an entity that is characterized as an expression or embodiment of *mono no aware*—be it a literary text, a painting, or the gesture of an actor on the Nō stage—is often so characterized because of the way that it refers to, recaptures, or reenacts a powerfully emotional moment, historical or imaginary, known or believed to have been experienced at some time in the past and continuously and repeatedly sought out again throughout successive time. I introduce this idea not because I intend to scrutinize the concept of *mono no aware* in detail, but rather because the present study seeks to explore something that I think is related to it—the idea that certain elements of *waka* language (that is, those that may be categorized as *utamakura*) function powerfully in and across texts and time, and that they are invested with such power and are cultivated consistently through time precisely because of their capacity to invoke this reverberating nostalgic sentiment, which is, in turn, invoked for a purpose, to produce a particular effect or effects.

The idea that nostalgia, which many think of as retrogressive, and even destructive, may also be a positive stimulus to creativity and change, was argued quite persuasively some time ago by Fredric Jameson. In his essay entitled "Walter Benjamin, or Nostalgia," Jameson explores Benjamin's "painful straining" amid mid-century Europe's crises "towards a wholeness or unity of experience which the historical situation threatens to shatter at every turn," but he concludes, after reviewing Benjamin's turns toward the past (particularly to Goethe), that "if nostalgia as a political motivation is most frequently associated with fascism, there is no reason why a nostalgia conscious of itself, a lucid and remorseless dissatisfaction with the present on the grounds of some remembered plenitude, cannot furnish as adequate a revolutionary stimulus as any other," and that "at its most poignant Benjamin's experience of time [was as] a pure present, on the threshold of the future honoring it by averted eyes in meditation on the past."[41] I am not sure whether a "remorseless dissatisfaction with the present" is always at play, but I would like to argue that what we may recognize in Japanese texts as moments of intense *mono no aware* are almost always intense moments of "meditation on the past" that do, at least in part, make it possible for both subjects and readers to accept the present and to await the future, in hopes that it, too, will somehow be graced by some of the same poignant traces of that past.

It was the early-modern philologist and nativist culture-critic (*kokugakusha*) Motoori Norinaga (1730-1801) who elevated and elaborated this concept into the far-reaching hermeneutic construct with which critics still grapple and contend today. It was he who argued, in various ways, that the purpose of making literature—whether a great work of fiction, such as *The Tale of Genji*, or a Japanese song or poem (*uta*), in any one of a large number of forms and genres—was to create a vehicle through which its audience (hearers, viewers, readers) might "come to know and appreciate *mono no aware*" (*mono no aware o shiru*). According to Norinaga, the only business of a literary work is, or should be, to demonstrate or make manifest the qualities and elements of experience that have the power to move emotionally those persons who take part in or observe that experience, and the only business of the reader is to understand and to feel empathy.[42] This position remains as influential as it is controversial, and its difficulties cannot be resolved here. Still, of the textual dynamics of *waka* that are explored here, it may well be said—with these notions in mind—that what moves both the maker and the hearer or reader of these poems is, fundamentally, recognition, remembrance, longing for another place and time, and that this is often enacted in a textual return to that time and place, launched and realized (as often as not) by the invocation, through utterance or inscription, of the name of a particular *place*, if not by some other deeply resonant word or words.

In *Jokes and Their Relation to the Unconscious* Sigmund Freud cites Karl Groos in support of the assertion that "the rediscovery of what is familiar, recognition," is pleasurable.[43] Groos, as translated by Freud's translators, wrote that

> recognition is always, unless it is too much mechanized . . . linked with feelings of pleasure. The mere quality of familiarity is easily accompanied by the quiet sense of comfort which Faust felt when, after an uncanny encounter, he entered his study once again. . . . If the act of recognition thus gives rise to pleasure, we might expect that men would hit on the idea of exercising this capacity for its own sake—that is, would experiment with it in play. And in fact Aristotle regarded joy in recognition as the basis of the enjoyment of art, and it cannot be disputed that this principle should not be overlooked, even if it does not possess such far-reaching significance as Aristotle attributes to it.[44]

Surely, this "pleasure principle" is hard to overlook and does reach far enough to be applicable (even if not a perfect fit) to certain aspects of the *waka* aesthetic, too—as a partial explanation for the habitual, repetitive returns to the familiar (or, the virtually unlimited experimentation with play) performed in so many *waka* texts. Some readers and critics may feel that these habitual methods of recycling, resorted to so often for the purposes of eliciting recognition in *waka*'s readers, govern, and in some cases tyrannize this poetry to its detriment, that it becomes all too mechanized an art, while I would argue that repetitions of and returns to the familiar are precisely what give, or gave, the tradition its vitality and its enduring shape. To be sure, there are moments of recognition that are not pleasurable, and there is also a pleasurability in that which is not quite familiar, and a pleasurability, as well as a pain, in that in which the familiar is overturned or otherwise altered. The *waka* tradition is replete with all these kinds of juxtaposition, interaction, subversion, and play. Indeed, such play lies at the heart of and is much of what constitutes the tradition, but, if so, its precise workings—the verbal and textual gambolings that make up this play—need precise examination. And, in fact, they have often been given such precise examination from within the tradition itself.

Sei Shōnagon, a lady-in-waiting of the late tenth-century Imperial court who is known today as the author of the so-called *Pillow Book* (*Makura no sōshi*), was perhaps one of this tradition's most exuberant and bemused examiners of its own habits of play. She was not always an overly enthusiastic player herself: descended from a line of distinguished poets, she was often vexed by the pressure to "perform," by composing verses to commemorate mundane court activities, when not particularly inspired to do so, but she was always well-prepared to do so, by her training, experience, and intelligence. Much of the vexation that she describes seems feigned, for she also displays a very thorough command of (or, some might say, a consuming obsession with) *waka's* canons and lexicons (as they were constituted in her day) throughout the *Makura no sōshi* and particularly in her lists or "poetic catalogues," as Mark Morris has called them, where she free-associates with various categories of poetic *topoi* (trees, mountains, rivers, and so on).[45]

In his study of these "catalogues," Morris draws a contrast between Shōnagon's recognition of and comfort with the flexible discursive roles of famous-place *utamakura* names (with which she amuses herself in list after list) and John Stuart Mill's controversial (and now rather easily dismissed) contention, in his *System of Logic*, that "the only names of objects which connote nothing are proper names; and these have, strictly speaking, no signification."[46] Those who have been willing to retrace Mill's steps may recall that some of the elements of his argument are more convincing than his conclusion: there is, for example, his assertion that the name of the city of Dartmouth would probably not be changed even if an earthquake or some other natural force were to change the course of the river Dart, so that the city was no longer at its mouth—the reason for this being that the name of the place has long since taken on the function of proper name and that it therefore has a significance that is independent of its origins.[47]

But it is just this sort of scenario, whether real or imagined, in which traditional Japanese poets—including Sei Shōnagon, a poet somewhat *malgré elle*—repeatedly found so much rich potential for signification; they reveled in taking names apart and putting them back together with new, often metaphorical significations piled onto them even while allowing them still to function semantically and syntactically as place-names. This is just what happens, for example, when the river Natorigawa is summoned into poems (like *Kokin wakashū* #650) that simultaneously name the river and offer a descriptive sketch of it—its shallows, rapids, and buried trees—but also carry out the exercise of the theme of falling so headlong and heedlessly in love that one finds oneself worrying about "getting a name for oneself" (that is, by punning on the syllables *natori*).[48] We can insist, if we choose, that these simultaneous functions are inseparable, that each is activated by the maker of the poem so as to effect and augment the reader's response to and understanding of the other; but Sei Shōnagon might have the last laugh at us in her gleeful insistence on deconstructing such procedures—as she does, for example, in her catalogue of rivers (*kawa wa*), where her free-association (structured by memory), or her paging through the annals of verse or through her own private notes on them, turns up Natorigawa and adds it to the list: then, having named it, she cannot help but add a quip, asserting that the sound of the name—and/or her recollections of poems that use it—makes her "crave to know just what sort of name one gets" for involvement in love affairs conducted there, or under its name, in verse.[49] What she is doing here is jokingly chastising the tradition for its addiction to conventional word-play, but she is also revealing her own taste for that play; and though she makes light of it, it is also clear that she wants to be sure that the tradition founded in such play does not lose its footing or suffer erosion through ignorance or neglect. She therefore explores and records it, in all its minutiae, along with all the minutiae of court life (as she lived it) as well, and preserves it all (against loss in time) in the deceptively casual *Pillow Book* text.

Too much enthusiasm for just this kind of play, tempered by too little discrimination, is just one of the shortcomings of a character in *The Tale of Genji,* a fictional work produced in the same social and cultural sphere and in the same era as the *Pillow Book*. The worst thing that the Ōmi Lady brings with her to the capital from her childhood in the "vulgar" east country is her countrified speech, and her poetry is almost as bad—yet she feels no shame for either. In an episode in the chapter called "Wild Carnations" (*Tokonatsu*) she becomes the butt of a joke, the protagonist of a burlesque on *waka* place-name word-play in which she is an all too willing, if unwitting, player. She composes a letter to her far more aristocratic half-sister (who is at court) which is full of misguided allusions and other misappropriations of the poetic language of love, sure to make the recipient wince—and, to make matters worse, there are altogether too many of them. She concludes the letter, as is customary, with a verse, but one in which these faults are compounded further:

> kusawakami Hitachi no ura no Ikagasaki
>   ikade aimin Tago no uranami
> Cape How of the grassy pastures of Hitachi
>   says, "how can the waves of Farmer Beach come see you?"[50]

The message, like that of the letter as a whole, is simply, "How can I arrange to meet you?": the rest is over-ornamentation, place-name play run amok. Ikagasaki (Cape How)—which Ōmi uses as a sonic "guidephrase" to *ikade*, the "how" of "how can I see you"—is actually in Ōmi's home province, not in Hitachi, the name of which is here adorned by an ersatz *makurakotoba*, *kusawakami* (young, fresh grasses). Tago no ura, Farmer Beach, is in yet another province, Suruga. So the poem is literally all over the map: these places are named as if their association through juxtaposition might make them contiguous, and as if their appearance together might make some sense. Ōmi should know better, but she doesn't—nor does she know that she doesn't know.

But the burlesque does not end here: Ōmi's disastrous poem is answered in kind by one Chūnagon, acting in Ōmi's half-sister's name.

> Hitachi naru Suruga no umi no Suma no ura ni
>   nami tachiideyo Hakosaki no matsu
> You waves of the Suma coast of Suruga-Hitachi,
>   the pine of Hakosaki waits.[51]

This poem goes one better than Ōmi's, with four utterly disjunctive place-names rather than three, and the joke of the poem, besides its mock-seriousness, which ridicules the addressee, is their rearrangement (just as in Ōmi's misguided attempt) into imaginary proximity, through a kind of semantic and syntactic hocus-pocus. The difference, in this case, is that Chūnagon knows just what she is doing, whereas Ōmi does not. But Chūnagon deliberately pushes Ōmi's unwitting error toward the brink of chaos, and, as a result, the fundamental geography of the Japanese poem itself is knowingly, if temporarily, defaced. All this for yet another laugh at Ōmi's expense—and, perhaps, for a gentle laugh (for author and reader) at the expense of the whole *waka* tradition and its propensity for just such play.

Yet the very same kind of word-play that is burlesqued so wittily in this episode is deployed and manipulated with considerably greater seriousness—and in a manner that is more in accord with eleventh-century aristocratic good taste—elsewhere throughout *The Tale of Genji*. The Ōmi episode is only a momentary spoof of a skill or art of which the author (Murasaki Shikibu) was herself a devoted and accomplished practitioner. In all the other appearances it makes in poems in the *Tale*, the place-name Suma, for example, evokes the pathos of lonely exile—Genji's own, and that of other exiles who are remembered as having dwelt and made poems there. This is still play, and it is not always heavy-handed; but it is always imbued with a zest for the plasticity of language itself and riven with reference to itself, open to inspection for traces of the process of its own manufacture. For, in episodes like that in "Wild Carnations," Murasaki Shikibu is amply ironic about her own endeavor, be it story-telling, poem-making, or the combining of the two, which is what her real business is in the *monogatari*. Like Sei Shōnagon, she too steps back from convention and praxis, to take stock and to tease, even while exercising and improving on them. She, too, documents a world, and particularly its use of language and the status of language therein, but she does so through fiction, where the world's habits and enthusiasms, and its pitfalls and disasters, can all be depicted in slightly altered but utterly familiar dimensions.

In their particular enthusiasm for the exploration of the multiple possible significations of place-names—this habit ingrained by training that has in turn become an instinctive reflex—many traditional Japanese poets before and after Sei Shōnagon and Murasaki Shikibu do things that may remind some readers of what Wallace Stevens does, for example, in his poem "An Ordinary Evening in New Haven," with its manipulations, inter alia, of the words *new* and *Haven* in a poem that is both about and of an "ordinary evening in New Haven" and about and of much else as well.[52] One difference, however, may be that Stevens' manipulations of "New Haven," for instance, have the effect of awakening us, with a start, to the place-name's ambiguities and its obscured etymology—that is, the implications of "new" and the intimations of "heaven," while in most cases in *waka*, the awakening experienced by the hearer or reader is rather a reawakening to a sense of a given place-name's familiar legacies, its layered weighting through use in poetry itself, rather than in speech, or in the mundane use of names, per se. In other words, if Stevens' play with a place-name like New Haven is, at least initially, disorienting, the analogous play in most Japanese poems has the intended effect of orientation, of grounding or anchoring the poem to its own literary precedents and its familiar resonances, and of making the hearer or reader thus feel, in a sense, textually at home.

Of course, if the reader's home happens to be or has ever been New Haven, that fact may have its own particular impact on the reading of Stevens' poem. But it will soon become plain that this place-name's work in the poem is as something in addition to that of being the name of the real, "ordinary" New Haven that the reader may know. The word *ordinary* in Stevens' title is also rich with ambiguity and implication—it also sets the reader up for the familiar, the everyday. But Stevens proceeds to disturb this expectation, too, and to make the ordinary utterly extraordinary in and through the poem. And he does so in ways that can be felt and understood by any careful reader—whether or not he or she has had an experience, ordinary or extraordinary, of "an evening in New Haven" in particular. The reader may seem to recognize the echo of Stevens' "dim-coned bells," or may conjure a familiar image of "such chapels and such schools," or may even see himself or herself in "the ephebe . . . solitary in his walk." So, at least for a while, the "land of the elm trees" may look very much like "home." But, sooner or later, the reader realizes that the poem is not about New Haven but about, at least in part, what making a poem of the sort in which the name New Haven has a part is all about. For, as Stevens puts it: "The poem is the cry of its occasion, / Part of the res itself and not about it. / The poet speaks the poem as it is. . . . Not as it was."[53]

For centuries, the Japanese poem, too, has been held to be nothing more nor less than "the cry of its own occasion, part of the res itself": on the other hand, though Stevens says that, "We seek / the poem of pure reality, untouched / by trope or deviation, straight to the word, / straight to the transfixing object, to the object / At the exactest point at which it is itself. . . ."[54] traditional Japanese poetry, on the whole, might well be described as a collective celebration of its own "tropes and deviations," its routes to "pure reality" which are by no means "straight" but rather often quite devious, and are therefore in themselves "transfixing." One might say that this tradition wallows in and glorifies its own "intricate evasions of as"—that *they* are its *makura,* its supportive cushion and nestling place—were it not for the fact that no such word as "as" is needed or used in most of its figurings.[55]

The evidence for these tendencies is not only in the poems themselves but also in the design of the texts in which we usually read them: as often as not, *waka* have been and are presented in framings that explain and display their occasionality, the "res" of which they are a part, which at the same time also draw our attention to the ways in which the figures therein— the "tropes and deviations"—irrupt from and also return to that occasion, that res. This is, in the end, the effect of what anthology editors do, in prose prefaces, when they can; it is also the effect of what diarists, who lace their journals with poems, and writers of fiction, who break up their prose with verse—or who, in some cases, encase their (or other poets') poems in prose —do as well.

For some illustrations of these effects, let us look at what is probably the earliest surviving poetic diary in Japanese, and certainly one of the best known: *Tosa nikki* (A Tosa journal, 930) is an account of a six-week sea voyage, "narrated" by a voice that is thinly disguised as that of a quasi-fictional female traveler but which is actually quite close to that of the author, Ki no Tsurayuki (872-945?), who actually made the trip from Tosa to the capital after completing a term of gubernatorial service there. The reader of this "journal" is presented with poem after poem, framed by prose updates on the journey's progress, as well as critical assessments of the poems themselves. Almost every poem—both the good and the bad, as they appear in the narrator's estimation—is portrayed as a composition inspired by the emotional highs and lows experienced by the seafaring gentleman-in-charge (Tsurayuki himself), his family, and their companions. These emotional moments begin with the party's farewells to friends and associates in Tosa and continue with their frustrations over the length and rigors of the journey, which are assuaged by the joy of first sightings of familiar but long-distant landscapes; and they end with the deflating discovery that the home to which they at last return has been abused and neglected by its caretakers. From time to time, along the way, there are also moments of mourning for a child who died before the departure from Tosa, and these moments of grief inspire poetry as well. But some of the most intensely poetic moments of the journey (in that they are productive of poems, and of thoughts and discussions about poetry) occur when the travelers simply gaze contemplatively at the passing scenery and commemorate their presence therein and their passage through those scenes by making new verse. In Tsurayuki's retelling (or imaginative and manipulative recollection) of these particular moments, the poems appear as if inscribed by their makers on those very scenes through which they have passed; they seem to serve not only as lasting records of their own occasions but also as intensifications of the poeticized experience itself.

Tsurayuki, or his disguised voice, narrates instance after instance like this as evidence in support of his belief (explicitly remarked upon at several points in the *Journal*—and enunciated even earlier in his preface to the *Kokin wakashū* in 905) that the drive to make verse is one that arises out of human experience in the natural and social sphere, and from the emotion that attends it; and that drive, in circumstances such as those described, will spontaneously and inevitably yield poems—good, bad, indifferent—but all worth keeping as records of their own occasions and as documentations of the relationship that men and women forge with their physical and emotional environments and then express as word, or song (*uta*). One of his best illustrations of these principles occurs in his account of a day about two weeks after the departure from Tosa, when

> the boat passed the pine woods of Uda. It was impossible to imagine how many trees might be standing there, or how many thousands of years they might have lived. The waves came up to their roots, and cranes flew back and forth among the branches. Too deeply moved to admire the spectacle in silence, one of the passengers composed a poem that went something like this:

> miwataseba matsu no ure goto ni sumu tsuru wa
>
> chiyo no dochi to zo omouberanaru
>
> As I gaze out at this scene, it seems to me that the cranes who have dwelt so
> long among the branches of those pines must think of them as their eternal
> companions.
>
> The poem was not the equal of the scene.[56]

The prose description that precedes the poem has many of the elements that one might expect to find in a verse about this place (or almost any seaside place like it), and it almost overanticipates the poem that follows. But Tsurayuki gives us both the prose frame and the poem, perhaps to suggest how organic the poem is, that it is the landscape itself, or the viewer's perception of it, that determines what the poem's words will be. Furthermore, the descriptive elements of both the prose preface or frame, and the poem—the vast grove of pines, the crashing waves, the soaring cranes—might also be the features of a painting of this place (or of almost any other seascape), the reproduction of which, in either language or in paint, might be exceedingly auspicious in and of itself and perhaps of almost magical effect. For both the pines and the cranes are symbols of enduring vitality, or eternal life, so that celebrating them may in turn bring new vitality and long life to the celebrant. But, beyond all this, what Tsurayuki emphasizes in the framing and presentation of this poem is the emotion of the occasion that drives the poet to formulate mentally and then to utter it, so that it then becomes part of the occasion itself, and of the written record thereof. The unnamed poet is portrayed as having been "too deeply moved" to remain silent, and unable to let the moment pass, or the place be passed, without some such utterance. And even if that utterance is a poem that does not measure up to the beauty of the sight that inspired it, its story must be told, and the utterance must be heard (and seen) again.

Two days later, we are subsequently told, "the boat reached a place called Hane," and then it is that place's name, rather than its scenery, that inspires a verse:

> "Does Hane look like a bird's wing [*hane*]?" asked a child who had heard someone
> mention the name. Everyone laughed at the naive question, and a little girl—the
> same one [who had composed a clever poem] as before—composed a poem:
>
> makoto nite na ni kiku tokoro hane nareba
>
> tobu ga gotoku ni miyako e mo ga na
>
> If, true to its name, this place consisted of wings,
>
> how nice it would be to return to the city like a flock of flying birds.
>
> "Exactly so," the other thought. Even though her composition was not very
> good, it was remembered by men and women alike, for everyone longed to reach
> the capital as soon as possible.[57]

Here, in child's play, is exactly the sort of manipulation of significance that Mill discounted. Indeed, the main point of Tsurayuki's retelling of this particular occasion is to show that even this child knew how to make a poem by playing with a place's name. In this case, as it happens, this *was* done with something like an "as" (that is, *gotoku ni*), the use of which is actually rather rare in *waka* and which might therefore, in some other circumstance, invite Tsurayuki's censure. But, his narrator says, the poem was memorable precisely because its playfuness and figuring also had real weight: the verse caught the emotional state of the whole group, who longed for home and for the journey's end just as much as did this naive child. In this case, then, a not very "intricate evasion of as" seems to have been right on target.

At last the party's boat is making its way up the estuaries and canals south of the capital city. A building called the Nagisa Villa (*Nagisa no in*) comes into view, and everybody in the party recognizes it:

> When we gazed at it, thinking all the while of the distant past, it was a delightful sight. On the hill behind it were groves of pine trees, and in the inner garden plum trees were in bloom. Someone said, "This has been a very famous place for a very long time, for it was here, when he came here in the party of the late Prince Koretaka, that Ariwara Narihira, the Middle Captain, wrote:
>
>> yo no naka ni taete sakura no sakazaraba
>> haru no kokoro wa nodokekaramashi"
>
> If only cherry blossoms did not bloom as they do in this world,
>> how tranquil springtime hearts might be![58]

What is being remembered here is another intensely poetic occasion, or one which has come to seem so through its repeated representations—most prominently, in the *Kokinshū*, but also later—probably after the writing of the *Tosa nikki*—in *Ise monogatari* (The tales of Ise, ca. 950), a collection of short narrative framings of poems, many of which are attributed to this same Narihira (825-880), who was, by Tsurayuki's time, one of the most admired of the poets of the previous generation, despite what Tsurayuki saw as his general tendency to try to "express too much with too few words" (*sono kokoro amarite, kotoba tarazu*).[59] In any case, it is through textual means that the *Tosa Journal* party knows of this poem-making occasion in the prior century, this moment that now seems so hallowed when viewed retrospectively through this famous poem. They therefore proceed to compound the emotion of the remembered moment with that of the present moment of remembrance (and of joy in being so close to home) and commemorate it all in their own verses, which they now inscribe upon this place and in memory alongside Narihira's. Two of these poems are as follows:

chiyo hetaru matsu ni wa aredo
   inishie no koe no samusa wa kawazarikeri |
These are pines that have endured for a thousand years, but there is no
   change in the chilly sound of the ancient wind
   [that blows through them now as it did then.]

kimi koite yo o furu yado no ume no hana
   mukashi no ka ni zo nao nioikeru
The blossoms of the plum in this house that has so long survived
   still yearn for their master and even now they pour forth the same sweet
   fragrance as they did in times long past.[60]

These verses eloquently celebrate the compounded moment and its emotional intensity by acknowledging but also minimizing the passage of time.
In fact, the antiquity of the occasion remembered here (and situated in the
past with the words *mukashi* and *inishie,* which both mean "a time long ago")
is not all that great—perhaps no more than fifty years or so; but the
occasion's dimensions are magnified by the party's admiration for and loving
recollection of the poem that it produced and that then became part of it.
And it is their reverence, abetted by the overwhelming sense of being
there—of knowing that they are standing where others have stood and are
seeing what they saw, or at least believing that they can—that supplies the
energy for their return, through memory, to that (only relatively) distant
time, and for the making of new verses that then cross that distance through
time. In short, these two poems are celebrations through allusion of the
illusion that past and present are as one.

This is neither the first nor the last of such celebratory returns: they
weave, or are woven, throughout the *waka* tradition and its texts, tying
strands here to others there, befuddling time. In this particular instance, the
story of the emotion-laden return also serves to retell and compound the
paradigmatic story of how Japanese poems are (supposedly) made, as human
feeling—here, incited by the viewing of a famous place and by recollection
of a famous poem said to have been made there—"flowers forth" in the
words of song. In the following pages, we shall see a preponderance of
instances in which the site visited by the makers of such songs is not a
physical place but the text of an older poem, and in which "feeling" is
something created or represented through the presence of and stimulation
provided by that poem's words, rather than the other way around. These
instances run counter to Tsurayuki's paradigm, but share with it the fundamental economy of word and feeling, which is perhaps best conceived of as
an economy constantly rearranging itself into new and renewable patterns
for creative stimulation. For the most part, it was by nurturing this economy,

by reaching for and raising "dead" times and by retrieving and revivifying inert but still potent words that the *waka* tradition kept itself alive, feeding on its own past for sustenance and filling its present with the sights and sounds of its own history.

2

Stories of the Tree, Stories of the River

At some moment in unmeasured antiquity, a tree that has grown old and tall beside a stream falls, uprooted by its own age or, perhaps, by a sudden tempest. For centuries thereafter the remains of the tree lie beneath the waters of the stream, buried under accumulating silts deposited by the ceaseless flow of the current. Over time, the tree's wooden fibers metamorphose to a different yet recognizably treelike substance — fossilized wood. And, over time, the river's shape and course are altered as well, so that when at last its waters run shallow where once they ran deep, the transformed remains of the tree are revealed, from time to time, to the eye of the observer. When dried and polished, these fossils are remarkable for the degree to which they preserve the original grain of the living wood while possessing the general characteristics of stone.

This metamorphosis of once-living trees into inert, stony fossils is one that must have occurred repeatedly in many environments in antiquity, but observers in the age of man see only its end result when they happen upon rare deposits of the remarkably transformed substance.[1] Their discovery reveals an untold tale of life, death, and transfiguration which, once that discovery has been made, can be told and retold again and again. But the very revelation to the observer of that which heretofore has been hidden from sight is itself an occurrence of note, the stuff of narrative. And the story of such a discovery is also rich food for metaphor. In Japan, the metaphor of the exposure of a deposit of fossilized wood, heretofore concealed, presented itself to early makers of song-poems (*uta*) as just one of many metaphors derived from nature (or, more specifically, from nature as observed by human consciousness) and found fitting or useful, and perhaps literally meaning-full, when they were moved to sing about what seems to have been a widespread preoccupation, or at any rate a favored topic, concerning a stage in a longer, larger story of love—specifically, a moment in which the desire to keep love between two people a private rather than a public matter is tested, as is that love. Eventually, the metaphor would also be used in song-stories about other preoccupations—in poems, for example, about other aspects and functions of the state of being hidden from view or in obscurity—and even in poems and other texts about the hidden or obscured state of Japanese poetry itself. The story that is to be told here about this figure is thus long, many-sided, and often self-referential.

It may be possible to say, with ample justification and without exaggeration, that every poem in the *waka* canon tells a story, or at least part of one—such as that part of a love story that is its occasion. One might say that every poem has a story that may be told, and that invariably that story is, at its root, a story that has to do with the making of that poem. This characteristic of *waka* has been recognized and explored, or exploited, for centuries, in the creation and development of a variety of texts. As we have noted, poems have been and are most frequently encountered by their readers in anthologies, where various arrangements of poems in sequences (coherent series and juxtapositions of what are in most cases otherwise unrelated poems) exploit this quasi-narrative potential to sometimes dazzlingly inventive effect.[2] In addition, this potential is often manipulated in anthologies (both those which bring together the works of various poets from disparate periods and those devoted primarily to the oeuvres of individuals) in yet another dimension, through the presentation of poems along with prose prefaces (*kotobagaki*) that indicate something of the circumstances of that poem's or those poems' composition. Even the barest details in such presentations can go a long way toward the re-creation of the story of a given poem's own genesis; and even the admission in these prefaces of the absence of those details—the anthologizer's indication that the poet is unknown (*yomi-bito shirazu*) or that the topic is unknown (*dai shirazu*)—indicates an assumption that there is a story that would be told about the poem (specifically, about its origins) if only it could be.

This inclination toward the narrative or quasi-narrative presentation of poetry is by no means confined to anthologies of poetry. Most of the earliest works of traditional Japanese narrative "prose" present poems in just this way, and make it their business to tell the reader, often quite explicitly, how the poems therein were made. In the *Kojiki* and the *Nihon shoki* (The record of ancient matters, 712, and The chronicles of Japan, 720), the earliest surviving works of Japanese prose, verses are always embedded in the midst of prose accounts of the events that produced them.[3] There are only a few poems in *Taketori monogatari* (The tale of the bamboo cutter, also known as The tale of the shining princess), the so-called progenitor of Japanese fiction (the standard versions of which date to the late ninth or early tenth centuries), but all are given as explicit responses by the protagonists to the events and circumstances that unfold around them.[4] *Ise monogatari* (The tales of Ise, ca. 950), the exemplar of the subgenre known as *uta monogatari* (literally, poem-narrative) is an episodic text, a collection of short narratives, all of which present one or more poems framed by an account (sometimes plausible or even confirmable, but sometimes much less so) of the circumstances in which they were (supposedly) first made.[5] (These frames are also often termed *kotobagaki*, writings of prose words, as opposed to the words of the verse or verses that they frame.) And there are many narratives of travel and other kinds of diaries—such as Tsurayuki's *Tosa nikki* (A Tosa journal) and its many descendants—in which poems are also framed by prose accounts of their occasions. In some of the most admired of the early works of this genre—*Kagerō nikki* (The gossamer journal, ca. 970-980, by the woman known as Fujiwara Michitsuna's Mother), *Izumi Shikibu nikki* (The diary of Izumi Shikibu, ca. 1007), and *Sarashina nikki* (The Sarashina diary, ca. 1058-64, by the woman known as Sugawara Takasue's Daughter)—the blend of prose and poetry approaches great sophistication and suggests, repeatedly, the intimacy and directness of the perceived connection between experience in natural and social environments and the making of verse by those who have (and tell of) that experience (in both poetry and prose). The further development of this sophisticated blending and the exploration of its potential in generating and structuring texts can be observed virtually throughout the Japanese literary tradition—reaching an apogee, many would say, in Murasaki Shikibu's *Genji monogatari* (The tale of Genji), but also manifesting itself in many later works and in works of various kinds, including such well-known poetic travel journals as Bashō's *Oku no hosomichi* (The narrow road to the Northeast, ca. 1694).

Because many historical and cultural factors gave rise to these works and genres and because the features and characteristics of each are so varied, there is a high risk of oversimplification in focusing too narrowly on any one of these factors or features. But one thing that they all share is a fundamental awareness of the potential of poetry to tell stories, or parts thereof, and in particular the potential that lies in each poem for the telling of its own story, or the potential awaiting discovery and teasing out—or even fabrication—by the reader or redactor. And Japanese poems have been read and reproduced in ways that demonstrate this awareness for as long as it has been possible to write them down. This appears to have been the case when, by the latter half of the eighth century, a system had been devised, through testing (with considerable effort and inventiveness) which made it possible to record and preserve in writing what had up to that time been preserved only through oral reproduction and memory. For it was then that the editors of the *Man'yōshū,* the earliest extant anthology of Japanese verse, culled some 4,500 poems from other (largely unknown) sources (perhaps oral, perhaps written) and wrote them down in the cumbersome but effective orthography we now call *Man'yōgana* (in which Chinese characters are used, for the most part, for their phonetic value, rather than for what they might otherwise semantically represent). These editors made the collective decision to present as many of these collected song-poems as they could as parts of and in the context of their own stories—as they did, for example, by presenting the following poem as just one among a very large number of poems in which feelings about love are expressed through reference to "things" (*kibutsu chinshi,* or *mono ni yosete omoi o noburu*).[6] In this case, the thing referred to is a buried tree (*umoregi*):

> amata aranu na o shi mo oshimi
>   umoregi no shita yu so kōru yukue shirazute[7]
> Anxious for my name, of which I have but one,
>   I keep my love concealed beneath a buried tree, and know not where its
>   future path will lead.

The editorial presentation of this poem, which emphasizes what we might think of as a technical feature—its recourse to the figure of a buried tree, as a means toward the expression of feelings of love—also invites the reader to read it as a story of love, or as a part or moment thereof—that is, as a verbal capturing of that moment in the course of a love affair when the possibility of exposure—and the loss of secrecy and its special intimacy—is recognized, with anxiety and fear. And the poem itself makes it its business to expose the voluble state of a passion concealed by that which is itself concealed from view. The poem-speaker admits that he or she allows concern for reputation (*na*) to govern action: it is because of care for what others may say that this passion must remain hidden, like a long-ago fallen and long-since altered tree (*umoregi*) that still lies concealed beneath protective waters. In the phrase that makes this admission, *na o shi mo oshimi,* the reduplication of sounds is probably intentional, and the structure of the phrase itself bespeaks reasoning—a kind of forced rationalism that overwhelms the inclinations of the heart.[8] But the poem-singer recognizes that time may alter this arrangement: he or she "knows not where its future path will lead" (*yukue shirazute*) and thus concedes that exposure may be inevitable.

The comparison of the secrecy of this uneasy covenant between intellect and passion to the concealed state of the buried tree is not made through simile (there is no equivalent to *like* or *as,* though it is tempting to use such words in translation). Most modern commentators treat *umoregi no* in this poem as a *makurakotoba,* a conventional five-syllable guide phrase preparatory to the word *shita,* "bottom [of something]."[9] This suggests that *umoregi* is used here as a kind of embellishment on the word *shita,* which stands not so much for "the bottom of a buried tree" but rather "the bottom of the yearning song-poem speaker's heart," wherein his or her passion abides in secrecy.[10] But if we recall that the compilers of the *Man'yōshū* read and presented this poem as one illustrating the technique or attitude of "expressing feelings through reference to things," we may want to think of the buried tree here as something more than an embellishment. Like an appoggiatura or other decoration on a musical note in an eighteenth-century Italian aria, which changes the character and impact of that note and perhaps of the whole aria as well, this decoration may be more than an incidental element of the poem: this figure, as much if not more than anything else in the poem, marks what might otherwise be straightforward utterance as poetry.

Furthermore, the figure may well be "meaning-full." By locating his or her abiding (but at least temporarily suppressed) yearning for the loved one as something that takes place "beneath a buried tree" (*umoregi no shita yu so*), the poem-speaker suggests that this passion may have some of the capacity to endure through time that the tree itself possesses, especially if it remains unseen. Still, though presently shielded by something once living that is now dead, this passion may yet (or most surely will) emerge from that place of concealment, and "go forward." For even while hidden, that passion, that yearning to which the singer admits with the verb *kōru,* but which is otherwise not named or personified except as the implicit subject of that which will take some unknown "future path" (*yukue*), is not wholly inert, nor as dead as the fossilized tree that is said to shelter it. And perhaps, by nurturing this passion in this concealed place, the poem-singer ensures that this love will develop further in some way—not necessarily happily— hereafter.

So, the song-speaker means what he or she says figuratively when he or she locates his or her action—that of desiring, yearning for a loved one—in an interior and fundamental part of him or herself identified as "the base of a buried tree," the foundation of a concealed and unseen organism. Loving and yearning continue there, unknown to all others, for a particular reason: the speaker fears that exposure of this love will tarnish his or her "name." Reputation and name are on the surface, and at risk: so, for the time being, love will remain safely buried, out of sight like the tree. But the speaker's own emotional volubility, as well as society's, may soon change everything: the situation is unstable (to the same extent that nature, which may expose the tree, is) because it involves love and human beings, and so it is unlikely that things will remain as they are for long.

Medieval practitioner-theorists of canonical Japanese poetry viewed this poem as exemplary, and worthy of special comment. In Fujiwara Norikane's handbook-treatise *Waka dōmōshō* (ca. 1118-1127) it is offered as the sole model for composition with what by that time had long been the conventional figure of the buried tree, and in Jōkaku's *Waka iroha* (1190) it is one of more than one hundred *Man'yōshū* texts singled out for detailed explication (in a group of some three hundred similarly "difficult" poems).[11] Modern readers, in turn, may think of it as the earliest *recorded* poem (though there may have been others) in which a link is forged between this figure, the buried tree, and the idea of name or reputation and the word used for them in poetry, *na*. But the possibility that such an associative scheme was already well formed and in place within *uta* compositional practice by the time of the compilation of the *Man'yōshū* (in which the latest dated poem is from 759) can be detected in yet another love poem which "refers to a buried tree" (according to the explanatory label—*umoregi ni yosu*—that precedes it in the text of the anthology):

> makana mochi Yuge no kawara no umoregi no
> arawarumashijiki koto ni aranaku ni[12]
> It is true that the trees buried in the banks of the Yuge
>   the river where they carve bows with planes—cannot escape notice,
>   and yet . . .

Here, the poem-maker's strategy of indirection—or of intensification of the utterance—produces a text that has the appearance of a meditation concerned not with love itself but rather with a natural scene and process that offers itself to the observer for contemplative comparison. The *umoregi* in the Yuge River (the name of which is here adorned with a *makurakotoba* or a *makurakotoba*-like embellishment that plays on the suggestiveness of the sound and orthography of its name, *Yu-ge,* "bow-carving") must sooner or later be exposed, if, for example, a drought dries up the river, or if its course is changed, or if humans intervene.[13] As inevitable as this, the poet says (though again avoiding simile per se), is the fate of a hidden love.[14] "I wish it were not so," the poet says, acknowledging what must eventually come to pass.

The linkage of *umoregi* here with the verb for "appearing (to the sight of the eye)," *arawaru,* like the connection with the concept of "name," may have been forged in still earlier poems; this poem, in the earliest surviving collection of such poems, probably demonstrates not the origin of a nexus of associations, but a stage in the development of those associations (and others like them) and the exploration of their potential for use in figural schemes. It is not possible to say who the agents of this development were, or to prove that those agents were in any documentable way systematic in the work of poem-making that drove this process. Modern readers can only imagine (but should not overromanticize) the relatively unhampered or un-supervised, if not necessarily wholly uninformed, conditions or settings in which the thousands of anonymous poems in the *Man'yōshū* (for example) were made. But eventually, by including these poems and placing them where they did, among others featuring parallel or analogous figural schemes and strategies, the compilers of the *Man'yōshū* drew attention to, and en-dorsed, what had by their time become (or soon thereafter became) the pervasive rhetorical mode in *uta*: the use of elements and aspects of the natural environment as figures in poems that do not primarily describe nature but which, rather, speak or sing (albeit through various strategies of indirection or re-direction) of such fundamental human yearnings as the desire of one person for another.

The person who made the Yuge River song sang of buried trees in its banks (whether they were actually there or not) and thereby drew his or her reader's or hearer's attention to them in order to convey a message not so much about those trees or that river as about himself or herself, or about some other person, or about a more abstracted love or lovers who are characters in a loosely contoured, open-ended, and easily accessible story.[15] In later times (as we shall see), the specific elements of such figural strategies (reliance upon which would become habitual and perhaps even definitive of *waka* rhetoric) would also often be read as literal evidence of historical or archaeological conditions. But a poem like this one offers no proof of the existence of *umoregi* in the Yuge River's banks other than its (the poem's) own existence. Similarly, the presence in the poem of the *makurakotoba makana mochi* ("wielding planes") tells us little that is reliable about the etymology of the river's name, other than that its sound suggested (to someone) or endorsed the introduction (by someone) of a manipulation of the associations and imagery of bow-making. Both the adorning *makurakobota* and the "datum" (the "fact" that *umoregi* are to be found in the Yuge's banks) are present in order that the poem may be a poem (rather than a simple statement, "I hope no one finds out that I'm in love with you"). Risking tautology even further, one might say that they are present because the poem *is* a poem.[16]

In either case, these two conspicuous elements are perhaps best understood as two distinct but ultimately related kinds of poetic language, examples of what would come to be called *uta kotoba*: elements of a poetic lexicon generated solely by use and governed wholly by convention. The linkage of the place-name *Yuge no kawara* with the phrase *makana mochi* may have had its origins (as do other *makurakotoba* collocations) in still earlier songs, where its function and meaning may or may not have had ritual significance, perhaps even some the power of a spell or charm. On the other hand, the "datum" (factual or otherwise) about *umoregi*'s presence there presumably comes from local lore—information (or perhaps misinformation) well known in the Yuge River area and circulated generally enough so that makers and hearers of song-poems elsewhere might recognize or would accept a reference to buried trees in Yuge's banks as plausible, perhaps simply because it is a river, the sort of place where such things might well be found. The figural operations of the poem are thus grounded in what its earliest hearers or readers might have in some way known, if only through the lore generated by song or poetry itself.

Though undated and anonymous, like the vast majority of the poems in the *Man'yōshū*, these two poems show us something of what was happening in the latter formative stages of the conventionalization of *waka* discourse—a process for which the *Man'yōshū* provides the best, though not the only documentation.[17] One cannot recapture much of a sense of what these anonymous poets thought they were doing, or why they did it as they did; but the ex post facto labeling and classifying of these poems (by the compilers of the anthology, most of whom also are anonymous) within groups that are designed to demonstrate an array of rhetorical possibilities has the effect of drawing our attention, as readers, to their central metaphors, as the most conspicuous elements of each; and the labeling and classifying also suggests, rightly or wrongly, that the composers of such poems were conscious of the figural operations they were carrying out as such, that they were in some sense aware that they were composing in what was, or would soon be seen as, a distinctive and predominant rhetorical mode.

These two *Man'yōshū umoregi* poems may also be seen as examples of the many hundreds of poems (far more numerous than those that survive) the composition and circulation (and, in some cases, recording and preservation in collections) of which led to the fixing of the system of lexical associations that would become the core of *waka* poetics and of the poetics of related genres. *Umoregi*, the buried tree, is one of the many elements or nodes in this system, chosen here for examination as just one example of the phenomenon as a whole. These two poems alone may not have defined for the *waka* tradition and its offspring just which particular thematic preoccupations or rhetorical stances would call for use of the word *umoregi* or, conversely, what *umoregi* would suggest whenever and wherever it was used; but these poems give us the earliest surviving examples of its use in what may already have been fixed (or, at least, not unprecedented) schemes even at the time of their composition, whenever that was.

The fact that these poems were read by the *Man'yōshū* compilers as love poems, and that they were grouped with others understood to be of their kind, was also an important factor in the process that would eventually fix the lexical-poetic roles of the word *umoregi*—just one among so many words so fixed and then recycled and re-fixed as *waka* and its history proceed. The result, in this case, was that for centuries one of the primary modes of usage of this word would be in various related anthropomorphizations and metaphorizations involving organisms that conceal passionate secrets; that is, in many of the thousands of poetic or poeticized stories of love.

The Yuge River plain was not the only place to yield the fossilized wood of buried trees to observers or excavators or to the makers of the figurative schemes of early *uta*. Another, as we know, was the Natorigawa, the name of which would serve most frequently and memorably as the quasi-geographical setting for such metaphorical accounts of a secret love's anticipated or reported exposure. The real Natorigawa rises in the mountainous uplands of old Rikuzen province—modern Miyagi Prefecture—and flows eastward through alluvial plains into Sendai Bay. Since ancient times, from time to time, its banks and bottom have indeed yielded up rich lodes of fossilized wood, which craftsmen have in turn rendered into various kinds of useful objects: it still is fashioned into elegant domestic implements (such as trays, small boxes, tea caddies and ladles), processed to be burned as a potent incense, and rendered into a fine aromatic charcoal that is used to heat water in tea ceremony urns.[18] But the Natorigawa *umoregi*'s other most prominent and conspicuous use through time has been that of providing substance for poems, and the artisans who have most frequently handled it are poets: its own name, *umoregi*, is also an extraordinary commodity—like the material itself and the things made from it (which are famous local products, *meibutsu* and *meisan*, of the Sendai region), prized both in the past and in the present and durably transformed as the matériel of poetry.[19]

We cannot know how early this lore of the place—the "datum" that the Natorigawa held such a special substance beneath its surface—was widely known elsewhere, and perhaps it only became known when it found its way into verse. It had clearly done so, however, by 905, the time of the compilation of the *Kokin wakashū* (Anthology of ancient and modern verse) (commonly called the *Kokinshū*), for it is among the love poems therein that we find the poems that would serve as the templates for all later Natorigawa poems (and there are many). The template of templates, as it were, is the previously encountered *Kokin wakashū* #650—a poem composed, as the compilers say, by someone whom they cannot name (*yomibito shirazu*), though they would apparently do so if if they knew who he or she was:

> Natorigawa seze no umoregi arawareba
>   ika ni semu to ka aimisomekemu[20]
>
> When we first met, did we consider what would happen
>   should our love be as exposed as are the buried trees
>   that come into view in the shoals of the Natori River?

As with Yuge, we can imagine that the name Natorigawa had been used as it is here in at least several other *uta* before this particular *uta* gained its place in the *Kokinshū*. But once the river's name had been manipulated in the manner thus recorded and enshrined, in what would become the most influential of all anthologies in the shaping of the canonical *waka* lexicon, then, thereafter, virtually every compositional moment which prompted invocation of Natorigawa would be shaped by recollection of this textual moment in the anthology. Even a deviation from the norm would advertise itself as such, and hence still be, perforce, a kind of gesture to (or against) the authority of known usages and associations. Most often, however, the recycling of this conventional usage would be (as in other cases, with other figures) an affirmative gesture (if not always wholly un-ironic, or un-trite), a way of enriching the matrix of signification of each poem in which it appeared anew.

But this is not the only such moment for Natorigawa in the anthology: just a bit earlier in the quasi-narrative sequence of the same chapter—the thirteenth, and the third of five chapters of love poems—is this poem (*Kokin*

wakashū #628), which the compilers credit to one among their own number—Mibu no Tadamine—but whose topic is nonetheless "unknown":

> Michinoku ni ari to iu naru Natorigawa
>   naki na torite wa kurushikarikeri[21]
> Natorigawa, "The River of Scandal," is in far-off Michinoku, they say:
>   and oh how terrible it is to have my name be used in a way it does
>   not deserve!

It is fairly reasonable to assume that, of these two *Kokin wakashū* Natorigawa poems, the sequentially later anonymous poem (#650) is the older
(representing, as it were, the *ko* of *kokin*, "ancient and modern") and that
Tadamine's (#628, a contemporary [*kin*] poem) may refer to it—at least
obliquely—or to yet other poems earlier than his that associated the name
of the river with "getting a name."[22] The presentation of #650 as both
yomibito shirazu (poet['s name] unknown) and *dai shirazu* (topic unknown,
i.e., in this case, "circumstances of composition unknown and hence un-
recountable") place it among that very large number of poems in the anthology that can be presumed to date not from the era of the compilers but from
some time beforehand—before the era of systematization of *waka* rhetoric
which the anthology itself both celebrates and advances. For their own
purposes, however—in their effort to craft an interesting patchwork of
poems from disparate times and sources, arranged in sequences which themselves have signifying functions—the compilers of the *Kokin wakashū* placed
#650 a bit later in the sequence of the third book of love poems than
Tadamine's #638; yet Tadamine's poem appears to be one that might be
informed by the existence of other, perhaps earlier or at least contempora-
neously known poems that also used the name Natorigawa playfully—#650
among them. Thus, when Tadamine writes of the river as one "of which one
hears" as being an important geographical feature—with an interesting name
—in far-off Michinoku, the distant (to dwellers in the geopolitically and
psychological central capital) and relatively wild and unknown Northeast, he
may be referring to impressions received or information heard in connection
with the name of the river as used one way or another in other *uta*, perhaps
including *Kokin wakashū* #650.[23]

Although Tadamine's poem is implicitly *dai shirazu* (topic unknown) in
the *Kokin wakashū* setting, in *Tadamine shū*, the so-called personal anthology of Tadamine's works, this same poem appears with a prose preface
(*kotobagaki*) identifying its compositional and topical context: "[he wrote the
following] when his name was linked in gossip with that of someone he had
not been with" (*awazarikeru hito ni, na o tachikereba*).[24] This may well be
a fabrication by those who devised and arranged the *Tadamine shū*, but,

whether authentically biographical or wholly imaginary, it effectively anchors the poem in imaginable circumstance, and thus offers a specific way of reading it.[25] The better-known presentation of the poem in the *Kokin waka-shū* lacks this particularized quasi-narrative contextualization, but constructs context (and perhaps narrative) in its own way by placing the poem among others that fret over "groundless gossip" about love (*naki na*)—the subtopic within the topic of love (*koi*) with which the compilers are working at this point in the sequence. Both settings of Tadamine's poem suggest, however, that he is turning to Natorigawa as a known device for poems engaged with the topos *naki na[tori]* ("getting a[n unwarranted] 'name'") rather than inventing that device.

And, indeed, such use of the name Natorigawa in association with the topos of secretive love, though unyoked from its *umoregi*, is also the chief feature of what is with fair certainty an *uta* from a still earlier period (even if it is not clear how much earlier it is): this is the Natorigawa song found among what are purported to be the earliest recorded songs from the northeastern region itself, the so-called *fuzoku uta* (local people's songs), also called *kuniburiuta*:

> Fuzoku uta: Michinoku no fuzoku
> Natorigawa seze ka wataru ya nase to mo yase tomo
>   shirazu ya yoru shi koshikaba ano[26]

This group of songs, it is said, were originally lyrics devised to accompany dances performed to entertain, cajole, or quell local deities of various districts or provinces (*kuni*) and were subsequently adopted (or appropriated) by the central urban aristocracy of the capital as a kind of pleasant and somewhat exotic set of folk-tunes. If so, then, we have strong evidence here, as elsewhere, that what came to be a conventional topos and the literary property of the court poetry tradition must be seen as having its origins in preliterate folk-culture.[27] But, by the time that this poem was reproduced in *Kokin waka rokujō*, a vast compendium of *uta* categorized by topic (the earliest version of which seems to have been compiled ca. 976–983), this *uta* (classified there among poems which have a body of water or aspect thereof as their major figural feature, and in the subgroup "shoals" [*se*]) had been recast, remade, and regulated: it is only in the *Kokin waka rokujō* version that the sounds of the song fall into the standard sequence of five, seven, five, seven, and seven syllables (whereas syntactically the older version breaks up into groups of something like five, eight, eight, four, seven, and two). Also, in the later version, the musical/rhythmic elements (*hayashi-kotoba*) *ya* and *ano* have been dropped, a neater, relatively more speechlike syntax has been substituted, and even the dialect word *nase* (seven rapids) has been "corrected" to *nanase*, more proper to the capital's idiom, yielding:

Natorigawa iku se ka wataru
   nanase to mo yase to mo shirazu yoru shi watareba[28]

In either case, the song's meaning is something like this:

I don't know how many of the Natorigawa's shoals I will cross
   maybe seven, maybe eight of them—
but when night comes I'll cross them [to see my love].

Although he (or perhaps she) who sings this song (or about whom it is sung) relies upon the cover of night to conceal an action prompted by passion, he or she also boasts that nothing will obstruct him or her from union with the object of this passion: no matter how arduous the task, this lover will make his or her way from shoal to shoal and thus eventually across the river. The existence of these shoals (*se*) is what makes the river-crossing feasible; in many other love song-poems, as well, these *se* are the relatively accessible places—around which more troubled waters stir and eddy—where lovers manage, against all odds, to meet (*au se*). And, as we have seen in *Kokin wakashū* #650, they are also the places in such rivers as the Natori where the remains of fossilized trees may be exposed and made detectable. Thus, the fact that shoals (*se*) are figured as the spaces (in space and time) where lovers come together may be part of the reason why the buried trees that are also found there (in more literal *se*) are also to be found in poems of love.

Looking back from the *Kokin wakashū* Natorigawa poems (as a pivotal moment or moments in *waka*'s history) to the Natorigawa *fuzoku uta*, the *Man'yōshū umoregi* poems, and beyond, we see what may not be a direct line of descent from poem to poem, but a handful of strands in a complicated network of genealogically interconnected texts. And these several poems share some key elements: a shared sense of the potential significance and function of those elements may also have been transmitted (however indirectly) among their manipulators (both the anonymous and the nameable poets). Thus, the poem canonized as *Kokin wakashū* #650, for example, may be a conflation of the previously established poetic significance of the figure of the buried tree with the (also apparently already established) practice of playing with the poetic potential embedded in and extractable from the river's name—a conflation abetted and affirmed by the fact that *umoregi* really did (and do) appear in the river's shoals. The result of this conflation, in turn, was the fixing of a rich node of reference within *waka*'s broad but circumscribed rhetorical repertoire. Once so fixed, that textual node could be replicated, elaborated upon, and re-fashioned—much as a lode of fossilized wood, or a segment thereof, might be—ad infinitum, in myriad forms and contexts. And, just as the grain of the once-living tree would show through to the surface of the refashioned fossilized wood, each refashioning of the textual node would display, in varying degrees of explicitness, the patterns of its original form, even as it would simultaneously display its altered character, its difference from its distant but ever-present forebears.[29]

While we can only speculate, in the above manner, about what we may call the process that led up to and shaped the *Kokin wakashū* Natorigawa poems, we can examine in great detail the process that unfolds thereafter. For generation after generation, makers of poems and of other kinds of texts made poems and texts with buried trees and the Natori River in them— sometimes separately, often together—and used those words and images in them as they did because they had found them in those earlier (classic) poems. The act of excavating these elements of the canonical *waka* lexicon and resetting them for display in new arrangements (new poems and other kinds of texts) itself had significance. As the process unfolded, that which had originated as metaphor (the figure of the buried tree) itself underwent metamorphosis: while it survived as metaphor, it also attained a new status, as a kind of archaeological artifact, the manipulation of which itself evoked a sense of the span of time and of an imagined or constructed continuity or contiguity in and of time. The figure itself was thus an entity (a kind of lexical item) and an image of an entity, both of which were at once thoroughly dead (having had to die in order to become what they became) and very much alive, pulsing with potential for signification.

And, of course, that potential might, at any one textual moment, find realization in multiple or manifold dimensions—as it did in one particularly key moment in *waka*'s history. Ki no Tsurayuki was striving to elevate the *waka* tradition itself and to augment its prestige (after about a century of overshadowing by Chinese verse) through the argument presented in his *kana* preface to the *Kokin wakashū*—the first and perhaps the single most influential essay on the history and character of the *waka* tradition—when he deployed the figure of the buried tree therein in prose. And he did so specifically to amplify (or meaningfully decorate) his account of the tradition's temporary loss of status and recognition, its relegation to what he suggests are relatively trivial private contexts and its removal (or concealment) from its rightful place as the preferred mode of formal public literary expression. "Disappearance from view" is the main signification of the phrase as Tsurayuki uses it in his argument, but its archaic linkage to the subject of love and its concealment would seem to underly its manipulation in a description of Japanese poetry as something that has itself fallen at present into a state of being unknown or unnoticed, that is, neglected because it has drifted into obscurity. As a result, Tsurayuki complains, the language and conventions of *waka* have become the mere toys of showoffs who abuse and trivialize them in pursuit of their own frivolous and amorous objectives (*irogonomi no ie ni mumoregi no hito shirenu koto to narite*).[30]

Tsurayuki's ideological agenda—his reason for arguing in this way for a restoration of what he claims was once the rightfully privileged status of Japanese poetry (*Yamato uta*)—has been discussed elsewhere;[31] what is interesting to note here is that Tsurayuki's figurative language takes shape and gains force against the background of its use in poetry itself—in the language and art whose decline he is both lamenting and attempting to stem. Most commentators treat this preposited *mumoregi no* as a *makurakotoba,* or as a *makurakotoba*-like deployment. From this point of view the usage resembles the function of *umoregi no* in *Man'yōshū* #2723 (*amata aranu*). This does not necessarily mean, however, that that particular poem was Tsurayuki's model for his own use of the phrase in the prose of the *Kokin wakashū* preface; rather, his usage may suggest that many other songs and poems no longer available to us did use the phrase in a similar way, and that Tsurayuki's reuse of the phrase is grounded in the familiarity of that hypothetically generalized usage. There is also the possibility, however, that Tsurayuki is here inventing a new way of using the phrase—new, especially for prose, but nonetheless strongly reminiscent of other uses in other kinds of structures.

More important, perhaps, is the fact that this passage also appears to be the earliest instance in which the figure of the buried tree is used in a way that suggests something about the status and condition of the *waka* tradition itself, and that it does so by replicating the significant or "meaning-full" use of a recognizably poetic figure in prose—as if to suggest yet another endorsement of the value (or the historical validation) of such poetic language.[32] But while Tsurayuki's manipulation of the figure in this manner may have been in some sense "new," its success as a signifier, and as rhetoric, depended on recognition of it as a *poetic* figure associated with the particular idea of concealment and obscurity, an "old" association that had to rest in turn on usage established in earlier texts, especially poems—perhaps including but by no means limited to *Kokin wakashū* #650, possibly reaching back as far as the *Man'yōshū umoregi* poems as well. While decrying the decline of *waka* praxis as a whole into a plaything of the amorously playful, Tsurayuki employs a figure whose use appears to originate (so far as we can tell) in songs of love. Although his rhetoric serves a lofty goal—the resuscitation and elevation of the art of native song—its roots seem to lie in humbler, quotidian soil. Tsurayuki himself recognized the status and historical importance of love songs in his account of the functions of *Yamato uta,* in the opening section of the *kana* preface: "It is song that moves heaven and earth without effort, stirs emotions in the invisible spirits and gods, *brings harmony to the relations between men and women* [*otoko onna no naka o mo yawarage*], and calms the hearts of fierce warriors."[33] In the structuring of the *Kokin wakashū* itself, more space (five of twenty chapters) is devoted to love poems than to poems on any other single topic or class of topics. And, although the chapters specifically devoted to "love" come after those devoted to what Tsurayuki and his confreres perhaps thought of as more dignified subjects— the four seasons, royal anniversaries, farewells, and travel—poems that could have been treated as "love poems" are to be found in virtually every chapter. There may have been an effort, in all this, to suppress the implications of frivolity in love poetry by emphasizing (through reclassification) other aspects of poems that might have been read as love poems, but these signs of their origins in the context and heat of *iro* (desire) show through, as does evidence that much of what would become *waka* rhetoric took shape in verbal (perhaps sung) exchanges between two individuals, yearning for and toward one another.

Nonetheless, or perhaps *because* of the character of its origins, such rhetoric as that deployed by Tsurayuki in his preface seems to have worked, or at least to have reflected a change in attitude toward "domestic poetry" (*Yamato uta,* i.e., *waka*) that was taking place anyway: in any case, *waka* thrived for centuries after Tsurayuki and his fellow *Kokin wakashū* compilers "rescued" it from neglect—and so, ipso facto, did *waka* rhetoric. And one of several important factors that insured the long survival of the *waka* tradition was the constancy and durability of *waka* rhetoric, the continuous presence of a communally available repertory of figures. The buried tree is but one example of this array of durable figures that underwrote the durability of *waka* itself, and one whose own durability is easily documented. It is also a figure that would show itself to be particularly useful as a figure for durability itself, for patient waiting for an opportunity to be taken notice of, to have its availability for reuse recognized once more, once its rescue from obscurity has been achieved.

Once again, we would be hard pressed to say just when and where the *umoregi* figure was first used as a sign of obscurity per se—that is, at something of a thematic remove, or modulation, from what do appear to be its earlier uses in songs about the concealment of love. If this was a process of modulation, it would seem to have been well advanced (if not initiated— which seems less likely) by the time that Tsurayuki wrote his *kana* preface. And the outcome of the process—the fixing of an alternative, common "reading" of the figure—seems already to have been achieved by the time (which we can only roughly approximate) of the composition of the previously discussed *umoregi* poem in the *Izumi Shikibu shū*.[34] That poem is presented therein, according to the prose preface (*kotobagaki*), as having been composed in response to a gift of flowers which the poet received on New Year's Day (*Shōgatsu ichinichi, hana o hito no okosetareba*):

> Haru ya kuru hana ya saku to mo shirazariki
>   tani no soko naru umoregi nareba[35]
> I/it did not know that spring had arrived, that the blossoms had come forth,
>   for I am/it is a tree that lies buried in the valley's depths.

Finding herself obliged to acknowledge the gift of flowers (presumably plum blossoms, the appearance and poetic celebration of which are often associated with New Year's festivities), the poet has seized upon the opportunity to complain, artfully and pithily, about her present condition. And she does so by portraying *herself* as the buried tree, living in obscurity and neglect, and in so doing she may be reproaching the person (*hito*) who sent the blossoms (from a *living* tree) for his or her neglect at some other time—or, perhaps, she is thanking him or her for this special attention while reproaching others who have neglected her. Despite the absence of anything quite equivalent to "I" in the language of the poem, the poet's identification with its subject—the *umoregi*—is more than readily apparent, precisely because of what must have been the extant and apparently obvious association of the figure with obscurity, the state of being out of sight or easily overlooked. Nothing is invented here, but that is just the point: the poet's message carries weight because it borrows weight from previous usage, and thereby takes on such meaning as it has.

Additional evidence of this modulation can be found in the private collection of poems attributed to Murasaki Shikibu, a contemporary and possibly an acquaintance of Izumi Shikibu's.[36] According to the prose preface (*kotobagaki*) to this poem, Murasaki Shikibu was on a brief leave of absence from her service in the retinue of the Empress Shōshi when she sent her mistress a spray of red plum blossoms plucked from the garden of her private home (*kōbai o orite sato yori mairasu to te*):

> mumoregi no shita ni yatsururu mume no hana
>   ka o dani chirase kumo no ue made[37]
> Oh you blossoms of plum that have hidden yourselves in obscurity
>   below a buried tree:
>   scatter your scent, at least, as far as the clouds on high!

This message (an apparently real communication, meant to be seen, read, and appreciated along with the object it accompanied, if the *kotobagaki* is accurate) also depends almost entirely on conventional resonances (as well as context) to convey its meaning. The plum blossoms come from a humble source (*mumoregi no shita*)—Murasaki Shikibu's relatively "obscure" dwelling, where she is temporarily out of sight, hidden from the Empress's gaze—but their strong perfume carries with it her affection and respect for the royal lady who dwells "on high" (*kumo no ue* is a conventional figure for the Imperial residence). The metonymic scheme of the poem toys knowingly with the status relation of the two personae in its scenario: the Empress is, of course, above (*ue*), and her correspondent is below (*shita*), even though intimacy and affection go a long way toward ameliorating the distinction. It may be that *umoregi no* here is but a (meaning-full) adornment of *shita* (as it may be in *Man'yōshū* #2723), but it may also engage (meaningfully) with the figure (just offstage) of the living, blooming plum tree. A tree removed from time and a branch of another tree that is still part of it—the one inert and hidden, the other active, showily displaying its vitality and marking the renewal of life in spring (with one of that season's most conventional poetic emblems)—are simultaneously present in this figural scheme, filling the poem with both timelessness and the specificity of a moment in seasonal, cyclical, and historical time.

In a slightly later poem we find the figures of a buried tree and a blossoming one interacting again; in this case, however, the blossoming tree is not a tangible thing in present time but a recollected emblem of a vitality of the past, and the old and new trees turn out to be one and the same. In 1105 or 1106, Emperor Horikawa commissioned sixteen of the most distinguished poets of his day to compose poems on a series of one hundred selected topics (*dai*). The poet in charge of the selection of topics (*daisha*) for what has come to be known as the *Horikawa hyakushu* (The hundred-poem sequences of Horikawa's reign) was the scholar Ōe Masafusa (1041–1111), and his own response to the topic *kaikyū* (yearning for the past) was:

> umoregi no shita wa kutsuredo
> > inishie no hana no kokoro wa wasurezarikeri[38]
> The bottom of the buried tree may have decayed,
> > but it has not forgotten how it felt to be in blossom long ago.

Here, the fossilized tree is the poem-speaker's anthropomorphized self which, though utterly changed in form and literally falling apart with rot and age, nonetheless retains its memories of a time of vibrant flowering forth. The resonances that generate such meaning in this poem may involve several conflations—or modulations—of precedent: at the very least, commentators point to two *Kokin wakashū* poems with which Masafusa's actively interacts.[39] The first, #875, is said to have been composed by the monk Kengei "when women laughed when they looked at him" (*onnadomo no, mite warai-kereba, yomeru*)—presumably because he was so old and decrepit (like a rotten tree), or because his monkish appearance (suggestive to some Heian women—such as Sei Shōnagon—of a "withered tree" or an "old stick") was itself a cause for mirth:

> katachi koso
> miyamagakure no
>   kuchiki nare
> kokoro wa hana ni
> nasaba narinamu
>   I may look to you
> like a tree rotting unseen
>   deep in the mountains,
> but if I should will it so,
> blossoms would flower in my heart.[40]

The second poem (#219) is one which Ōshikōchi no Mitsune (another *Kokin wakashū* compiler) supposedly wrote (according to the *kotobagaki*) while conversing with an old companion (perhaps a former lover) encountered by chance in a meadow full of autumn flora:

> akihagi no
> furue ni sakeru
>   hana mireba
> moto no kokoro wa
> wasurezarikeri
>   The flowers blooming
> on the autumn bush clover's
>   aged branches
> tell us that the plant, at least,
> remembers former feelings.[41]

This reading of Masafusa's poem's intertextual matrix—its interdependence with Kengei's and Mitsune's poems, at least, and perhaps with others—defines his achievement as one that consists, again, of nothing that is particularly new but rather in the ingenious re-arrangement of resonant elements familiar to readers of other poems. Masafusa's buried tree comes by its capacity to recall the past through the poem's direct inheritance of the language ascribing the same capacity to Mitsune's "aged branches," and it derives its residual resiliency in part through its kinship with Kengei's "rotted" tree, unseen deep in mountain recesses but as willing as ever to put forth a show of blossoms.

Intertextual complexity of this kind is compounded even further in a poem by Fujiwara Shunzei on cherry blossoms (*sakura*) from a *hyakushu* series of 1140 or 1141. On this occasion, Shunzei took up the hundred topics of the *Horikawa hyakushu* of 1105-06 and treated each one with a layering of yet another conventional topical attitude called *jukkai* ("expressing one's feelings" [of dissatisfaction, often over having grown old]):

> mumoregi to narihatenuredo
>   yamazakura oshimu kokoro wa kuchizu mo aru ka na[42]
> Though I have become an altogether buried tree,
>   I still have enough heart left in me to feel regret about the mountain cherry blossoms.

This poem has been read as one of several from this same period of Shunzei's life—his late twenties—in which he laments his low court rank but defies his destined obscurity by trying to distinguish himself through the virtuosity of his verse.[43] It seems as likely, however, that it is a kind of overdetermined masquerade—a performance in the pose of the "discontented courtier," depersonalized by the conventionality of that pose and of the rhetoric employed in that very performance, yet enriched through its evocation of textual memories of the *Horikawa hyakushu*—Shunzei's memories, and his readers'. That previous and now exalted moment of composition is recalled with reverence and perhaps with regret—or with the fear that such achievements cannot now be equaled, but can only be eulogized. Still, if Shunzei—or, the singer, the performer of the masque—is now an "altogether buried tree," he nonetheless claims that he has not lost the capacity to feel the most basic but also the most refined of poetic sentiments—a reveling in the moment of flowering and a simultaneous mourning of its passing. And, by reaching beyond the *Horikawa hyakushu* moment in particular, through its conventional figurations, this poem transparently engages itself with virtually every other known and remembered buried tree and rotting wood poem, as well as with all "mountain cherry" and "regretting heart" poems, which are practically innumerable. Shunzei has no need to gesture to any *one* specific other poem to make his point, or to carry out the performance: his referential matrix here is (conceivably) *all* poetry, both extant and potential.

Still, Shunzei anchors this broad gesture by invoking one particularly potent figure, polished by time and repeated handling—that is, the buried tree, which here becomes his (or, his masque character's) aging but far from incapacitated self. Thus, this poem suggests that for Shunzei, as for so many of his predecessors (and successors), the figure of the buried tree was not only an available and almost irresistibly attractive figure (especially given the contours of the compositional moment he created for himself on this occasion) for an entity in decline or in obscurity which nonetheless remains vital, awaiting notice in a space and time at once central and peripheral. It was also a figure of *fixedness*—an object submerged and immovable in the river's banks, but resolute and secure alongside the constant motion of the river itself. As time wrought change in the world around it, the buried tree, having reached an equilibrium, a solid state, has ceased to change: beneath the shifting, flowing waters, it lies motionless, just below the visible surface, awaiting rediscovery, excavation, and new use as a tangible piece of the past—an exhumation embodied in the language of *waka,* a language itself shaped in its own past and transmitted through time, seemingly unchanged and representing (in a fragile but forceful way) the passage of time itself. And, like the buried tree itself, the language of *waka* was or at least could be viewed as a fixed constant past which the currents of time might flow, changing the form if not the character of that (supposedly) constant object while all the world might change even more radically around it. It may have been for this reason, above all, that the language of *waka* became a thing to be treasured as much as some might treasure a bit of a buried tree, as a rare residual deposit from the past, the embodiment both of this seeming changelessness and of inevitable change: something to cling to, even if desperately, while the value and viability of virtually everything else was at risk, if not already lost forever; something to fashion, again, into objects (poems) of inherited and inherent value at once old and new, dwelling simultaneously in past and present and, as if magically, diminishing the distance and the difference between the two. And, of course, to use the figure of the buried tree, or, for that matter, any other figure as deeply embedded in time and textual tradition, was to align and connect the new text in which that figure was used to virtually every other that had every used it: through that figure, the new text would place itself both in its own moment and in all of history.

Eventually, in the literary tradition's collective memory (as much as in its textual record), it would come to seem as though the figure of the buried tree (like so many others) had always been there, awaiting exhumation by anyone who might be moved to employ it for a variety of ends—many of them quite far removed from its apparent origins in love song. Its continued and varying use would bridge gaps in time, even while revealing how great those gaps might be; and its knowing and knowledgeable use and reuse would become ever more effective (and time-layered) as rhetoric, even as it already may have been when Tsurayuki used it (ca. 905). In yet another rhetorical modulation, for example, a buried tree allegory—a variant on the figure's association with obscurity—might be an appropriate way to vent frustration over failure to advance in office and rank. We have seen something of this in Shunzei's usage, but we questioned whether his was a real complaint, given the circumstances of that composition. But there were, of course, other poets before Shunzei who had things to complain about—and perhaps their example also helped determine the contours of his subsequent performance. One such predecessor—perhaps an equally knowing performer, also acting on the basis of poetic precedent—would be Minamoto Shigeyuki (ca. 939-ca. 1000), a poet who, upon finding himself in the provinces on the day of the ceremonial announcement of new appointments and promotions to administrative positions in the capital (*tsukasameshi*), is said to have written:

> haru goto ni wasurarenikeru mumoregi wa
>   hana no miyako o omoi koso yare[44]
> The buried tree that has been forgotten spring after spring
>   longs nonetheless for the city of flowers.

And again, at the time of another *tsukasameshi* some decades later, a poet of the next generation, Fujiwara Akinaka (1059-1129), apparently remembered Shigeyuki's plaint. Though, unlike Shigeyuki, he was fortunate enough to be in the capital at the time of the announcement of posts, the results seem to have been no less disappointing: the *kotobagaki* for Akinaka's poem in *Kin'yō wakashū* says that he composed it "because he heard nothing at the time of the *tsukasameshi* but that which caused him to feel envious resentment" (*tsukasameshi no koro urayamashiki koto nomi kikoekereba yomeru*):

> toshi furedo haru ni shirarenu mumoregi wa
>   hana no miyako ni sumu kai zo naki[45]
> The buried tree, ignored each spring though years go by,
>   gains nothing by living in the city of flowers.

Though both of these poems vent personal rancor against an exclusive system (which neither of these poets could hope to change), both were given a place in Imperially commissioned anthologies, as if in recognition of the fact (or, to reaffirm the notion) that such rancor itself might give rise to that which might be viewed as elegant poetic statement. Presumably, it is at least in part because of the way that this rancor is expressed—through recourse to the figure of the buried tree, the bearer, by this time, of a remarkable pedigree—that these poems merited admiration and inclusion in these two anthologies. And, for the knowing reader, Akinaka's poem builds on the precedent of Shigeyuki's, which in turn builds on the precedent of all its forebears: at each stage, the layers of reference become deeper, the web of interrelation broader.

To be sure, the weight of precedent did not preclude all flexibility: rather, it offered a language that could be adapted to multiple circumstances, even as each reuse of that language referred itself to other uses. Thus, at a moment somewhat later in the history of these usages, Fujiwara Tameuji (1222-1286) could turn Shigeyuki's and Akinaka's self-pity into a blander (but not unrelated) humility, in a poem "among those he presented [as an offering] to the Kasuga Shrine" (*Kasugasha ni tatematsurikeru uta no naka ni*):

> mumoregi no mi wa itazura ni furinu to mo
> > kami dani haru no megumi arawase[46]
> This buried tree has lived through all this time in vain,
> > but grant it the blessings of spring, oh god of Kasuga!

Here, Tameuji takes the figure into a new context—or, rather, takes it back to a very old context, the use of poetic language to induce and assuage the gods—in hopes of receiving the reward of renewed vigor from a divine source. The figure's presence in his poem may be as that of an emblem of time-weariness, of the need (apparently sensed by Tameuji) for revivification which he attributes, through it, to himself; but, recast here in the context of what at least purports to be a form of religious supplication, the time-worn figure of the buried tree does seem to be on the verge of attaining a new vitality, through a kind of alchemical dialectic with the forces of life. In an offering to a shrine dedicated to his clan's tutelary deities (and, in effect, to all his ancestors), Tameuji pleads for the blessings of vitality, and, perhaps, for worldly recognition—an antidote to the obscurity and lassitude of the buried tree. Many other poems—Izumi Shikibu's, Murasaki Shikibu's, Shigeyuki's, and Akinaka's, for example—had juxtaposed the buried tree and spring, projecting the figure of age and decay into a temporal context teeming with renewed and renewable vigor; here, however, that tactic is given extra texture, and perhaps a kind of residual ritual potency, by the fact that *Kasuga* is written with the two characters for "spring" and "sun"—representing the season of rejuvenation, and the ultimate source of energy. Thus, the poem and the preface given it upon anthologization combine as a quasi-narrative that is also quasi-acrostic: spring is written into the poem itself, while the spring sun is an implicit, potent presence.

In another compositional circumstance with rather particular contours, a buried tree allegory made itself useful to the poet Fujiwara Suemichi (1097?-1158?)—perhaps in order to get some wry smiles out of his readers. He was called in as one of three late substitute participants in the composing of *Kyūan hyakushu* (The hundred-poem sequences of the Kyūan era), after three poets previously named had died before making their contributions to the project.[47] As the last of the poems in the section of twenty "spring poems" in his execution of the sequence, Suemichi wrote:

> mi wa fuyu no umoregi naredo
>   choku nareba haru no kotoba no hana o chirashitsu[48]
> I may be a buried tree in the winter of my life,
>   but since it is His Majesty's command, I scatter here these flowery
>   spring words.

Suemichi jibes good-humoredly at himself, at his situation, and even at the contrivance of the *hyakushu* enterprise itself. He portrays himself as one who has been overlooked and marginalized until called upon to contribute to the *hyakushu* project; now, though that status has not altogether changed, the buried tree has been injected with new life: it can still create new foliage—and so, in response to a royal request (*choku,* a word read here in its Sino-Japanese pronunciation rather than as *mikotonori,* and hence a somewhat jarring presence, but perhaps deliberately so), it "scatters" words, in poems.[49] The phrase *haru no kotoba no hana* of course refers to the spring (*haru*) section of the sequence for which the poem was prepared, but also to the allegorical spring which Suemichi now experiences: the words of his poems are thus "words about the flowers of spring" but also the embodiment and evidence of his own revivification. The effect of the overlapping here of multiple, simultaneous referentialities is almost dizzying, but this should not obscure the fact that the poem is fundamentally light—an amusing move (only contingently consequential) in an elegant game: and the rules of the game clearly do not forbid the participants from joking about what they themselves are up to.

    In 1201, the poet known as Shunzei's Daughter (1171?-1252?) was a participant in similar game, a collective fifty-poem sequence project designed (and also participated in) by the Retired Emperor Gotoba and other members of his literary coterie.[50] The assigned topics for this project (known as the *Sentō kudai gojūshu*) were fifty elegant phrases in Chinese (*kudai*): on one of these, *kokeika* (flowers in an old ravine), Shunzei's Daughter wrote:

> furihatete shirarenu tani no mumoregi mo
>   haru wa mukashi no hana zo kuchisenu[51]
> Even the buried tree in the aged and abandoned ravine
>   has not yet let the blossoms of long-ago springs entirely decay.

This is a more abstract allegory than Suemichi's: it lacks an explicitly anthropomorphized subject, but, rather, celebrates enduring vitality itself. It is also a deft execution of a specific task—the call to seize upon the implications of the topic (*dai*) and to respond fittingly. Shunzei's Daughter knew her canons well: it is not surprising that a "buried tree" should lodge itself in her "old ravine," for the association was ready-made. Her labor was its repositioning in this particular setting, in a poem which, like the old ravine and the buried tree in it, looks back through time immeasurable but which also seizes its moment in the present. She thus seems to say that the way to respond to present tasks (such as this one) is to revert to the past; if sought out, there are abundant "flowers" in the past which, despite or *because* of their antiquity, can imbue the moment at hand with pungent color and perfume. Perhaps, for Shunzei's Daughter, her father/grandfather Shunzei's *umoregi* poesy was the strongest source of such redolence: she does not point directly to it as the font for present play, but lets its vestiges mix freely with other derived and now conjoined flavors and scents, in an amalgam that is hers and yet not entirely her own.

While the records of these assorted courtly projects show participants turning deftly to the figure of the buried tree to meet specific needs or to convey specific messages—in circumstances where the demanding but motivating pressure on the poet came largely from the need to make fitting response to a topical challenge, and to do so in good time—two works in another genre, the narrative tales of warfare in the twelfth and thirteenth centuries, give us examples of poets who seize upon the figure of the buried tree in rather different circumstances: that is, the composition of some of the most memorable (and best known) buried tree poems in the tradition is depicted in these works as having been occasioned by moments of fatal crisis. Within these narratives, these *umoregi* poems serve to cap the retelling of tragic episodes: both are used to poeticize these tragic moments, and are meant to give the telling of them a special grace. Though their effect when read today may verge on bathos, they were no doubt conceived as lyrical beautifications of these accounts of frightening, bloody, and real events. They are, yet again, a kind of deeply signifying embellishment—but can also be read, of course, as yet further examples of stories (within other stories) about how particular poems (or, poems in general) come to be made: and these particular poems are shown as having been made in emotional environments that are extremely dire.

The first of these poem-stories is found in "The Death of the Prince," a chapter in *Heike monogatari* (The tale of the Heike), which is one of a sequence of chapters that describes the rout of rebellious forces led against the Taira dictatorship by the hapless Prince Mochihito at Uji, in the summer of 1180. Mortally wounded, the elderly commander in the field, Minamoto Yorimasa, asks a junior officer, Watanabe no Chōjitsu Tonō, to decapitate him, but Tonō cannot bring himself to do it; he promises only to remove his commander's head after Yorimasa disembowels himself. Then,

> Yorimasa turned toward the west, chanted ten Buddha-invocations in a loud voice, and spoke his last sad words:
>
>> umoregi no hana saku koto mo nakarikishi ni
>>> mi no naru hate zo kanashikarikeru.
>> No flower of fortune
> has blessed a life resembling
> a long-buried tree —
>> yet how bitter is the thought
> that all should end like this.[52]

A second, similar poem-story is to be found in one of the variant texts of *Jōkyūki*, a chronicle of Retired Emperor Gotoba's abortive coup against the Kamakura shogunate, in 1221. In the aftermath of this poorly organized outburst of royalist resistance, the victorious Kamakura authorities lashed out ruthlessly at almost everyone who had been close to the defeated Emperor, who was sent into exile.[53] One of the most pathetic victims was the adolescent son of Gotoba's military commander, Sasaki Hirotsuna. This fourteen-year-old boy, called Seitaka, was the beloved page-companion (*chigo*) of Gotoba's son, the Priest-Prince Dōjo, abbot of the Ninnaji monastery in the capital city. According to the *Jōkyūki* (*rufubon* version), Dōjo tried to plead for the boy's life, promising to take responsibility for any misdeeds that might be committed in his name, but in the end he could only stand by helplessly while Seitaka was put into the carriage that would take him away to await execution. Dōjo did manage, however, to utter this poem in parting:

> umoregi no kuchihatsubeki wa todomarite
>> wakaki no hana no chiru zo kanashiki[54]
> How terrible! The buried tree that ought to perish remains behind,
>> while the blossoms on the youthful tree shall scatter.

While neither of the accounts from which these episodes come can be treated as reliable documentary history, they are significant in another way: they show that the makers of these *monogatari*—ex post facto narratives meant to be both read and sung, to musical accompaniment, to share with diverse audiences a poignant sense of what had happened to the nation and its people in these trying times—saw fit to portray these protagonists (a professional soldier and a cloistered prince) as the kind of men who could manipulate such figures, even in extremis, as deftly as their counterparts in courtly life in peace-time. In both these perilous moments, the characters who make these poems seize upon the figure of the buried tree as the emblem of their own age. While Yorimasa was "more than seventy" at his death, Dōjo was only in his late twenties when Seitaka was taken from him. At the end of a long life, Yorimasa looks back and declares that he has never accomplished anything; he has dwelt all this time at the margins, waiting for his moment of glory, and now all ends in ignominy. Dōjo, on the other hand, is really in the prime of life, but, comparing himself to the even more youthful Seitaka (*wakaki*, a "sapling"), he is already "aged wood" which now, sustaining this loss, cannot hope for anything but speedier decay.[55] Yorimasa's poem juxtaposes the unrealized possibilities of life (*hana saku koto*, "the blooming of the flowers") with his ignominious end (*mi no naru hate*); in much the same structure, Dōjo's poem poses the aged tree beside the sapling, then focuses on their parting, and both contrasting situations are predicated as *kanashi,* cause for grief.[56]

In both these cases, the figure of the buried tree becomes a metaphorical player in a tragic scenario, a node of irony, as the protagonists look back (on the one hand) and look forward (on the other) and assess or predict a final and complete loss of vitality. To the audiences for these narratives, the deployment of this figure in these moments must have rung with resonance—and would have needed little explication, for it was already packed with associative significance, and could serve well to heighten the pathos (if not the bathos) in the retelling of these events.

A figure as heavily packed and resonant as the buried tree was bound to be useful in yet another genre—Nō drama—in which allusive language is strategically deployed as an economical and powerful code. In *Sekidera Komachi* (Komachi at Sekidera), a Nō play of unknown date and uncertain authorship but known and performed at the time of the great playwright Zeami (1363-1443)—and perhaps revised by him—the *shite* (protagonist), an old woman eventually identified as the spirit of the famed poet Ono no Komachi, describes herself as having fallen into an obscurity like that of the buried tree, and therefore into estrangement from the art and traditions of poetry (*umoregi no hito shirenu koto to nari*).[57] The speech is a thematically appropriate and dramatically effective borrowing from Tsurayuki's *Kokin wakashū kana* preface—strands of which are woven elsewhere into the play's texture. But its utterance on the Nō stage in the fifteenth century may also be thought of—along with the *Heike* and *Jōkyūki* poem-stories—as yet another step in a far-flung and multi-faceted process that served to perpetuate and also to spread recognition of the figure's significance, as did its continued use in poetry per se—or, conversely, its use in the Nō libretto may demonstrate how widely recognized and understood the figure was likely to be among literate audiences.

Similarly, the transmission of the figure of the buried tree from the *waka* tradition to that of *renga* and *haikai,* as part and parcel of the adopted and adapted rhetoric of a "new" textual tradition that very transparently displays its roots in the "old"—also gives evidence of the figure's capacity to endure and the means whereby that endurance was ensured. This particular phase of the figure's circulation and transformation in multiple genres can be traced as far back as *Tsukuba shū,* the first authoritative anthology of linked verse, compiled by the Regent (and *renga* enthusiast) Nijō Yoshimoto with the aid of the poet-monk Gusai in 1356 and submitted for Imperial imprimatur (as a new kind of *chokusenshū*) in 1357. In the section of the anthology devoted to a selection of Gusai's own *renga* is the following pair of linked verses:

> ari to mo mienu koke no shitamizu
>> mumoregi no eda ni wa nami no hana sakite[58]
> Beneath banks of moss flows a stream that one can scarcely discern;
>> on the branches of a buried tree, flowers blossom in rippling waters.

And the first link in the section devoted to the works of Gusai's literary disciple Eiun is:

> mumoregi nagara haru o wasurezu
>> tanikawa no seze no shiranami yuki kiete[59]
> Though it is a buried tree, it has not forgotten about spring;
>> in every shoal in the valley stream, snow melt feeds waters that toss up white waves.

As the *renga* scholar Ijichi Tetsuo has pointed out, the first part of Eiun's link offers the conventional ambiguity of subject (who or what is the buried tree that persists in blossoming?), but the latter part suppresses anthropomorphization in favor of seasonal landscape.[60] Thus, at the juncture of late winter and early spring, a recently frozen stream visually and audibly displays its newly amplified torrent, and the ancient tree on its banks displays new vibrancy as well. The descriptive content of the second part of the link forces a rereading of the first part, obscuring some possibilities of signification and bringing others to the fore. But such dynamics are possible precisely because of the extent to which the figure of the buried tree was an at once deeply embedded and exposed "lode," and hence a richly malleable resource for poets like Gusai, Eiun, and their contemporaries as they labored to adapt the associative schemes of *waka* for use in new forms, in what would emerge, through them, as a newly distinct genre—one which would, in time, overtake and displace *waka,* even while exploiting and affirming its genealogical ties to the foundation genre, and thereby, if indirectly, contributing in yet another way to its survival.

The name of the Natori River was likewise both securely embedded and invitingly exposed as durable and malleable poetic matériel through these same centuries of textual and intertextual development. During most of this long period, relatively few poets actually journeyed to its banks and reported what they saw there: as a result, and as is the case with so many famous places in the *waka* tradition, it is imagined presences, rather than real ones, that set the stage for the greater part of those poems that form the corpus of Natorigawa poesy. And though the preponderance of moments in which poetic gaze would be turned upon this river would occur at a far remove from its "real" geography, the very fact that Natorigawa (like other remote *meisho*) was so often sung of from such distances must have served, in turn, to increase its exoticism, and to make its remoteness seem even greater to those who actually made their way to it.

One of those who did so was Saigyō (1118–1189), perhaps the most famous of those medieval poets whose literary personae took shape through their movements and activities in the twin modes of travel and aesthetic eremitism. It is believed that Saigyō took Buddhist vows and adopted the guise of a mendicant at the age of twenty-three, in 1140; his subsequent peregrinations are believed to have taken him to Michinoku, the remote northeast, at least twice, perhaps for the first time as early as 1147, when he was thirty.[61]

In his private collection, *Sankashū,* the reader follows Saigyō through a poeticized Michinoku landscape—a terrain already enriched, for Saigyō as for so many others, by the prior presences (both factual and fanciful) of so many other poets (also both real and imaginary, named and unnamable) before him. The *kotobagaki* for the poem that records Saigyō's Natorigawa crossing is quite transparently dependent on the poem itself for such information as it conveys, and hence may seem almost superfluous; yet, in the anthologized setting it serves, in poetic-diary or poem-tale fashion, to tell the story of how this particular poem came to be made. It also contributes to another larger story, about how Saigyō experienced travel, how he saw things, and how he made these experiences into poetry.[62]

> Natorigawa o watarikeru ni, kishi no momiji no kage o mite
>   Natorigawa kishi no momiji no utsuru kage wa
>   onaji nishiki o soko ni sae shiku[63]

When he crossed the Natori River, he saw the reflection of the colored autumn foliage on the banks, and wrote:

> At Natori River, the reflected image of the colored foliage on the bank
> spreads the very same brocade beneath the water's depth.

In its intent focus on descriptive conceit—on the poetic mistaking of autumn foliage (*momiji*) for brocade (*nishiki*)—this poem seems almost deliberate in its avoidance of the Natorigawa/*umoregi* conventions: it shuns all association with the site's traditional but abstract linkage with the subject and imagery of love to view this autumnal land- and waterscape from an equally traditional pose, one adopted in conscious imitation of a *Kokin* aesthetic.[64] For Saigyō, this moment beside the Natorigawa was not one for an excursion (even in the abstract) into the territories of poeticized love traversed by previous poets in their manipulations of the place's name; rather, Saigyō's own gaze upon the river itself, and the resulting confusion (in which he takes a knowing delight) were what demanded (or merited) poetic reporting. What Saigyō says he saw at Natorigawa is a scene he might have seen beside many another river at this point in autumn; its description, as well as the moment, are particularized only by the river's name. The trees that hold the brilliant foliage Saigyō sees may be descendants of others long buried—literally and poetically—in that river, or may be the antecedents of others that will be, but Saigyō does little if anything with that nuance of their appearance: he is all involved with their present, living form, and with the visual impact that they, and their reflections, produce in him, as viewer.

Yet, even in adopting this descriptive (or hyperdescriptive) approach, Saigyō is by no means out of step with all precedent for the poetic treatment of the site; for, while the object of his gaze is, at least ostensibly, the real river, there had been more than one previous poet who had imagined an analogous scene or scenes in verse. These, too, were Natorigawa scenes without buried trees—scenes from which that feature of the landscape may have been deliberately excluded, to heighten the effect of difference from the norm—but scenes which were nonetheless enriched by a consciousness of virtually all other poetic "viewings" of that site. What moved these poets to imagine Natorigawa scenes in the particular compositional moments in which they found themselves was their awareness that the name itself evoked such riches—the exoticism of the far Northeast, the romance of earlier Natorigawa poesy. A pantomimed presence at the river (in contrast to Saigyō's "real" presence) was, therefore, a kind of elegant stunt, a creation through text of an experience these poets had never had, except in the imagination.

This was, for example, quite likely the effect that Minamoto Shigeyuki sought when, during his days of service in the retinue of the Crown Prince

who would become the Emperor Reizei in 969, he composed the following
and included it in the twenty winter poems section of a *hyakushu* sequence:

> Natorigawa yanase no nami zo sawagu naru
> momiji ya itodo yorite seku ran[65]
> What a din the waves breaking in the sluices in Natorigawa are making!
> I suppose it is because so many colored leaves carried in the downstream
> current are blocking the flow.

It is primarily the sensations of sound, rather than sight, that are imagined
here, as Shigeyuki adopts the conventional pose of one who cannot discern,
through sight, the source or cause of a sound perceived, but who nonetheless
speculates (or is *therefore* moved to speculate) about its nature and origin.
Though conventionally staged and wholly imaginary, this sonic pantomime
may exercise the exoticism of its imagined setting in a particularly powerful
way: through its sounds, or through its graphic recording as text (which
might act as guide to the re-production of sound), it may have had the almost
magical capacity to transport the capital-bound hearer or reader to that very
imagined site in his or her own imagination, or rather, to close the distance
between the capital and that site. Though arising from an immeasurably
distant (abstracted and idealized) source, this watery noise may have
sounded very close at hand to those who received and savored Shigeyuki's
poem, thus joining with him as actors in the pantomime (figure 4).[66]

There is also a Natorigawa poem among the collected works of Nōin
(988–ca. 1050) that seems intended to be another sort of pantomime, a *faux*
performance of a provincial song (*kuniburiuta*): it is one of five poems
apparently composed in imitation of the east country songs (*tōkoku fuzoku
goshu*) of pre-*Kokin* times, but is otherwise very much a poem of its own
time (the first half of the eleventh century):

> Natorigawa kawa naku tori zo nagarete mo
> shita yuku mizu no masu moto zo omou[67]
> Look how these crying birds are drifting off in Natorigawa's stream—
> yet I cannot help but think of how the waters that flow beneath the surface
> must be surging!

This poem enacts another dialectic, or an act of choice, between that which
can be seen and heard and that which can only be imagined; Nōin, or rather
the "singer" of the ersatz *fuzoku*, acknowledges the action on the river's surface
but is ineluctably drawn (by the birds' cries and the roar of the surging waters
themselves, as it were) to speculate about what is taking place beneath them,
out of sight. This dialectic may be readable as parable (an urging to look past
surfaces and diverting noise to hidden depths), but it may also be a narrative

4. Scene from Ōshū meisho zue *(author and artist unknown; early nineteenth century): Minamoto Shigeyuki composes his poem about Natorigawa,* Shin kokin wakashū *#553 ("Natorigawa/yanase no nami zo/sawagu naru /momiji ya itodo'yorite seku ran"). The artists shows Shigeyuki on horseback among his attendants beside the stream, in which maple leaves flow swiftly past the sluices mentioned in the poem. Although Shigeyuki did travel to the far northeast, this poem was actually composed in the capital for a* hyakushu *sequence in 969. Courtesy Miyagi-ken Toshokan.*

of observation of a specific scene, albeit one transportable from the environs of Natori to any riverine locale, but in any case one in which sight and sound so capture the observer's attention that he is compelled to try to penetrate the scene still further, through intellect. All this may be out of keeping with the enterprise of *fuzoku* imitation: indeed, all this poem may have in common with the traditions of song to which it apparently links itself is its Natorigawa setting—but the resulting interplay between archaic performances and practices (however dimly recollected or understood) and Nōin's (relatively) modern sensibilities is, perhaps, its essence.

Nōin is known or at least is reported to have travelled to the far Northeast, perhaps repeatedly.[68] There is nothing to suggest that this Natorigawa poem is in any literal sense a "song *he* sang in the east country"; yet, like Saigyō's poem, made when he was "really" there, and like Shigeyuki's, made when he certainly was not, it enacts a visit, a presence on the spot. This tension, then, between being there and the imagining of being there may shape our reading of one or another of these poems alongside or against one another—

and, in some instances, it becomes a part of the Natorigawa topos itself. Thus, for example, what must have been, for some, the shock of being there at Natorigawa, after a lifetime of merely hearing about and imagining what it was like, or what it might mean to *be* there, becomes the transparent subtext of an episode of riverside composition—once more, in extremis—in yet another narrative of medieval warfare. The *Taiheiki* is an account of Emperor Godaigo's mid-fourteenth-century revolt against the Hōjō family's dictatorship, and its aftermath. In an early section we are told that the monk Enkan, abbot of the Hosshōji monastery, had been one of several prelates who, in 1331, at the behest of Godaigo's son, Prince Morinaga, had performed exorcisms designed to rid the country of the Hōjō; retaliating, the Hōjō order the arrest of the exorcists, and Enkan finds himself under escort to his place of exile—the town of Yūki, in distant Mutsu, a Michinoku province.[69] The *Taiheiki* narrator emphasizes the severity of such exile (in "a far place among distant barbarians")[70] in preparation for the reproduction of the poem Enkan supposedly composes on the spot when, having almost reached his destination, he prepares to cross Natorigawa:

> Michinoku no uki Natorigawa
>   nagarekite shizumi ya haten seze no umoregi[71]
> I have drifted to this place, Natorigawa, famed in Michinoku for its sad name,
>   and shall I sink forever beneath its waters, a buried tree amidst its shoals?

The deftness of this poem belies the tension of the moment in which it is said to have been made—and thus it may be read as a means of capping and overcoming that tension, of imposing a kind of order, and perspective, on the moment at hand. Enkan is shown as placing himself in history—a history shaped largely by poetic practice—as he stands by the Natorigawa shore and makes his poem. The current of events has borne him thither, to a place of which he has long known but which he has certainly never seen, and he records the moment of "being there" by seizing upon the poeticized contours of the place, and reconfiguring them. The word *uki* doubles in this poem (as in many another about many rivers and other bodies of water) as floating (a gerund) and sad (an adjectival) descriptive of this river and its reputation, and it temporarily forms the word *ukina* (ignominious name) before syntax pushes the poem onward. The verbs *nagare[kite]* and *shizumi[hate]* (drifting [and reaching this place], "sinking [completely]") are also linked through conventional association to watery *topoi* in general, but have special relevance to Enkan's situation. Once again there is transparent anthropomorphization, as the poem takes the form of a kind of prayer: "Must it be my fate to end my life here in oblivion, like this river's buried trees?" By this time, the phrase *seze no umoregi* was a litany, one that might well be addressed to the river, or to the whole site, to beg for its compassion. And, in this case, the charm seems to have worked: Enkan survived his banishment, was reinstated to his post at Hosshōji (in the capital) by Godaigo, assisted in the founding of a number of other important monasteries in various parts of the country, and died in 1356 at the age of 76.[72]

In this episode describing the nadir of Enkan's career, however, the anonymous author of the *Taiheiki* is chiefly interested in melodramaticizing the moment of the prelate's river-crossing, or in capitalizing on the historic circumstance that brought him to it: for here was an opportunity for the poeticization of the narrative, not to be missed. Whether Enkan actually wrote such a poem, or whether it is an embellishment of his story, cannot be known; but its appearance in *Taiheiki*—a text that is known to have been performed orally by itinerant singer-reciters before audiences of *samurai* and of peasant alike as late as the early eighteenth century[73]—ensured that it, in turn, would become part of the lore of Natorigawa itself, another stratum in its textual history.

The *Taiheiki* account (factual or otherwise) places Enkan in that small fraternity of poem-makers whose poems on Natorigawa can be presented as having been made when, or soon after, they saw the river with their own eyes. But far more numerous, as we have noted, were the men and women who made Natorigawa poems at a distance—a liberating distance, for some, since some compositional situations allowed certain poets to bring new elements to the treatment of this "old" topos without straying far from convention and precedent.[74] The twelfth-century poet known both as Kōtaigōgū no Daijin (Lady Daijin, from the Empress Kinshi's Retinue)[75] and as Wakamizu does this in a poem in her personal collection (*Kōtaigōgū no Daijin shū*, compiled by the poet herself and presented as an offering to the Kamo Shrines ca. 1182-1183).[76] The *kotobagaki* indicates that this particular poem is an exercise on the topic (*dai*) "maidenflowers growing on the opposite bank of the river" (*ominaeshi kawa o hedatsu*):

> Natorigawa ochi no migiri no ominaeshi
> nami ni tawarete nureginu ya kiru[77]
> The maidenflowers that grow at the edge of the opposite shore of Natorigawa
> have frolicked in the waves, and now wear sodden robes, I fear.

Contemplating the topic before her, this poet seems to have come up with what may well be the only known poem that plants these flowers (*ominaeshi*) into the Natorigawa landscape. Still, she does not stray entirely from precedent; rather, she manipulates and elaborates upon it. In *waka*, these flowers, with their suggestive name, had long been used to portray various kinds of women—quite frequently, women much given to erotic dalliance.[78] It would seem that Lady Daijin/Wakamizu remembered Natorigawa as the poeticized site of passionate encounters, secret and otherwise, and then made her "maidenflowers" the protagonists of a scenario in which they have been enticed into its waters, only to reap ruined reputations and regret. Added to this concoction are the verb *tawar[u]*, which denotes illicit play between the sexes, and the noun *nureginu*, which identifies a garment soaked through with moisture, the source of which is invariably the wearer's own tears. This, then, is the state of the flowers that the poem-speaker views from the opposite shore; she is not one of them, but, as it were, a detached observer. In an imagined scene on the bank of what is here a wholly imaginary river—again, particularized by its name alone—Daijin/Wakamizu begins to sketch an anthropomorphized pantomime, with a hint of moral censure (or of mock censure, perhaps). But the poem's main goal is to meet the challenge of the *dai*, and it does so adequately, maybe even inventively—and leaves things at that.

Topical challenges posed in several late Heian and Kamakura-period poetry competitions (*utaawase*) also, not infrequently, prompted the use of Natorigawa, usually in fairly strict adherence to precedent; but the degree to which a competitor adhered to or strayed from the precedents of Natorigawa poesy seems often to have determined his or her success or failure in each given match. In the *Roppyakuban utaawase* of 1193 (Poetry competition in six-hundred rounds), Jakuren (d. 1202) ended up in a tie when, in the eighteenth round in the seventh series of "love" rounds—a round governed by the *Man'yō*-esque topic "love, through reference to a river" (*kawa ni yosuru koi*)—he offered this reworking of the Natorigawa matériel:

> ari to te mo awanu tameshi no Natorigawa
>   kuchi dani hateyo seze no mumoregi[79]
>
> If I live, yet we never are to meet—as in the Natorigawa's fabled example—
>   then let this old tree buried in its shoals rot to the core!

Neither team could find any fault with this poem, or with the one paired with it, by the host Fujiwara Yoshitsune, and the judge, Shunzei (Jakuren's uncle and adoptive father), declared: "Both poems are quite good; this is a good tie" (*Ryōhō tomo ni mottomo yoroshi. Yoki mochi to su*).[80]

But in round 1,227 of the *Sengohyakuban utaawase* of 1201 (Poetry competition in fifteen-hundred rounds)—a round governed by the general topic "love"—Fujiwara Yasusue, on the left, offered

> omou koto shinobedo ima wa
>   Natorigawa seze no mumoregi arawarenikeri

> Though I have tried to hide my love, now word is out, and I've made a name
>   for myself:
> the buried trees in Natorigawa's shoals are all exposed.

The entry from his opponent on the right, Fujiwara Tadayoshi (1162–1225), was

> nerareneba makura mo utoki
>   toko no ue ni ware shirigao ni moru namida ka na
> Unable to sleep, even my pillow is alien to me,
>   and my own tears fall heartlessly, soaking my bed.

The commentator and judge (*hanja*) for this section of the contest, Fujiwara
Kenshō (1130–1209), had quite a lot to say:

> The poem on the left takes the first three lines of the [*Kokin wakashū*] poem,
> "*Natorigawa seze no mumoregi*" as its own last three lines; only the first two lines
> are new. The poem on the right recalls the [*Kokin wakashū*] poem [#504],
>   wa ga koi o hito shirurameya
>   shikitae no makura nomi koso shiraba shirurame
>   [How can that person know about my love?
>   If anyone or anything knows, it is the pillow that lies upon my bed that knows,
>   and no one else.]
> and then sets down the lines "Nerareneba makura mo utoki/toko no ue ni"
> [Unable to sleep, even my pillow is alien to me, and upon my bed . . .]. The end
> of the poem, "ware shirigao ni moru namida ka na" [my own tears fall heartlessly,
> soaking my bed] is so interesting that one cannot say there is anything the least
> bit old-fashioned about the poem: its relationship to the old poem is confined to
> turning "makura bakari zo shiraba shiruran" [if anything or anyone knows, it is my
> pillow that knows] into "makura mo utoki" [even my pillow is alien to me]; so it
> *is* a new poem, and for this reason I must say that it is the winner.[81]

The deciding factor in this judgment is the nature and degree of relationship
to the foundation poems: Kensho's preference here, like that of many of his
contemporaries, was for inventive use of "old" material in the creation of the
"new," and that is why he preferred Tadayoshi's transformation of the foundation poem's sympathetic pillow into one that makes itself remote (*utoki*)
from the suffering lover (the poem-speaker) who would drown it with tears.
This poem's newness lay in that transformation, a linkage of Tadayoshi's
poem to the anonymous *Kokin wakashū* poem forged in such a way as to
suggest a continuum of situation and time, in which unfolding (un-narrated)
events have made the subject lover's anxiety and frustration still more acute.
Unfortunately for Yasusue, no comparable newness was to be detected in
his haplessly matched verse, the sameness of which, vis-à-vis its *Kokin* template, was far more marked than any difference.

Such, then, was the danger of Natorigawa's status—the danger, that is, that its name, and that of its *umoregi* (like other tried and true names and figures) might be allowed to surface too often in *utaawase* and similar situations and thereby cease to be able to inspire ingenious, transforming (or even acceptable) treatment. In a later round (number 1,337) in the *Sengohyakuban utaawase*, Yoshitsune would win the honors with a poem combining the same old (*furushi*) Natorigawa matériel as Yasusue's with elements from another "old" poem—which is, as it happens, Motoyoshi's *wabinureba* poem, the poem from which elements were also woven into Teika's Natorigawa *sōmonka*, *Shūi gusō* #2503[82]—but only because Kenshō found a serious fault in the poem paired with Yoshitsune's, by Prince Kore-akira.[83] But, at the love-poem contest held at the Imperial villa at Minase in 1202 (*Minase koi jūgoshu utaawase*), Shunzei held that his son Fujiwara Teika's entry, which used Natorigawa to treat the topic "love by the riverside" (*kawabe no koi*), was inferior to Yoshitsune's, which deployed the name of another famous place, the Hatsuse River:

> Hatsusegawa ide kosu nami no iwa no ue ni
> onore kudakete hito zo tsurenaki[84]
> I shall dash myself upon the rocks in the channels over which waves crash in
>   Hatsuse River,
>   for the one I love has no love for me.

In this case, Yoshitsune's poem won Shunzei's praise for the elegance of its allusion to a specific *Man'yōshū* verse, the recognized foundation-poem of Hatsuse River poesy:

> Hatsusegawa nagaruru mio no se o hayami
> ide kosu nami no oto no kiyokeku[85]
> Waters run swift in the shoals amidst the currents that flow in Hatsusegawa,
>   so the sound of the waves that spill out of the channels is pure and bright.

But Teika's was dismissed for its reliance on "stale language" (*koto furite haberubeshi*):

> Natorigawa watareba tsurashi
> kuchihatsuru sode no tameshi no seze no umoregi[86]
> Here is trouble, now that I have crossed Natorigawa:
>   my sleeves will follow the example of the buried trees in its shoals, rotting to
>   the core from dampness.

In a sense, both poets' resort to *meisho* poesy puts their poems on a level playing field, but, in Shunzei's judgment, Yoshitsune's gesture to one archaic poetic moment, and its language, was *en*—that is, possessed of and producing a highly valued charm—while the not-quite-so-old but perhaps overly familiar (and possibly overused) language of the *Kokin* Natorigawa template could not yield anything like the same effect—at least, not as used by Teika here.

The results may have been better on a somewhat later occasion, in a contest for both Chinese and Japanese versification at the Imperial Palace (*Dairi shiika awase*) in 1214, when Teika addressed the topic "flowers [cherry blossoms] on the surface of a river" (*kawa no ue no hana*) with:

> Natorigawa haru no hikazu wa arawarete
>   hana ni zo shizumu seze no mumoregi[87]
> In Natorigawa the number of spring's days is revealed:
>   the buried trees in its shoals are drowned in blossoms.

No judgments or commentaries on the poems for this contest survive, nor do we know what the Chinese poem or poems devised on the same topic may have been like, or how they may have interacted with the *waka* composed on the same occasion. But Teika has responded to the openness and flexibility of the topic (much as he did at the Minase contest) by introducing specificities: "a river" is "the river," the Natorigawa, and the moment is a particular one, when the clutter and mass of fallen blossoms drowning the buried trees inform the imagined, imaginary, or imagining viewer that "the number of this spring's days" that have come and gone (*haru no hikazu*) are many—that is, that few days of spring remain, for its natural signs have already reached this advanced stage. Like Saigyō, standing at the river's edge, or like the many other poets who conjured their Natorigawa scenes from afar, Teika could have omitted the buried trees from his vision, but their inclusion allowed him to make his poem into yet another dialectic meditation on time and timelessness: the swirling blossoms that drown the buried trees expend the passing color and scent of this special, passing moment, all of which will be borne away in the river's (or time's) current, while the trees remain fixed, unchanging, certain to reappear again (figure 5).

In these contests, and in other similarly structured collective compositional settings, place-name poesy was just part of a battery of tools that participants could bring to bear on the diverse topical challenges presented to them; but, in some other structured settings, place-names were themselves the central matter, and the challenge presented to the participants became that of manipulating the selected place-name topics and their attendant figures into diverse new arrangements. A *meisho utaawase* organized in 1041 in the name of Emperor Gosuzaku's four-year-old daughter, Yūshi Naishinnō, is the earliest known such exercise; among the fragmentary records of its products is a Natorigawa poem by an anonymous competitor:

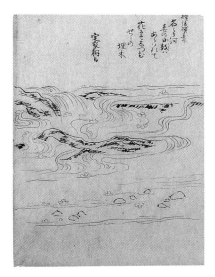

5. *Scene from* Ōshū meisho zue: *Fujiwara Teika composes a poem about Natorigawa,* Shūi gusō #2073/ Shoku gosen wakashū #135 *("Natorigawa/haru no hikazu wa/arawarete/hana ni zo shizumu/seze no mumoregi"). To create a companion piece to the Shigeyuki scene (figure 4), the artist shows Teika and his companions gazing across the river, but, unlike Shigeyuki, Teika never traveled to the Northeast. Courtesy Miyagi-ken Toshokan.*

> Natorigawa soko sae zo teru natsu no yo wa
>   hotaru himanaku miewataritsutsu[88]
> On a night when moonlight shines to the very depths of Natorigawa
>   fireflies flash everywhere I look.

The intrusion of fireflies may be a response to the assignment of the site-name to a group of summer poems. As is so often the case with competition poems, the evocative scene—swarms of fireflies filling the air and, as it seems, the waters as well—could be sited anywhere, for nothing particularizes the venue as Natorigawa per se, other than that name. This may have been the competitor's intent: to produce a "new" effect by forsaking conventional Natorigawa imagery and introducing in its place a new scenic element—the fireflies, figures from the standard summer repertory. But, if so, he or she seems to have had no subsequent imitators.[89]

Still, as this one example may suggest, *utaawase* sessions and *hyakushu* projects were not simply workshops for the production of poems for future anthologies; they were also (sometimes) laboratories in which poets might experiment with conventions and test expectations, even though innovation

might invite criticism and defeat as easily as praise and the prize of heightened prestige. Or, viewed in another way, a topically structured *utaawase* or
hyakushu might function as a test of the participant poets' ingenuities, and
of a kind of courage as well; it might measure their command of precedent,
as well as the degree to which they were able and willing to work within it
or to test or even defy its authority over them.

In the *Kenpō meisho hyakushu*, the hundred-poem famous-places sequences composed by twelve court poets in 1215—among them the reigning
Emperor Juntoku, the project's patron—such dynamic play or tension in and
with tradition, leading simultaneously to its preservation and its alteration or
redirection, is readily apparent. Natorigawa was the last of the twenty *meisho*
selected for treatment in the "love" portion of the sequence, a topical assignment that duly reflects the project planners' (probably Juntoku and
Teika's) cognizance of the site-name's long *koi no uta* pedigree. Dealing with
it, however, was only one step in each participant's execution of the sequential composition: it was the last of twenty place-names that had to be worked
into twenty different (but stylistically consistent) love poems, which, in turn,
comprised just one fifth of the entire set, all of which demanded similar
ingenuity and flexibility, in poem after poem. Conscious of the Emperor's
desire that the completed sequences should collectively advertise the literary
accomplishment, erudition, and adaptability of his coterie and of the era of
his reign, each invited participant must have felt extraordinary pressure to
perform at least creditably, if not brilliantly—and many must have felt pressure to perform rapidly, as well: Teika's diary, for example, suggests that he
completed the composition of all of his one hundred verses in about six
weeks.[90]

All these pressures, and more, must be kept in mind as one reads and
examines the results, and one can do so in several ways: in the collected
works of several participants—Juntoku, Teika, Ietaka, and Shunzei's Daughter, for example—one may read each individual's hundred-poem sequence
as a whole, and consider it in the context of each individual's entire oeuvre
(and each individual's style, if such there be); but, in records of the composite
hyakushu, all twelve poets' assays at each *meisho* topic can be seen side by
side, in sequence, and this approach reveals patterns and divergences within
the group's collective approach to the project, showing the extent of their
adherences and their departures from prior praxis.[91]

Within the group of twelve Natorigawa poems alone, the contours of just
such a multi-dimensional compositional landscape come into view. For example: six of the twelve *Kenpō* poets place the place-name Natorigawa at
the beginning of their poem—as its first word, and first five syllables—in the

manner of the *Kokin wakashū* template (#650), and, in effect, as an obvious if partial echo of it. Three poets reproduce the *seze no* litany in some form, and two feature *yanase* (as in Shigeyuki's *Shin kokin wakashū* #553). The word *mumoregi* is included by six, as is some form of the verb *arawar[u]*, and a form of *kuts[u]* appears in three—but in one case, in Teika's poem, it appears, for the first time in Natorigawa poesy, as a transitive verb, *kutas[u]*:

> Natorigawa kokoro ni kutasu mumoregi no
>   kotowari shiranu sode no shigarami[92]
> My sleeve is an overflowing weir that refuses to heed the lesson
>   of the buried tree made to rot to the very core in Natorigawa.

One recognizes the packed and convoluted syntax of this poem as characteristic of the mature Teika (he was fifty-four in 1215), and one also recognizes his masterful blending of familiar figures, from various sources, in a poem that is nevertheless entirely "new"—almost disorientingly so. Teika builds upon the base of known and given Natorigawa poesy, yet adds to and transforms it, not only with a verb (*kutasu*) that advertises its relation to convention while at the same time departing from it, but also with the introduction of a figure, the weir (*shigarami*). As a scenic device, this weir would be contextually harmonious and appropriate in any depiction of a river; yet Teika does not use it as an aspect of the Natorigawa scene but rather (more complicatedly) as a metaphor (as in many another love poem) for the function of the tearful poem-speaker's sleeve (*sode*). And, though imagistically and thematically legitimate in a Natorigawa/love poem, both *sode* and *shigarami* are "new" to the Natori poetic landscape, and their presence, along with the introduction of the verb *kutasu*, goes a long way toward reconfiguring that landscape, making it at once familiar and strange.

The structural ambiguity and shifting syntactic contingencies in this poem increase its disorienting effect to yet another degree: the poem opens with the solid, substantive place-name, but Natorigawa immediately loses its stability as a site and becomes, rather, the talismanic means of invoking (through automatic recall of all that has gone before in poesy) the thematic context of illicit love and its effect upon reputation. *Kokoro* (heart, core of being) may be the river's core, the locus of feeling in an anthropomorphized place where affairs of the heart are known (through poetic legacy) to happen, but it is also the poem-speaker's heart, wherein the lesson (*kotowari*) of the buried tree has been made known by memory. Yet the poem-speaker's sleeve (*sode*) "doesn't know" or refuses to understand the lesson thus to be learned: it is a *kotowari shiranu sode,* a sleeve that is unaware of the principle for which the buried tree stands. Then, just when this sleeve seems to be stabilized as a subject, Teika predicates it with the destabilizing attribution of a metaphorical status: it is a weir (*shigarami*) which, implicitly, must strive to stop a flood of tears (which flow because the sleeve "does not recognize the principle" known so well within the lover's heart). In this way, Teika insures that his reader or hearer will feel as if at home in familiar poetic territory—every word and image is fitting in a treatment of the specific Natorigawa topos or in the more general topic of "love" evoked for the specific topos by its placement in the sequence—yet it is also as if everything seen and heard in this revisited territory has been re-arranged, that the relationships among familiar elements have been altered, and may never seem the same again.

Three other *Kenpō* poets—Juntoku, the prelate Gyōi (1177-1217), and Shunzei's Daughter—give prominence to the image of the sleeve (*sode*) in their Natorigawa poems, too—as if in joint conspiracy, to add this figure to the river's evolving poetic scheme. In an exercise bound by convention to treat the theme of love's frustrations, the figure of the sleeve is an almost inevitable presence, taking the role of that part of each poem-speaker's clothing that must try to absorb his or her flowing tears; yet, as noted above, this figure seems to have had little or no prominence in Natorigawa poesy prior to the *Kenpō* project.[93] On the other hand, however, its presence in the Natorigawa group of Kenpō poems is presaged in many of the poems on the preceding nineteen *koi* (love)-plus-place-name topics, and its reappearance in the Natorigawa group serves to link the poems in that group to several of those that come before it—an effect that would be apparent in a sequential reading of the *hyakushu* of some of the individual contributors but even more obvious in a reading of the composite *hyakushu* of all twelve poets. Thus, following what happens to this sleeve as the sequence evolves becomes, in itself, an object of readerly interest—particularly where it is used to upset readerly expectations. In Juntoku's Natorigawa poem, it is this sleeve—one that cannot stop the torrent (of tears)—that is the subject of the verb *arawar[u]*, rather than (as might be expected) an *umoregi* or a secretive love:

> orokanaru namida zo ada ni Natorigawa
>   sekiaenu sode wa arawarenu to mo[94]
> Those tears, shed in vain over the gossip about our love, can scarcely be
>   sincere,
>   even if your sleeve which cannot hold them back is seen by all the world.

Here, Juntoku forges a new alloy using elements from a love poem by Ono no Komachi:

orokanaru namida zo sode ni tama wa nasu
  ware wa sekiaezu tagitsuse nareba
Those tears which, you say, turn into jewels upon your sleeve, can scarcely be
    sincere;
  mine are a torrent whose flow cannot be stemmed.

Komachi's poem appears in the *Kokin wakashū* as a response to a letter-poem from a male admirer, but Komachi characteristically transforms the poetic matériel thus offered her and reassembles it in such a way as to reject the gentleman's show of interest.[95] This posture, in turn, gives Juntoku's poem its reproachful perspective and tone, which in themselves depart from the self-pitying and excuse-making of the classic Natorigawa poems. In other words, his poem's intertextual nexus is not controlled or dominated by extant Natorigawa poesy alone, but rather resists it, or dilutes and thus complicates it, by giving prominence, in this *new* variation on precedent, to the imagery and diction of another specific and very different but equally canonical *old* love poem; thus, through hybridization, Juntoku opens new possibilities, and, at least potentially, initiates a new genus within the family of Natorigawa poems.

Other *Kenpō* poets achieve the effect of "newness" within a lexical and stylistic framework redolent of the "old" without going to Juntoku's cross-breeding lengths. Ietaka, for example, confines himself largely to old Natorigawa matériel but nonetheless radically alters the perspective in his contribution:

Natorigawa kokoro no towaba
  mumoregi no shita yuku nami no ikaga kotaen[96]
Natorigawa: if the heart interrogates,
  how will the waves that billow beneath its buried trees respond?

Here, again, is the language of the earliest (known) *umoregi* poesy (*umoregi no shita* yu so kōru *yuku*e shirazute), remodeled and made very much at home in the Natorigawa setting. But now Ietaka proposes to penetrate these turbulent waters in search of some new clarity. He anthropomorphizes "the waves that billow beneath its buried trees") so that inquiry can be made of them, and that implicit inquiry ("what are their true feelings?") is posed by a *kokoro*—another locus of feeling, one that "remembers" having forsaken love to protect reputation but which now delves below the surface in search of the abiding, unaltered passion so long hidden in the depths beneath the tree. Again, as in Juntoku's and Teika's poems, all the elements in this scenario are exceedingly familiar, but a fresh perspective has rearranged them. Ietaka seems to say, "Let's go back to the beginning [of a story begun, as it were, with the first Natorigawa poem] and rediscover the truth, and perhaps even change the course of history." Yet he does not prejudge the results; rather, he asks the reader-hearer to join with him in speculating as to what the personified waves' response will be.

Similar tactics, for grounding these "new" Natorigawa poems in old territory, then seeing it with new eyes, or from new attitudes, are adopted by three other contributors—Hyōe no naishi (one of the two female *Kenpō* contributors, along with Shunzei's Daughter), Fujiwara Norimune (1171-1233), and Fujiwara Yasumitsu (dates unknown):

(Hyōe no naishi)
mumoregi no na zo arawaruru Natorigawa
   awanu tameshi wa sate mo kuchinan
Natorigawa, where the buried tree's fame is exposed to view:
   if only this example of "not meeting" might perish once and for all!

(Norimune)
Natorigawa soko no mumoregi arawaru na
   momiji wa ue no iro ni izu to mo
O buried trees on the bottom of Natorigawa, do not show yourselves!
   —even if the color of your autumn foliage comes to the surface.

(Yasumitsu)
Natorigawa shizumu mokuzu ni
   na o kaete omoikeri to wa hito ni shirasen[97]
I want to let the one I love know that I have decided to change my name
   to "flotsam that sinks to the bottom of Natorigawa."

Hyōe no naishi's innovation is to force "the example of 'not meeting'" for which Natorigawa stands to serve as the subject of the verb *kuts[u];* then, it is her poem-speaker's wish that the river, its story, and its name might cease to function as such—that, by erasing this exemplar of failed love, happier outcomes may be insured. Or, one might say, Hyōe no naishi imposes the conventional subtopic *awanu koi* (a love affair characterized by the lovers' failure to meet) on her treatment of the Natorigawa topos, and then suggests, as it were, an end to that topos' susceptibility for treatment in that vein: the result would be the loss of one means for writing about such sad affairs, and, perhaps, fewer such disappointments. Like Saigyō, who saw them, Norimune introduces colored autumn leaves (*momiji*) into the Natori landscape —here, through imagination—but primarily to prepare and augment the function of the word *iro* in his poem: here, as elsewhere, it stands not only for the color and aura of that foliage but also for sexual passion. And, his poem-speaker says, this *iro* may force its way to the surface and be seen—

but, even if it does, the river's buried trees are adjured to remain out of view, with their secret, conflicted memories concealed. Thus, the conventional scenario is to be reversed: the buried trees (repositories of inert and ancient love) may not be seen, but the present passion will be. Finally, Yasumitsu's alterations and augmentations are just as striking, in their own way. In place of the buried tree it is flotsam that sinks to the bottom of Natorigawa, and his poem-speaker boldly declares that he will "let his name be 'trash'" and that he wants his loved one to know of his determination: "No matter what they say of me, I will pursue this love. To hell with my name!"

Driven to be inventive within the parameters of their undertaking, simultaneously inspired to experiment yet constrained by convention, these and the other *Kenpō* poets contrive new contortions (perhaps, distortions) of the Natorigawa poetic legacy. Then, once recorded, their accomplishments thereafter joined with those of all their predecessors to form the points of reference for still later exercises, as Natorigawa surfaced again and again, in later times and in a variety of compositional settings. In this way, the course of poetic history and practice moved forward in time, retaining while changing its former contours through internal reference to its own previous path. For example: the *Shoku gosen wakashū*, a *chokusenshū* compiled in the middle of the thirteenth century, puts two Natorigawa poems by two contemporary poets side by side among a group of verses in which this and other famous place-names (*meisho*) are deployed in "expressing one's feelings [of dissatisfaction]" (*jukkai*) poems; these two are by Fujiwara Akiuji (1207-1274) and Fujiwara Korenaga, respectively:

> toshi furedo kawari mo yaranu Natorigawa
>   ukimi zo ima wa seze no mumoregi
> Natorigawa changes not at all though years go by,
>   and now this sorry self of mine is yet another of the buried trees among
>   its shoals.

> ukimi yo ni shizumihatetaru Natorigawa
>   mata mumoregi no kazu ya souran.[98]
> This sorry self of mine has sunk as far as it can go in this world, at Natorigawa,
>   and now adds itself to the number of its buried trees.

Akiuji explicitly invokes the language of Akinaka's *tsukasameshi* poem (*Kin'yō wakashū* #525); Korenaga invokes its spirit and that of others of its kind. In a sense, all that has really changed is that the generalized, geographically unfixed *umoregi* of those earlier poems of complaint is now sited at Natorigawa—a location in which, one might say, it was bound to come to rest—but, as Akiuji observes, all else is (seemingly) the same in the terrains of aristocratic professional life and traditional poem-making.

A somewhat different view is taken by the *Shoku gosen wakashū* compiler, Fujiwara Teika's son Tameie (1198–1275), in poems from a *hyakushu* sequence included in his *Chūinshū* (the private collection in which are gathered the works of his later years):

> seki no meisho
> hito zo uki yamato kotoba no michi taete
>   kayowazu nari shi ashigara no seki
>   on "a famous barrier":
> People are faithless: the Way of Japanese speech has disappeared,
>   and no one traverses Ashigara Barrier these days.

> kawa no meisho
> mukashi yori tsutauru michi no Natorigawa
>   nado ka nageki mo mumorehatsuran[99]
>   on "a famous river":
> At Natorigawa, which belongs to that Way passed down to us from
>   ancient times,
>   why should the timbers that feed the flames of love be so completely buried
>   as well?

Both poems are petulant, almost self-righteous (and, in a way, self-serving) complaints about a perceived decline in the quality of Japanese verse and in the status of the genre. (Tsurayuki, in a very different time, felt the need to elevate *waka,* too—and turned to *waka's* own rhetoric in his effort to do so.) In making these complaints, Tameie makes a point of reviving ancient usages: he says that Ashigara Barrier—one of many such checkpoints much featured in *meisho* poems (though not one of the most famous among them) —is now deserted, for no one now follows the Japanese "Way" (that is, *waka [no michi])* to reach it.[100] Likewise, Natorigawa is part of and also representative of the whole of the inherited tradition, yet it too lies in neglect, while such words as *nageki*—used since *Kokin* times (at least) to mean both "sighs [of love]" and "timber that is thrown [*nage-ki*] onto a fire" (thus causing the flames of passion to leap still higher)—also languish, buried in obscurity and disuse.[101] What Tameie may bemoan here is the deleterious effect (as he sees it) caused by interference in the Way of *waka* (embodied in the *chokusenshū*) by Kamakura-backed poets—that is, relative outsiders—who were usurping what had become his family's almost exclusive control over the canon. (Tameie had had the privilege of compiling the *Shoku gosen wakashū* by himself, in 1248, but in 1259 he was forced to accept the participation of several rivals in putting together the *Shoku kokin wakashū*.)[102] But in these poems, Tameie focuses his fears about the future of *waka no michi* on the very words of the Way, for that which is under threat of being buried, in his view, is the very understanding of the use of language on which the whole tradition (of which he deems himself guardian) is built. It is imperative, therefore, that he resuscitate and protect it, by using it, since no one else can or will do so (in the right way): he must therefore enact these returns to deserted terrains and, by invoking these names, give new life and meaning to the whole of poetry.

But, of course, *waka*'s Way was not yet lost: what was changing, however, was the status and orientation of those who followed it. While Tameie and his descendants strove for preservation and control—sometimes through innovation, sometimes through reactionary resistance to change—the language of *waka* was being acquired and manipulated by an increasingly diverse array of men and women, and not only by those of the highest aristocratic lineage. The canon would accept, for example, the works of such poets as Matsuda Sadahide (active in the mid-fourteenth century), a professional administrator and magistrate (*bugyōnin*) for the Ashikaga shogunate. That acceptance, and the resulting preservation of his oeuvre, allow us to learn that Sadahide was apparently the first to interpolate Natorigawa and its *umoregi* into what is ostensibly a devotional poem, or at least one made to look like one:

> Fumon bon: moshi daisui no tame ni tadayowasaren ni, sono myōgō o tonaeba, sunawachi asaki tokoro o en.
>
>> Natorigawa fukaki ni shizumu mumoregi no
>> asaki se yori ya arawarenikemu[103]
>
> The "Gateway to Everywhere" Chapter: "If he should be carried off by a great river and call upon this bodhisattva's name, then straightaway he would find a shallow place."[104]
>
>> The buried tree that was sunk so deep in Natorigawa
>> has now, it seems, come into view from shallow shoals.

Repeating an exercise performed by many poets in the generations before him, Sadahide addresses a passage from a revered Buddhist scripture—here, the *Lotus Sūtra*—as his topic (in this case, a quotation-topic [*kudai*]) and transforms its (originally) Chinese prose and its imagery into an emphatically Japanese verse. The result is a poem so deeply ensconced within the language of traditional *waka* that, were it not paired with the scriptural topic-text with which it is meant to be read, as a single, hybrid textual unit, it might not appear to bear any relationship to Buddhist scripture or ideas.[105] But the deep waters in which the subject of the *Lotus Sūtra* passage founders (he is a hypothetical seeker of rescue from various dire perils) become, in Sadahide's rendering, the waters of a specific "great river," the Natorigawa; and whereas rescue is achieved in the scriptural source when the imperiled one "calls upon the name" of the bodhisattva (Avalokiteśvara, Kannon) and then finds safety in a "shallow place," the protagonist in the poem becomes the buried tree which now surfaces in placid shoals. It is as if the imaginary terrain of the sūtra text, with its depths and shallows and its promise of help through the reverent use of the bodhisattva's *name,* have spontaneously reconfigured (in Sadahide's poetic imagination, aided by literary memory) as a Natori terrain, one where such "depths," "shallows," and "names" have had other meanings but which now undergo alchemical change under the conditions of the poet's own design: the secular (if not profane) language of ancient love poetry is thus made sacred, or quasi-sacred, and Sadahide does homage to both these textual and canonical realms by conjoining them in a single verse.

In several poems in *Sōkonshū,* one of the "private anthologies" of the works of Shōtetsu (1381–1459), homage is paid to the tradition in yet another way, through a different interaction with the conventions of topical composition.[106] In several sequences of poems in the collection, Shōtetsu addresses a variety of topics typologized as "three-character *dai*" (*san moji dai*), "four-character *dai*" (*shi moji dai*), and so on.[107] This exercise is perhaps less mechanical than it first appears, for it is an exercise recollective not only of various *utaawase* enterprises but also of the *Man'yōshū*'s figure-based system of classification: that is, certain *Man'yōshū* classifications and subclassifications are here treated as *dai,* as subjects unto themselves, and their original function, as description, has been turned into prescription, in order to provide a structure within which Shōtetsu can challenge himself and at the same time re-enact and transform the compositional postures of old. And what are the results? In one group of three-character *dai* poems, Shōtetsu disposes of the topic "a love that makes its appearance in the autumn" (*aki ni arawaruru koi*) much as one might expect:

> Natorigawa hito no chigiri no asagiri wa
>   taete ato naki seze no mumoregi[108]
> At Natorigawa, the fog of my beloved's shallow pledges
>   disperses, and leaves no trace other than the buried trees still in the shoals.

And similarly, when Shōtetsu confronts the *Man'yō*-esque *dai* "on love, through reference to a tree" (*ki ni yosuru koi*) he produces (among several examples),

> nagarete no Natorigawa naru mumoregi wa
>   ukiidete koso shigarami mo are[109]

Even if the buried trees lodged in Natorigawa's flow
   should float to the surface, there will surely be a weir to stop them.

The four-character *dai* "on love, through reference to a buried tree"
(*mumoregi ni yosuru koi*, a descendant of the classifying label under which
Man'yōshū #1385, the "Yuge River" poem, was found) yields:

Natorigawa minawa nagaruru adanami ni
   ukabi idetaru seze no mumoregi[110]
Amidst the fickle waves that carry off the foam in Natorigawa
   the trees that were buried in the shoals have floated to the surface.

All of these appear to be exercises in which Shōtetsu is self-consciously
honing his intertextual skills, imposing upon himself a challenge much like
those imposed upon his literary forebears in various *utaawase, hyakushu,*
and other competitive, structured settings. But in each of these poems, he
self-consciously does "new" things with the "old," in a manner not unlike
that of his favored and revered model, Teika. The morning fog (*asagiri*) in
#7427 is a new feature for an imagined Natorigawa-scape, but the word
incorporates a double reading, as *asa-* (shallow), descriptive of the poem-
speaker's beloved's pledges (*chigiri*). The *shigarami* (weir) in #7815 is a
legacy from Teika's *Kenpō meisho hyakushu* Natorigawa verse, but it has
been freed from its metaphorical linkage to Teika's "sleeve" and has been
returned to the river, where it is expected to halt the drifting buried tree
when the forces of passion release it to the river's flow.[111] And, likewise,
minawa (foam), in #8427, is new to Natorigawa poesy per se but very much
in place in any literal or figural aquatic scene: it also offers a hint of a pun,
since *mina wa nagaruru* may also mean "its [the river's] name is the subject
of gossip." In such quasi-archaic exercises, the *seze no mumoregi* litany
resounds, an echo from another place and time (or, places and times)
brought forward to the present (Shōtetsu uses it in many other poems, too,
including *Sōkonshū* #7821, another in the *ki ni yosuru koi* set): through it,
and through the other elements of traditional poesy of which he makes use
here, Shōtetsu moves through time, condensing the past into the present,
and creates texts that are as patently old as they are insistently new.

Yet another recollective dimension is added to similar compositional exercises recorded among the collected works of Sanjōnishi Sanetaka (1455-
1537): on several occasions, Sanetaka undertook to write *hyakushu*
sequences governed by *dai* used by Fujiwara Teika in *hyakushu* projects of
his own day. In one such "summer solo *hyakushu*" (*Hyakushu waka, natsu
dokugin*) composed during the Meiō era (1492-1501) on "four-character *dai*

used by Lord Teika," Sanetaka treats the topic "a spring moon above a river" (*kawa no ue no haru no tsuki*, or *kajō shungetsu*) with:

> kokoro to wa kumoranu tsuki no Natorigawa
> nakina torite mo kasumu koro ka na[112]
>
> As for my heart, it is Natorigawa on the night of a cloudness moon,
>   at that season where mists will gather if I earn a name for something that I
>   have not done.

Teika composed on this same topic in the *Fujikawa hyakushu waka*, a famous "solo" undertaking of his mature years (ca. 1224, when he was sixty-four, according to Kubota Jun),[113] and the poem he produced at that time depicts the same spring mists and shifting clouds that also spread across the moonlit night sky in Sanetaka's.[114] This *Fujikawa hyakushu* was much revered in later times, and was a central canonical text for Teika's descendants in the Nijō school of poets, who often used it as a training text for aspiring practitioners of *waka* art.[115] Sanetaka, who was the foremost literary scholar of his day—a master of *renga* as well as *waka*, and an authority on other literary genres, too—was far beyond the training stage when he returned, on this occasion, to the *Fujikawa hyakushu*, but he must have been intimate with such texts throughout his life, and must have been happy to return to them frequently; and, for him, reiterating and reproducing the *Fujikawa hyakushu* structure in his own work was yet another way of preserving and possessing the past and making it his own.

Other exemplary compositions of Teika's received similar treatment in Sanetaka's hands: on a winter day in 1496 (Meiō 5), for example, he took up the model of Teika's poems for a *hyakushu* presented at the residence of the Minister of the Center Kujō Michiie on an autumn night in the year 1215 (*Naidaijinke hyakushu*). On the topic "Amida" (the Buddha who promises to create a paradise, or "Pure Land" for all those who place their faith in him), in the group of five Buddhist poem (*Shakkyōka*) topics at the end of the model text, Sanetaka wrote:

> fukakarishi chikai no mama no Natorigawa
> hikarete ukabu seze no mumoregi[116]
>
> As promised in that deep vow, the buried trees that have dwelt so long in
>   Natorigawa
> have been pulled up to float upon the surface.

Like his predecessor Sadahide, Sanetaka reconfigures the conventional Natorigawa imagery to suit the contours of quasi-devotional poetic discourse; the poem is itself the record of that reconfiguring, just as it is the record of the reliving of a moment in the revered Teika's artistic life. But Sanetaka manages to do homage to Amida even as he makes obeisance to Teika as well. His poem owes nothing in particular to Teika's *Naidaijinke hyakushu* poem on the same *dai*,[117] except perhaps the attitude of reverence which all such *Shakkyōka* share: it is, rather, Sanetaka's own idea to cast the Natorigawa's "buried trees" as metaphors for the vast numbers of sentient beings whom Amida promises to save through his deep vow (*fukakari shi chikai*). The word *chikai* (vow), very much at home in love poetry, here bears nuance from Natorigawa's conventional realm, but that nuance is all but quashed in this devotional setting; like all else in Natorigawa poesy, it lingers beneath the surface of Sanetaka's poem, complicating its meaning and effect. And Sanetaka (or the transcriber of the poem) complicates the interplay in one more way as well: the *seze no mumoregi* litany is here not written with the character for "shoal" repeated twice, as is usually the case, but rather with the doubled inscription of another *se*, a character that means "age" or "lifetime"; thus, Sanetaka's *mumoregi* are buried trees that have lain beneath the Natorigawa's waters "for many an age" (*seze*).[118] Like suffering sentient beings who have not yet reached Amida's Pure Land, they have been caught in time and circumstance: at death, they did not cease to be, nor did they leave the earth, but were held in an intermediate state of life-that-is-not-life, as fossilized trees. But now everything will change, as Amida "pulls them" up from the depths to the surface, into the light.

Of course, experiments like Sadahide's and Sanetaka's could not incontrovertibly change Natorigawa poesy—nor were they meant to. Rather, such diversions from the mainstream of praxis probably served, as much as did more conventional usages, to perpetuate the status quo; and though it might occasionally be redirected, the flow of Natorigawa poesy would continue virtually unabated toward the subject of love. Thus, among the love poems (*koi no uta*) in the collected works of Nakanoin Michikatsu (1556–1610)—a poet prominent in that group of men who would strive to see that *waka* might survive beyond the dawn of the transformational Tokugawa age—one is not surprised to see a self-conscious return to the point of origin:

> mumoregi ni yosuru koi:
>> ause araba itowade yoshiya Natorigawa
>>> mi o mumoregi to kuchinan wa ushi[119]
> on "love through reference to 'a buried tree'":
>> If there is a chance for us to meet, I shall not shun it,
>>> but shall say "Very well, Natorigawa!";
>>> it would be too sad to be a buried tree, to let my whole self rot away.

Once more, like Shōtetsu before him, Michikatsu takes the *Man'yōshū*'s classifying label as his *dai*, his compositional challenge. He meets it with a poem that turns back to the beginning of the Natorigawa story, and gives it a new ending: faced with a choice, his poem-speaker opts for love. He says that "if there is a chance to meet" [with his beloved] (*ause*—that is, if they can find a "shoal" or "shallow place" amidst the teeming waters of life across which they struggle toward one another), he will take it. The fate of the buried tree will not be his, for he will not let fear of exposure control him; rather, he will face whatever this bold acceptance of love may bring upon him (and his name). His exuberant *yoshiya Natorigawa* voices his exhilaration: this time, he will let no fear or compunction stand in love's way.

Thus, across the centuries and amidst the vicissitudes of time and historical change, Natorigawa and its own buried trees were also truly always there: at compositional moment after moment, in the Natori environs and, more frequently, elsewhere as well, the figure of the buried tree and the name of this most famous of its burial sites proved easily and effectively portable, or importable, from the past to the present; the love story (or stories) in which they originally figured proved flexible as well. And, as the passage of time increased the distance from the moments of their classical usage (in the *Kokinshū*, and earlier), their accrued weight, or value, increased in proportion to that increasing antiquity. We might also call that accrued weight or value power—a recognized and much used power of durability and malleability, a power to remain present even when overlooked, a power to signify in ways that could be made known to all who might hear or see these artifacts in old or new settings. This story of the accrual of that value or power—that is, the etiology of these figures (as Thomas M. Greene defines it)—obviously has no end points: it is, rather, a continuum, and documentation of its contours must always be incomplete and selective, a mere sampling of those moments that most readily come to the observer's eye and install themselves in the tale-teller's memory, there to launch, in turn, the repercussions and resonances that seem to link one moment in time to another, or to all others. And sometimes, it seems, this time-spanning etiology appears to collapse into a single moment—a moment in which one jarring of the memory by new experience reshapes that experience to fit the contours of the past and thus to prepare it for and propel it toward the future. Such, it would seem, is what apparently occurred when the Buddhist prelate Dōkō (1430-1501)—abbot of the Shōgoin monastery in Kyoto, participant in palace poetry parties as well as in *utaawase* sponsored by the shogun (Ashikaga Yoshihisa)—found himself standing beside the Natorigawa in the spring of 1487, after a journey northward from the capital that had already taken him some nine months, as he tells us in his poem-filled journal entitled *Kaikoku zakki* (Jottings from my travels 'round Japan) and which had included a stop to worship Sanekata's remains as well as visits to many other famous Michinoku sites. We can almost see him at this point just where the journal breaks off: gazing at and across the river, and back at the path along which he has come, and back through time, and then looking below the surface, and sifting through his memories—and then composing these two poems:

> hito shirenu umoregi naraba
>> Natorigawa nagarete no yo ni nado kikoyuran
> itsu no yo ni arawaresomete
>> Natorigawa migakurehatenu seze no umoregi[120]
> If these "buried trees" are secret, unknown things,
>> why does one hear so much about Natorigawa even now, after all these years?
> When was it—in what year, what time—that they first appeared,
>> these buried trees in Natorigawa shoals which have not yet disappeared from view?

Once more, like so many others who had seen the view from that shore, or imagined it, Dōkō celebrates its timelessness by refashioning the same words that have so often before been written onto the scene: once more, Natorigawa's buried trees appear—having never disappeared—and once more their name, and fame, echo through the ages. Dōkō's time—the late fifteenth century—was emphatically the age of *renga*;[121] but, for certain poets like him, in such places and on such occasions as this, *waka*'s idiom was as alive as ever, and the power of that idiom was as assertive as it had always been—demanding to be seen and heard, asking, or insisting, to be handled lovingly at least once more and to have its story told once again.

3

Fetishes and Curios

On the shores of another storied stream, almost three hundred years prior to Dōkō's northward journey, another recollective moment bequeathed a special treasure to the *waka* tradition and to its patrons and participants. It was a moment as deeply enriched by intertextual memory as Dōkō's moment beside the Natorigawa, similarly summoned and orchestrated by echoes of innumerable poems from the past; and, in turn, it was a moment which would, in the future, be marked and remembered for its own significance in *waka* history, and it would be recollected and reenacted in both actions and words, through the making of new, time-layered poems.

In the early thirteenth century, when these particular events occurred — that is, in the era of the compilation of the *Shin kokin wakashū* — the *waka* idiom was very much alive, but its vitality was as much a product of recollection of the textual and other kinds of artifacts of the past as of the creative (or recreative) energies of the present. It was the Emperor Gotoba (1180- 1239), both during his reign (1193-98) and even more so after it — especially in the first decade of the thirteenth century — who drove and directed much of this recollective and reconstructive surge of text production. Most of this production took place within the precincts of the capital, in the royal palaces and in the mansions of the elite; but some of it took place when Gotoba and his elite attendants took themselves on the road, beyond the confines of court and city. The particularly rich intertextual moment whose story will be told here—a moment of recollection in several overlapping dimensions—occurred early in this active and productive decade, on one of the several occasions when, on his way back from one of his many pilgrimages to the holy shrines of Kumano, on the southeastern tip of the Kii peninsula, Gotoba paused with his retinue at a place called Nagara before boarding boats that would take them to the mouth of the Yodogawa estuary and along the coast to Sumiyoshi, where the Emperor and his party would give thanks for the successful completion of their pilgrimage.

This itinerary closely followed the precedent set by Gotoba's forebears, many of whom, like Gotoba, made the same trip repeatedly: Emperor Shirakawa (1053–1129; r. 1072–86) made fourteen Kumano pilgrimages; Emperor Toba (1103–56; r. 1107–23) made twenty-two, and his consort Taikenmon'in (1101–45) made thirteen; and Gotoba's grandfather Goshirakawa (1127–92; r. 1155–58) outdid them all, with twenty-nine pilgrimages.[1] For all, the pilgrimage was an arduous undertaking. It would begin with a four-day period of special abstinences and purifications. Then boats would carry the royal party from the capital down the Yodogawa to its mouth at Tenma in Naniwa; obligatory obeisances would be made at the nearby Tennōji temple and at the Sumiyoshi shrines; and the party would proceed along the sea road skirting the coast of Izumi Province and on into the mountains of the province of Ki, stopping periodically at one or another of the many subsidiary Kumano shrines along the way until at last reaching the main shrines (at Hongū, Shingū, and Nachi) on the far south coast of the Kii Peninsula. The return journey was usually made more quickly, with fewer stops along the way, but there was always an obligatory stop back at Sumiyoshi before the return to the capital.

Our knowledge of what took place at Nagara on this occasion—during this particular repetition of the devotional circuit, which probably took place in the third or seventh month of 1203, although the exact date is not known —comes to us from the diary of Minamoto Ienaga (d. 1234), one of the trusted courtiers who often accompanied Gotoba on such journeys.[2] "The day was drawing to a close," Ienaga reports,

> but we were to travel up to Sumiyoshi by boat that evening, and so we were all very busy and bustling about, absorbed with the outfitting of the royal bark; but my Lord was somehow so taken with the deeply affecting look of the place that

he simply sat gazing upon it in reverie. On the shoreline, as if stretching endlessly into the distance, a grove of young pines filled the scene with deep greenery; the wind blew, raising a fearful noise, and shower after shower swept past. Memories of the many past days of travel flooded our minds in this extraordinary place; the sounds of horses' hooves pounding across Watanobe Bridge rang through the air, and the shouts of travelers calling for ferries filled our ears.[3] But none of this disturbed my Lord's serene concentration. He wondered whether the ancient Nagara Bridge were not close by, and he thought that, since he had for so long known it by its name alone, he would now like to see such remains of it as there might be.[4]

Oblivious of the tempest and aloof from the bustle around him, the Emperor enters into a reverie about the place itself. In this pause between his public obeisances at Kumano and Sumiyoshi—two of his nation's (and his family's) most important pilgrimage sites—Gotoba's memories take him on another sort of pilgrimage: this one, experienced in the mind rather than in the body, is a journey into *waka*'s past, as embodied in this particular poetic site.

When Ienaga reports that Gotoba "had for so long known the ancient Nagara Bridge by its name alone" (*na bakari o kikiwataru ni*), he refers, of course, to a familiarity obtained through the medium of poetry. For, at least since the appearance of the *Kokin wakashū*, Nagara and its bridge had been frequently celebrated in song, and, as in the case of Natorigawa (and so many other famous places), that prominence had been in great part due to the plasticity of the place's name. The sound of *Nagara* is evocative of several words containing the element *naga* ("length"), especially two homophonous and etymologically related verbs, *nagarau* ("to flow continuously," usually said of streams of fluid) and *nagarau* ("to persevere or prevail through a long period," usually said of persons). In a verse included in the fifth book of love poems in the *Kokinshū*, Sakanoue Korenori exploits this plasticity and in so doing establishes a lasting association between the Nagara Bridge and enduring, if frustrated, passion:

> au koto o Nagara no hashi no nagaraete
> koiwataru ma ni toshi zo henikeru[5]

Helen McCullough's translation of this poem is:

> Never seeing you
> I live on like the ancient
> bridge of Nagara,
> and now long years have gone by,
> all spent in ceaseless yearning.[6]

This rendition, like most modern Japanese paraphrases as well, treats the *no* that associates *Nagara no hashi* with *nagaraete* as the marker of a simile. But it may be better to think of this particle as marking *Nagara no hashi* as a referent figure related both metaphorically and metonymically to the subject speaker, in an association that is more complicated than that suggested by the English *like*. The poem's main statement—*koiwataru ma ni*, "during the years that have passed while I have gone on longing for you"—is prepared for and enriched by the language that precedes it and which turns strategically at the sonically evoked *nagaraete* ("I, *persevering through time* despite my disappointment"). But even prior to that, the name of Nagara plays another punning role, in *auto koto o Na[gara]*, where both sound and syntax invite the hearer or reader to anticipate *au koto o na[mi]*, or a similar construction signifying the state of *"being without* opportunities to meet (*au*) with the one I love." This is, then, a fine example of a *Kokin* poem that plays meaningfully with the *sound* of a place name in the process of making a poetic statement that, in itself, has little to do with that place but that, subsequently, contributes to the redefinition of the poetic significance, or signifying potential, of that place-name. In other words, Nagara, Nagara Bridge, and their several other variants are prototypical *meisho utamakura*, in that their later usages are defined, or launched, by the patterns of their use in the *Kokin* era.

But Korenori's *Kokin wakashū* #826 is not the only template for Nagara poesy: the anonymous *Kokin wakashū* #890, included in the first "miscellaneous" book, is of equal if not greater genealogical importance. It offers an analogical juxtaposition of the aging of the Nagara Bridge, as it perseveres across the span of time, with the aging of a mortal poem-speaker, and this juxtaposition itself would become a feature of innumerable later poems that make figural use of the name of this bridge:

yo no naka ni furinuru mono wa
   Nagara no hashi to ware to narikeri[7]
Things that have grown old in this world, I find,
   are Nagara Bridge and I.

The idea that the bridge has grown old (*furu*) may be traced to its association, through the sound of its name, with "perseverance through time" (*nagarau*); but such aging also suggests decay, in the man-made bridge and in the mortal who compares him or herself to it. Here, again, factual data concerning the "real" bridge (like the "facts" about buried trees in the Yuge and Natori rivers) may have played a special role in the development of Nagara's particular poetic identity. While one official court history, the *Nihon kōki*, reports the dispatch of an Imperial courier to oversee construction of a bridge at Nagara in 813, another, the *Montoku jitsuroku*, reports that by

853 the bridge was in such terrible disrepair that it could not bear the traffic of men or horses.[8] There are many subsequent accounts of the bridge's gradual decay: according to *Eiga monogatari*, for example, a single pillar of the bridge (*hashibashira*) was all that was visible when a party accompanying Retired Emperor Gosanjō on his pilgrimage to Sumiyoshi halted at Nagara, in 1073.[9]

These and other chronicles of the bridge's repeated collapse and reconstruction may not have been their source of information, but poets from the ninth century onward seem to have been well aware, perhaps through hearsay, of the bridge's "story," or stories, of decay and renewal. Ise, for example, shows this in a poem that also seems to suggest her familiarity with *Kokin wakashū* #890—or with a poem or poems like it—and its equation of the aging bridge with an aging human subject:

Naniwa naru Nagara no hashi mo tsukuru nari
    ima wa waga mi o nani ni tatoen[10]

Ise says, "I hear that even Nagara bridge *has fallen apart*" and "*is to be rebuilt*" (*tsukuru* means both, if it is heard or if it is written phonetically). "To what," she then asks, "shall I now be able to compare myself [in my own state of age and decay]?" This poem may be read as a light comic commentary on poetic analogy itself: Ise may be as much concerned with this conventional posture—the hyperbolic comparison of dissimilar things, the (forced) discovery of a likeness where likeness might not otherwise be sought —as she is with her own "aging and decay," or the bridge's. What will she use for analogy now? she asks. If the bridge perishes, or is made anew, it will in either case cease to be useful to her—and to others—in the making of comparisons carried out under the topical category of "aging." Such a reading of Ise's poem, as a reflexive commentary on poem-making itself, may not be altogether anachronistic: the *Kokin wakashū* compilers classified this as an unorthodox or "joke" poem (*hikaika*) in book 19, which is devoted to "poems in miscellaneous styles" (*zattai*): they may indeed have seen it as a light variant of the topical category *jukkai* (poems that lament aging), which are usually serious, although they often engage in similar play.[11]

In his *kana* preface to the *Kokinshū*, introducing and justifying the text in which the template Nagara poems were first canonically enshrined, Tsurayuki also refers to them, as well as to some others of their kind, as emblematic of waka *poesy* itself. He does so at the conclusion of an encomium for the poets of the past (that is, those who practiced the art before it became "the province of the amorous, as unnoticed by others as a log buried in the earth") and their effective use of analogical reference (i.e., metaphor)—in particular, their reference to things in nature and to the names of places in the natural environment as a means for singing of or praising very different subjects. "Men found comfort," Tsurayuki claims,

> in composing poems in which they expressed wishes for a lord's long life or for patronage through comparisons with pebbles or allusions to Mount Tsukuba . . . or in which they compared romantic passion to Mount Fuji's smoke . . . or in which they thought of growing old in the company of the Takasago and Suminoe pines, or recalled past days when they were like Man Mountain [Otokoyama] . . . or linked their love to the waves at Matsuyama . . . or made reference to the Yoshino River to complain about the ephemerality of relations between the sexes.

The coda to this celebration of the past successes of poetic reference goes on to observe that "today"—in Tsurayuki's own time, that is—"when people hear that smoke no longer rises about Mount Fuji, or that the Nagara Bridge has fallen apart/been rebuilt [Nagara no hashi mo tsukuru nari], poetry is their sole consolation [uta ni nomi zo, kokoro o nagusamekeru]."[12] When all else has changed, Tsurayuki claims, poetry, both old and new—and, perhaps not just any poetry, but *Japanese* poetry per se—is the only available and effective medium for recuperation of what has been lost, not only because it is a repository of the experiences, sentiments, and utterances of the past, but perhaps also because the very mentality that produces analogical reference seems familiar, and offers itself as a position to which a return can be made. Later poets, including Tsurayuki himself, gaze back upon that position *and* reoccupy it, and thus can make themselves (or imagine that they can make themselves) into analogical recreations of their forebears, the poets of the past. In other words, poetic creation—the making of analogies, singing through metaphor—is here seen as an ever-present and eternally rich cultural field, specifically defined as a Japanese landscape through citation of the names of prominent sites in that geographic and literary terrain.

But, rich as it is, this field has sometimes lain fallow. In Tsurayuki's portrayal of *waka*'s history, the tradition of Japanese poetry itself has waxed and waned: having flourished in antiquity, it has more recently fallen into neglect, but even more recently—in his own hands and in those of his contemporaries—it has been rediscovered and "rebuilt," in a regenerative cycle like that which has become the poetic story of the Nagara Bridge itself. In Tsurayuki's figural rhetoric, then, Mount Fuji's dwindling smoke and the Nagara Bridge's state of disrepair are signs of an ancient vitality that is giving out, but the process of debilitation can be halted, or reversed, through poetry—that is, through the recollection of the poetry of the past alongside the creation of new poems for the present.

In the early thirteenth century, when Gotoba was engaged in his own project of celebratory recuperation of the *waka* tradition—the creation of a *new* "collection of ancient and modern verse"—and in that particular moment when he found himself at Nagara, all these texts, and more, and all the associations they carried with him, were present—virtually audible, or visible, in the ear and eye of memory—and they offered themselves, as they and their kind had offered themselves to Gotoba's forebears, as havens of comfort, mantras of consolation and regeneration—or, at the very least, as antidotes to the rigors and dislocations of travel. In this moment of repose and reverie at the Nagara landing, the "sound" of what Tsurayuki had written in reference to the bridge may well have been among the most resonant of the echoes that Gotoba "heard": so too, no doubt, were many of the other poems enshrined in other anthologies—poems composed at the site itself, as well as poems composed from other aestheticizing perspectives, as *byōbu uta* (poems on or suggested by landscape paintings on screens), for example, or as an entry in response to an assigned topic in an *utaawase*. Perhaps because it lay on such a well-traveled pilgrimage route, Nagara was more often the site of poems composed on the spot (*X nite yomeru*, the *kotobagaki* would say, with X standing for one or another *utamakura meisho* name) than were many other famous places; yet that very fact (along with the multivalent significance of the name and the place itself) may well have increased the likelihood of its appearance in a felicitous landscape painting-and-poem program or its mention at a courtly poetry gathering.

There is ample evidence of this dual role of Nagara—as a place visited in person, as a place imagined from afar—in the *chokusenshū* alone, and it may well have been echoes of the Nagara poems therein that Gotoba would have heard most distinctly as he sat in reverie beside the stream; and even if he did not think of these or other particular poems, it would have been these works, in the selective Imperial anthologies, that would have done most to determine what the place and its name stood for, for him. Among these determinant texts there was, for example, a poem in the *Goshūi wakashū* (#1073) said to have been composed by Akazome Emon "when she saw Nagara Bridge on her way to worship at Tennōji":

> ware bakari Nagara no hashi wa kuchinikeri
>   Naniwa no koto mo fururu kanashisa[13]
> The Nagara Bridge is as dilapidated as I am:
>   oh, how sad it is that every single thing must grow old!

Naniwa, the name of the province in which Nagara is located, doubles here as "anything one can think of" (*nani wa no koto*). This particular play was Akazome Emon's addition to the established convention of manipulating the names of the bridge and its locale in poetic complaints about aging. Whether accurately or not, the anthology records this contribution as having been made when the poet had the bridge itself in sight; what she made there, then, is a poem that describes the state of the bridge itself (*kuchinikeri*) as she "observed" it which at the same time transforms the bridge into an emblem for the universal process of decay and, even more particularly, an object against which the poem-speaker's own "age" can be measured, a figure for her own inevitable decline.

On the other hand, the bridge, or rather its remains, are celebrated as escapees from this universal process—exceptions to the natural rule—in a poem in the *Senzai wakashū*, which was compiled late in the twelfth century under the auspices of Gotoba's father, Goshirakawa. *Senzaishū* #1031 is said to have been composed when its author, Dōmyō (974-1020), "crossed Nagara Bridge":

> nanigoto mo kawariyukumeru yo no naka ni
> > mukashi Nagara no hashibashira ka na[14]
> In this world where every single thing seems to keep changing,
> > here is a pillar of the Nagara Bridge, just as it was so long ago.

Here, the name of the bridge also functions first in the phrase *mukashinagara*, "just as of old": the syntactic doubling (*kakekotoba*) literally makes the bridge-pillar a part of the past (*mukashinagara no hashibashira*); and Dōmyō's celebration of the apparently visible pillar—a man-made architectural element that somehow defies the forces of time and change, or which, having repeatedly been remade, offers the *illusion* that it, at least, has not changed—seems designed to ensure that this remnant of the past will remain close at hand to conjure it back into material existence. However, the next poem in the sequence, which is introduced as one "composed in the same place" (*onaji tokoro nite yomeru*) by the monk Dōin (b. 1090), is emphatic in its recognition that every last trace of the bridge is now finally gone:

> kyō mireba Nagara no hashi wa ato mo nashi
> > mukashi ariki to kikiwataredomo[15]
> As I gaze upon it today, there is nothing left at all of Nagara Bridge,
> > though I have always heard that it was here, long ago.

As if well aware of what has already been done by others in their manipulations of the Nagara matériel, Dōin seems to search for and find another gambit for his reiteration of the by-now-standard poetic idea of the place. His poem poses his act of "seeing" the site of the bridge in the present (*kyō mireba*) against the experience of "hearing" about it in days gone by (*mukashi . . . kiki*), and that juxtaposition, of course, underscores the fact that observation of the site belies the expectations raised by its reputation. To this Dōin also adds a pun commonly seen in poems about bridges: *-wataredo* in *kikiwateredo* means, literally, "*I have crossed a span* of years hearing this talk about the bridge," but, in isolation, the verb construction also stands for the action of crossing the bridge—which is what Dōin, ostensibly, was doing as he composed the verse that reflexively mirrors that very action.

In *Shūi wakashū* #468 the bridge pillar is viewed and celebrated by Fujiwara Kiyotada (d. 958) as he examines its representation in a screen painting (*byōbu no e*):

> Composed during the Tenryaku era [947-957] upon seeing the depiction, in a screen painting, of only the bare remains of what had once been a pillar of the Nagara Bridge (*Nagara no hashibashira no wazuka ni nokoreru kata arikeru o*):
> ashima yori miyuru Nagara no hashibashira
> mukashi no ato no shirube narikeri[16]
> The pillar of the Nagara Bridge just visible amidst the reeds
> is a guide to the remains of the ancient past.

Then, the same pillar apparently reappears, in this same role of guide to the past, in a poem by one of the great courtier-poets of the next generation, Fujiwara Kintō (966-1041); but the poem in which it does so is introduced in the *Goshūi wakashū* (and in Kintō's personal anthology) as one "composed on the spot" (*Nagara no hashi nite*):

> hashibashira nakaramashikaba
> nagarete no na o koso kikame ato o mimashiya[17]
> If this pillar had not survived
> we might know this bridge's famous name, but how might we discover its remains?

Here, none too surprisingly, is the same posing of "hearing" against "seeing" that would re-sound and reappear in Dōin's poem, supposedly composed on the same "spot" at least several decades after Kintō was there. The evocation, and contrasting, of auditory and visual stimuli thus seems to have become a fixed gesture in Nagara poesy, and the topos thus seems to have been made into a figure not only for the passage of time but also for the inevitable discrepancy between report and fact. And then, in the later stages of the evolution of this etiology, we see some modulation away from these quasi-allegorical leanings toward a mode of quasi description of what can, and cannot, be heard and seen at the Nagara site *itself*, whether one is there or not. The poet Gotokudaiji Sanesada (1139-1171) is the author of a poem in this later vein—one that Gotoba would select for inclusion in a Nagara group in the seventeenth (miscellaneous) book of the *Shin kokin wakashū*:

kuchinikeru Nagara no hashi o kite mireba
 ashi no kareba ni akikaze zo fuku[18]
When I reach the spot and gaze at the dilapidated Nagara Bridge
 the autumn wind is blowing through the withered reeds.

The *kotobagaki* for *Shin kokin wakashū* #1594, which opens the Nagara minisequence that concludes with Sanesada's, says that Mibu no Tadamine composed it "on the topic 'Nagara Bridge,'" and because there are no intervening prefaces this information also governs the reading of Sanesada's poem.[19] In fact, Sanesada's poem also appears in the records of a contrived Poetry Competition for Thirty-six Poets (*Jijō sanjūrokunin utaawase*) assembled in 1179—that is, nine years after Sanesada's death—where it is specifically identified as a poem composed "on the topic 'the Nagara Bridge.'"[20] So it would seem that it was indeed in the context of an *utaawase* or a *hyakushu* project, or some other topically structured program, that Sanesada composed the poem; nevertheless, he artfully and deliberately contrives to create the impression that his poem-speaking subject is actually on the spot and seeing what was "seen" (if only in a painting) and described two centuries earlier by Kiyotada. Here, still standing before Sanesada's (or, the poem-speaker's) eyes, as it were, are the same reeds described by Kiyotada, but now what is also "seen" in their vicinity is not the real bridge but an image of it that has by now been firmly fixed in the poetic imagination, and what is heard is not the story of the bridge's decay but the same withering autumn wind that rustles through desiccated plants in so many *Shinkokin*-era poems, as a sonic emblem of an aura of aesthetic desolation that was favored and savored by many of the poets (and other artists) of Sanesada's generation and by their heirs, including, in particular, Gotoba.

Within the textual space formed by the conjunction of these poems in these anthologies, then, we see the bridge and its parts as they are made to function in multiple, adjacent dimensions and are made as if to appear accessible through different but complementary functions of perception; Nagara is, or was, a real place that one might see with the eye (*mi[ru]*), in its real place, or through the artifice of representation in paint; and it was also a name (*na*) that one might hear (*ki[ku]*) when no such visual stimulus was to be had. We also see, and hear, how Nagara becomes a site in and across which these poems resonate and seem even to speak to one another, impressing their sounds, forms, and poses on one another across time and gathering together into a cacophony that is as loud, and demanding, as is the tumult of horses' footfalls and travelers' calls described in Ienaga's diary entry. Amid the aggregated noise of remembered poems, a "new" poem like Sanesada's poem may have been most likely to have echoed most clearly in

Gotoba's memory when he finally "saw" Nagara himself; but Kintō's "old" one must also have spoken to him and impressed upon him its insistence that contact with a *meisho* such as this one in the dimensions of *both* sight and sound is preferable to contact limited to *one* dimension alone—but that, if anything, visual contact is more valuable than aural. It is not enough, Kintō rhetorically implies, if he or we only are able to hear the bridge's long-lasting (i.e. "far-flowing," water-borne) name (*nagarete no na o . . . kik[u]*), without seeing what remains of its parts (*ato o mi[ru]*). The currents of fame have borne that name far and wide and have made it a commonplace. Aural experience of it is now nothing special; but visual perception of its remains is much more rare, and can occur only because a single surviving pillar is still at hand, in situ (that is, stationary, unlike the "flowing name"). So, when Kintō takes himself on the road and finds himself at Nagara (*Nagara nite*), he realizes that he can now add to and deepen the dimensions of his experience of that place: it is no longer a name alone—a fetish to be brandished at will when the conditions of poem-making may demand or avail its use—but a visible, tangible thing, as it was in the beginning of its poetic career (whenever that may have been).

Gotoba, it seems, came to the same realization at Nagara—or arrived there having already realized it, perhaps under the influence of just such poems as these. In any case, this same desire to *see* and thereby to verify, enrich, and alter the experience of the outer and inner ear is clearly evident in Ienaga's account of what Gotoba *appeared* to be thinking as he sat beside and amid these same currents some two hundred years later, occupying the same spot that had been occupied in one way or another by so many poets before him. The quasi-aural resonance and presence of aggregated Nagara poesy seems not to have been enough to satisfy the Emperor's expectations for experience in and with this place: beyond what memory could supply, or alongside it, Gotoba also sought contact with those same vestiges (*ato*) of the bridge itself as Kiyotada had seen painted on a screen and which Akazome Emon, Kintō, Dōmyō, Dōin, and so many others had apparently seen in reality. The name and the name-repeating poems Gotoba heard in memory were themselves vestiges of *waka*'s past, but Ienaga understood that it was the Emperor's hope to augment and concretize his own experience and knowledge of Nagara, based on its name, and rooted in texts, by *seeing* whatever might remain of the ancient bridge *with his own eyes* (*tada na o ba kikiwataru ni, ato o dani miteshigana to oboshimeitari*). For, were he able to do so, the *waka* idiom, so alive in one dimension—that generated in consciousness by text—might seem even more alive, in yet another: a place and thing whose name had served so frequently and effectively in figural play and which had been so many times uttered in speech and song and inscribed in writing (*and* iconographically represented) might become tactile once again. The place and thing so often referred to, then, would reappear in its grounding in the visible and palpable nature- and man-made environment. This completion of the circle—a return to the thing referred to, after all the referring that had taken place in textual (or pictorial) time and space—would go a long way toward making all of *waka*'s history seem whole and immediate, and would return that tradition to, and also reground it in not only text and memory but also the soils and waters from which it had originally sprung.

But Gotoba's companions seem to have been at a loss as to how to fulfill their master's wish. "Some of us just laughed," Ienaga reports,

> for no one had even the slightest idea of how to go about looking for the remains of the bridge. But Captain Masatsune,[21] who was with my Lord, said, "It so happens that I own a piece of one of the pillars of that bridge." He was told to present it as soon as the party returned to the capital. Some others noted that it could only be a mere fragment of the dilapidated bridge, and some wondered what proof might be given our Lord to convince him of its authenticity. But, Masatsune said, "It was handed down into the possession of a local man, one Takiguchi Morifusa. An ancient ancestor of his was crossing this river here in a small boat when something struck the boat and stopped it, so all the passengers got out and a search was made of the river bottom, whereupon this object was dredged up. When it was examined closely it was found to have iron spikes driven into it, which strongly suggested that it had been a pillar. Concluding that it must be a piece of a pillar from the old bridge, Morifusa's ancestor kept it, and it has been handed down in his family ever since."[22]

So, it seems, the single surviving pillar that poets of the past had seen, in one way or another, was no longer in situ; yet a fragment of it, somewhat miraculously, was even now in the hands of one of Gotoba's own men. Masatsune does not explain just how it was that this fragment of the pillar had passed from the Takiguchi family to himself, but Gotoba seems to have accepted his story as sufficient proof of authenticity (in much the same way as an ex post facto *kotobagaki* account of compositional circumstances might be taken as authentication of a poem's origins). And he assumes that this treasure should now be his. Ienaga reports,

> Two or three days after the party's return to the capital, Masatsune presented it, accompanied by this poem:
>> kore so kono mukashi nagara no hashibashira
>> kimi ga tame to ya kuchinokoriken[23]

> This is, indeed, the pillar of the Nagara Bridge, just as it was of old;
> it seems to have survived for you while all the rest has rotted away.

Along with the proffered object itself, Masatsune offers a poem about the object, in the manner of countless earlier poems of presentation of fine, aesthetic objects to exalted or beloved persons; and, like many earlier composers of such presentation poems, he plays in the poem with the name of the presented object itself. Here, Nagara serves doubly as the name of the object's putative source and in the phrase *mukashi nagara*, "just as of old"— and the whole phrase, "mukashinagara no hashibashira" is, of course, a distinct and direct borrowing from Dōmyō's *Senzaishū* poem, and Masatsune no doubt expected Gotoba (and anyone else who might hear or see his poem) to recognize it as such. But there is more: in addition to these phrases, the poem in its entirety is made in a manner "just as of old," from its formulaic opening with an emphatically deictic phrase, *kore so kono* ("This, this very"), which here performs another act of authentication of the object at hand, to its extravagantly flattering gesture to Gotoba, the royal addressee —that is, the suggestion that the fragment of the pillar of the bridge has weathered all this time just in order to please him (*kimi ga tame*, "for Your sake").[24] All of these are timeworn courtly postures, replicated in innumerable verses, and replicated now, by Masatsune, as a way of linking the present moment of presentation to innumerable other moments of courtly exchanges of goods, of flattery, and of poems. Thus, the poem's "just as of old" quality (*mukashi nagara*), which it claims explicitly for the proffered object (it *is* a part of a pillar of the bridge, just as it always was) and implicitly for itself, through its own recollective gestures, is meant to please the Emperor as much as the object it accompanies. It does so by telling him what he presumably wants to hear, in a quasi-arcane manner that, it is assumed, would be pleasing to him as well. And so, like the fragment of the pillar, which although it has decayed has yet survived (*kuchinokori*), the poem celebrates, through replication, an idiom that has itself waxed and waned and yet survived to serve again in courtly communication between a dependent aristocrat and his Imperial lord. And if the claim can be made that the object is "just as of old" (which, of course, it is not), so, implicitly, poetry, as a language shared between the ruler and the ruled, can be celebrated as essentially unchanged, even if it and the relationship of ruler and ruled are by no means what they once were.

Masatsune's presentation of the object and his poem in turn required acknowledgment in verse:

My Lord said, "Compose a reply," and so [I, Ienaga, wrote]:
kore made mo michi aru miyo no fukaki e ni

nokoru mo shiruki hashibashira ka na[25]
   Clearly it is due to the righteousness of his rule
      that deep affinities have preserved it in the water's depths
      —this pillar from the bridge.

Ienaga recapitulates and elaborates on Masatsune's courtly attitude: he, too, celebrates the miraculous surfacing of the pillar (*hashibashira*—the fragment stands here for the whole structural element) as a predestined or inevitable event brought about through the cultivation of intimate ties linking Gotoba, the land, and the people of the land. In deep waters (*fukaki e*) figured as "a reign [i.e., Gotoba's] that is in keeping with the Way [of ideal rulership]" (*michi aru miyo*) this treasure has lain, awaiting the moment when the powerful and deeply rooted causal forces (*fukaki eni*) generated by this ruler's presence in the world and his adherence to its divine Way might bring the precious object forth, to grace that reign (which is the same as his "life," *miyo*) with marks of timeless divinity, signs of continuity and contiguity with the past. It does not seem to matter, for the purposes of this discourse, that Gotoba is at this time a Retired Emperor: his "reign" continues as long as his life does; and it is a reign "in keeping with the Way" precisely because it is an era marked by a flourishing of poetry. *Michi* may in fact also refer to "the Way of Poetry" (*waka no michi*)—but that Way may have been indistinguishable, from Gotoba's and Ietaka's point of view, from the Way of righteous rulership. Thus, the discovery of this fragment becomes an occasion for celebrating something much larger than that discovery itself: it becomes an opportunity for the production of poems that expand upon an ongoing discourse of poetic celebration of Imperial rulership itself—poignantly so, in an era when the very status of such rulership was in doubt. But both poets seize upon the opportunity to suggest that even such events as the discovery of a fragment of the Nagara Bridge occur precisely in order to add a kind of luster to Gotoba's semidivine aura. Their poems marking the conveyance of the pillar fragment into his possession interpret the exchange as a commerce between him and the physical texture of history: his existence made the discovery possible, and that which was discovered further endows him with the potency that has accrued to it through all the years that it was hidden from mortal view.

Having already invested the unexpectedly discovered fragment of the bridge with such significance, and having used it as the occasion for such politically significant text production—much of it turning on the multiple meanings of the place-name Nagara and the multiple significances of an object found there—Gotoba and his friends next do something else with this object to concretize and expand upon its productive utility: "It was made into a reading desk [*bundai*] and installed in the Wakadokoro [Poetry Office]."[26] In other words, it was refashioned as another and wholly different object, a surface on which the old and new poems collected and created for the purpose of the forthcoming "new collection of ancient and modern poetry" would be placed for copying, study, and criticism, both in the Poetry Office in the Imperial compound and elsewhere.[27]

Ienaga's diary continues with an account of the debut of this new and extraordinary accoutrement. He reports: "The first poetry gathering at which it was put into use was the one held during the excursion to Uji"—on the eleventh day of the seventh month in the year 1204 (Genkyū 1).[28] And he continues with further details:

> At Uji a temporary residence was constructed by the river opposite the first set of weirs, with river water running naturally through the gardens. My Lord spent some five days in residence there. As it was just the beginning of autumn, the rustling of the full heads of grain and the sound of the wind in the pines was overwhelming; the shouts from people on the Isle of Cypresses calling through the mists for boats to bear them away, the distant echo of the footsteps of travelers trudging across the bridge—the days of our journey had mounted up for those of us unused to travel, so these sights and sounds made everyone feel quite desolate and deeply moved. We understood then what a trial it must have been to live as did that poet of old who seemed to be dissembling when he wrote about his hut on Ujiyama, "mountain of all the world's grief."[29]

Ienaga sets the scene with all the features of Uji that had come to be so well-known to courtly visitors, who for generations had viewed Uji as an attractive resort, a few hours' journey from the capital city yet wholly unlike it in its terrain and atmosphere. These were the same features that had come to characterize depictions of Uji in both poetry and prose, particularly in the Uji chapters of *The Tale of Genji*, where the roar of the river waters through the weirs and the sights and sounds of traffic on and around the Uji Bridge had filled the ears and eyes of "the Eighth Prince" and his daughters and their princely visitors, producing a mood of discomfiture and depression mixed with a relish for the misty beauty of the relatively exotic site.

In this connection, Ienaga also invokes the spirit of the ninth-century poet Kisen, whose repute rests almost entirely on a single poem in the *Kokin wakashū*:

> wa ga io wa miyako no tatsumi shika zo sumu
>   yo o Ujiyama to hito wa iunari[30]
> My dwelling is a hut, southeast of the capital, and I live quietly there;
>   people say, I hear, that it is because I found the world distasteful that I came
>   to live on Ujiyama, the mountain of grief.

Very little is known about Kisen, but this poem has long served to identify him with a tradition of reclusion at Uji, and that is certainly its role in Ienaga's pastiche account of the place. Even if he was not the first to live in relatively modest retreat there, Kisen's name and his presence—or, memory of his having played thus with the name of the place—were intimately bound up with the place itself; even an account of a retreat to Uji like Gotoba's, ostensibly undertaken for pleasure, would be likely to prompt reference to Kisen's verse. In this particular instance, Ienaga claims that he and the others in Gotoba's party could feel what Kisen felt about life at Uji, and thus he literalizes Kisen's pun on the name of Uji Mountain. (*Yo o ushi*, another way of reading the sounds in the phrase that leads into the name, means "because I found the world distasteful").[31]

From all these parts, then, Ienaga concocts a depiction of Uji in autumn as a locale in which every topographical feature, every sight and sound, evokes memories of past poetic experience; at the same time, of course, the site invites new compositions into which those features, and the words of poets of the past, may be reset. Gotoba apparently was in no hurry to leave such a place, and (according to Ienaga) his host, the Regent, Fujiwara Yoshitsune, who had arranged the whole excursion, did his best to make his guest comfortable there:

> My Lord rejoiced in this freedom to enjoy himself at leisure without hurrying back to the capital, and his host went to great lengths to provide appropriate delicacies for his pleasure.[32] Everything was beautifully arranged, and it seemed that nothing had been overlooked in his preparations. It was in these circumstances, then, that the reading desk made from the Nagara Bridge pillar was put to use. Among the poems composed at that gathering was this one, in which our host took special note of the occasion of its introduction:
>
> > koyoi shi mo Yasoujikawa ni sumu tsuki wo
> >
> > > Nagara no hashi no ue ni miru ka na
> >
> > Here tonight at Ujikawa, River of the Eighty Clans,
> >
> > > we gaze at a moon from the vantage of the Nagara Bridge.[33]

Yoshitsune "takes special note of the occasion," and takes special advantage of the new poetry desk's presence at hand: he ushers the Nagara Bridge from which it was reportedly fashioned into the Uji setting of his poem—in a position that should, by rights, be occupied by the equally hallowed Uji Bridge—and thus crafts an artful analogy to the introduction of the new *bundai*, the new instrument for the support of poem-making made from a part of that fragment found and reclaimed at Nagara, transferred to the capital, reshaped, and then borne hither for the specific purpose of festive poem-making. Again, the old and the new are potently mixed into this poem:

the river's name is given its alternate, archaic name, Yasoujikawa ("river of eighty [innumerable] clans"), but the moon that has been seen shining over and in it for so long, and which has been seen and sung of so many times before, is now seen from an entirely new and wholly artificially contrived perspective. The desk that was a fragment of something that once was a part of a bridge is now a bridge again, or is willed to be. "Tonight, we gaze at the Uji moon from Nagara Bridge," says Yoshitsune: "We write poems about the sight of this moon once more, as of old, but tonight we do so with a new sense of ourselves in time, reshaped by the knowledge that a remnant of the ancient Nagara Bridge—itself so rich with poetic potency—is supporting, re-orienting, and energizing our perception of what we see and do here."

Although Ienaga does not tell us so, we know from other sources that five topics (*dai*) were selected on this occasion to challenge the creative capacities of the members of Gotoba's Uji party, in what was apparently a sort of mini-*utaawase*. Yoshitsune's "Koyoi shi mo . . ." poem addressed the second of these, "the moon in the water" (*mizu no tsuki*); the other topics were "the wind on the mountain" (*yama no kaze*), "dew in the fields" (*no no tsuyu*), "love at night" (*yoru no koi*) and "travel in autumn" (*aki no tabi*)—all highly appropriate to the site and the season. Gotoba's own poems on the five topics appear together in his personal anthology, and every one makes its explicit gesture to the poetic past while simultaneously commemorating the moment at hand, as in his "wind on the mountain" poem:

> Uji no yama Kumo fukiharau akikaze ni
>   miyako no tatsumi tsuki mo sumikeri[34]
> In the autumn wind that sweeps the clouds off Uji peak
>   the moon also shines clearly, here where it dwells "southeast of the capital."

This is a clear echo of Kisen's Uji verse, transformed and reshaped as it reverberates across time and then enters the mind of a man who now—some three centuries later—finds himself in the locale where Kisen's spirit still seems to dwell. In the hands of this man, the cultivator of a new style that retains but redirects the mannerisms of the old, punning play must yield deeper effects. Now, the sounds of Kisen's verb *sumu* ("to dwell") take on the additional meaning of "shining pure and bright," just as they do in Yoshitsune's "Koyoi shi mo . . ." Thus, through allusive moves that explicitly underscore his substitutions, Gotoba suggests that the moon now dwells and shines just where Kisen dwelt, and he reports that he can see it doing so, in a sky swept clear of clouds by the autumn wind. In place of Kisen's elaborate riddles, but with much of the same material, Gotoba creates an old/new description of a new viewing of Uji, a record of something seen in the present that speaks through the revivified language of the now-distant past.

The same moon, and the same wind, are also part of the scene drawn in Gotoba's "moon in the water" poem, for the second *dai*:

mukashi yori taenu nagare ni sumu tsuki o
  migakite wataru Uji no kawakaze[35]
The wind off the Uji river adds to the luster of this moon
  that shines as it has always shone in this stream that flows as it has always
  flown.

The moon that "dwells" and "shines" in the Uji sky *and* in the Uji waters that catch its reflection is also fixed in time, and so it can be claimed that what is seen now has been seen before: it is a vision caught in waters that have "never ceased to flow since antiquity" (*mukashi yori taenu nagare*), for this moon has never given up this dwelling/shining place (*mukashi yori . . . sumu*). The implication, not far beneath the surface, is that poetry's presence, its flow, is concomitantly uninterrupted, equally active and accessible in this site—perhaps even more so here than elsewhere—and that this can be demonstrated in the making of just such old/new poems as these. Yoshitsune follows Gotoba's lead in conflating time and space in his "Koyoi shi mo . . ." poem on this same *dai*: when he carries Nagara into Uji through word and text, he replicates the time- and space-conflating renovation and transfer of the quondam bridge-pillar fragment. In both the textual and physical spheres, both poets—as well as their companions—find surfaces onto which they impose their poeticized vision of space and time, collapsed into unities through the alchemy of verse.

Teika—one of the masters of such alchemies—was another member of this party. His poem on the fifth *dai*, "travel in autumn," is recorded as *Shūi gusō* #2541:

waga io wa mine no sasahara shika zo karu
  tsuki ni wa naru na aki no yūtsuyu[36]
For my traveler's hut I cut thus the bamboo grass that grows on the peak
  [which the deer also cut]:
  do not grow too fond of the moon, o dew of this autumn night.

In this refashioning of the matériel at hand at Uji, Teika casts himself as Kisen's successor, making a temporary dwelling for himself in these environs and then asking the dewy autumn skies not to rob him of the moon's companionship. He also ably negotiates the unresolved debate about the meaning of Kisen's *shika zo sumu* by letting his own *shika zo karu* read two ways, too: as "*thus* do I cut [the grass]" and as "*deer* cut the grass."

Still other poems composed for this mini-*utaawase* suggest that Kisen's was not the only spirit whose presence in Uji was felt by the members of the party: they were equally well aware that the place was also inhabited by the spirit of a mysterious Lady of the Bridge, *Uji no hashihime,* and so her presence also inhabits some of the poems they made on this occasion. Her persona was actually an amalgam of several Uji presences—a female guardian deity of the river crossing, courtesans who, from ancient times, plied their trade among travelers through the area—but it crystallized in and through a *Kokinshū* poem (#689) in which an anonymous male voice pictures the Lady's patient nightly vigil:

> samushiro ni koromo katashiki koyoi mo ya
>   ware o matsuramu Uji no hashihime[37]
> Spreading only her own single robe on her woven rush matting,
>   does she wait for me again tonight—the maiden at Uji Bridge?[38]

Gotoba's Uji "love at night" verse seems deliberately to avoid direct reference to this famous poem, yet that very avoidance seems to strengthen the link he forges to it:

> ashihiki no yamaoroshi fukite samuki yo no
>   nagaki o hitori koitsutsu zo furu[39]
> Chilled by the winds that sweep down from the peak,
>   I pass this long night yearning but alone.

The voice that speaks Gotoba's poem is that of a new persona who now displaces the Lady of the Bridge as the solitary lover but is just as chilled as she, with only her own robe to cover her, lying just as exposed to the night winds. Again, archaic language—including the *makurakotoba ashihiki no* (sometimes translated as "foot-wearying") preceding *yama* (*oroshi*), "wind that sweeps off the *mountain*"—is present to mark the poem as one crafted in homage to the poetic diction of the past, here deployed in a scheme to create an old/new tableau of lonely waiting under the cold Uji night sky. The poem is thus another linking of the present visit to Uji to the ancient past: it is a reclamation of that past for the purposes of new creation in the present, performed and directed by Gotoba in order to create a record of his own maneuverings in and across spatial and textual time.

Ienaga also invokes this beguiling female persona as he describes the end of the Uji excursion: "Truly, the place was so extraordinary that we all could have wished to spend the rest of our days there in the company of the Lady of the Bridge, but we all knew that we must eventually return to the capital, and so we did so, though my Lord's manner showed how loathe he was to tear himself away."[40] Here, the siren's erotic allure is a metaphor for the allure of the place itself. There, in the sights and sounds of that place as it existed both in real and textual time, Gotoba and his companions had found rich materials for new poem-making in the old/new style they were then cultivating. They brought with them to Uji the physical embodiment of such material—the poetry desk fashioned from the fragment of the absent/present, "just as of old" Nagara bridge, an instrument designed to form a base on which to make new verse; and they availed themselves of its contrived presence just as they availed themselves of the textually present language of old verse. Thus they made poetic records of their own presence in this place, records that gave that presence an elegant, courtly cast and which added further to the mystique and the multilayered literary heritage of the place itself.

But an entry in Teika's diary *Meigetsuki* for the fourteenth day of the seventh month—three days after the night of the Uji *utaawase*—reveals a very different aspect of the outing than that portrayed by Ienaga in his diary and collectively represented in the poems by Gotoba and his men:

> The weather was fine. I joined the Retired Emperor's party. He had gone upstream to bathe in the river. Various gentlemen ran about naked in the courtyard in front of the Byōdōin. Others, also naked, rode horses. (They did not use saddles.) The sight of the procession they made was shocking. With [Lord Ariie], I watched from behind a doorway. In secret, I gasped—it was like a dream. I wondered what the Kami and Buddhas thought of it. Making my obeisance to the Buddha [in the Amida hall], I returned to my lodging.[41]

Teika withdraws in disgust from this scene, after watching from the sidelines (with Fujiwara Ariie, a fellow senior member of Gotoba's entourage and of the *Wakadokoro* staff), but his description of it helps us to remember that the Uji excursion was a pleasure outing—an all-male one, and, it would seem, an opportunity for complete, if temporary, abandon of courtly decorum. The *utaawase* was part of the program of entertainments, along with the gustatory novelties, the bathing, and the rest. In the playfulness exhibited therein—in the manipulation of Uji and other poetic icons—we may perhaps also detect a lighthearted dimension, a wiseacre's knowing and clever display of the ability to toy adeptly with images and themes treated more seriously in other settings, a gentle mockery of courtly poetic production performed amid the revels of a suburban holiday. The same may be true, to some extent, of much of what was done and said at Nagara on Gotoba's way back from Kumano, and subsequently, when the fragment of the bridge was given over to him. None of the participants in this sequence of events seems to have been inclined to resist the temptations offered, to *play* in the manner dictated by the prevailing mood of the moment. Poetic composition was one among the several modes of play, and in these circumstances poem-making may have been something to play at with less of the sober constriction that prevailed over the same practice elsewhere and on other occasions.

Or, to put it another way, these were circumstances somewhat different from but equally productive of poems as were others, and the men involved in them showed how the *waka* idiom could function in lighthearted play, in the relatively liberated atmosphere of a junket, in ways that were similar to, but perhaps almost subversive of, the ways it functioned in more formal conditions. The manufacture and use of the Nagara poetry desk, employed at Uji amid all the elegant trappings deployed for Gotoba's pleasure, may also have been a kind of genteel joke, another amusing manipulation of something old and of intentionally exaggerated value fashioned into something new and of equally exaggerated and artificial value, prominently displayed and given lavish attention if for no other reason than to create the opportunity to make more genteel jokes about it, in the form of poems. The men who played with it perhaps knew that it was a fetish—yet they went ahead and used it, and made poems about it, in knowing celebration of their own fetishism, and in imitation of the fetishistic manipulation of the language and tradition of poetry for which they had caused it to stand. Likewise, everything in Ienaga's account of these events—from his description of Gotoba's reverie at Nagara to the use of Hashihime as an emblem for Uji's allure—may also be read as an artful, purposeful, and stylish exercise in such fetishism, a cult performance dressed in the trappings of a time-enriched cultic language, adorned with specimens hauled out of the store of literary memory for yet another act of amusing display in a new arrangement (a new text) which, in turn, could become part of the cult's historical record. The Nagara poetry desk was a centerpiece for this performance, generated by and generative of the cultic displays in which it so prominently figured.

This was not the end of its career. Upon the return of the party to the capital, the Nagara *bundai* was deposited in the Wakadokoro—the cult's head office, as it were. Teika was the first to use it there, he tells us in his diary, just a couple of days later, on the sixteenth, when he went to the Poetry Office to act as lector (*kōshi*) at the formal recording of the poems recently composed at Uji (figure 6).[42] Although it surely made other appearances in the intervening years, the desk's next recorded use occurred in 1251, in a setting that prompted direct reference to the occasion of its Uji debut. On the evening of the thirteenth day of the ninth month of that year (Kenchō 3), forty-two court poets gathered at the Sentō Palace, the residence of Gotoba's grandson, the Retired Emperor Gosaga (1220-1272), for an *eigu utaawase*, a poetry contest conducted in honor of and in the presence of a portrait of Hitomaro, the deified sage of the *waka* tradition.[43] The Nagara

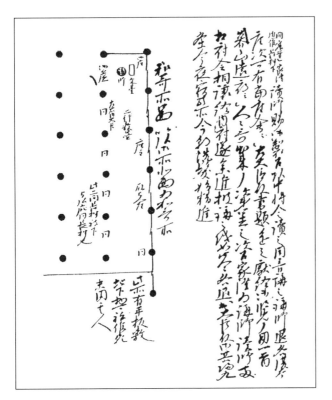

6. Copy of page from Fujiwara Teika's diary Meigetsuki, *dated Kennin 1.7.26 (1201), with diagram of the* Wakadokoro *(Poetry Office in the Imperial Palace). The location of a* bundai *(poetry desk) of the kind made for Retired Emperor Gotoba from a fragment of the Nagara Bridge is indicated in the upper right corner of the diagram. Courtesy Kyoto Furitsu Sōgō Shiryōkan.*

poetry desk was placed near the portrait, and the lectors for the contest held forth from it. In the one-hundred-and-sixth round of this contest, under the topic "moonlight in famous places" (*meisho no tsuki*), Gosaga took the opportunity to make a direct gesture of salute to the desk. The poem he then offered was simultaneously a recollection of the 1204 Uji *utaawase* and was thus also an indirect but fairly transparent act of homage to his grandfather's memory:

> tsuki mo nao Nagara ni kuchishi hashibashira
>   ari to ya koko ni sumiwataruran[44]
> Even now, the moon still shines in such a way to make us think
>   that the pillar of the bridge that disappeared so long ago from Nagara is here
>   at hand.

At Uji, Yoshitsune had deliberately conflated one locale with another in his claim that the Nagara Bridge was now part of the Uji landscape; now, the bridge is once more reconstructed, as it were, in the grounds of the Retired Emperor's palace, where it provides the same perspective on the moon, and basks in the brightness of the same moon as it did in its other sites. The suggestion first made by Yoshitsune at Uji and now doubled in Gosaga's recapitulation—a suggestion patently contrary to fact but therefore contingently valid, or at least possible, in the context of *waka* discourse—is that both space and time can be and have been rearranged, and that something that "disappeared long ago" (the bridge, and all that it stands for) can be reconstructed, through word and will, if imagination and rhetoric are allowed to have their way. Like Yoshitsune and the rest of the Uji party, Gosaga summons all the spirits of *waka*'s past into presence at the *eigu utaawase*: the moonlight, posited as the same as that which shone on the Nagara Bridge in its original site, carries with it all the collective and lasting potential of the *waka* idiom, now made magically accessible—"here," close at hand (*koko ni*)—through the presence of the *bundai*, to be shared by and manipulated once again by every poet in the Sentō assemblage.

Gosaga's poem was matched with one by "the former Minister of the Center," Fujiwara Motoie (1203–1280), a son of that same Yoshitsune who had been Gotoba's host at Uji. Motoie chose the storied Akashi coast as the *meisho* in which to set his moon:

> kotoshi koso ke ni kazu soite nagatsuki no
>   tsuki mo Akashi no uraji narikere[45]
> This year, once more, in yet another long ninth month,
>   the moon shines brightly yet again on the road along the Akashi shore.

Like Gosaga, Motoie forces the present time of his poem into a continuum with all that time that has passed at the selected famous place. At Akashi, in Motoie's poem, the moon that shines at the time of the composition of the poem—in the "long ninth month," *nagatsuki*—marks the repetition of an endless cycle of shinings, reaching back into the literary past, when the hero of *The Tale of Genji*, for example, trod moonlit paths to make his way to the Akashi Lady, and even farther, to that unknown moment when the place's very name was first associated with "the brightness of the moon" (*akashi*).[46] The poem may reveal another agenda as well: it may be a thinly veiled complaint, from the "former" Minister, that "this year, in truth" (*kotoshi ke ni*) he is without office, as Genji himself was during his sojourn in Akashi.

We know, however, that Gosaga's poem won the round: the detailed judgments rendered on the spot have not survived, but shortly after the

contest one of the judge-participants, Teika's son Tameie (1198–1275), recorded his preferences. Of this round he wrote,

> As I pondered the excellence of this "Nagara Bridge" poem in both its underlying
> meaning and its outer form as well [*kokoro mo kotoba mo*], I recalled for the first
> time that there was a special story about the poetry desk that was in use on this
> occasion.
>
> During Emperor Gotoba's time, when he went on an excursion to Uji and poems
> were being composed and discussed there, one of those present, hearing about
> the origins of this desk, wrote, "we gaze at the reflection of the moon in Yasouji-
> kawa from the vantage of the Nagara Bridge."[47] But in "the moon shines in such
> a way to make us think that the pillar of the bridge that disappeared so long ago
> from Nagara is here at hand" there is an excellence that even surpasses that
> achieved at that former time. Some skill has been put into the making of the
> "Akashi shore" poem, but there is no respect in which it even approaches a level
> of excellence, so from every point of view "Nagara Bridge" must be the winner.[48]

It is not altogether surprising that Tameie should have lavished such praise
on the poem composed by the grandson of one of the Uji participants while
dismissing that composed by the son of another. In this particular competition, the scales were already tipped in Gosaga's favor, not only because of
his royal status but also because Tameie and Motoie were ranged on opposite
sides of the current struggle for dominance in court poetic matters; and, if
anything, Gosaga leaned toward Tameie's side. And, in view of the actual
presence of the Nagara poetry desk at the site of competition, Gosaga's poem
appears to be the more ingenious: it also transparently displays his recollection of Yoshitsune's Uji verse, using the moon and its shining and dwelling
and the Nagara Bridge's decay and transformation in much the same way as
his predecessor, yet with a new arrangement of those same elements. In so
doing, it may even constitute a conciliatory gesture of honor to Yoshitsune's
son, Gosaga's temporary "foe" in this phase of the match. Tameie's claim that
the new poem exceeds the old one in its excellence may be hyperbole, but
it shows an appreciation of Gosaga's adroit achievement just as much as it
shows his own desire to flatter his patron.

Both at Uji, when Gotoba and his male friends went there for amusement,
and, decades later, at the Sentō palace, when his grandson and his court held
a relatively more sober, quasi-religious rite presided over by the visually
present spirit of Hitomaro, the extraordinary Nagara poetry desk was given
a central, instrumental role and was treated as if it held extraordinary energies that could be knowingly tapped by those poets who were exposed, or
exposed themselves, to its special aura. Or, one might say, these poets, in
providing themselves with and making use of this desk in this way, in full

knowledge of the story of its origin, were fetishizing that which might otherwise have been a completely insignificant scrap of rotten wood, even as they fetishized that language of which that piece of wood was held to be both embodiment and emblem—a language which, without such special treatment, might otherwise have lost the special significance that had accrued to it through time. In these settings, as in many others, both the semi-sacred fragment of the ancient bridge and the semi-sacred language of ancient verse, miraculously rediscovered, were made available to serve as equally malleable tools, hallowed by time yet not so sacrosanct as to prohibit such manipulation. Their semi-sacred status never put them beyond reach; they were, rather, accessible and attractive and eminently portable implements of pleasurable and meaningful play, and such play with them was at once a form of (not necessarily very solemn) worship at the altar of poetic cult and a step toward the production of new material for future (not necessarily very solemn) worship. Equally potent, both the object and the idiom it stood for generated new poems which could in turn serve as surfaces on which still more poems might be inscribed in future time, in similar mixes of the sober and the gay, the heavy and the light.

This same mix of seriousness and light-heartedness also characterizes accounts found elsewhere of fetishism involving the manipulation of other fragments of the Nagara Bridge and of similar objects that attained similar cult status through their association with *waka*'s past and the tradition's survival into the present. Such accounts, which are available to us in texts that date from many periods, collectively suggest that *waka* fetishism, particularly in the form of the search for and preservation of poetic memorabilia—the physical bits and pieces that had come to stand for the tradition's venerable past—was both a serious business, diligently pursued, and one from which both participants and observers could step back, to assess such obsessiveness with a mixture of admiring awe and wry amusement. Take, for example, the story found in two Kamakura-period tale collections—*Uji shūi monogatari* and *Kohon setsuwa shū*—concerning a lady known as Prince Yasusuke's Mother, or the Mother of the Chief of Rites (Yasusuke-ō no haha, Haku no haha), who was active in court poetry circles from the middle to the end of the eleventh century. Among the gifts that this lady sent to a certain monk named Yōen, who had performed a Buddhist rite under her sponsorship, was an object wrapped in fine writing paper dyed a pale shade of purple. The poem she had written on this paper explained just what the gift was, and why it was special:

kuchinikeru Nagara no hashi no hashibashira
    nori no tame ni mo watashitsuru ka na[49]

This pillar from the rotten bridge of Nagara
> has been saved by the power of the Law which now enables me to pass it on
> to you.

Inside, Yōen found, was a sliver (*kire*) of wood, authenticated by the donor's accompanying poem as a genuine fragment of the famous Nagara Bridge.

In the exchange of the bridge fragment between Masatsune and Gotoba, the suggestion was made that the survival and rediscovery of the precious object was a minor miracle ultimately attributable to the Emperor himself and indicative of his authority (*kimi no tame*); here, it is Buddhism itself (*nori no tame*), as expounded by the hired monk, that has preserved another fragment of the bridge and has now brought it forth and motivated its passage from one collector's hands into another's. This message, and the gift itself, are deftly conveyed through the verb *watasu*, which bears three simultaneous connotations: it stands for the act of "saving" something or someone, as in the Buddha's saving of sentient beings and their transportation from a realm of suffering to a realm of bliss; for the construction (or reconstruction) of the bridge, which is transitively made to "cross" the body of water which it spans; and for the actual act of exchange, the handing over of the object. The poem finds its place in the story as part of the account of this exchange—part of the social nicety of it—but it also demonstrates Haku no haha's understanding of the object's greater significance: she conveys this, along with the object, in a poem that replicates, in its attitude, the gestures of many other presentation poems and which celebrates, in its verbal play, the very idiom for which the presented object has come to stand.

Early on the morning following Yōen's receipt of this gift (the story continues), he received an unexpected visit from another prelate named Ryūgen—a monk described in both versions of the tale as an *utayomi*, a poem-maker, or devotee of verse.[50] "He must have heard about the gift," Yōen is reported to have thought; and, indeed, Ryūgen deferentially presented his name-card to Yōen and then asked him for the fragment of the bridge. When Yōen responded by asking Ryūgen why he should give up such a precious thing, Ryūgen said something to the effect of, "Indeed, why should you?" or "That's what I thought you would say. Too bad!" (*Nani shi ni ka, torasetamawan. Kuchioshi*) and then went away.

Both versions of this story conclude and assess it in the same way, with the same words: *Sukizukishiku, awarenaru kotodomo nari* ("These were moving, impressive acts of elegant devotion [to the traditions of poetry]"). What is here termed "elegant devotion" is the attitude that was to be detected in the tastefulness of Haku no haha's choice of gift to Yōen, the manner of its presentation, the poem that accompanied it, and, perhaps above all, in Ryūgen's keen desire to have it for himself and Yōen's equally keen desire to keep it. All are demonstrations of *suki*, tasteful if sometimes extreme or eccentric recognition of and attachment to things that are invested with rich aesthetic weight, however small, mundane, and insignificant they may otherwise seem to be. Stories of those who seek out or display such things, those who understand and therefore are held in the thrall of the cult of *suki*, and who perpetuate it, are often found by those who tell such stories to be *aware* as well—that is, "deeply moving" and memorable, and hence worth telling and writing about, so as to be preserved and savored.

Closely related to *suki* in accounts of such *waka* fetishism is yet another term, *fūryū*: it denotes a style of behavior that is held to exemplify the height of fashionable taste (literally, behavior in consonance with airs [*fū*] and currents [*ryū*]). One of its earliest and greatest exemplars, according to literary lore, is Minamoto Tōru (822–895), an Emperor's son-made-civilian, whose tasteful accomplishments were deeply admired by his contemporaries and then, through literary representation, attained legendary dimensions after his death. Tōru's *fūryū* was most memorably embodied in his construction, in the grounds of his mansion (the Kawara no in) in the capital city, of a replica of the land- and seascape of Shiogama, a famous place in the far northeast. The illusion created by Tōru's miniature Shiogama was made as complete as it could be when he had salt water hauled from Naniwa and other harbors so that it might be boiled within his own garden to produce an imitation of the salty smokes and steams so often associated with the real Shiogama in travelers' accounts and in poetry—not only because salt-fires were a real feature of such seaside locales, but also because the very name Shiogama means "salt-cauldron" or "salt-kiln."[51]

When Tōru built his Shiogama garden there was not yet a *Kokinshū* proto-catalog of famous poetic places; rather, what he constructed became, in turn, a part of that catalog, and interacted therein with that other Shiogama which he and his contemporaries knew from song, if not from direct experience—that is, the Shiogama that was sung of in the regional songs of Michinoku collected by the Poetry Office of their day, two of which eventually made their way into the twentieth volume of the *Kokinshū*:

> Michinoku wa izure wa aredo
>   Shiogama no ura kogu fune no tsunade kanashi mo
> Say what one may of places here and there in Michinoku,
>   how moving it is to watch a boat making its way
>   across Shiogama Bay!

> wa ga seko o miyako ni yarite
>   Shiogama no Magaki no shima no matsu zo koishiki

7. Scene from Ōshū *meisho zue:* Minamoto Tōru, *seated on the veranda of his* Kawara no in *villa, looks out on the ersatz* Shiogama *scene constructed in his garden; with inscription of* Kokin wakashū #1088 *("Michinoku wa/ izure wa aredo/Shiogama no/ ura kogu fune no/tsunade kanashi mo"). Courtesy Miyagi-ken Toshokan.*

> I have sent my man off to the capital,
>> and now, how sadly I wait, "pining" like the pines of Magaki Isle at Shiogama.[52]

But, as a story in *Ise monogatari* (The tales of Ise) (*dan* 81) tells it, Tōru's artifice was one into which others, invited into the garden to share in the pleasure of contrived illusion and imaginary travel, entered in a light mood, aware that this was a place for genteel play, even if the rising steam and smoke might otherwise, in poetry, be taken as emblems of sadness, loneliness, and grief. The *Ise monogatari* narrator tells us that, on one such occasion,

> an old gentlemen, lurking under the veranda of the house, composed this poem after everyone else present [at an all-night autumnal banquet] had read his own:
>> Shiogama ni itsu ka kinikemu
>> asanagi ni tsurisuru fune wa koko ni yoranan[53]
> When was it that I came to Shiogama?
>> Perhaps that boat that is trolling in the morning calm will come close to me.[54]

The fishing boat on Tōru's lake was, of course, no more genuine than the body of water—the ersatz Shiogama Bay—upon which it sailed, but the

8. Scene from Ōshū meisho zue: *the Kawara no in episode,* Ise monogatari *(Tales of Ise) dan 81, in which an elderly man (at lower left) composes a poem in praise of the Shiogama scene in Tōru's garden. Courtesy Miyagi-ken Toshokan. The inscription reproduces the* Ise monogatari *text including the elderly man's poem ("Shiogama ni/itsu ka kinikemu/asanagi ni/tsurisuru fune wa/koko ni yoranan").*

anonymous old gentleman (*kataiokina*) nonetheless treats them both in a manner that shows that he, too, can get into the spirit of the place, while poking gentle fun at it. He asks, "How did I get so quickly, so easily, to distant Shiogama?" That is, "How has this imaginary transportation through space and time been accomplished? Am I really there, or somewhere else—in an improved, controlled 'Shiogama,' perhaps, rather than in that wild, remote, unknown locale? In any case, the imaginary exoticism is here to be indulged in, offered for the pleasure of any who may enter this beguiling space with (at least partially) suspended disbelief—so I will make myself one of them, and I will play the game." This was both flattery of the host and a jibe at his affectations; it is also the best known of the poems supposedly composed in Tōru's Shiogama garden while it was in its prime.

The creation of such elaborate, beguiling illusion required not only Tōru's will but also his wealth, and the conjuring could only work, it seems, as long as he was there to pay for it and keep up the ruse. The delight he thus provided for his friends turns to regret, and the previously effaced gloom inherent in the Shiogama scene (the real *and* the imaginary one) reasserts itself in a poem that Tsurayuki is said to have written after Tōru's death, when he found himself back at the Kawara mansion, gazing once again on the now-deserted garden:

kimi masade kemuri taenishi Shiogama no
   urasabishiku mo miewataru ka na[55]
The smoke has vanished from this Shiogama Bay
   now that its master is not here, and everywhere I look I see only desolation.

This poem literally turns on the double function of *ura* in Shiogama *Bay* (Shiogama no *ura*) and in the adverbial *urasabishiku mo mieru* (literally, "has a look of utter desolation"). The semantic shift (*kakekotoba* or zeugma) replicates the transforming turn that Tōru's artificial bay seems to have undergone, in Tsurayuki's eyes, since its owner and creator has left it behind; it also replicates the garden's own amalgam of playfulness and melancholy, in that it, too, is a carefully crafted display of its own maker's combination of ingenuity and solemnity. In this new scheme, the poem-speaker's (i.e., Tsurayuki's) memory of the salty smoke that Tōru caused to fill these precincts, to please himself and others, now calls to mind the smoke from Tōru's funeral pyre as well; but now it, too, has already drifted away (*taenishi*), leaving only absence and a void. (There is perhaps also some significance in the fact that the occasion described in *Ise monogatari dan* 81 was a banquet at which the guests took particular pleasure in the garden's autumnal aspect. Perhaps the garden's melancholy beauty was at its height in autumn, and so the melancholy of autumns after its owner-creator's death would seem even more intense. The pathos would seem to increase even further if the garden were to show signs of resisting autumn itself.)

Another poem placed in the same chapter ("Laments") of the *Kokinshū* as Tsurayuki's similarly memorializes Tōru by noting how his absence seems to have upset the natural order of things in the garden. The *kotobagaki* says that Minamoto Yoshiari (a.k.a. Kon'in no migi no ōimochigimi, 845–897) was passing the mansion in the autumn following Tōru's death when he noticed that the leaves on the trees in the garden had not changed their colors as much as others elsewhere. He then composed the following poem and had it delivered to those who remained inside the house:

uchitsuke ni sabishiku mo aru ka
   momijiba mo nushi naki yado wa iro nakarikeri[56]
This makes me feel his loss more deeply than before!
   The maple leaves in this house that has lost its master
   have also lost their color.

During his lifetime, Tōru reordered the natural form of his garden so that it might artificially represent another natural form, the Shiogama coastline;

now, Yoshiari suggests, even in his absence the foliage in his garden is somehow unable to regain consistency or harmony with the cyclical forces of nature. Tōru disrupted these forces in the forging of his new order, and now his plantings seem to continue to honor his memory by setting themselves apart, delaying their participation in the process of aging and decay.

Yet, with the passage of just a few years, poetic discourse in memory of Tōru would honor him by attempting to claim that little really did change in his garden after he was no longer there. By the middle of the tenth century, the Kawara mansion had been turned into a monastery, and its chief resident was Tōru's great-grandson, the monk Anpō.[57] His personal anthology (*Anpō Hōshi shū*) is arranged as a poetic journal of his life there: at one point in it, he introduces a pair of poems with a *kotobagaki* that says that he "sought to say in them what others had left unsaid" in their own memorial poems in Tōru's own time (*hito no yomanu o kokoromi ni to te*). "Unspoken" poems thus themselves become a site to return to, like the garden and the other poems written in its praise and in that of its designer. In the first of these poems, Anpō catches sight of the smoke from Tōru's artificial salt-fires, rising once again over his artificial Shiogama—a place still populated by artificial fisherfolk, among whom Anpō now numbers himself:

> toshi furite ama sonaretaru Shiogama no
>   ura no keburi wa mada zo nokoreru
> Though years have passed, the smoke that fisherfolk
>   are so used to seeing at Shiogama Bay still is here.

And in the second, he focuses on a celebrated feature of both the real and the man-made Shiogama scene, an offshore island evocatively named Ukishima ("Floating Isle"):

> okitsunami tatete tadayou Ukishima wa
>   mukashi no kaze no nagori narikeri[58]
> Ukishima, the "Floating Isle," drifting amidst waves that rise in these sea
>   waters:
>   it is a memento left by a breeze that blew here a long time ago.

In both poems, Anpō reclaims the perspective of Tsurayuki and other observers of the post-Tōru Kawara site: he insists that he sees just what they saw (or thought they saw), that the illusions wrought by Tōru decades before are still at work; and when he says that the artificial "Floating Isle" (also, potentially, "Isle of Sadness" [*uki*-shima]) has been left here by an ancient wind (*mukashi no kaze*), he may even be toying with the etymology of *fūryū* (or even its graphic evocation of currents [*ryū, nagare*] of "wind" [*fū, kaze*]) and thus identifying that "wind" with the aesthetic energy that drove Tōru to make the model Shiogama in the first place. Everything in the garden, he thus suggests, was placed here and invigorated by that transforming and reordering energy as it moved through this space, and its lingering effects (*nagori*) are still visible, still energized by his spirit. It is the continued presence of his transforming spirit that makes the place the *meisho* that it is. It gained its fame through ingenious artifice—the making of a convincing faux-Shiogama—and now, additional artifice—the willful insistence that that faux-Shiogama is unchanged—perpetuates and compounds that claim to fame.

In the aforementioned *kotobagaki* preceding these two poems, Anpō uses a telling verb as he briefly recounts the story of the design of the garden: *utsushitsukur[u]*, written phonetically to allow, perhaps, for more than one interpretation, suggests that Tōru both "copied" (*utsushi*) and "moved" (*utsushi*) Shiogama, from its original site in the far northeast to the (central, accessible) Kawara site.[59] The facsimile thus manufactured (*tsukur[u]*) was thus both a simulacrum of *and* a real Shiogama, or, at least, a bona-fide surrogate brought close to hand for the delectation of aristocrat-aesthetes who might never have had the opportunity to see it otherwise. It is precisely this dialectic of the artificial and the genuine, productive of so much elegant confusion, that is celebrated in all these poems about the garden, and this intentionally produced confusion is, perhaps, the very essence of Tōru's *fūryū*.[60] Those who admired the Kawara garden, both in Tōru's time and later, knew very well that it was a fake, but that knowledge seems only to have increased their admiration, which then took the form of poems in which the deception was compounded. The *Ise monogatari* narrator (or, perhaps, one of the early annotators whose marginalia have made their way into the body of the text) also compounds the confusion, observing, after recording the "old man's" poem: "If one goes to Michinoku one does find many strange and wonderful places. Yet there is no place in all of the more than sixty provinces in this land that resembles Shiogama. And that is why this 'old man' praised *this* Shiogama, too [*sara ni koko o medete*], by composing this poem."[61] The ultimate effect of these artifices is a suspension of the fake-real dialectic in favor of a kind of contractual acceptance of and reveling in the elaborate illusion: its sequel is the attempt, like Anpō's, to reinstate that illusion even in the absence of its originator.

To live in the post-Tōru Kawara no in, as Anpō did, was in and of itself a kind of revelry in this extended illusion and an occupation of a double *utamakura* site—a Shiogama that was and was not Shiogama, a place that had attained its special aesthetic status and appeal precisely by being neither entirely the one place nor entirely the other. One might also say that the illusion was, in itself, an allusion: the garden referred to and manipulated the real Shiogama, and that act of play in turn made possible a seemingly unlimited number of acts of further allusive play. To indulge oneself by residing in such a place was itself a form of *suki,* as well as an act of homage to Tōru's *furyū,* and so, perforce, was the making of poems in that poetically enriched environment. Anpō freely admits to this in the preface to his own *Anpō Hōshi shū:*

> Those who read this in ages to come may think of it as aesthetic self-indulgence (*sukeru yō ni omoubekeredo*), but as I have been unable to resist being so deeply moved by things (*aware naru koto no taegatakereba*) in the many moments of solitude that I have experienced during my residence in the Kawara mansion — when the spring blossoms reached their peak, when the colored autumn leaves were scattering, when the wind in the pines soughed in the depths of the night, when the mandarin ducks called to one another at dawn, when the moonlight floated on the surface of the lake, when the wild geese lighted in the tufts of grass — at these deeply moving moments (*aware naru orifushi ni*) I secretly gathered together a few words (*koto no ha*) on these and various subjects: and what follows is just a sampling thereof.[62]

It may have been aesthetic self-indulgence (*suki*) to allow himself to be "moved" by these things, as Anpō suggests, and it may have been similarly self-indulgent to write poems on them as a result, and to share them in this way. But Anpō does not expect censure for having done so: what he offers, by way of self-justification, is, in fact, an almost deliberately trite catalog of those things in nature which were conventionally understood to be the quintessential producers of that emotional impact he calls *aware* — the effect of seeing and hearing such things which, it was understood (at least since Tsurayuki's day) is what inevitably prompts the observer to make verse (*koto no ha*), to expel *and* capture that impact and thereby make it available, through text, to be shared or appreciated by others. Any poet of Anpō's time (and others) might have offered a similar apologia for his or her poems (and many did); what is special here is simply the fact that Anpō's moving experiences — his observation of nature, the unfolding of the cycle of the seasons — took place in an exceptional place, the Kawara mansion, a space still charged by Tōru's lingering presence.

It was perhaps quite fitting, then, for Anpō to brandish these fetishes of the *waka* tradition — the seasonal sights and sounds that he says he could not ignore and could not fail to be moved by — in the context of a preface to a collection of poems produced in a place that was itself a fetish. When Tōru conveyed Shiogama to the capital — just as when Gotoba and his friends conveyed Nagara Bridge to Uji—one kind of artifice unleashed others: the creation of these new spaces and surfaces, invested in the process of their manufacture with special literary potency, gave rise, as expected, to more creation, in the form of poem texts. The Kawara no in inevitably became for Anpō what Nagara and Uji were for Gotoba's party, and what so many other spaces and places were for other poets: charged fields displaying the powerful elements of old verse, always available (even when overlooked) to the makers of new. Finding himself or herself in such a place, a *waka* poet might well have reason to believe that poem-making remained, in a sense, what it had always been, a craft intimately bound up with a cult of places and the things made in or found in and around those places. The manipulation of such places—even when represented in copies or miniatures, or by their names alone—and the manipulation of those things (features of the landscape, local products, and the like) that might ultimately be traced to them—whether physically handled, or when rendered as figure—had been productive of verse for at least as long as there had been records of verse-making. So, whether they believed in the magical force of these places and things or not, poets who found themselves in their proximity, or imagined themselves there, inevitably repeated these manipulations, in one form or another, as they set about to make new verse. Indeed, it must often have seemed to some that there was no other way to go about it.

Nōin (b. 988), the compiler of the first surviving *utamakura* handbook, must have been a believer in such powers and potentialities, judging from what he did and said in and about poetry in his time, or from what he is said to have done and said, according to others. Minamoto Toshiyori (1055-1129) reports (in his *Toshiyori zuinō*, the written version of his own abundant store of knowledge about the *waka* tradition) that Nōin always "carefully rinsed his mouth and throat with water before speaking about poems—and as for books of poetry, he always washed his hands before picking them up and opening them."[63] But his fussiness did not stop there: Toshiyori also tells us that Nōin insisted on getting out of a carriage and proceeding on foot when he realized that he was passing what had once been the residence of the great *Kokin*-era poet Ise, and that as long as a giant pine tree—which he insisted was one that Ise herself had planted—remained in sight, he would not get back in.[64]

Nor was Nōin the only poet to demonstrate his respect for the poets of the past so literally; in time, Nōin, and a place associated with him, would also become the objects of similar obeisances, as Toshiyori reports:

> When the poet (*utayomi*) Ukon no Taifu Kuniyuki was setting off on a journey to Michinoku, some fellow poets gathered to give him a farewell party.[65] One of

them told him, "On the day that you pass through the Shirakawa Barrier, you should dress your side-locks with water and change into formal traveling attire."

"Why is that?" asked Kuniyuki. "Will the local people be there to see how I look?"

"Really, now!" retorted the other. "How could one pass through the barrier where the monk Nōin is said to have composed the poem 'aki kaze zo fuku Shirakawa no seki' [the autumn wind is blowing at Shirakawa Barrier] in one's everyday clothes, or with one's hair in disarray?!"[66]

It seems that everybody laughed at this, but [the one who had undertaken to instruct them] said, "If you wish to show your love for the Way of Poetry, you must do such things as this, and by doing them you will become able to make poems."

"Therefore," Toshiyori concludes, "those who would indeed show their love for this Way—even in these degenerate days—should revere these examples."[67] In his reiteration of the words of Kuniyuki's instructor, whereby he applies them to Nōin's example as well, Toshiyori fully endorses the idea that such behavior is peculiarly conducive to the development of poetic skill; thus, he offers these stories as prescriptive exempla, emulation of which he holds to be a necessary part of a program of cultivation that is meant to lead to success in the field of poetry (or, at least, a subtle advancement from the status of the *utayomi* to that of a more serious, genuine poet, or *kajin*). He adds only that this is true "even in this degenerate age" (*yo no sue nari to mo*), suggesting that in an era which, in his view, has seen a falling off from the level of literary achievement of the past, such actions and attitudes are perhaps even more necessary than ever, that indeed they may be the only kinds of actions that will be of any help or efficacy in the process of becoming a true poet.

The rhetoric of a "degenerate end of an age" (*yo no sue*) used here is the secular counterpart to the Buddhist eschatological doctrine of *mappō*. Many of Toshiyori's contemporaries held and taught the view that, by the end of the Heian period, the world had entered a period so far removed in time from that in which the Buddhist teachings were originally propounded that it was now impossible for individual mortals to understand them, or to observe Buddhist precepts with any efficacy, so that the only remaining effective path to salvation was to rely upon the power of others—such as the salvific powers of Amida Buddha, which can be effectively invoked only through the most simple practices, such as sincere, respectful utterances of his name. Similarly, Toshiyori suggests that in a "degenerate age," "perfect practice" of "the Way of Poetry" is likewise impossible, but aspiring poets can nevertheless make progress through such displays of respect for their quasi-divine literary predecessors as those that he here describes.

Toshiyori apparently took his own advice on this point. According to Fujiwara Kiyosuke's *Fukuro zōshi,* a slightly later twelfth-century compendium of literary lore, Toshiyori surprised his companions when they were on their way to Ōhara for a pleasure outing by suddenly getting down from his horse at what seemed to be an insignificant spot. In response to queries he explained that the place was one formerly inhabited by the poet Ryōzen (998?–1064?), a contemporary of Nōin's; duly impressed, his companions got off their horses as well. Kiyosuke brackets this story with his own version of the story of Nōin's behavior at Ise's house, which he cites as the example to which Toshiyori was deliberately adhering when he behaved as he did at Ryōzen's.[68]

In the passage quoted above from *Toshiyori zuinō,* "to love the Way of Poetry" is *kono michi o konom[u],* and this verb *konomu* is very closely related in such discourse to the verb *suku,* the active form of *suki.* Nōin himself is reported to have offered similar advice, in similar language, according to one of Kiyosuke's many stories about him in *Fukuro zōshi*:

> Every year, when the blossoms were at their peak, Nōin would travel up to the capital from [his residence at] Kosobe.[69] He always stayed at Ōe Kin'yori's house, at Gojō Higashi no Tōin.[70] There was a flowering cherry tree in the south garden of this house, and Nōin went there for the pleasure of viewing its blossoms. . . . On these occasions, he often told Kin'yori's grandson, Kinnaka, to "Cultivate *suki*; if you do so thoroughly, you will be able to make poems" (*Sukitamae. Sukinureba uta wa yomu zo*). [This was reported by Kinnaka's son Aritsune.][71]

Nōin's annual pilgrimage to the capital was itself a demonstration of thoroughgoing *suki,* an aesthetic self-indulgence which allowed him to witness a spectacle that generations of poets had witnessed and written about so many times before him. His behavior, therefore, gave context and substance to the advice he offered, and his words, *Sukinureba uta wa yomu zo,* are self-descriptive as much as they are prescriptive for others; he, too, is equating "total *suki*" with the path to poetry itself, and he is inviting others to follow him in that direction.

In yet another episode recounted in *Fukuro zōshi,* a younger poet, Minamoto Yoritsuna (1024?–1097), is quoted as having reported that, when he first met Nōin and spent time in "pure [aesthetic] conversation" with him, Nōin averred that "It is through *suki* that I have achieved excellence in poetry" (*Ware, uta ni tassuru tokoro wa sukitamauru nari*). The pronouncement seems to have been understood both as a justified boast and as valuable authoritative advice to Yoritsuna and other aspiring poets.[72] But there were other sides to Nōin's *suki.* Alongside his admiring, if bemused, accounts of Nōin's words and deeds, Kiyosuke also accuses him of humbuggery, at least in the case of his famous Shirakawa Barrier poem. After giving his own version of the Kuniyuki story, Kiyosuke reports, "the fact of the matter is that Nōin did not actually travel to the far north. In order to produce this poem, they say, he stayed hidden in his own house and spread a rumor that he had gone off to the far north. On the other hand, there is evidence that he went there twice; it may indeed be true that he went there at least once."[73]

Kiyosuke seems to be of two minds here: he gives credence to the view, which henceforth came to be widely accepted, that the poem, or its pretext, was a fraud, but he also admits that this may not have been the case. Elsewhere, however, the allegation is rendered with less ambivalence, yet still without overt opprobrium. In *Kokon chomonjū,* for example, Nōin's ruse is described quite sympathetically:

> Since Nōin was such a complete devotee of *suki* (*itareru sukimono ni te ari-kereba*), when he composed the poem,
>> Miyako o ba kasumi to tomo ni tachishikado
>> aki kaze zo fuku Shirakawa no seki
>> I left the capital in the company of the rising mists
>> but now the autumn wind is blowing at Shirakawa Barrier
> he thought it would be a shame were he to give it out in the capital (which is where he was), and so, unbeknownst to anyone, he kept himself out of sight for some time, and exposed his face to the sun so that it might darken, and then released the poem, saying, "I composed it while I was off practicing austerities on a pilgrimage in Michinoku" (*Michinokuni no kata e shugyō no tsuide ni yomitari*).[74]

This account would have us understand the whole episode as an exercise of *suki,* an aesthetic which here seems to be achieved through recourse to deception and masquerade; the subterfuge, however, is not condemned but, rather, seems to be reported in order to illustrate the depth and extent of Nōin's commitment to and desire for *suki*—the extremes to which he was willing to go in its pursuit. Neither the poem nor the poet is explicitly taken to task for being something less than honest or genuine: if anything, there is an implicit admiration, in this telling, for Nōin's peerless ingenuity, his unfettered chutzpah.

That ingenuity in this instance first called forth the manipulation of the exoticism of "far-off" Michinoku in general and of the Shirakawa Barrier site (and name) in particular, as well as manipulation of the image or persona of the *shugyōja,* the ascetic wanderer. The chutzpah then came into play with Nōin's desire to ensure that this poem would achieve maximum effect upon its "release to the public" (*hirō*), and his belief that it would do so only if his readers could be led to believe that he was really in Michinoku, in the course of his austerities, when he wrote it. To this end, he took himself out of social circulation for a while, but went to some lengths to produce the impression that he had actually hgone away, to subject himself to the elements in pursuit of spiritual development. Yet, what he was actually pursuing was a much more worldly reward, in the form of acclaim for a poem which, according to this account, he released in such a way as to give the impression that its production was merely incidental to a greater spiritual quest (*shūgyō no tsuide ni*)—as incidental, it would seem, as the sunburn he also pretended to come home with.

The poem thus produced does not insist upon but nevertheless amply suggests that it might well have been written "on the spot," at the barrier where the winds were blowing. The impression it gives of immediacy—that it is a report of sensations recently felt, realizations recently achieved—is largely dependent on the manner of its presentation, in the control of which, according to this account, Nōin expended far more energy than in the making of the poem in the first place.[75] But, according to this account, the only winds that were really blowing were the winds of elegant literary artifice (*fūryū*). We are thus invited to read the poem retrospectively, as a celebration of just such artifice, of adroit manipulation of instruments found at hand, and of poem-making and poem-presenting as performance, the combined effect of which is an achievement to be admired *even if* exposed as a sham; for such shamming, in this tale, is valorized as consummate *suki*.

The debate as to whether Nōin was really there or not when he wrote the Shirakawa poem has gone on for centuries, and it continues even in modern scholarship, which generally holds that he *was* there.[76] Proof that the whole business was or was not a sham may make the poem seem more or less artificial but can make it no less an artifact, a contrivance, a display of knowledge, an almost (but not quite) transparent record of the process of its own manufacture. As a product of its own time, and now, the poem can be understood and appreciated as a bravura performance by an artist who has deliberately prepared himself to play his role in an equally carefully prepared scenario. His script brandishes the fetishized name of Shirakawa Barrier and the fetishized traveler's persona alongside still other thoroughly fetishized figures—the mist (*kasumi*), quintessential emblem of spring, and the "rising and parting" (*tats[u]*) of that spring mist, which here occurs and is described contiguously with the poem-speaker's act of taking his departure (*tats[u]*) from the city. All work together to emphasize the passage over and through space and time that constitutes a journey from the capital to the remote far northeastern site of the barrier, and the whole scenario works whether it is staged in the capital or at that remote site, whether it is a real or fictitious journey, precisely because these figures are all so richly invested with meaning through their prior use, and are so conspicuously available for reuse.

Thus, though it makes no overt gesture to any particular earlier poem, it is by no means difficult to see Nōin's Shirakawa Barrier poem as one that takes shape within and then in turn becomes part of a rich intertextual nexus; and this, too, is true no matter where Nōin was when he wrote it. There was, by his time, ample precedent for using this place-name in poems composed at the site as well in more playful references composed elsewhere; what it usually stood for, in both cases, was distance and separation from the capital, from the center.[77] It was to this aspect of the place's literary significance that Nōin had to address himself, in pursuit of the desired-for effect, whether he was there or not. And, by addressing it as he did, Nōin simply but effectively created a new scenario that featured himself as reenactor of the experiences of others who had previously been there, in person or in imagination; and, of course, he also created a scenario that would be recalled and reenacted by others in the future.[78]

One of those who previously had been there—or so it was understood— was Taira Kanemori (?–990). When this court poet wrote what would become (and, by Nōin's time, certainly was) one of the most conspicuous of the foundation poems for Shirakawa Barrier poesy, the site's remoteness was already fixed as the most important element of its potential poetic significance. One of the three major Heian-period barriers (check-points) in the northeastern provinces, it marked the place where an eastbound traveler entered Michinoku, the most remote province. It is the realization that he has come as far as that and must still go farther which Kanemori seeks to convey in the poem that would eventually find a place of prominence in the "Parting" chapter of the *Shūi wakashū*. The *kotobagaki* in that anthology claims that he wrote it at the site, and the poem has always been read as a reliable record of what he thought and felt there:

> tayori araba ikade miyako e tsuge yaramu
>   kyō Shirakawa no seki wa koenu to[79]
> If only I had a messenger, I certainly would send word to the capital,
>   to let them know that today I have crossed the Shirakawa Barrier.

To say what he wishes to say, Kanemori has no need of words for "far," "distant," or "remote:" the name of Shirakawa Barrier itself conveys this for him, as does the finality of the verb form *koenu*, which suggests that the act of crossing is complete and irreversible; the anticipated increase of the traveler's sense of remoteness from home has come upon him in its fullness.

He stresses his awareness that his lines of communication with home are virtually cut off by this distance; yet, even as he laments this situation, his poem itself becomes its maker's means of conveying these sensations to those with whom he wishes to communicate in the capital, even if it can only do so at some time long after those sensations were originally felt. Thus, a poem in which Kanemori portrays himself pathetically, grieving for his losses and his dislocation, also becomes a medium for renewal and reaffirmation of his links with home.

And what he seeks to convey in this report of his emotions on reaching and crossing the barrier is not only the distressed disorientation and anxiety of the traveler, who has come a long way and still has a long way to go, but also something of the satisfaction of having done something and been somewhere that has value in terms of *suki,* or *fūryū*: it is the exhilaration of that traveler who finds himself, at long last and after much effort, in a place that previously has been only a name—but a significant name—to him, and to many others as well. Thus, the verb construction *koenu* may also mean "at last I've crossed it"—"at last I have had *my own* experience of this famous place!" Here, that direct experience is not seeing, as at was for Kintō and others at Nagara, but *passing over* the barrier, moving physically across the significant border that it marks. It is this news—that he has reached this distant place, and has done what one is expected to do at such a barrier (that is, "cross it," *ko[yu]*, and that he now faces all that lies beyond it—that Kanemori says he would like to convey to those whom he has left behind in the capital, were there means to do so. By making a poem out of this experience and thus providing himself with the means of communication that he says he otherwise lacks, Kanemori converts the stress of separation and dislocation into the comforts of *fūryū,* or *suki*; he sentimentalizes his actions by "singing" and writing about them, and the lyrical expulsion of the emotion he feels upon crossing the barrier serves, in turn, as evidence of his retention of the courtly sensibilities that he has brought with him from home. Even at this distance, he announces, he can turn experience into verse—verse which is made in and for the idiom of those in the capital (*miyako*), and which therefore demonstrates, once again, the accessibility, portability, and utility of that idiom, as well as the determination of its advocates to take it with them wherever they might go, even into the farthest reaches of their nation, and beyond the borders of what they viewed as its civilized core.

Bracketed with Kanemori's, Nōin's Shirakawa Barrier verse looks like yet another such demonstration of the mastery of this far-flung idiom, and a celebration of its plasticity and capacity for constant renewal through repeated, adroit manipulation—and that is perhaps exactly what it was meant to look like, whether is was composed at the geocultural margin marked at Shirakawa, as Kanemori's was believed to be, or as an act of elegant masquerade performed in the capital. In either case, it is clear that Nōin was seizing upon extant and easily recognized associations and sentiments that had accrued to Shirakawa Barrier, through both direct and other kinds of poetic experience, and that he was exploiting those accruals to their maximum effect. Compared to other famous places, the corpus of poems and the historical experience supporting this particular place's fame may have been of relatively limited scope and of relatively recent invention, but these shortcomings could not lessen the site's (or the site's name's) latent potency. *Suki*, for Nōin, meant knowing (among other things) that such potency existed and knowing how to use it; he knew, as well as anyone, that the spring mists that rose and departed with his poem-speaker/protagonist—that solitary traveler from the capital who may or may not be himself—and the autumn winds that blew through the barrier, and the barrier itself, were powerful tools of the poet's trade, and his poem showed just what he could do with them.

His *Utamakura*, or what has survived of it, was also a display of the tools of that trade and a guide to their use, just as such poems as "*Miyako o ba*" were, or came to be.[80] "Shirakawa Barrier" is there, of course, listed in two different but complementary entries: it is second in the list of the barriers that "one ought to compose upon, if one is composing about barriers" (*Seki o ba, Ausaka no seki, Shirakawa no seki, Koromo no seki, Fuwa no seki nado o yomubeshi*), and the first of some forty-two *meisho* in the list of Michinoku famous places the names of which, it is implied, should be familiar to the poet, or which are likely to be used or are appropriate to use in verse (*Michinokuni: Shirakawa no seki, Natorigawa*).[81] The first listing is a good example of what Nōin seems to be trying to do in the *Utamakura* in that it is gently prescriptive, if not exhaustive: *yomubeshi* suggests that "if one is writing about barriers, writing about *these* is likely to work out best, because these are the ones that have been written about (successfully and memorably) by others," while *nado* ("and such") seems to leave the list somewhat open-ended, for the possible consideration or inclusion of other items.[82] The second listing seems to be more straightforwardly informative, while attempting to be as thorough in its coverage of acknowledged Michinoku famous places as it is with those of the rest of the sixty-six provinces of eleventh-century Japan.[83]

If one were a traditional *waka* poet of Nōin's time, or thereabouts, one might have occasion to compose about barriers, or one of these specific barriers, or about Michinoku, in all sorts of situations, as the foregoing discussion of Kanemori's *"Tayori araba . . ."* and Nōin's *"Miyako o ba . . ."* (and other poems) has shown. The two entries in Nōin's *Utamakura* that list "Shirakawa Barrier" are designed to serve in two different but related ways, as parallel avenues of access to the poet's essential data set, the evolved and evolving *waka* lexicon; either listing, or both, might be of help should one find oneself with the task of writing a poem from any number of directions but in circumstances that might prompt one to deploy one of the previously used, and hence sanctioned, lexical items listed therein. But the *Utamakura* offers guidance in the use of much more than the names of places alone, and it is for this reason, among many, that we must understand that, for Nōin, *utamakura* probably meant something like "the specific lexical items, and the aggregate lexicon, of poetry"—as well as the systematized presentation of that lexicon, in textual format—rather than simply the place names used in poetry. Many of his entries are brief but clear explanations of words used in poetry whose meanings seem obvious, but which, without specification, might be ambiguous—for example, *Yamakawa to wa, yama ni nagaruru kawa o iu*: "The word 'mountain river' is used to mean 'a river that flows among mountains'" (that is, it does not mean "mountains *and* rivers," as the compound *sanga* might mean in Chinese). Others are glosses on figures and phrases whose meanings, without explanation, might well be missed, or which one might misuse in ignorance—for example, *midori no sode to wa, rokui o iu nari*: "'green sleeves' is used to mean 'a person of the sixth court rank.'"[84] Conventional substitutions and euphemisms are sorted out, too, as in the entry *soragoto o ba, itsuwari to iu,* which advises the reader that one word for lies, *itsuwari,* is the one to be used in poetry, whereas another, *soragoto,* might be the word more likely to be used in other styles of discourse. The entry *"Dairi, momoshiki no miya to iu"* similarly indicates that the flat (two-syllable) Chinese word *Dairi* for "Imperial Palace" is the prosaic cognate of the mellifluous, figuratively rich, and thoroughly Japanese (seven-syllable) phrase *Momoshiki no miya,* which one might be likely to encounter in a verse, and which one might therefore want to use (correctly) oneself if one needed to mention that building or its precincts.[85]

Occasionally, of course, such explanations include information about famous places, too: for example, concerning two words, one poetic and one conventional, for frog, Nōin writes: *Kawazu to wa, kaeru to iu* to explain that the word *kawazu,* used since antiquity (i.e., beginning in the *Man'yōshū*) for one kind of frog or another, is simply the equivalent of the word *kaeru,* and to imply that, if a frog is to be mentioned in verse, the word *kawazu* is preferable to *kaeru*; but he also goes on to observe that *kawazu* "are to be found in the neighborhood of a place called Ide, and in the waters of seedling fields" (*Ide no watari ni ari, nawashiro no mizu ni mo ari*).[86] He does not mean, of course, that these are the *only* places where *kawazu* are to be found, but rather that, if one is composing about *kawazu*, one would do well to place them (in one's poem) at Ide, or in a flooded rice field; conversely, if one is writing about Ide, or a flooded rice field, one would do well to put some *kawazu* there as well.

What was Nōin's basis for the formulation of such guidelines? He was, of course, not inventing the rules; he was simply recording that which he understood to have been established as (some of) the conventions of *waka* praxis—*his* praxis and that of his forebears and contemporaries. And, as previously noted, he was probably not the first poet to record such guidelines in an *utamakura* handbook; Kintō, for one, is believed to have done so, and his *Utamakura* could have been a model or source for Nōin—but nothing survives of it except its title, and, in any case, Nōin gives no explicit indications of his sources of information. Yet it is not difficult to see that what produced and supported an entry like the one on frogs, above, was the practitioner-compiler's thorough knowledge of poetry itself—the substantive minutiae derived from and definitive of *suki*—and, specifically, his knowledge of the canonical prominence of such poems as *Kokin wakashū* #125, the locus classicus for the locating of *kawazu* at Ide:

> kawazu naku Ide no yamabuki chirinikeri
> hana no sakari ni awamashi mono o[87]
>
> The kerria flowers at Ide, where frogs cry, have scattered.
> If only I had come here when they were in full bloom!

There is no poem of comparable prominence, in an imperial anthology, to support the additional locating of *kawazu* in "flooded rice-seedling fields," but there is nonetheless ample evidence elsewhere to show that the phrase *kawazu naku nawashiro mizu . . .* was as well-established in the repertoire as was *kawazu naku Ide . . .* There is, for example, a poem that begins with the former phrase in the collected works of Shigeyuki (ca. 939–ca. 1000):

> kawazu naku nawashiro mizu ni kage mireba
> toki suginikeru ware ika ni sen[88]
>
> When I see my reflection in the waters of a flooded seedling-fields where frogs sing,
>> I wonder what I can do with myself, now that the times have left me so far behind.

The phrase can also be found in use in a poem in Nōin's own private collection:

miminagusa uubekarikeri
   kawazu naku nawashiromizu no chikaki yado ni wa[89]
They should have planted those "flowers that have no ears"
   here at this inn that is so close to a flooded seedling-field where frogs sing.

Nothing is said, in *Shigeyuki shū,* as to the circumstances in which Shigeyuki made his poem; Nōin's, on the other hand, is introduced, in *Nōin Hoshi shū,* as something written "when I/he was in a place where frogs were making a terrific noise" (*kawazu no itaku naku tokoro nite*) which may be a factual contextualization but which may equally well be an afterthought. In any case, these two instances of the use of this single phrase, in poems in two clearly different moods—one self-pitying (in the conventional *jukkai* mode), the other self-consciously flippant—show us that these two poets, in two successive generations, held the phrase in common in their respective mental lexicons, and could turn to it readily as a resource in quite different compositional moments. Someone before either of them—perhaps several someones—had also said and/or written, "*kawazu naku nawashiromizu . . .,*" and so both Shigeyuki and Nōin were able to remember hearing, or seeing, those words, and knew that they would do well to reuse them.[90] Nōin's frog entry in the *Utamakura* also records such recollection, and implies that both *kawazu naku nawashiromizu . . .* and *kawazu naku Ide . . .* are phrases that are not only sanctioned for use but are, or have proven to be, durable and versatile; their portability into an array of compositional situations has been duly proven, in his view, and so both should be part of *any* poet's repertoire, just as they are a part of his own.

While Nōin's *Utamakura* is, as a whole, a concretized, written version of this personal and collective mental lexicon, rendered as an accessible and authoritative resource to be turned to for guidance either in preparing for or in the very midst of the task of composition, it is, perforce, eclectic rather than encyclopedic. Inclusions and exclusions seem arbitrary—perhaps reflecting a somewhat casual or unsystematic approach to the task of handbook-making, or perhaps reflecting the subsequent fragmentation of the text—but that very arbitrariness, coupled with the text's gently prescriptive rhetoric, also seems to reflect the evolving state of *waka* itself as it lies somewhere between the two poles of "pure," spontaneous self-expression (such as that which was believed to have produced Kanemori's Shirakawa poem), on the one hand, and self-consciously crafted, conventional composition (such as that which was suspected in Nōin's), on the other. The habit of looking back for matériel, for models, and for ideal (or idealized) principles of composition was, by his time, a defining characteristic of the *waka* tradition itself, and, in this *Utamakura*—this "foundation for poem-making,"

as it were—Nōin looked back at what had been done in the past, and also
looked at what he and his contemporaries were doing, and then recorded
what he and they knew, and what seemed to matter, concerning how poems
had been made in the past, because such knowledge was of the utmost
importance in determining how they were to be made in the present, and
would, presumably, continue to be of utmost importance in the future. The
data he shared may appear to be a mass of trivia, but, to him, each item, and
all such items collectively, were elements of a body of irreplaceable know-
how, of inestimable value. Writing them down was one way not only to make
them more accessible, but also to ensure their preservation. In a sense, it
was also an ultimate exercise of *suki*—a utilitarian display of Nōin's personal
store of expertise, a brandishing of the contents of his poetic armory. It
revealed both his pride in his personal possession of this body of knowledge
and a willingness to share it, by opening it up for inspection and use by
others.

One more story, once more from *Fukuro zōshi*, allows us to see Nōin
sharing in an analogous display of things, not words—but they are things
that have value precisely because of their relationship to the words of poetry.
The story also shows Nōin meeting his match, as it were, in the field of *suki*,
in a gentleman named Fujiwara Toshinobu:[91]

> Toshinobu, the head of the Crown Prince's archers, was a great connoisseur
> (*sukimono nari*). When he met Nōin for the first time, both men were deeply
> impressed by one another. "I have something that I would like to show you," Nōin
> said, "to commemorate your gracious visit," and he drew from within his robes a
> brocaded pouch. Inside it was a single piece of wood-shaving. Showing this to
> Toshinobu, Nōin said, "This is my great treasure. It is a shaving made at the time
> of the construction of the Nagara Bridge."
>   Toshinobu was thrilled, and then he also took an object wrapped in paper from
> within the folds of his own robe. He unwrapped it and showed that inside lay the
> dried body of a frog. "This is a frog from Ide," he explained. Both men were
> extremely pleased. Then each returned his treasure to its place of safe-keeping,
> and the two parted company. People of the present would no doubt call them
> foolish.[92]

Neither his contemporaries nor any of his later admirers have left us any
detailed description of the process of data-collecting that led up to the
production of Nōin's *Utamakura*, and so we can only imagine what that
process involved; here, however, is a glimpse of him in the guise of another
sort of collector, the *suki*-aficionado of *waka* memorabilia, of curios rendered
invaluable by their capacity for standing for the value, and the history, of
waka itself. Kiyosuke, the latter-day rapporteur of this incident, realizes all

too well that few in his own time would understand or sympathize with these two *sukimonos*' antiquarian zeal and pride, their insuppressible delight in the private possession of these tangible fragments of *waka*'s past. Others might call it foolishness (*oko*), but Kiyosuke himself seems to have understood their exhilaration in being able to hold in their own hands objects that had for so long been celebrated, along with the names of their places of origin, in the language of verse—objects of such antiquity that their existence seemed now to be limited almost exclusively to the realm of verse, confined to the dimension of words—but which now were reconfirmed and rematerialized as *things* once more. And the story of their delight in the discovery of their mutual fetishism itself needed telling and needed to be preserved, as much as did these bits of the past that they held in their hands, if that understanding and that sympathy were to be kept from dying out altogether. So, Kiyosuke collected this tale of collectors, and added it to the store of words that he and others would collect and circulate as part of the process of keeping the *waka* tradition and its receding past alive for the present.

One of his many successors in that effort was Kamo no Chōmei (1153?-1216), who is best known as the author of the reclusionist memoir *Hōjōki* (An account of my ten-foot-square hut), but who was also an active and authoritative participant in court poetry circles, and, like Toshiyori, Kiyosuke, and many others, also eventually put together his own miscellaneous collection of *waka* lore, the *Mumyōshō*.[93] There, inter alia, Chōmei describes some of his own direct encounters with the residues of *waka*'s past—some of them at the very sites, or the reputed sites of that past's unfolding; and in these descriptions we see the development of his concern with the problems involved in preserving knowledge of that past, and his efforts to participate in its preservation. He tells, for example, of going all the way to the Miidera monastery (Onjōji, over the mountains to the east of the capital, near the banks of Lake Biwa) to meet a certain monk named Enjitsu, who claimed to be the only living person able to identify the precise location of a freshwater spring that had often been featured in poetry as one of the prominent features in the vicinity of the Ausaka Barrier.[94] Enjitsu told Chōmei at their precisely dated encounter—in the tenth month of the first year of the Kenryaku era (1211)—that "There seems to be hardly anyone who takes any interest, as you seem to do, in learning about ancient matters; this is a rare pleasure. I can hardly do less than show you where to go," and so the two men proceeded together to a spot in a little hollow, marked by a small stone stūpa, which apparently was the site of the spring. "It is only some thirty meters off the main road," says Chōmei, "and it lies behind a cluster of small buildings; but, since there is no water in it, there is really nothing to see. Still, the lingering residues of its ancient past seemed to float up in visions before my eyes (*mukashi no nagori omokage ni ukabite*), and I was able to sense something of its wonted elegance (*yū ni nan oboehaberishi*)."[95]

After his scramble through the brush with Enjitsu, Chōmei is understandably disappointed to find that "there was really nothing to see" at this famous place, but he nonetheless claims to have been able to see, or sense, the aura of the place's past, bequeathed to it and preserved through the medium of poetry. It is in his conjured vision (*omokage*) of the richness of that past that Chōmei feels the impact of what he calls its "elegance" (*yū*, a word often glossed as the equivalent of *fūryū*).[96] Thus, in place of a place that has become (or perhaps always was) rather mundane—just a little spring, in what is now a dry hollow—Chōmei "sees" a substitute, parallel place, still fed, or fed again, by refreshing waters; once again, as it was with Nōin and Toshinobu, *fūryū*, or *suki*, has become a force for preservation, or reconstruction, of what otherwise might be or actually has been lost.

On another occasion, Chōmei hears with great interest, and records in detail, a friend's report of a visit to Ide, with an emphasis on the friend's dismay in finding that no kerria bushes were to be seen there—since they had all apparently been cut down to make way for more profitable crops—and that, furthermore, no trace could be found of the ancient villas of the Tachibana family, the Nara-period aristocrats who, it was believed, played a role in bringing the *Man'yōshū* into being and thereby caused Ide to be associated in another way with poetry itself.[97] The friend is happy to report, on the other hand, that the famous Ide frogs, at least, are still there in profusion, and he urges Chōmei to go to Ide and hear them for himself. This, Chōmei regrets, he has been unable to do:

> This story made a very deep impression on me, but alas, three years have passed since then and I have not gone there yet. I have grown old, and find foot-travel difficult, and so, though I have given it much thought, I still have not heard the voices of those frogs. . . . And when I think about it, I fear that in the future there will be precious few men who, even if they happen to have some reason to go there and see the place for themselves, will be inclined to stop and listen to the song of the frogs. This is because there is less and less inclination toward such aesthetic matters, and less and less sympathy for them, with each passing year [*hito no suki to kokoro to wa, toshitsuki ni soete otoroete yuku yue nari*].[98]

If his friend's story made a "deep impression" on Chōmei, as he says (*kono koto, kokoro ni shimite imijiku oboeshikado*), it must have been, in part, because it told of the partial survival of Ide as it once had been: though it has lost its *yamabuki* and its grand villas, it still has its frogs, and Chōmei agrees that he, too, should make haste to go and hear them, before their song is lost as well. He wants to do so, as he explains, not only to satisfy his own antiquarian curiosity, but also to help, in some small way, to stem the decline of *suki*, to assist in the cultivation of understanding of and sympathy with the past. Yet, Chōmei says, age and infirmity have deprived him of his chance at having the direct, unmediated experience of "hearing the song of the frogs"; failing that, however, he must be satisfied with writing about the desirability of having that experience and thereby implicitly urging others to try to have that experience for themselves, before it is too late.

The efforts of men like Kiyosuke and Chōmei, to preserve knowledge of the ways in which knowledge of the way of *waka* had been preserved by men like Nōin, were not in vain; for centuries, their various efforts to collect the memorabilia of *waka*'s past, in the form of things as well as words, would serve as reminders of what poem-making had been, how it had shaped and been shaped by the aesthetics of *fūryū* and *suki*, how *sukimono* eccentricity or foolishness (*oko*) had often come to the rescue of perishable sentiments and sympathies, and of perishable goods as well—goods that were fetishized by the *sukimono*-aesthetes as emblems of the *waka* tradition itself. And even when that tradition had, in a sense, been eclipsed, or displaced by the emergence of more popular, contemporary genres—in the seventeenth, eighteenth, and nineteenth centuries, for example, by which time the arts of *haikai* (light verse) and especially the *hokku* (or *haiku*, the seventeen-syllable verse of the kind that might open a *haikai no renga* sequence) had long since flowered over and out of the remains of *waka*—there would still be poets who would remember these "eccentric" acts, and would model some of their own creative and recreative efforts on them.

One of those who did so was Yosa Buson (1716–1783). The *Shin hana-tsumi* memoir (written in 1777 about experiences in the 1740s, including the acquisition and relinquishing of a bit of Natorigawa *umoregi*, and his friends' recovery and reuse of it)[99] reads, in part, like a fragmented commentary on such eccentricities, and a meditation on their meaning for later times. Buson is none too sympathetic with the fetishism of those whom he here remembers, but he does seem to understand what motivated their avid coveting and collecting. At one point, for example, he writes:

> A certain person was deeply attached to a dagger-guard which, it was said, had been fashioned from a decorative nail-head cover from the Xian-yang Palace [of the first Chinese Emperor]:[100] the owner wore it constantly on his hip and treasured it fervently. How richly do such ancient objects of metal molded into

representations of flowers and birds evoke a thousand years and more of antiquity! But it is useless to fuss about what proof there may be that this is a Xian-yang Palace nail-cover. The thing would be something to treasure even if it were not said to be a Xian-yang Palace nail cover, but, unfortunately, no one seems to think of it this way.[101]

Here, as in many of the thematically related episodes in the memoir, Buson deems the cited example of antiquarian fetishism worthy of recollection and retelling—yet he seems to question the process that placed such great value on the coveted, treasured "thing." If anything, he suggests, he would prefer to seek such value as it possesses in the thing itself, rather than in the claims made by its owners and manipulators, who would estimate that value by their own lights. To Buson, the tale of this object's ancient and exotic provenance is dubious, and in the absence of "proof," he seems to argue, that tale cannot be the guarantor of the object's value: so, instead, its inherent qualities—its visual beauty and the marks of craftsmanship—must be seen for what they are, and left at that.

Next, as if in free-association on matters of this kind, Buson writes, "If someone of the present day were to say that he owns one of the pillars from the Nagara Bridge, or the preserved body of a frog from Ide, I'm sure that most people would think that person an utter fool, and would refuse to believe his claim" (*Nagara no hashikui, Ide no hoshikawazu mo, ima no yo no hito mochitsutaetaramashikaba, asamashiku obotsukanaki koto ni hito mōshiasamihaberame*).[102] Buson, it is clear, has read his *Fukuro zōshi*, and remembers, in particular, the Nōin and Toshinobu episode. He remembered it a few years later, as well, and, in letters to disciples written in the winter of 1782 and again in the following autumn, he wrote an abridged version of their story as a *kotobagaki* for one of his own *hokku*:

> Kakuya no Osa Tachihaki Toshinobu was a *sukimono* without equal. Remembering how, at his first encounter with the Kosobe Monk [Nōin], the two men felt the need to show one another their treasures, and how Nōin proved his elegant connoisseurship by displaying the contents of a brocade bag—and, deeply stirred by the sights of spring—I wrote [the *hokku*],
>
> yamabuki ya
> Ide o nagaruru kannakuzu.[103]
> Kerria roses!
> and, flowing down Ide's stream, wood shavings.

Furthermore, in one of these letters, Buson adds these comments on this composition:

> I wrote the poem you see here with this amusing old story [of Nōin and Toshi-

nobu] in mind. But on the surface it will appear that I have simply described a pleasing scene, with gentle spring sunlight and a suggestion that the wood shavings are drifting down from some place upstream on the Ide River, where peasants are building a cottage. It is frequently the case that the reading of a Chinese poem can be explained in two ways; the same holds true for *haikai*.[104]

Thus does the poet and painter instruct his followers, revealing "what was on his mind" (*shitagokoro*) as he wrote the poem while spelling out what he thinks most readers, lacking this knowledge, will be likely to make of it. But, of course, the *kotobagaki* says as much—that Buson recalled the story of Toshinobu and Nōin and found it amusing (*omoshiroki*); and that then, on some warmly sunlit late spring day, in a reflective mood, he composed this gentle paean to their elegant eccentricity (*suki, fūryū*). The poem opens with *yamabuki*—Ide's other most famous feature, along with its frogs—as its seasonal emblem-word (*kigo,* emphatically marking the setting as "late spring"); and then its speaker espies what, to the knowing reader, need not be shavings from some peasant's plane but Nōin's very own fragment of the Nagara Bridge, drifting even at this moment in the strong (spring) current of the Ide stream—that is, in the very waters from which the dried frog that Toshinobu matched with Nōin's shaving was said to have been obtained. In either case, these wood shavings catch the eye of an observer, who would otherwise see nothing that is not natural in the scene, and, as Buson suggests in his letter, they may be read as a disruption of this timeless and elegant setting by evidence of quaint human labor going on "upstream," out of sight if not undetected. By this means, the *hokku* imitates, in miniature, a range of poems as old, if not older, than several in the *Kokinshū,* in which observers of a stream at hand detect conditions that pertain upstream through evidence brought before their eyes in the flowing current.[105] The overt juxtaposition of stillness against movement—here, the kerria roses (stationary on the banks) posed vis-à-vis the wood shavings (flowing in the stream) is also a legacy from *waka* translated into the tighter spaces of this *hokku*; and the ostensible peasant cottage under construction upstream—as it appears—is also a latter-day rustic counterpart to the wonted grandeur of the Tachibana villas that gave Ide its first fame. The result of all this is both an adroit rearrangement of Ide's poetic properties and a deliberate deflation of the elegance that would attend upon the naming of that place in *waka*: or, to put it another way, it is a discovery of (or, an insistence upon) Ide's *ordinariness*, not unlike the disappointing discoveries made there by Chōmei's friend—as well as an acknowledgement that there is, nonetheless, a beauty to be found in that very ordinariness—that is, in whatever can still be (or might be) seen at Ide, in that very juxtaposition of its kerria roses and those mysterious wood shavings.

Thus, in several simultaneous dimensions, Buson nods to his inheritances, in a mixture of reverence and bemusement; and, in this sense, his Ide *hokku* is a very good example of *haikai* insouciance vis-à-vis the literary past. It is an exercise infused with that spirit (or pose) by means of which the practitioners of *haikai* sought to lighten the load of tradition that weighed upon them, while stopping short of totally shedding that weight. Buson's own insouciance is, as we have seen, a part of what he is chronicling in the *Shin hanatsumi* memoir, and it is evident, again, in the section that follows the reference to the Nōin-Toshinobu episode:

> The ancient Korean tea bowl formerly owned by Tokiwa Tanpoku was once the treasured possession of Ōtaka Gengo, one of the famous "loyal retainers of Ako."[106] It was passed down from hand to hand from Gengo and eventually came into my own possession. Its transmission from owner to owner is a matter of record, yet what serves as the basis for its authenticity? It will hereafter end up just like that Xian-yang nail-cover, and for this reason I soon gave it away to someone else.[107]

Again, Buson insists that he is immune to the attractions of "treasured objects" (*kibutsu*) whose fame rests largely on such claims as may be made about their past ownership, and again the problem seems to be lack of proof. In this case, there is a very clear record of ownership, but Buson doubts that that record will count for much for long. Aware, however, that others may not feel the same as he—or, perhaps, to save himself the trouble of caring for such a supposedly precious thing—he simply bequeaths it to another owner.

It is as this point, then, that Buson tells his Natorigawa *umoregi* story— about its provenance, its presentation, its weight, its loss and recovery. It, too, was an object with a pedigree—but, even if the Ten'rin'in abbot seemed to make much of this, Buson was not inclined to do so. It, too, bore the marks of past, loving possession: polished to a dazzling gleam, it was an object beautiful to hold and behold, and the grains of the wood that it had once been did catch Buson's eye, and did hold his attention—but not for long. It was too heavy; it could not be borne. It was left behind. And then it was found again, and made into something new and of use in the ongoing business of poem-making (like Gotoba's Nagara poetry desk)—but by others. Buson refused, in this instance—as in others?—to play the role of *sukimono* that others would have thrust upon him; toward their *fūryū*, and its fetishes, he maintained his attitude of indifference and nonchalance. And yet the story is worth his telling, though decades have passed since these events occurred. Telling it, Buson places himself inside the circle of his friends but outside the circle of their fetishism; still, he lets us know that their avidity— their way of cultivating their ties with their past—deserves to be remembered, and he lets his readers try, if they will, to understand, even if he claims that he can not.

And perhaps, in retrospect, Buson felt some regret for his own insouciance; perhaps, looking back upon these events, he did in fact understand the sentiment that had moved his friends but which had, it seems, at the time left him untouched—until now. For he did, after all, write thus in the memoir: "One should do whatever one can to take possession of things that one seeks to possess and one should make haste to see things that one wishes to see. Do not casually assume that there will be other opportunities to see or possess such things. It is very unlikely that another chance of obtaining such satisfaction will come along."[108]

So the abbot's gift—that gleaming, heavy piece of what had once been a buried tree—was, indeed, "a thing not to be taken lightly" after all: its weight had meaning, but it would take time, and a rereading of the past, to prove it.

4

The Saishōshitennōin Poems and Paintings

The Saishōshitennōin monastery was built by Retired Emperor Gotoba in 1207, in a votive act designed to recapitulate the votive architectural projects of his royal ancestors and also to enlist divine aid for his drive to undermine the recently established Kamakura shogunate. Within a few years, however, the Saishōshitennōin was literally deconstructed, and, if reports in contemporary sources are accurate, it seems to have been dismantled, moved, and partially reconfigured on a site not far from its original location where Sanjō (a major east-west thoroughfare) crossed the Shirakawa River in eastern Kyoto. So almost as soon as it was completed it ceased to be, or in any case ceased to be what its creator, Gotoba, had intended it to be. Although in a material sense it was, then, as ephemeral as the river's bubbles and froth and the mansions of the mighty described in the opening lines of Kamo no Chōmei's *Hōjōki* (composed ca. 1212), its brief existence nonetheless marks the intersection of significant cultural, political, and historical forces. And, in another dimension, the Saishōshitennōin does survive—in the written records of the circumstances and processes that brought it into being and then so quickly obliterated all but a few of its traces.

The most substantial of these traces are poems that were written for inscription on sliding doors (*shōji*, what are now called *fusuma*) in the Emperor's quarters within the building. Both the poems and the paintings on these *shōji* celebrated selected famous places—*meisho* or *nadokoro*—from various parts of Japan, and thus they also celebrated Gotoba, the quondam sovereign of these representative places, who had caused their images to be made. This was, then, an important moment in the long history of *utamakura meisho* poetry and painting and their interaction, especially within the context of Imperial patronage and the inculcation of an evolving ideology of Imperial rule. That the decorations of the monastery should have featured the themes and imagery of famous places was, of course, no accident, nor simply an exercise of the current fashion in interior decor. Fashionable and elegant it may have been; but this pictorial and textual scheme was also designed to give visual form to the objective that underlay the construction of the monastery in the first place—that is, the revivification of a vision of national unification under the Imperial house. Moreover, the poem-and-painting program was itself a means toward that end, embodying, as did the building itself, a magical or ritual invocation, an assertion of Imperial sovereignty and Gotoba's personal authority, and an enactment of his relationship to the lands ruled—or, once ruled—by him and by the Imperial house. Thus, poetry, painting, architecture, and religious symbolism were all called into play here in an effort to reassert Imperial claims to supremacy in a time of uncertainty and change.

But the effort was in vain, at least insofar as Gotoba was concerned, for the shogunate prevailed, and Gotoba did not. The powers of the words and images invoked in the Saishōshitennōin seem to have had little or no lasting effect, except for the fact that we can remember and try to understand what was attempted in and through them—a kind of last-ditch effort to work a kind of magic, by summoning, through text and picture, powers that had been invoked repeatedly in ages past to protect and promote the interests and ideologies of Imperial rule.

It is in *Jōkyūki*, a literary chronicle of the events leading up to and beyond Gotoba's abortive attempt to overthrow the Kamakura shogunate in 1221, that we find the most explicit account of Gotoba's apparent motive for constructing the Saishōshitennōin: he built the monastery, we are told, as a curse upon the *bakufu*—that is, as the embodiment of a vengeful prayer, formulated in the exorcistic phrase *Kantō chōbuku* (Subdue the Kantō).[1] If this report is at all accurate—even as an interpretation in hindsight—it suggests that the Saishōshitennōin project was but one of the several means through which Gotoba sought, over a period of several years—and, in the event, unsuccessfully—to bring about the downfall of the paramilitary government, based in the east ("Kantō"), which was causing him so much irritation through its de facto usurpation of what had heretofore been the exclusive prerogatives of Imperial rule.[2]

Jōkyūki goes on to say that immediately after the assassination of the shogun Minamoto Sanetomo in Kamakura in 1219 (a deed in which Gotoba appears to have had no direct involvement)—and also because of fears that the curse would also cause pollution of the waters of the Shirawaka—the Saishōshitennōin was "deconstructed," at Gotoba's behest. Other records give conflicting information about the building's eventual fate, but it is nevertheless clear that the Saishōshitennōin itself (and not the *bakufu*) was caused to collapse, and that this occurred in tandem with the collapse of Gotoba's hopes for the restoration and revival of the Imperial institution in a form something like that it had had when he inherited it from his forebears but which, in fact, had been forever altered by events that unfolded during his lifetime and as the result of crises in which he himself played a major part.

The reliability of the *Jōkyūki*'s retrospective reading of Gotoba's purposes may, of course, be questioned; but even without this reading of the Saishō-shitennōin (and its contents) as the manifestation of a politically motivated curse, there is ample evidence—in the building's other extant "traces"—of what it seems to have been about. The surviving poems and plans for the paintings that decorated the Saishōshitennōin *shōji* themselves suggest that the project embodied a bravado display of Imperial—and Gotoba's—claims to authority over the Japan that had been, the Japan that was, and the Japan that would be. These were claims that needed reiteration, for they had been, were being, and would be tested in these times to the point of negation. The form that this reiteration took was recollective: it involved the manufacture of images (in poem texts and landscape paintings) that were simulacra of other images that had been made and used again and again for similar purposes, though perhaps never in such extremis. Or, one might say, Gotoba's desperate nostalgia for another time—for a way of life that was fast slipping away—took form, at his request and with his input, in the production of poems and paintings for the Saishōshitennōin *shōji* that served his purposes precisely by being just as deeply intertextual—in every sense—as were most of the famous-place poems and famous-place paintings that had been made, either separately or in joint programs, on virtually every prior occasion. Those prior occasions were, in turn, evoked here, individually and in aggregate, through the allusive gestures to the "old" that were incorporated in these "new" poems and paintings.

And these allusive gestures, and this display of this intertextuality, were themselves a part of the casting of the building's spell. By reaching back to their past in this way, the makers of the Saishōshitennōin program—Gotoba and nine of the most accomplished members of his *waka* coterie, led by Teika, and the four painters who worked at their direction—sought change through the imposition of a discourse of continuity and idealized harmony, as expressed and represented in the landscapes forged in these poems and paintings, upon the real political landscape of a Japan caught up in the irresistible currents of change and in the process of a reconfiguration characterized (as it had been and would be for some time) rather by *dis*continuity and *dis*harmony. Within the Saishōshitennōin, upon its sliding doors and inside the spaces that they enclosed, a deeply nostalgic, sentimental, and defiant orchestration of sounds and sights (poems, their texts, and paintings based upon them, all sharing the same surfaces) was briefly played, in what seems to have been yet one more attempt to alter (or reread) history through these means; but, very soon, the performance was interrupted and the score for its orchestration was deliberately destroyed—by its very makers—and the attempt to change the world through *this* means was, perforce, abandoned.

The Saishōshitennōin program can be understood as yet another creative and re-creative moment in which the deeply intertextual poetics of place-name poetry were exercised and manipulated, in this case—and not for the first or last time—in circumstances shaped in large part by political conditions and in media which, while certainly decorative, are also highly energized by the precedents and objectives of ritual or "religious" praxis. The context or intertext of the Saishōshitennōin program extends far beyond the "foundation poems" to which the poems composed for it allude, and far beyond the paintings (and other sources) that provided the precedents and models for the paintings created for it. The age-old practice of creating poems and paintings celebrating the lands ruled over by Japan's sovereigns as a gesture of loyalty and of fealty and the presentation thereof at the beginning of each new reign (in association with the royal thanksgiving rite called the *Daijōe*) in the name of the people of those lands and as an embodiment of their prayer for each new Emperor's or Empress's long life and long rule (*miyo*) is but one of the many practices recapitulated, albeit in altered form, in the Saishōshitennōin plan.[3] Another is the practice of composing poems (and sometimes making paintings) in commemoration of the special visitations (*miyuki*) of Emperors and their retinues *in* their lands, on those relatively rare but

significant occasions when they left the confines of their palaces and journeyed—not necessarily far afield, nor for very long—to other parts of the
realm.[4] The poems composed for the Saishōshitennōin speak much the same
language of celebration, and often adopt the same adulatory poses, as do the
poems composed (and sometimes mounted on screen paintings) for innumerable *Daijōe* presentations (settings in which, according to many literary his-
torians, many of the most familiar patterns in the language of place-name
poesy itself took shape); and the paintings mounted on the Saishōshitennōin
doors themselves created spaces wherein their royal commissioner, Gotoba,
and his companions could enact, or reenact—or, at least, be prompted to
remember—innumerable real or imaginary *miyuki*.

Gotoba could, and did, dwell briefly among these images and texts *as if
they were* his lands, or what had once been his lands: passing through these
rooms, or seated within them, he was surrounded by representations of what
had once been and what he perhaps wished might again be *his* idealized
realm, arranged before him as a harmonious nation-scape, shaped and colored by the ordered and timeless sequence of the seasons. And the space
thus decorated was one within which both words and images might seem to
retain the meanings they had always had, or seemed to have had. The
recovery and resuscitation of those meanings, through words and pictures,
was the means chosen on this occasion for recovering and resuscitating a
geopolitical order that had given meaning to the lives of all the Emperor's
ancestors, even long after that order had ceased to be politically "real," if
indeed it ever had been. In the Saishōshitennōin, Gotoba indulged in the
illusion that such an order could be reinstated, and he deployed toward that
end the symbolic means most readily at his disposal. But perhaps even he
knew, all along, that none of this would work.

Still, the grand effort was made: the building briefly stood, the Emperor
briefly took up residence therein, and there he found surrounding him the
poems and paintings that he had caused to be made. Making them was his
whim: so was their destruction. By this time it was really only in such spheres
that his whim, and word, had such authority: otherwise virtually powerless,
this was, perhaps, all that he could do. And this was certainly a costly,
perhaps wasteful, way to exercise his will. Still, in what may have amounted
to little more than a desperate (and perhaps cynical) exercise of his royal
ego, he caused the Saishōshitennōin to be made and then soon caused it to
be taken down. The building and its contents soon were gone, but the marks
of their presence were not totally erased: the poems—the score for the
orchestrated act of conjuring—remain, and through them we can still read
the Saishōshitennōin intertext and try to recover some of what it meant.

In 1207, Gotoba was twenty-eight years old. He was not Emperor but something rather better—a Retired Emperor, enjoying immense prestige without the encumbrances of the throne itself. Some nine years had already passed since his abdication; his very young son Tsuchimikado was the reigning Emperor. In Kamakura, Minamoto Sanetomo was the nominal shogun, but *bakufu* authority—still in the process of consolidating and defining itself vis-à-vis Kyoto, the Imperial system, and other vestiges of the old order—really lay in the hands of his Hōjō relations. Also, in 1207, Gotoba's great literary project, the compilation of the *Shin kokin wakashū* (the new collection of ancient and modern Japanese poetry), which he had officially initiated in 1205, was slowly making its way to completion. Throughout this period, Gotoba was also travelling frequently—to the Kumano shrines (as we have seen in chapter 3) and elsewhere—and sponsoring and participating in gatherings at various sites for the composition of Chinese poems (*kanshi*) and linked verse (*renga*) as well as *waka* (the latter primarily, or sometimes secondarily, as part of the process of generating fine "new" poems for the new anthology), and enjoying various athletic pursuits—archery, hunting, and especially football (*kemari*)—too. And, it appears, if the *Jōkyuki* account of the Saishōshitennōin is accurate, that he was already spoiling for a fight with Kamakura. It would be some fourteen years, however, before hostilities would break out openly, in what has come to be called the Jōkyū War of 1221.

While the fine-tuning of the contents of the *Shin kokin wakashū* continued, amid the above-mentioned and still other activities, Gotoba and the favored poets of his circle continued to meet in several formal literary gatherings to match new poems: in the spring of 1207, for example, Gotoba and his coterie offered the products of two *utaawase* (held in the second and third months) to each of the Upper and Lower Kamo Shrines in turn. Among the participants on both occasions were some of the chief contributors to the ongoing *Shin kokin wakashū* project, including the Tendai prelate Jien, Teika and his friendly rival Fujiwara Ietaka, and Teika's adopted sister—actually, his niece—who is usually referred to in the records of these events as Shunzei's Daughter. All four of these poets would be among those recruited for the Saishōshitennōin project just a few weeks later.

Also, at various times leading up to and through the *Shin kokin*-editing period, various members of this coterie planned and carried out some compositional projects that specifically brought poetry and painting together for celebratory purposes, as they were for the Saishōshitennōin as well. Back in 1190, when the powerful regent Kujō Kanezane's daughter Ninshi (later Senshumon'in) was presented at court as the very young Gotoba's new consort, a celebratory screen depicting scenes of the twelve months on its four panels (that is, a *tsukinami byōbu*) was ordered for presentation at the welcoming ceremonies. (This was, in itself, a "revival," and extension, of such presentation practices, some early instances of which—from various courtly celebrations held during the last decades of the ninth century—are recorded, for example, in the "Felicitations" [*ga no uta*] section of the *Kokin wakashū* and in the fifth book of "miscellaneous" poems in the *Shūi wakashū*.)[5] The eight contributing poets included Kanezane himself and several other august senior members of the extended Fujiwara-clan hierarchy, including Ninshi's brother Yoshitsune, who would soon become a great favorite of Gotoba's and a mainstay of his poetic coterie (until his early death, at age thirty-eight, in 1206) as well as Fujiwara Shunzei, the preeminent poet of the day, and his heir, Teika.[6]

Some thirteen years later, on the occasion of Shunzei's ninetieth birthday, Gotoba himself ordered the preparation of another screen, and poems to be inscribed upon it, to honor the revered poet's attainment of this great age. (By this time Shunzei had retired and had taken Buddhist vows and a priestly name, Shaku'a.) In the eighth month of 1203, Gotoba announced the topics for the four panels of the four-season screen to a select group of coterie poets, including six men—Gotoba himself, Yoshitsune, Jien, Teika, Fujiwara Ariie and Fujiwara (a.k.a. Asukai) Masatsune, and four distinguished women —Shunzei's Daughter, Kunaikyō (a Shunzei protégée), and two of Ninshi's ladies-in-waiting, the cousins Sanuki and Tango. Six of these poets—Gotoba, Jien, Teika, Ariie, Masatsune, and Shunzei's Daughter—were among those brought together again in 1207 for the Saishōshitennōin project, and some of what they would do then—in the manipulation of a time-tested vocabulary of festive figures, adaptable to several kinds of celebration—would, not surprisingly, bear some resemblance to what they did to honor Shunzei in 1203.[7]

It was in the fourth month of 1205 (Genkyū 2) that Gotoba issued an order for the construction of a new religious complex (and residence for himself) at Sanjō Shirakawa, in a sector of the city in which several of his royal ancestors had also built their votive temples.[8] The site for the new building had been ceded to the Retired Emperor by Jien, who held it by right of descent in his capacity as Abbot of the Shōren'in monastery (a major Tendai establishment), which was nearby.[9] Like the names of several of its neighbors, the name chosen for Gotoba's monastery would refer to the title of the "Sūtra of Wondrous Golden Light and the Supreme King,'" the *Konkōmyō saishōōkyō*, a scripture particularly favored by Japanese Emperors ever since their first formal adoption of Buddhism because of its promises to bring celestial aid and protection to royal sponsors of its worship.[10]

In what amounted to an allusive gesture to this sūtra and to the institutions that were its predecessors in the Sanjō-Shirakawa quarter or nearby—among them, the Hosshōji, the Sonshōji, the Saishōji, the Jōshōji, and the two Enshōji—the names of all of which suggested complete, enduring victory to be achieved through the scripturally guaranteed alliance of royal and celestial forces—Gotoba's institution was to be called the Saishōshitennōin, "the monastery of the Four Conquering Deva Kings [as described in the *Konkōmyō saishōōkyō*]."[11]

Thus, even in its name—as well as in its contents—the Saishōshitennōin was a replication and extension of precedent, an exercise in retrospective reconfiguration, and a public demonstration that some (if not all) royal practices of the past could still be revived, and continued, as if in flagrant defiance of the changing times. And, of course, the name of the monastery was also a literal sign of Gotoba's hope of enlisting the aid of the Four Deva Kings (*Shitennō*) in the advancement of his own grand cause. The monastery was thus shown, through this appellation, to be the material manifestation of Gotoba's belief in and worship of the words of the sūtra in which such aid was pledged, and a signal that the erection of the building was in itself an act of supplication in their honor and a grand display of Gotoba's powers—alongside which, he prayed, their far greater powers might also be aligned.

But the Saishōshitennōin project was in fact conceived by Gotoba on a more modest scale than that of the royal temples to which its name bore such strong resemblance and which also, in their way, had invoked divine favor for his ancestors. According to the account of the project in Minamoto Ienaga's diary, Gotoba feared that the new building, like so many of the grandiose structures of this and other kinds raised by his royal predecessors, might all too soon be reduced to "dust and ashes."[12] This may have been one reason why he built, on this occasion, what was at least in name a cloister (*in*) rather than a full-scale temple (*ji, tera*). Another reason may have been an anticipated need to preserve resources for other causes. Still, the project was one that drew heavily upon the financial wherewithal and organizational skills of many groups and individuals who were in one way or another beholden to Gotoba. Thirty courtiers took it upon themselves to sponsor the preparation of *keman* ("garlands" of wrought metal) for the Buddha images, and donations of other votive implements, including the image platforms (*daiza*) and backdrops (*kōhai*), were also pledged from "aristocratic sources" (*kisho*).[13] And Ienaga, perhaps without a great deal of exaggeration, says that, despite Gotoba's relatively modest intentions, the project nonetheless inspired "peasants and farmers from the various provinces to turn their backs on their fields and head up to the capital to assist in the project by digging the ponds, raising the dikes, and laying the foundations."[14] For the moment, then, it seems that the Saishōshitennōin project became a temporary focus for the energies and resources of many of those, in many social strata, who in one way or another owed Gotoba their cooperation and support.

Participation in the planning of and contributions to the program of poems and paintings planned for the building was, of course, yet another way that courtiers (particularly those of relatively modest means) could give something of their own to the Saishōshitennōin votive project as a whole; and, once invited (and thus obliged) to donate in this manner, these and the other participants—both high and low—may have had reason to expect to share in such merit as the monastery's completion and dedication might generate. And there were, apparently, multiple avenues for participation that did not necessarily involve either great expense or intense physical labor. From early on, it seems, Gotoba planned to have Chinese poems (*shi*) inscribed on his *shōji* along with the famous-place *waka* and the landscape paintings that would also be prepared. Teika reports in his diary that a meeting was held to plan these *shi* at the home of the regent, Konoe Iezane, on the twentieth day of the fourth month of 1207. During this session it was argued that, because the *uta* (*waka*) on the screens would be new, the *shi* should be old (which means, presumably, that they would be quotations from classic Chinese verses). It was felt, furthermore, that the *kanshi* poets of the day might not be equal to the task of composing new *shi* that would be good enough for the occasion. But Gotoba insisted on new *shi* anyway, and ordered Iezane and three other courtiers (Fujiwara Yoshisuke [the younger brother of Ninshi and Yoshitsune], Fujiwara Sukezane, Fujiwara Mitsunori, and Fujiwara Nagakane) to prepare them.[15]

Thus, the program that was in preparation at this stage was not only in multiple media (poetry and painting, as well as architecture) but in multiple genres (*waka* and *kanshi*), too. In this way, one might say, the Saishōshitennōin plan called for simultaneous and overlapping use of several of the most revered and prestigious textual and visual/spatial languages of the day—that is, *waka* and Chinese poetry, painting and architectural design—in a no-holds-barred attempt to get "results" through the application of the best of several available means of supplication to the divine powers-that-were. Even if these *kanshi* were completed and inscribed as Gotoba ordained, they do not now survive in any records, so we can only guess at how they might have interacted with the Japanese poems and paintings of Japanese scenes alongside which they were meant to be seen and read.[16] One may suppose, however, that, in contrast to the *waka* that were eventually made and which make no reference whatsoever to the Buddhist setting of the Saishōshitennōin or to Buddhist ritual or scripture of any kind, the *kanshi* commissioned from Iezane and company may well have featured some relatively direct engagement with Buddhist texts, because their language—Chinese—would have been one and the same as that of the translated sūtras that lay at the heart of Buddhist liturgy and of both monastic and lay devotion. But, of course, the composition of *kanshi* in entirely secular modes was by no means unheard of—it was, indeed, the most common sort of Chinese verse written by Japanese poets—and so the *kanshi* for the Saishōshitennōin may well have borne a rather close resemblance to the Saishōshitennōin *waka*, and may well have differed from them largely in form (including visual, graphic form, if inscribed on the *shōji*) rather than in content.[17]

At about the same time that Iezane held the meeting to discuss the proposed *kanshi* program, Teika was informed that Gotoba wanted him to head a team of courtier-poets in the selection of a series of the famous places that would serve as the topics of the Japanese poetry-and-painting part of the decoration program. And so, on the day after the gathering held at Iezane's, Teika attended a Wakadokoro meeting with Ietaka, Ariie, Minamoto Michitomo, and other courtier-poets and proceeded to prepare a list of suggested *meisho* and to select the positions in which the poems and paintings representing those sites would eventually be mounted. Teika's record of the resulting designations is incomplete, but it does give us some idea of how the program was envisioned at this stage:

> In the southeast quarter, on the south façade, in the public rooms (where the curtains will, on occasion, be raised), there will be three *shōji* bays: this is were the *meisho* of Yamato (Kasugano, Yoshinoyama, Miwayama, Tatsutayama) should be drawn. To the west thereof, on the south façade, the *meisho* of Settsu (Naniwa and the like) should be drawn.
>
> In the farthest reaches of the eastern quarter is the hall of musical instruments (*gakuso*). (This is quite spacious, with several rooms.) This is where Michinoku should be drawn. (There are a number of "famous places" of great mysteriousness in this province, and they may be difficult to work with. This is why they are to be treated in the remote quarter of the *gakuso*. This cannot be done satisfactorily on balustrades; this is why it will be done in these relatively hidden spaces.) In the Emperor's living quarters, depict Yamashiro. On one side of the bedchamber: Toba and Fushimi, and among the *shōji* on the west side (in his sitting room): Minase and Katano. In front of these, depict Harima; and near the shelves (on one side of the dining room): Shikama Market.[18]

What is most striking in these partial notes for the plan is the emphasis placed on "famous places" that were literally close at hand, in the home province of the capital, Yamashiro, and its closest neighbors, Yamato and

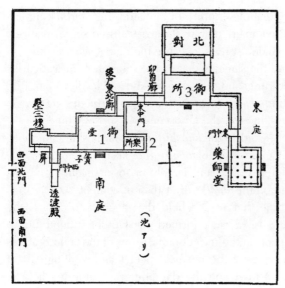

9. *Plan of the Saishōshitennōin buildings, adapted from
the reconstruction by Fukuyama Toshio (plate 37,*
Nihon kenchiku shi no kenkyū) *based on a description
in Son'en's* Mon'yōki. *The structures marked (1) Midō,
(2) Gakuso, and (3) Gosho are those in which the program of* meisho *poems and paintings was mounted on
sliding doors.*

Settsu, and the placement of the scenes and poems representing these
relatively familiar sites in those rooms that would be most frequented by
Gotoba and the most intimate members of his extended family and retinue,
while, on the other hand, the representations of "exotic" Michinoku are
relegated to a relatively remote quarter (figure 9). Thus, even this plan for
the distribution of the selected *meisho* topics mirrors a geopolitical priori-
tization of sites, ranging from the center to the periphery, that had governed
and would govern other arrangements of such "famous places" and their
names in other settings—in *utamakura* handbooks, in other *meisho* poem
sequences, and elsewhere.

Furthermore, the plan also seems to be tailored for Gotoba's anticipated
pleasure in the recognition of what the represented sites might mean to him,
personally, and, perhaps, to other informed observers as well. Accordingly,
in the most public of Gotoba's Saishōshitennōin rooms, the *meisho* of Yamato
—the Imperial family's ancient seat, represented by sites of the greatest
prominence in the traditions of poetry nurtured for centuries under Imperial

auspices—would command the stage: here, the eye would be treated to scenes of festive courtly outings in Kasuga's fields on New Year's Day, and by scenes of Mount Yoshino, since ancient times the site of palatial royal retreats, and by scenes of Mount Miwa and Mount Tatsuta, locales in the vicinity of the ancient Yamato capitals that had long been given pride of place in the positioning of poems naming them in anthologies prepared at royal behest, from the *Kokin wakashū* onward. Then, to the west and facing the south would be the scenes of and poems about Settsu, a province that lay southwest from the capital (and from the Saishōshitennōin itself). The Yamashiro scenes and poems, representing the places best known to Gotoba's eyes, geographically most close at hand, and hence most frequently visited by him and by his royal ancestors, would fill the rooms reserved for his greater privacy: Toba and Fushimi, royal outing sites that were particularly close to home, would decorate his sleeping space; and Minase, site of his own favorite villa, and Katano, a long-time and still favored royal hunting ground, would be featured in the room where he might well spend the better part of his day. A lively market scene, Shikama-no-ichi (from westward Harima), would be the theme in the room where he would take his meals.

Meanwhile, however, the renderings of the topics chosen to represent distant Michinoku, in the far northeast, would be consigned to the most distant (and easternmost) rooms—where, as Teika says, the special problems of dealing with these topics might best be resolved. This region, he says, is one with a large number of "mysterious" sites that are "hard to judge" (*kono kuni toku ni yūgen no meisho ōku wakimaegatashi*),[19] by which he means, presumably, that the names and features of these Michinoku sites are not so easily manipulated or readily rendered in *waka* or in painting—in this setting, at least, if not elsewhere as well—as are the names and features of *meisho* that lie closer to home. Teika's use here of the word *yūgen*—which both his father and he used often as a term of high praise in their *waka* criticism, particularly in the rendering of *utaawase* judgments (and which would eventually become a key aesthetic term of critical discourses in other arts, perhaps most notably in Zeami's Nō theater)—seems to have a somewhat negative or at least cautionary connotation: the mysterious Michinoku sites, Teika seems to suggest, would have to be handled with care. Their exotic flavors, in his view, would not be welcome in other parts of the structure, and he advocated that they be hidden away in rooms which might be used only rarely but which would offer relatively expansive spaces in which their "strange" forces might be released without deleterious effect to the inhabitants. In any case, and despite this plan for special treatment, the six Michinoku *meisho* chosen for this location would prove just as rich in positive associations as were the place-names treated in the more accessible parts of the building, and Teika's fear that they might prove hard to work with seems to have proven false when it came time to write poems about them.

The charge to the Wakadokoro group that assembled on the twenty-first also called for decisions about which scenic features (*keiki*) of these places would be emphasized in their textual and pictorial representations, and which season (*jisetsu*) would be featured in those representations as well (table 1). This was no simple task. It demanded nothing short of a masterful orchestration that would reconcile, retain, and, at points, accentuate a variety of facets of each *meisho* topic—as independent integers of the program, and in their relationships to one another—so as to ensure their pleasing and effective programmatic function in several overlapping registers (geographical, topographical, seasonal, etc.), the contours of which were themselves laid out by long-standing precedent. A desire and need to conform with convention in the treatment of each *meisho* must have been the governing principle in the Wakadokoro discussions pursuant to this goal—but, judging at least from the poems that eventually were written under these guidelines, there must also have been some interest in departing, in subtle but telling ways, from the confines of precedent, so as to infuse the program with an air of newness in combination with its evocation of the old.[20] The result is very much in the *Shin kokin wakashū* mold: the program as a whole, like its individual elements, reveals and revels in retrospection at every turn, yet it also makes it clear that it was created under the governance of contemporary taste, something made for delectation and utilization now—to meet present contingencies—but under the guidance of an understanding, admiration, and affection for things (poems, paintings, buildings and their parts) that had been made long beforehand and which, if no longer extant, had not been forgotten.

In the end, it seems, this plan for the program's "orchestration" bore the stamp of Teika's discretion, taste, and preference more than anyone else's— but, as he describes it, this came about largely by default. In his diary entry for the day of the Wakadokoro conference, Teika expresses his annoyance with his recalcitrant colleagues, who for some reason (perhaps out of deference to Teika, or lack of a clear sense of their role in the business at hand, as Kubota Jun has suggested) refused to voice their opinions or to contribute their own suggestions even as the deliberations were under way. "I myself am deeply ignorant about such matters, and am lacking in imagination," Teika writes, "but considering my obligations to the nation" (here embodied in Gotoba), "I just went ahead and said what I thought, without regard for the possibility of incurring His Majesty's wrath or for the objections that

Table 1. The Saishōshitennōin Program

Locations: A = public *(hare)* rooms on south facade, southeast quarter; "where curtains will, on occasion, be raised;" three rooms (three bays on east and west, one bay on north and south); B = to the southwest of the above; C = easternmost quarter, *gakuso* ("spacious, with several rooms"); D = *Tsune no gosho* (Emperor's living quarters); D^a = *on-nedokoro* (bedroom) therein; D^b = "the *shōji* on the west, in his sitting room"; D^c = in front of the above; and D^d = "near the shelves on one side of the dining room."

Spatial mood: hare and *ge* designations, as assigned to the painters

(Source: *Meigetsuki,* Jōgen 1.4.21 and 5.14)

"WI" means that meisho is listed in *Waka iroha.* If features are mentioned in *Waka iroha,* they are listed first. Other features listed after slash are most prominent in the composed poems. (*Source:* Sasaki, ed., *Nihon kagaku taikei* 3:158-74.)

Meisho	Province	Season[1]	Poet of Chosen Poem	Painter	Location/ Spatial Mood	Features
1. Kasugano 春日野	Yamato	Spring	Michiteru	Sonchi	A/hare	WI/shoots, plum blossom
2. Yoshinoyama 吉野山	Yamato	Spring	Gotoba[2]	Sonchi	A/hare	WI/cherry blossom
3. Miwayama 三輪山	Yamato	Summer	Michiteru	Sonchi	A/hare	WI/cuckoo, cedars
4. Tatsutayama 竜田山	Yamato	Autumn	Gotoba	Sonchi	A/hare	WI/momiji, mountain wind, stag's cries
5. Hatsuseyama 泊瀬山	Yamato	Winter	Jien	Sonchi	hiroma[3]/ hare	WI/snow, cedar clouds, temple bell
6. Naniwa no ura 難波浦	Settsu	Spring	Teika	Kaneyasu	B hiroma/ hare	WI/mist, geese, new leaves of reeds
7. Sumiyoshi no sato 住吉里	Settsu	Spring	Gotoba	Kaneyasu	B/hare	WI/mist, "forgetting grass"
8. Ashiya no sato 芦屋里	Settsu	Summer	Ietaka	Kaneyasu	B/hare	[WI (Pine Grove of Koya]/ fireflies, rain
9. Nunobiki no taki 布引滝	Settsu	Summer	Ariie[4]	Kaneyasu	B/hare	WI/crickets, summer robes
10. Ikuta no mori 生田杜	Settsu	Autumn	Jien	Kaneyasu	B hiroma[5] /hare	WI/dew, momiji, wind, stag's cries, drizzle

1. Distribution of topics per season, based on predominant figures in composed poems (in some cases confirmed by subsequent inclusion of some poems in seasonal section of anthologies): spring 10, summer 8, autumn 19, winter 9.

2. Poem appears as *Shin kokin wakashū* (SKKS) #133, Spring 2.

3. Hatsuseyama is paired back-to-back with Tatsuyama.

4. Poem appears as SKKS #1651, Miscellaneous 2.

5. Ikuta no mori and Nunobiki no taki are a pair.

Table 1. The Saishōshitennōin Program, continued

Meisho	Province	Season	Poet of Chosen Poem	Painter	Location/ Spatial Mood	Features
11. Waka no ura 若浦	Kii	Autumn	Michiteru	Sonchi	hiroma /hare	WI/moon, frost
12. Fukiage no hama 吹上浜	Kii	Winter	Tomochika	Sonchi	hiroma[6] /hare	WI/snow, plovers, frost
13. Katano 交野	Kawachi	Winter	Jien	Mitsutoki	D^b hiroma /ge	WI/hail, snow, hunting
14. Minasegawa 水無瀬河	Settsu	Autumn	Gotoba	Mitsutoki	D^b hiroma[7]/ge	WI/wind, chrysanthemums, deer's cries
15. Suma no ura 諏磨の浦	Settsu	Autumn	Jien	Kaneyasu	B waki/ hare	WI/evening, breezes
16. Akashi no ura 明石浦	Harima	Autumn	Ietaka	Kaneyasu	B[8] hare	WI "splendid moon"
17. Shikama no ichi 飾麻市	Harima	Autumn	Jien	Kaneyasu	D^d/hare	WI/indigo, market commoners (*tami*)
18. Matsurayama 松浦山	Hizen	Winter	Teika	Mitsutoki	ge	WI/night, momiji frost
19. Inabayama 因幡山	Inaba	Autumn	Gotoba	Kōshun	ge	WI/wind, frost
20. Takasago 高砂	Harima	Autumn	Hideyoshi[9]	Kōshun	D^c/ge	WI/pines
21. Nonakano-shimizu 野中清水	Harima	Summer	Shunzei's Daughter	Kōshun	D^{c}[10]/ge	WI/deep grass, dew
22. Ama no Hashidate 海橋立	Tango	Spring	Jien	Kōshun	hiroma/ge	WI/"Sayo no umi; pines"/geese
23. Ujigawa 宇治川	Yamashiro	Winter	Gotoba[11]	Sonchi	D/hare	WI/"weirs" (*ajiro*)/ ice, momiji, plovers
24. Ōigawa 大井川	Yamashiro	Autumn	Masatsune	Mitsutoki[12]	D^a /hare	WI "rafts, cormorant fishing"/fallen momiji
25. Toba 鳥羽	Yamashiro	Autumn	Gotoba	Mitsutoki	D^{a}[13]/ge	fulling of robes, fog, geese
26. Fushimi no Sato 伏見里	Yamashiro	Autumn	Teika	Mitsutoki	D waki/ ge	WI/geese, *hagi*, deer's cries, dew, etc.

6. Fukiage and Waka no ura are a pair.

7. To be on a *waki* screen, according to *Meigetsuki* Jōgen 1.5.14.

8. Akashi and Suma are a pair.

9. Poem appears as SKKS #290, Autumn 2.

10. Nonaka no shimizu and Takasago are a pair.

11. Poem appears as SKKS #636, Winter, and Jien's Ujigawa poem follows as SKKS #637.

12. Originally assigned to Sonchi; change ordered by Gotoba. Ōigawa and Ujigawa are a pair. Although Mitsutoki's other assignments are designated *ge*, it may be assumed that the Ōigawa painting/location retained the designation *hare* despite the change of painters.

13. To be on a *waki* screen, according to *Meigetsuki* Jōgen 1.5.14.

Table 1. The Saishōshitennōin Program, continued

Meisho	Province	Season	Poet of Chosen Poem	Painter	Location/ Spatial Mood	Features
27. Izumigawa 泉河	Yamashiro	Autumn	Teika	Kaneyasu	D/hare	WI "vicinity of *Mika no hara*"/waves, *Hahaso no mori*
28. Oshioyama 小塩山	Yamashiro	Spring	Jien[14]	Kaneyasu	D waki[15] hare	WI "in Ōharano; kami present; pines"/mist, storms
29. Ausaka no seki 会坂関	Ōmi	Spring	Teika	Sonchi	hare	WI "well, springs"/paths, mist, warbler
30. Shiga no ura 志賀浦	Ōmi	Winter	Jien	Kōshun	ge	? ice, drizzle, snow, frost
31. Suzukayama 鈴鹿山	Ise	Autumn	Gotoba[16]	Mitsutoki	ge	WI/"barrier"/leaves, drizzle, momiji
32. Futami no ura 二見浦	Ise	Summer	Masatsune	Mitsutoki	ge	WI[17]/summer robes, moon
33. Ōyodo no ura 大淀浦	Ise	Spring	Teika[18]	Mitsutoki	[19]/ge	geese, *mirume* (kelp)
34. Narumi no ura 鳴海浦	Owari	Winter	Hideyoshi[20]	Kōshun	ge	plovers, snow
35. Hamana no hashi 浜名橋	Tōtomi	Autumn	Tomochika	Kōshun	ge	WI "it crosses the beach"/mist, geese, dusk
36. Utsunoyama 宇津山	Suruga	Autumn	Masatsune	Kōshun	ge	wind, leaves
37. Sarashina-yama 更級山	Shinano	Autumn	Shunzei's Daughter	Kōshun	[21]/ge	WI "splendid moon; at the foot of Obasuteyama; Sarashina River"
38. Kiyomi no seki 清見関	Suruga	Summer	Michiteru[22]	Sonchi	ge	WI "near sea; refer to 'the barrier guard who watches the waves'"[23]
39. Fujiyama 富士山	Suruga	Summer	Gotoba	Sonchi	[24]/ge	WI/sky, sun, cuckoo
40. Musashino 武蔵野	Musashi	Spring	Ariie	Kōshun	ge	WI *"murasaki, okera"* (flowers)/mist, dew
41. Shirakawa no seki 白河関	Michinoku	Winter	Ietaka	Kōshun	C waki/ ge	WI/snow

14. Poem appears as SKKS #1900, Jingi no uta.
15. Oshioyama and Izumigawa are a pair, occupying one *waki* screen.
16. Poem appears as SKKS #526, Autumn 2.
17. Listing is for site in Harima, with note that a place with the same name is in Ise.
18. Poem appears as SKKS #1723, Miscellaneous 1.
19. Ōyodo no ura and Futami no ura are a pair.
20. Poem appears as SKKS #259, Summer.
21. Sarashinayama and Utsunoyama are a pair.
22. Poem appears as SKKS #259, Summer.
23. *"Nami no ma o hakarite sugureba nami no sekimori to yomu."* Apparently a reference to a template poem, but no such poem has been identified.
24. Fuji and Kiyomi no seki are a pair.

Table 1. The Saishōshitennōin Program, continued

Meisho	Province	Season	Poet of Chosen Poem	Painter	Location/ Spatial Mood	Features
42. Abukuma-gawa 阿武隈河	Michinoku	Winter	Ietaka[25]	Mitsutoki	C/ge	WI/mist, plovers ice
43. Adachi no hara 安達原	Michinoku	Autumn	Ietaka	Kaneyasu	C/hare?[26]	*momiji*
44. Miyagino 宮城野	Michinoku	Autumn	Jien	Mitsutoki	C/ge	WI *"hagi* are profuse" grass, dew, insects' cries, traveler's sleeves
45. Asaka no numa 安積沼	Michinoku	Summer	Masatsune[27]	Mitsutoki	C waki[28] /ge	*hanakatsumi* (iris), rain
46. Shiogama no ura 塩竈浦	Michinoku	Spring	Jien	Kaneyasu	C/hare?[26]	WI *"kami* present"/ama, clouded moon, mist, pines

25. Poem appears as SKKS #1577, Miscellaneous 1.

26. Application of the *hare/ge* designations in the painters' assignments here does not seem to make sense; Kaneyasu, whose assignments are supposed to be *hare,* has two subjects ("Adachi no hara" and "Shiogama no ura") in a location otherwise given over to paintings by Kōshun and Mitsutoki, who are supposedly responsible for spaces designated *ge.*

27. Poems appears as SKKS #184, Summer.

28. Abukumagawa, Miyagino, and Asaka no numa are a group, to be mounted in proximity to one another.

Order and manner of listing is as found in the complete composed poems published in *Shinpen kokka taikan,* vol. 5: *Utaawase hen,* pp. 896-905.

bystanders might raise."[21] Thus, in a roundabout way, Teika admits (or boasts) that the poem-and-painting plan was, for the most part, of his own making. He also says that he took it upon himself to recommend that, although plans originally called for the distribution of two *meisho* representations to each two-paneled door, the distribution rather should be one *meisho* per door, to allow for ample and readily recognizable paintings. The Emperor's approval of this adjustment was obtained, with the proviso that on selected *shōji* sufficient room for two *meisho* subjects might yet be found.[22] At the end of these discussions, which dragged on far into the night, Ienaga, who was also on hand, made the list of the forty-six *meisho* thus almost unilaterally decided upon by Teika; an unnamed Wakadokoro staff priest (*azukari no hōshi*) sketched their assigned positions on a plan of the building; and another courtier, Fujiwara Kiyonori, took detailed notes about the recommended landscape elements and seasonal designations. Then, all of these minutes from the all-night planning session were presented to the Retired Emperor for his approval.

According to *Meigetsuki,* a five-day-long ritual reading of the *Konkōmyō saishōōkyō* (a *Saishōkō*), sponsored by Gotoba, began in the Seiryōden, in the Imperial Palace, on the twenty-second—the morning after the Saishōshitennōin planning session.[23] *Saishōkō* were regularly held under royal auspices, but usually in the fifth rather than the fourth month, so the timing of this particular reading may be significant: perhaps Gotoba was striving, in yet another way, to be sure that the Four Deva Kings would shed their blessings, and grant their protection, to the building program that was being prepared to honor their name and that of the sūtra that invoked them.[24] And even as the ritual proceeded over its five-day course, Gotoba continued to turn his attention to the details of the program. On the twenty-third, Teika was called into Gotoba's presence and was asked why Waka no ura—admittedly one of the most famous of famous places in the *waka* tradition—had not been included among the forty-six chosen *meisho*. There was apparently no argument: two sites recommended by Teika—Koya and Nagara Bridge—were forthwith dropped and were replaced by Waka no ura and Fukiage.[25] The full rationale for these maneuvers is not reported, and perhaps there was no real basis for the substitution other than Gotoba's own preference and his desire to exercise the privilege of *veto*. We know, of course, that Gotoba was interested in the Nagara Bridge and its *meisho* status; the poetry desk that he had only recently had fashioned from a fragment of the bridge was presumably still in use in the Wakadokoro at the time of these deliberations. But, for some reason, the bridge and its associations did not fit into his vision of the Saishōshitennōin program—or, even if it did, it was nonetheless expendable if room was needed for some other *meisho*.[26]

With these plans now in place, orders soon went out (on the fifth day of the fifth month) to the ten coterie poets chosen to contribute poems that might be selected for inscription on the painted doors. These ten were listed as they would eventually appear in the complete records of the program (table 2).

1. Gyosei, i.e., Retired Emperor Gotoba
2. Daisōjō Jien
3. Gon Dainagon Minamoto Michiteru
4. Kōtaikō no miya no taifu Shunzei no Musume [Shunzei's Daughter]
5. Ōkura no kyō Fujiwara Ariie no Ason
6. Sakon no chūjō Fujiwara Sadaie no Ason [Teika]
7. Kunaikyō Fujiwara Ietaka no Ason
8. Sakon no shōshō Fujiwara [Asukai] Masatsune
9. Sakon no shōshō Minamoto Tomochika
10. Saemon no kami Fujiwara Hideyoshi

And, at the same time, Teika learned that he was expected to direct the initial preparations of drafts by the four court painters Gotoba had selected for the

Table 2. Poets and Painters of the Saishōshitennōin Program

Poets:

Gyosei 御製 Retired Emperor Gotoba (1180–1239)

Son of Emperor Takakura and Shichijōin. Reigned 1184–1198. Commissioned and edited *Shin kokin wakashū*, 1205. Exiled to Oki 1221. Eight poems selected:
2. Yoshinoyama = *Shin kokin wakashū* #133, Spring 2
4. Tatsutayama
7. Sumiyoshi no hama
14. Minasegawa
19. Inabayama
23. *Shin kokin wakashū* #526 (Winter)
25. Toba
31. Suzukagawa = *Shin kokin wakashū* #526 (Autumn 2)

Daisōjō Jien 大僧正慈円 (1155–1225)

Son of Regent Kujō Tadamichi; tonsured 1167. Appointed Chief Abbot of Tendai School (Tendai zasu) four times. Ten poems selected:
5. Hatsuseyama
10. Ikuta no mori
13. Katano
15. Suma no ura
17. Shikama no ichi
22. Ama no hashidate
28. Oshioyama = *Shin kokin wakashū* #1900 (*Jingi*)
30. Shiga no ura
44. Miyagino
46. Shiogama no ura

Gon Dainagon Minamoto Michiteru 通光 (1187–1248)

Younger brother of *Shin kokin wakashū* editor Michitomo. Participant in *Sengohyakuban utaawase.* Four poems selected:
1. Kasugano
3. Miwayama
11. Waka no ura
38. Kiyomi no seki = *Shin kokin wakashū* #259 (Summer)

Kōtaikō no miya no taifu Shunzei no Musume 皇太后宮大夫俊成女 (1171?–1252?)

Shunzei's granddaughter, and Teika's niece; adopted by Shunzei as "daughter"; married Minamoto no Michitomo but continued to serve in Gotoba's retinue. Two poems selected:
21. Nonaka no shimizu
37. Sarashina no sato

Ōkura no kyō 大蔵卿 Fujiwara Ariie 有家 no Ason (1155–1216)

A Rokujō-family poet sympathetic to the Mikohidari faction. Participant in *Roppyakuban utawase, Sengohyakuban utaawase, Shin kokin wakashū* as Wakadokoro member and editor. Two poems selected:
9. Nunobiki no taki = *Shin kokin wakashū* #1651 (Miscellaneous 2)
40. Musashino

Table 2. Poets and Painters of the Saishōshitennōin Program, Continued

Sakon no chūjō 左近中将 Fujiwara Sadaie 定家 (Teika) no Ason (1162–1241)

Shunzei's son and chief heir of his literary legacy. Participant in major pre-*Shinkokin utaawase;* Wakadokoro member and editor. Six poems selected:
6. Naniwa no ura
18. Matsurayama
26. Fushimi no sato
27. Izumigawa
29. Ausakayama
33. Ōyodo no ura = *Shin kokin wakashū* #1723 (Miscellaneous 1)

Kunaikyō 宮内卿 Fujiwara Ietaka 家陸 no Ason (1158–1237)

Son of Fujiwara Mitsutaka. Tutored in poetry by Shunzei. Gotoba coterie member; Wakadokoro member and *Shin kokin wakashū* editor. Six poems selected:
8. Ashiya no sato
16. Akashi no ura
39. Fujiyama
41. Shirakawa no seki
42. Abukumagawa = *Shin kokin wakashū* #1577 (Miscellaneous 1)
43. Adachi no hara

Sakon no shōshō 左近少将 Fujiwara [Asukai 飛鳥井] Masatsune 雅経. (1170–1221)

Tutored by Shunzei. Gotoba coterie member (and *kemari* athlete); Wakadokoro member and *Shin kokin wakashū* editor. Progenitor of influential Asukai poetic lineage. Four poems selected:
24. Ōigawa
32. Futami no ura
36. Utsu no yama
45. Asaka no numa = *Shin kokin wakashū* #184 (Summer)

Sakon no shōshō 左近少将 Minamoto Tomochika 具親 (dates unknown)

Murakami Genji. Elder brother of poet Kunaikyō; joined Gotoba's coterie with his sister; Wakadokoro member. Two poems selected:
12. Fukiage no hama
35. Hamana no hashi

Saemon no kami 左衛門尉 Fujiwara Hideyoshi 秀能 (1184–1240)

Gotoba coterie and Wakadokoro member. May have led forces on royal side in Jōkyū War; in its aftermath fled to Kumano and took tonsure. Two poems selected:
20. Takasago = *Shin kokin wakashū* #290 (Autumn 2)
34. Narumi no ura = *Shin kokin wakashū* #649 (Winter)

Painters

Taifubō Sonchi 大輔房尊智 : *hare* subjects

Udoneri Sōnai Kaneyasu 内舎人宗内兼康 : *hare* subjects

Shinano no bō Kōshun 信濃房康俊 : *ge* subjects

Hachiman Heizō Mitsutoki 八幡平三光時 : *ge* subjects

project—[Taifubō] Sonchi, [Udoneri Sōnai] Kaneyasu, [Shinano no Bō] Kō-shun, and [Hachiman Heizō] Mitsutoki.[27] Teika demurred, claiming that his lack of familiarity with landscapes outside the capital (*rakugai*) made him unfit to serve as the painters' supervisor. In response, Gotoba told Masatsune and Hideyoshi—two of the participating poets who were, in fact, somewhat more widely traveled than Teika—to assist. This trio then proceeded to work out the assignments of groups of the *meisho* topics to each of the four painters: Sonchi and Kaneyasu would be responsible for the relatively public (*hare*) rooms, and Kōshun and Mitsutoki would prepare work for the more private (*ge*) spaces.[28] Assignments were also made on the understanding that fundamental features in the three major segments of the representation of each site—the field contours (*nosuji*), sky spaces (*kumo*), and bodies of water (*mizu*)—should be painted as if flowing naturally from one site into the other.[29] The result of such depiction would of course be contrary to "natural" fact, but would nonetheless have yielded the *illusion* of contiguous, con-joined spaces somewhat miraculously rendered from matériel that, in fact, represented discontiguous locales; thus, a new, idealized reality would re-place another, and a nation that was actually in disarray would be portrayed —selectively, partially, and in miniature scale—as a harmonious whole.

Two days after these assignments and designations were made, Kaneyasu came to Teika to discuss a problem. His assignment included the depiction of two especially famous places in Settsu Province, Akashi and Suma—best known, perhaps, through their association with the chapters devoted to the account of the protagonist's years of exile in *The Tale of Genji,* but in fact so treated there largely because of associations that had long ago accrued to them in poetic usage. The cumulative weight of these associations, and the plenitude of conventions decreed by prior treatment of these particular subjects in both poetry and painting, apparently was causing confusion for Kaneyasu. "There are so many views about the proper way to treat these *meisho*," he complained, "that I am finding it difficult to paint. Akashi and Suma are no great distance from here. If I were to go there and then were to present my plan for painting those scenes, after seeing them with my own eyes, would it cause too great a delay?" Teika reports that he replied as follows: "This project does need to be completed as quickly as possible. But we would not want to commit errors, either now or for future viewers. If you paint these scenes after having traveled there yourself, your paintings will no doubt earn the praise of future generations. I suppose it will not matter, then, if you take a bit more time."[30] And so, apparently, Kaneyasu made his trip to Suma and Akashi, applied what he observed to what he had learned from precedent, and proceeded with his sketches.

As the art historian Chino Kaori has noted, this episode shows that by this point in the development of *meisho* painting programs, there were fairly strong expectations on the part of some of those involved—in this case, Teika (and Kaneyasu)—that depictions of famous places should be accurate, and not based solely on the imagination of the artist or on fixed models derived from what had been imagined by earlier artists.[31] But Teika's anxiety over the possibility of error may also be based in his understanding of the special nature of the Saishōshitennōin project itself—that is, its conception as an undertaking that would generate words and pictures meant to bring about certain positive effects—and his fear may have been not only of censure for inaccuracy by critics in his day and in posterity, but of the consequences of any failure to produce the right mix of words and pictures, which might lead in turn to a failure to bring about the whole project's hoped-for goals.

None of this, however, is expressed in his diary; rather, what surfaces quite conspicuously, and repeatedly, is his irritation with Gotoba, who several times undid or overturned what Teika, his fellow poets, and the painters working with them had already put in place. During the early summer months of 1207, Gotoba was reviewing drafts of those paintings that had been prepared so far. On the twentieth day of the fifth month, he ordered the site-topic Ikuno dropped in favor of Inabayama (but no explanation for this was given).[32] And on the seventh day of the sixth month, Gotoba sent word that he was dissatisfied with Sonchi's drafts for the Ōigawa scene—which was to feature a representation of that site as a favored locale for royal outings (*miyuki*)—and that Mitsutoki should take it over. To aid him—and perhaps to avoid further interference from Gotoba—Teika writes that he then studied "the chronicles of the Jōhō era [1074–1077]" and that he offered the painter these and other "old records of royal hunts [*no no miyuki*] of previous times" as the basis for his new sketch.[33] Most likely this means that what Teika found in these Jōhō records (which no longer exist) were descriptions of Emperor Shirakawa's Ōigawa *miyuki* of 1077—a grand affair that was in turn modeled on the accounts of the excursion of Retired Emperor Uda to the same site in the ninth month of 907. The 907 excursion had been celebrated with poems composed on the spot, some of which eventually made their way into several later anthologies, including the *Kokin wakashū*, the *Shūi wakashū*, the *Kokin waka rokujō*, and, eventually, the *Shin kokin wakashū* as well; still others, along with some descriptions of the event, had been preserved in the personal anthologies of several of the participants (including Ki no Tsurayuki, Oshikōchi no Mitsune, Ōnakatomi Yorimoto, Sakanoue no Korenori, Mibu no Tadamine, and Fujiwara Tadahira).[34] Poems composed on subsequent Ōigawa excursions, or on other occasions when Ōigawa presented itself as a topic, invariably made reference to those earlier poems and to that particular earlier occasion. The Saishōshitennōin Ōigawa poems would do likewise (as we shall see); and Teika, by referring to "records" of Ōigawa *miyuki* as a guide for the painter, was insuring that both the visual image of Ōigawa and the words that would be inscribed upon it would jointly display their engagement with the conspicuous specificities *and* the general richness of the past of that particular site (figures 10 and 11).

Also, as Fukuyama Toshio has suggested in his study of the Saishōshitennōin program, there may have been other useful models for its *miyuki* representations that were fairly close at hand, in paintings that Teika and Mitsutoki—and, for that matter, Gotoba—might well have had some opportunity to see, at another royal-votive monastery, the Saishōkōin. This building had been erected in 1173, as a subtemple in a larger complex called the Hōjūji, under the sponsorship of Gotoba's grandmother Kenshunmon'in (the consort of his grandfather Goshirakawa). While the doors in the main rooms and corridors of this building were painted with scenes of the twenty-eight chapters of the *Lotus Sūtra*, with the relevant passages from that scripture inscribed on *shikishi* (appliquéd paper slips), the rooms reserved for Kenshunmon'in's and Goshirakawa's private use were painted with specific, and historically recent, *miyuki* scenes: that is, Goshirakawa's apartment featured scenes of his own royal visits to the religious complex on Mount Kōya, and Kenshunmon'in's were fitted with depictions of her pilgrimages to the Hirano shrine, at the time of her elevation to the rank of consort, and to the Hiyoshi shrine some time after Goshirakawa's abdication. There may, of course, have been yet other paintings of Ōigawa *miyuki* in particular, and Teika and Mitsutoki may have consulted them as well; but, if there were not, these Saishōkōin paintings may have served as their most useful and accessible models.[35] In any case, there seems to have been no further trouble over the Ōigawa paintings, at least.

There were, however, other causes for Teika's vexation, and at times they seem to have got the better of him. He reports that, on the day after his special consultation with Mitsutoki over the Ōigawa depiction, he spent the entire day at home, feeling depressed and ill, and fretting over the poems that he himself was preparing for the project. One of his sisters, known as Ken gozen, dropped by to comfort him, and he read her what he had written so far; but he also bemoaned the fact that, in his view, he had failed to absorb their father's wisdom sufficiently, and that, since death had recently robbed him of Yoshitsune's company, he now had no good (male) friend to whom he might show his poems while they were in the making, and no one from whom to seek reliable advice.

10. *The Ōigawa (photo by the author).*

Still, Teika was ready to submit his completed set of forty-six poems to Gotoba two days later (as was Ariie) (figures 12 and 13). But other contributors, and other phases of the project, were reported to be running behind schedule, and so the dedication ceremonies that had been planned for the following month were now postponed to the eleventh month.[36] Then, as one by one the contributing poets completed their work, Gotoba began the process of selecting those poems that would be inscribed on the finished *shōji*. When he called a Wakadokoro meeting for this purpose on the twenty-fourth day of the ninth month, he revealed that he had already, unilaterally, chosen twenty-six out of the forty-six poems, but was willing to hear comments and suggestions about his selections—and, once again, the discussion over the fine points of the submitted poems went on far into the night. Teika records in his diary that he was pleased that the Emperor had selected some five or six of his poems in this first round, but that he had actually objected

11. Detail from Festive Boating on the Ōigawa, *six-panel screen painting by Ukita Ikkei (1795-1859). Parties of aristocratic gentlemen and a few women (in the covered boat) are accompanied by musicians, all in court dress typical of the*

to the selection of his poem for the Kasugano scene (which would have special prominence, on the first panel on the south side of Gotoba's main sitting room, and hence was, in effect, the first poem-and-painting moment in the entire program) and had suggested that that honor should go to someone else.[37] As it turned out, Gotoba eventually chose Michitomo's poem for Kasugano.

Then, one month later (on the twenty-fourth day of the tenth month, and with the dedication ceremony date fast approaching), Hideyoshi brought Teika the news that Gotoba had personally reversed many of the choices that the group had managed to agree upon during their joint selection session with him. Teika's ire simmers on the surface in his diary: "He does such things," he writes, avoiding direct reference to Gotoba but obviously mean-

mid-Heian period—in particular, the time of the famous Ōigawa excursion of 907. Courtesy Sennyūji, Kyoto.

ing no one else, "as lightly as turning his hand from one side to the other" (*tanagokoro o kaesu ga gotoshi*).[38] At other times, as the process dragged on, Teika seems to have been even less discreet about his annoyance with Gotoba, and apparently he expressed his irritation openly enough for Gotoba to have known all about it. Years later, writing his memoirs while in exile on Oki Island (after the failure of the Jōkyū revolt), Gotoba would chastise Teika in turn for having grumbled to others—though not to himself—when he chose Jien's poem on the Ikuta no mori site over Teika's.[39]

Finally, toward the end of the eleventh month, the monastery and its furnishings were deemed complete. On the twenty-third, Gotoba himself watched the rehearsals for the dedication ceremony (*kuyō*). Four days later, he and his mother, the Dowager Empress Shichijōin, left the Kōyōin mansion, where they had been living for the last several months, and took up

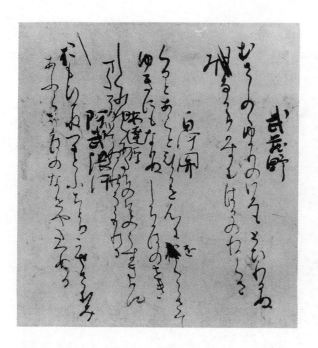

12. Teika's Saishōshitennōin poems on Musashino,
Shirakawa no seki, Adachino, and Abukumagawa, in
Teika's hand. "Musashino: Musashino no/ yukari no iro
mo/toiwabinu/mi nagara kasumu/haru no wakakusa" (I am
worn out from searching for the colored [murasaki] grass
that has such an affinity with Musashino, for the fields are
all enshrouded in mist.) "Shirakawa no seki: kuru to aku
to/hito o kokoro ni/okurasade/yuki ni mo narinu/Shira-
kawa no seki" (By night and by day, I've kept thoughts of
my beloved in my heart as I have traveled, and now snow
is falling at Shirakawa Barrier.) "Adachino: shigure yuku/
Adachi no hara no/usugiri ni/mada somehatenu/aki zo
komoreru" (As showers fall on Adachi Plain, an autumn
not yet touched with colors by the mist still lies concealed.)
"Abukumagawa: omoikane/ tsumadou chidori/kaze
samumi/Abukumagawa no/na o ya tazunuru" (It must be
because it is so cold that the plovers that cry out with longing for their mates must be seeking out the river, Abukumagawa, whose name says, "Let us be together"). In the
Musashino poem, the kanji for mi in minagara has been
crossed out and replaced with the hiragana letter mi. In
the Shirakawa no seki poem, the hiragana o in okurasade
has been crossed out and replaced with wo. The Adachino
poem appears to have been inserted between the
Shirakawa no seki and Abukumagawa poems, almost as an
afterthought. Courtesy Maeda Ikutoku Kai, Tokyo.

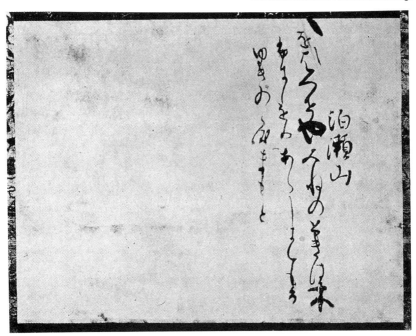

13. *Teika's Saishōshitennōin poem on Hatsuseyama, in Teika's hand.*
"Hatsuseyama: Ohatsuse ya/ mine no tokiwaki/fukishiori/arashi ni kumoru yuki no
yamamoto" (Hatsuse: the storm winds have come blowing through the evergreens
on the peak, and now they hide the foot of the mountains under snow). Courtesy
Yōmei Bunko, Kyoto.

residence in the new Saishōshitennōin; and, two days after that, on the
twenty-ninth, the formal dedication ceremony (*rakkei kuyō*) took place, with
the Emperor (Tsuchimikado) himself in attendance. A *ganmon*, or dedica-
tory prayer in Chinese, was offered by Fujiwara Chikatsune (who also had
written the Chinese preface for the *Shin kokin wakashū*), and the services
were led by two distinguished prelates: Shin'en, an official of Kōfukuji, and
his younger brother Jien—donor of the land on which the monastery now
stood, and author of ten of the poems that now graced the *shōji* within it.[40]

Teika, however, does not seem to have been there. Several months later,
in the sixth month of the following year (1208), he records in *Meigetsuki*
that, finding themselves in the vicinity, he and several companions went to
the Saishōshitennōin in hopes of viewing the decorations that he had worked
so hard to prepare. Gotoba had moved on to other quarters: a priest left in
charge had hidden his keys and refused the party's entreaties to be let in.
Ban'i no chi no gotoshi, Teika writes: "That place is like some barbarian
country."[41] Thus, as it had been for much of the time while preparations

were underway—and, for that matter, as it had been in many of the other projects into which Teika was drawn by Gotoba, including the *Shinkokinshū* compilation itself—Teika's involvement with the Saishōshitennōin ended in irritation and gall. But, perhaps, such was the inevitable cost of working for a royal master who was as adamant about his own tastes and judgments—and as eager to have the last word—as Teika was himself; and, though it had seemed to be a privilege to be asked to participate as much as he had, it must also have seemed to Teika that it was inevitable, as well, that in the end Gotoba would take complete control, and would shut him out. The locked doors meant, in short, that Teika's privileges did not extend to viewing the results of his own labors, on Gotoba's behalf, with his own eyes, and that the special pleasure of seeing a few of his own poems inscribed on the finished screens, and of savoring the total effect of the program to which he had contributed so much, would be denied him.

Meanwhile, Gotoba—though residing elsewhere—was continuing to make some use of the building, largely for religious undertakings. In the fourth month of Kenpō 1 (1213) it was the site of a ceremonial copying of the entire Buddhist canon in one day (*ichinichi issaikyō shosha kuyō*) convened under his sponsorship, and *Mon'yōki,* the diary of the Retired Emperor's son, Prince Son'en, has a description of *kanjō* ritual (a Buddhist initiation ceremony) held there in the last month of 1218, along with an architectural sketch of the monastery's main halls and altars.[42] But soon thereafter, it seems, those halls and altars were no more. *Hyakurenshō,* a fairly reliable late-Kamakura-period history, reports that the monastery was in the process of being dismantled and moved to a new location, within the precincts of another of the Emperor's residences, at a place called Itsutsuji, in the seventh month of the following year, 1219, while an entry in *Mon'yōki* for the fourth day of the tenth month of the following year, 1220, says that on that date the Saishōshitennōin was completely "torn down."[43] (Whether this report of the final destruction refers to the building remnants at the original site, or at Itsutsuji, or elsewhere, is unclear.) The dates cited in these accounts are in general agreement with the report of the building's dismantling in *Jōkyūki,* but they differ from it in that *Jōkyūki* pointedly implies some causal connection between the Saishōshitennōin's destruction and the assassination of Sanetomo, which took place while the shogun was paying his New Year's respects at the Tsurugaoka Hachiman shrine in Kamakura, in the first month of 1219.

Still another contemporaneous chronicle, *Rokudaishōjiki* (a narrative of events in the reigns of Takakura, Gotoba's father, through Gosaga, his grandson, told from a sympathetic courtier's point of view), offers yet another perspective on the causes of the monastery's demise: in a passage describing Gotoba's state of mind as he made his way to his place of exile on the island of Oki, after the failure of the Jokyū revolt in 1221, it suggests that "he must then have recalled with deep sorrow the disappointment he had felt when the Saishōshitennōin (along with so much else that he had made) was destroyed by celestial demons" (*Saishōshitennōin dani mo tenma no tame ni kobochikogasarenishi, hoinaku ya oboshimeshiideken*).[44] Exactly who these "demons" (*tenma*) might be—that is, which of Gotoba's enemies, in heaven or on earth—is not made clear, but the passage does seem to attribute the Saishōshitennōin's "collapse and immolation" to forces that lay beyond the Retired Emperor's control, and in opposition to him, whereas most other sources would seem to suggest that its vicissitudes were directed by his own hand.

In Teika's diary, in an entry dated Tenpuku 1.8.18 (in the autumn of 1233), we read that the poet has heard that the monastery's remaining structural elements have once more been recycled: they have now been reassembled for use in the reconstruction of a recently burned-down temple called Kannōji in Kawasaki (a district in the northeastern quarter of the capital, near the banks of the Kamo River), where a rededication ceremony has taken place on that day. Teika here expresses some mild regret that what was once Gotoba's grand votive monastery (*gyoganji*) is now no more, but he also makes a point of noting that "pictures from its pillars and doorways" have been transferred to the new location and installed there intact.[45] It is uncertain whether these "pictures" (*hashira-e* and *tobira-e*) are or are not the *meishoe* prepared in 1207; those paintings are consistently referred to in Teika's diary entries at that time as *shōji(no)ga*, or simply as *shōji*—but *shōji*, of course, were positioned between pillars and could serve as doors. In any case, this is the last mention of the Saishōshitennōin in Teika's diary: from this point, he puts his memories of the project—and his dealings with Gotoba—behind him, and carries on with the more current affairs of his life.

Son'en's *Monyōki* reports that, in 1222, after Gotoba's exile, title to the property on which the Saishōshitennōin had stood was returned once more to Jien, the original donor.[46] The poet-prelate apparently made some effort to bring about the reconstruction of the monastery but had failed to do so by the time of his death in 1225, and the site lay fallow until some ten years later, when his successor as Shōren'in abbot, Jigen, built a new residence for himself on the old monastery's grounds. This was but the first of a series of such residences constructed on this location for the use of the Tendai abbacy and known as the Shirakawa Sanjōbō palace; some of these palaces seem to have been much grander in scale than the original Saishōshitennōin—which, it will be recalled, Gotoba had tried to build on a relatively modest scale, as if in anticipation of its short life span.[47]

As is the case with so many buildings of ancient and medieval—and even more recent—times, one will find no physical trace of the Saishōshitennōin on its former site, even if one goes looking for it. For that matter, there are no physical traces of the Shirakawa Sanjōbō, either. Sanjō, the avenue, is still a major thoroughfare across the modern city, and there are still a number of other major Buddhist institutions in the general vicinity of the Sanjō/ Shirakawa intersection, in what is now the Higashiyama ward of modern Kyoto. But if this busy avenue still crosses the river at the same point as it did in the early thirteenth century—and it may not do so—the spot is, in any case, unmarked as the one-time site of a building that was once called the Saishōshitennōin. What once was there lives only in memory, and in textual traces of the sort that have been assembled here in an effort to conjure images and create memories of what once was. But the effort is fitting: for the Saishōshitennōin poems and paintings, and the building itself, were themselves designed to serve, among other things, as the media for an engagement with cultural memories of other poems, other paintings, and other projects. That engagement in turn was not brought about simply as an aesthetic indulgence, but in the context of a personal political agenda, to- ward the realization of which it was but one means. This was a risky business; the times being what they were, the sponsor and the designers of the building's various parts seem to have known all too well that little of it would last for long. But perhaps it occurred to them that the poems might outlive them and the rest of what they had made, in one form or location or another.[48] In any case, the poems did survive, while little else has—and we can still see in them the intertextual means by which they helped bring about this calculated engagement between that particular present and those varied pasts. We can also see, then, how the recollective gestures operating within and enacted by those poems abetted the casting of the monastery's "spell"— which, if it had really succeeded, would have amounted to a reversal of time, a return to how-things-were, or seemed to have been, at least in memory. Again and again, the program's poems—both those selected for inscription and others—make just such gestures of return: it is thus, then, that word is here again employed in a (failed) attempt to remake the world as it was nostalgically imagined once to have been.

Let us take, for example, the Ōigawa poems. We have seen, already, that special pains were taken over the preparation of the Ōigawa painting—per- haps because of the richness of memories of real royal excursions to that site, and perhaps, as well, because of the richness of the significance of royal excursions per se. The painting does seem to have been designed through reference to earlier Ōigawa visitations, or perhaps to records of *miyuki* elsewhere; the poems composed on Ōigawa likewise manipulate the past in such a way as to relate the present occasion for which they were made to previous and well-remembered occasions. This is clearly not accidental: such depiction, in both word and image, of a place so long associated with special royal presences—and with commemorative and celebratory poem-making carried out under royal auspices—in a program of this kind must indeed have demanded special care, and may well have excited special efforts. For here, in the topic of Ōigawa—an exemplar, in turn, of the associated theme of *miyuki* itself—was an excellent opportunity for the invocation, through multiple media, of divine protection for the nation, in association with the act of asserting power over and through the land and, hence, reinforcing the relationships among lands, the people who inhabit them, and their rulers.

Real Imperial progresses and pilgrimages were powerful symbolic acts because they involved the direct physical visitation of royal persons to landscapes and buildings which they did not normally frequent: the royal personage would make himself or herself manifest in these precincts in order to make contact and be allied with the forces—divine and otherwise—based and active therein. Thus, *miyuki* were at once acts of supplication to these local powers and a preempting of them.[49] Any depiction of such acts—in painting or poem, for example—was both memorialization and repetition of that act, and might carry some remnant of its symbolic and magical weight. It seems quite likely, then, that that weight, and the possibility of its transference to the Saishōshitennōin, was felt quite keenly by its designers and executors as they confronted the Ōigawa topos in particular but also as they contemplated the project as a whole. For, in a sense, the Saishōshitennōin program was a program for the creation of an ersatz *miyuki* to multiple (and artificially adjacent) sites in miniature; its manufacture and installation would make it possible, at least in theory, for Gotoba to imagine himself and his companions in movement in and through a succession of famous, scenic places, displayed upon the walls surrounding them in artificial stasis and under his absolute (and equally artificial) control. And instead of celebratory poems composed on the spot for subsequent recording elsewhere, the words inspired through the imagining of royal presence in the Saishōshitennōin program sites would appear right on those mounted surfaces, as if part of those sites, and would guide the viewer to a particular reading of the word-and-image representation of each site and of the program as a whole.

It should be pointed out, however, that Ōigawa was not, in and of itself, a ritual site: its appeal as a *miyuki* destination lay largely in its natural scenic beauty, and it was for this reason—and also because it was in a relatively wild and unspoiled area not far from the midtown Heian palace—that the place was visited in several generations by Emperors and their retinues in autumn, for the enjoyment of the colorful Ōigawa scenery at its seasonal peak. The appealing conjunction of mountain, colorful foliage, and flowing water that would meet the ear and eye there could be counted on to inspire commemoration in verse; the presence of an Emperor would make composition even more de rigueur and would inevitably prompt the use of these stimuli to the ear and eye as figures of celebration of that presence and prayers for returned visits and perpetual royal attention.

This was certainly the case on that noted occasion in the ninth month of 907, when the Retired Emperor Uda and a group of favored courtiers went out to Ōi to enjoy the sights and then made poems about what they saw (or claimed to have seen). When the poems that have survived from that occasion are assembled from the various anthologies and other sources in which they have been preserved, it becomes quite clear that one of that fall day's literary agendas was to make skillful use of the site's scenic offerings, and of the occasion itself, to pay court to Uda through flattering and congratulatory verse. The mood was set, in part, by the fact that this *miyuki* took place on the morning after the court had held its annual all-night revels in celebration of the "double-nine" or chrysanthemum feast (*Chōyō* or *Kiku no sekku*), the predominant theme of which was "long life."[50] Taking this cue—and also with full awareness of what was no doubt expected of them when traveling to such a place on such a day, and in the Emperor's company—the poets in attendance sought and found ways to address the nine *waka* topics assigned to them in suitably celebratory and felicitous ways. Some did so explicitly, while others were more indirect; but, in one way or another, all made poems that were tantamount to prayers for their Emperor's and their own long lives. This was accomplished through the manipulative representation of those elements of the actual or putative Ōigawa scene that were already marked, and available, as poetic figures for lasting vitality and as emblems of agelessness. For example, on the topic "chrysanthemums [lingering on the banks]," one courtier-poet, Mibu no Tadamine, wrote:

> shimo wakete sakubeki hana mo naki mono o
>   iro o nokoshite hito o tanomuru[51]
> It is not a flower that can bloom through heavy frost,
>   and yet it has kept its color, trustfully waiting for this visitor.

Other participants wrote on the same topic in a very similar vein; for example, Ōnakatomi Yorimoto's *kiku* poem is:

miyuki o ba kyō to ya kanete kiku no hana
 kinō no iro mo asede nokoreru[52]
It looks as if these chrysanthemums heard in advance of today's Imperial visit,
 for they are showing the same fine colors as they did yesterday.

The same poet, and his colleagues Sakanoue no Korenori and Fujiwara Tadahira, also manipulate the topic "pines aging in the river's lagoons" in the same vein, to imply by various means that these symbols of longevity par excellence (and, by extension, all living things that inhabit the Ōigawa environs) are pleased to be the subjects of Imperial inspection, and that all that is natural—and timeless—hearabouts has joined to welcome the ruler, to make his visit memorable, and to place it in the context of the flow of history (as represented by the river itself, and by all that it has "seen"):

Korenori:
kono kawa no irie no matsu wa oinikeri
 furuki miyuki no koto ya towamashi[53]
The pines that stand in the lagoons of this river have attained a great age:
 if only we could ask them, then, to tell us about the *miyuki* of ancient times.

Tadahira:
e ni fukaku toshi wa henikeru matsu naredo
 kakaru miyuki wa kefu ya miruramu[54]
They are pines that have dwelt here with deeps roots in this lagoon for many years,
 and yet they are here to witness a *miyuki* like this!

Yorimoto:
e ni fukaku toshi furu matsu wa
 minasoko no kage ni sae koso iro wa miekere[55]
The vibrant color of the aged pines—whose roots lie deep in this lagoon where they have dwelt for all these years—
 can even be seen in their reflections on the river's bottom.

Both Tadahira and Yorimoto further imply that deep and powerful forces are responsible for bringing Ōigawa and its denizens—here represented by the aged pines—into contact with their royal visitor. The phrase *e ni fukaku*, with which both begin their poems, and which is here translated literally as "deep in the lagoon," can also be construed as *eni fukaku*, in which case it evokes a Buddhist-tinged view of causality—that is, the idea that particular states or phenomena come about through deeply rooted causal connections (*eni*). Thus, these poets suggest that the Ōi pines (like Tadamine's and

Yorimoto's Ōi chrysanthemums) have been preserved and are uniquely energized by an unnamed, invisible, but readily apparent force which long ago
ensured their capacity to await the Emperor's coming and empowered them
to greet him in a state of undiminished vitality and unrivalled beauty at the
time of what is now seen as a predestined and inevitable encounter.

And in other poems, these and other attending poets go on to suggest
that, now that this foreordained encounter has taken place, the moment is
one that should be captured and, if possible, extended, so that the stirring
sights made available to their eyes through the miraculous conjunction of
this peak of seasonal beauty with the Emperor's presence may continue to
be available for viewing throughout time.[56] Thus, Korenori writes on "scat-
tering maple leaves":

> momijiba no chirite nagaruru Ōigawa
>   seze no shiranami kaketodomenan[57]
> Scattered maple leaves are drifting in the waters of Ōigawa:
>   I wish that the white wavelets on the shoals might stay them!

Tadahira writes similarly, though not necessarily on the exact same topic:

> Ogurayama mine no momiji kokoro araba
>   ima hitotabi no miyuki matanan
> Maple leaves on Ogura mountain: if you had a heart,
>   I would have you wait for one more royal visit!

This is perhaps the best-known of all Ōigawa *miyuki* poems.[58] It is usually
associated with the 907 excursion, although the *kotobagaki* that accompanies
its appearance in *Shūi wakashū* does not specify a date of composition other
than "in the time of the Retired Emperor Uda" (Teishiin). This after-the-fact
preface does suggest, however, that Tadahira wrote the poem while that
particularly noted *miyuki* (or another one quite like it) was in the planning
stages: the idea of going to Ōi is attributed to Uda himself, and the poem is
presented as having been made to serve as a means of informing the reigning
Emperor (Uda's son Daigo) of his father's plans. Thus we can read the poem
as a go-between's (i.e., Tadahira's) invitation to join the party—perhaps on
the second day of a two-day sojourn.[59]

But Tadahira, of course, evokes more than a two-day span of time in his
poem: he goes so far as to ask the leaves on the slopes that overlook the river
to understand (with some humanlike capacity to see into time) that there
may always be yet other royal visitors, that beyond each encounter there
surely will be at least another (*ima hitotabi no miyuki*). His request to them
is, in effect, an exhortation to fix themselves in time, in defiance of other
natural forces and in obedience to their own desire to accommodate the

royal pleasure; and the reward that is promised them is yet more contact with the preserving and transforming force of Imperial charisma, which will carry them along with it toward eternity—in resistance to what would otherwise be their fated and rapid decay.

Exactly three hundred years after the 907 excursion, when the Saishōshitennōin poets were at work on their contributions, the Ōigawa they imagined and represented was, indeed, a place of fixed character, preserved and defined for all time by its contact with royal charisma and by the poems that other poets had written about that place and those contacts. Its decay had been arrested: its visual attractions were as vibrant as ever. As they wrote the poems to be submitted for possible selection, these poets perhaps imagined, as well, a similarly idealized Ōigawa that would be fixed in paint and mounted—with one of their poems inscribed upon it—on a *shōji* in a room that would serve as the ex-Emperor's private bedchamber. To this task they brought such knowledge as they had of the conventions of Ōigawa poesy—from the 907 occasion onward—which had so firmly defined its features for poets and painters alike. The seasonal designation for the site, inevitably, was autumn; and as the Saishōshitennōin poets then wrote, accordingly, of the river's lapping waters and colored maple leaves, drifting "now," as "then," in the trailing wakes of Imperial excursion boats, they thereby offered the inviting (if patently false) impression that the present imagined Ōigawa scene (constituted jointly by their poems and by the accompanying painting) was "contiguous" and perhaps even identical with the scene seen in the recollected past, and still ordered by the same eternal forces.

Gotoba's own Ōigawa poem typifies this pose:

Ōigawa nami no kayoiji tachikaeri
  ato aru kaze ni konoha chiritsutsu[60]
In Ōi River the path of the returning waves turns back again,
  and leaves are falling in a wind marked by the past.

The poem itself is full of the marks of return to a site where time seems to stand still, or where disparate moments in time seem to overlap one another: *kayoiji*—"the path taken in return"; *tachikaeri*—"turning back"; *ato aru kaze*—"a breeze that bears the marks of former times." Teika's Ōigawa poem is even more explicit about this overlapping or collapse of many moments into one:

Ōigawa mare no miyuki ni toshi henuru
  momiji no funaji ato wa arikeri[61]
Royal visits to Ōi River now are rare, yet through all the years
  the leaf-strewn wake of their pleasure boats remains.

In Gotoba's poem, the marks of the past (*ato*) have somehow been inscribed upon the wind, which tosses the scattered leaves now just as it did in former times, so that the observer cannot tell whether what he sees is happening now or then—but the distinction is unimportant, for the point is that the place and the conditions that prevail therein are unchanged, even in minute detail. In Teika's poem, the same word, *ato,* is still the unmistakable mark of time's imprint upon the scene, but it is also a wake left upon the river's surface by boats that have been rowed upon it again and again, on the occasions of storied *miyuki* that now, sadly, are few and far between. This wake, Teika claims, is a permanent, lasting fixture of the scene, inscribed upon it for all time: it moves in the currents of the river's flow, but never dissipates, so even if the Ōigawa *miyuki* of which it is evidence should occur no more, there will, at least, be an image of it upon a sliding door in the Saishōshitennōin—or, at the very least, there will be this poem, preserving that image even when that painting is no more.

Teika's Ōigawa poem seems to take the same cue as Gotoba's, in its play on *ato*; but, more directly, it owes its diction, and its perspective on the scene, to a poem in the *Gosen wakashū* by Ariwara Yukihira, which is itself a commemoration of yet another Emperor's return to a particularly favored place in the Ōigawa vicinity—a feeder stream called Serikawa:

> Ninna no mikado, Saga no ontoki no tameshi ni te, Serikawa ni miyuki
> shitamaeru hi:
>> Saga no yama miyuki taenishi
>> Serikawa no chiyo no furumichi ato wa arikeri[62]
> Composed on the day that the Emperor Kōkō, following the example of Emperor Saga, went on an excursion to Serikawa:
>> Royal visits to Saga Mountain have long since ceased,
>> but traces of the old paths of a thousand ages past are still here beside
>> Serikawa.

The occasion of Yukihira's poem, as reported here, was a moment in which one Emperor, Kōkō (Uda's father, who reigned 884-887), deliberately revived and recapitulated the movements of his grandfather, Saga (who reigned 809-823).[63] This recapitulation took place in the generation before Uda's memorable visit to Ōi, the poems about which, as we have seen, were also shaped by a rhetoric of return and repetition, as were the poems that would subsequently recapitulate those rhetorical gestures in turn. But just as Teika would, some three centuries later, Yukihira claims that traces left by previous royal passages along the river are still visible, even after an interval of many years and a falling-off in royal attention to the site. Both poems—Yukihira's and Teika's—thus make the same affirmation, by claiming to see that which cannot be: both, by collapsing time, confirm the seemingly unchanged relationship that has pertained between generations of rulers and the land they rule, for both insist (against all odds, against normal expectations of what can and cannot be seen) that the marks of former visitations, and of the ancient "way" of rulership (*chitose no furumichi*) of which they are a sign, are still visible in the river's waters. And thus, by this means, these marks and signs *are* made visible—if not in nature, in the real river, then in a painting of it (such as might be made in conjunction with this poem), or in the mind's eye.

The recapitulative depiction or manufacture of such a scene, in the joint medium of a new poem and painting—as in the Saishōshitennōin—would be yet another reenactment or re-creation of those moments in the past, and a means toward the preservation, or reinstatement, of the ideally unchanged relationship that they would celebrate. We cannot tell whether a viewer gazing at the new Ōigawa painting made by Mitsutoki for the Saishōshi-tennōin would have found it reminiscent of other particular paintings of that site; but if we read the poems submitted for inscription upon it as guides to or commentary on the program, or as its script, we can assume that at least some of the painting's features (the poses or gestures of human figures, or the configuration of the river's course or of the adjacent pathways) may have suggested the themes of return and repetition to the viewer. And Teika's *honkadori* Ōigawa poem, with its overt gesture to Yukihira's and, through it, to other moments of recapitulation, is in itself an enactment, or pantomime, of return—like Kōkō's return to Serikawa, and like the entire Saishōshi-tennōin program's return to the visual and textual gestures of the distant but not yet forgotten past. In other words, it would appear, a particularly complex but lucid intertextuality here energizes the Ōigawa moment in the program, shapes its meaning, and projects its message—which is a prayer for the lasting revival of Imperial sovereignty over a harmonious, ordered land. And at other points throughout the program, that same meaning and that message will likewise surface as motifs that may be drawn out, accentuated, and elaborated upon, thus imparting that meaning and message to the program as a whole—or, rather, bringing that underlying message of the whole into full view.

The poem finally selected for inscription on the painting of the Ōigawa scene, Masatsune's, uses intertextual means of a similar kind to invoke the past; but, in this case, the gestures are toward the rhetoric of *waka* in and of itself, and the recapitulation is of the oft-repeated act of poetic viewing, and interpreting, an idealized autumnal scene at a moment of transition:

Kono kawa ni momiji wa nagaru
  ashihiki no yama no kai aru arashi fukurashi[64]

Colored leaves are flowing here in the river:
   storm winds must be blowing in the mountain gorges.

Here, the echoes are of such well-known poems as *Kokin wakashū* #284
(Tatsuta*gawa momijiba nagaru*/Kamunabi no Mimuro *no yama* ni shigure
fururashi—"Colored leaves are flowing in Tatsuta River: / showers must be
falling on Mimuro, the divine mountain")[65] and #320 (*Kono kawa ni momijiba nagaru* / Okuyama *no* yukige no mizu zo ima *masarurashi*—"Colored
leaves are flowing here in the river: snow-melt waters must be gathering
into torrents in the heart of the mountains").[66] These are poems that purport
to be about other (specific) rivers viewed in other (unspecified) autumns;
but these positions, and the diction exercised therein, provide a pattern
which Masatsune can readily transfer to his own imagined stance at Ōi (or
to that of another imagined viewer of the river or its painted image). These
are, yet again, exercises in seeing that which cannot be seen, through a
process of deductive reasoning which gives all three poems their balanced
rhetorical structure: evidence in the waters before the eyes of the anonymous *Kokin* poem-speakers moves them to suspect that it is a shower on
distant Mimuro Mountain that has caused the Tatsuta River to fill with
maple leaves, or that snow melt in deep mountain valleys is causing the
leaf-strewn river at hand to flow so swiftly. When Masatsune adopts the
same pose and claims to see and surmise something so much like what
others have seen and surmised (in verse, if not in real nature), he marks
his poem as a simulacrum of those poems and others that have been made
in their mold: he thereby invests his poem of imagined return to Ōigawa—
and the painting upon which it was to be inscribed—with the dimensions
of return to the hallowed history of *waka* itself, with all its associations
with royal patronage, presence, and protection, and its rich traditions of
verbal "gazing" upon the land. Celebration of that history, and of such
traditions, is a more than fitting way to celebrate the occasion of the Saishōshitennōin, which was soon to be (or already was) a moment in that history
as well: for, through such intertextual means, all such power as might still
reside in hallowed words such as these, and others, that have been used
again and again by *waka* poets and other singers, and inscribed again and
again, in places of honor in their hallowed canons, could be invoked for
and incorporated into the program's "spell," invigorating its action through
the reinvigoration of these time-tested nodes of verbal energy. The program
generated to abet or embody that spell was one that would propel *utamakura meisho* (as particularly potent nodes of such energy) into action again,
as so often before; throughout it, the power of their intertextuality is unleashed and is wielded at large and on a grand scale across the panoply of

poems and paintings *and* on the intimate scale of each individual verse
(and, perhaps, in each individual *meishoe* as well).

The rhetoric of return across time—and, in particular, the enactment of
a deliberate (and meaning-full) feigning of confusion about where one stands
(as poem-speaker or scene-viewer) in time—is perhaps most prominent in
the Ōigawa segment of the program, and there, without doubt, it serves as
the defining direction for the participating poets' intertextual moves; but it
appears elsewhere, and in some other forms, throughout the program. Because it turns out to serve so well in this vein, it seems almost surprising, in
retrospect, that Waka no ura should not have been among the *meisho* topics
originally programmed by Teika and his associates; but, perhaps, Gotoba
insisted subsequently on its inclusion because he anticipated just how well
it would fit in, and how effectively it would add to the development of this
motif—and to the configuration of the entire program as a recapitulated
royal journey in miniature. As we have previously noted (in chapter 1), Waka
no ura poesy often involves itself in punning play with the name of the place
itself (as Poetry Bay). The poems composed by the Saishōshitennōin poets
largely leave this potentiality untouched, though by its mere presence the
name evokes the history of poetry itself; instead, or in addition, they busy
themselves with the scenic imagery long associated with the *place*, Waka no
ura—perhaps, one imagines, in order to provide a useful "script" for Sonchi,
the designated Waka no ura painter, but also, of course, to produce an
illusion of contiguity with disparate other moments in poetic time. The poem
chosen for inscription on the finished product is Michiteru's:

> Waka no ura ya shiohi o sashite yuku tazu no
>   tsubasa no nami ni yadoru tsukikage[67]
> At Waka no ura, moonlight lodges on the beating wings
>   of a crane that flies toward the ebbing tide.

As script for this moment in the unfolding sequence, Michiteru's poem bears
with it the prominent marks of memory, in the form of figures transferred
from the most famous of all Waka no ura poems, Akahito's *Man'yōshū* #919:

> Waka no ura ni shio michikureba kata o nami
>   ashibe o sashite tazu nakiwataru
> At Waka Bay, when the tide is high, there is no beach,
>   and so the cranes are crying as they make their way
>   toward beds of reeds.

As it happens, Akahito's poem, as well as the *chōka* (#917) that precedes it
(with another *hanka* as well) in book 6 of the *Man'yōshū*, are also *miyuki*

poems: they commemorate a royal visit, that of the Emperor Shōmu, to the province of Kii in the early winter of 725. In the *chōka* that anchors this sequence, Akahito—who went along on the trip to record in verse what the Emperor's party saw and did—lays out the Waka no ura scene that then filled Shōmu's commanding gaze even as he (temporarily) occupied it himself:

> yasumishishi
> wago Ōkimi no
> tokomiya to
> tsukaematsureru
> Saikano yu
> sogai ni miyuru
> okitsu shima
> kiyoki nagisa ni
> kaze fukeba
> shiranami sawaki
> shio hireba
> tamamo karitsutsu
> kamiyo yori
> shika zo tōtoki
> Tamatsushimayama[68]
> From the fields of Saika,
> where our gracious lord, sovereign of the earth's eight corners,
> has built the palace in which we serve,
> the offshore island can be seen at one side.
> On the pure strands,
> when the wind blows, the waves crash;
> when the tide falls, they cut the jeweled sea grass.
> Since the age of the gods
> it has been awesome like this—
> Tamatsushima, jeweled sea island![69]

There is more here than courtly celebration of the stirring seaside panorama, although Akahito vividly reproduces the sheer pleasure of viewing it. He also reminds us of the significance of his sovereign's having established a temporary residence in this locale and on a vantage point from which he can admire and lay claim to a site where time seems to stand still: from there, he sees just what was seen in the age of the gods, his ancestors, and knows that this aged, ageless land is his as it was theirs. Then, in the envoys, there is a shift in focus, to narrower segments of the scene, and a shift in mood as well: though longing intensely for home, the viewer finds it hard to tear himself away, even as the passage of time and the shifting of the tides alters the configuration of the scene before his eyes. But by recording these moments of transition as he claims to have seen them, Akahito effectively fixed this particular Waka no ura scene in time: and one result of his having done so is that Teika and his colleagues must have had this poem in mind when they addressed the Waka no ura topos for the Saishōshitennōin, and that they therefore treated it—as they did Ōigawa—as a place defined largely by its history of royal visitation as recorded in verse.

Their task, in addition, was to place Gotoba's and their own collective moment in that continuum. The reference that their poems and, presumably, the painting both made to the history of Imperial presence at the site is more subtle than in the Ōigawa case, but their route through the language of Akahito's *Man'yōshū* #917-919 nevertheless does lead straight back to Shōmu's *miyuki* there. Thus, as in the Ōigawa poems, the verses created to mark the Waka no ura moment in the Saishōshitennōin program are poems that unfold with layers of time: their allusive gestures position the present moment of poem-making and poem-reading, and of visual interaction with a painted representation of this scene, as yet another moment in a long and seemingly uninterrupted series. This is particularly clear in Shunzei's Daughter's offering, which reaches beyond Akahito's famous *hanka* to figures in the *chōka* itself:

> chiji no aki no hikari o kakete
> waka no ura no tamamo ni nabiku ariake no tsuki[70]
> With all the brightness of a thousand thousand autumns
> the dawn moonlight is spreading over the jeweled sea grasses of Waka no ura.

While looking thus backward, Shunzei's Daughter's poem also peers into the future as well. Her dawn moon, the source of light that now, as in so many autumns before, is shedding its radiance upon the glistening Waka no ura kelp beds (and on the wings of the crane, in Michiteru's verse), surely stands for Gotoba himself: he is, of course, Shōmu's direct descendant, as a commanding observer of the Waka no ura scene and as a font of that energy which even now, as then, causes poems to be made and provides for occasions and sites for their inscription—and which, presumably, will do so for a long time to come. Thus, like Akahito's ancient *chōka,* which describes Shōmu's occupation of a site occupied by his own divine forebears, these new poems take possession of the site in Gotoba's name, and direct its incorporation—in reduced scale—into the Saishōshitennōin spatial program which is also so emphatically his. By means of the spell thus cast, Gotoba is himself transported, in imagination, to this fabled site, which is also "his"; there, with the aid of his trusted companions, he harvests his own "jeweled sea grass," and adds this precious product of the site to his personal hoard of timeless treasures and other charms of immortality.

Another site depicted in the program which was also very emphatically "his" was Minase. Emperors in several generations had built retreats for themselves in that vicinity, and Gotoba's villa there was one of his special favorites. (It was also the site of several notable gatherings held there, at his invitation, for competitive, programmed poem-making.)[71] It is perhaps not surprising, therefore, that Gotoba eventually selected his own composition for inscription on the Saishōshitennōin Minase scene. This poem is a fine example of his art and of *Shinkokin* style, particularly in the way it captures the sights and sounds of a moment near daybreak with understatement and restraint that are nonetheless as deeply resonant and clear as a temple bell:

Minaseyama konoha arawa ni naru mama ni
  onoe no kane no koe zo chikazuku[72]
On Minase Mountain, leaves on the trees gradually come into view
  as the sound of the dawn bell from the peak comes ever closer.

Like Waka no ura and so many other topoi, Minase is an *utamakura* that underwent a transformation in usage as *waka* history proceeded through time. At a very early stage, it was the sound of the word *minase* itself—a common rather than a proper noun—that was manipulated for reference to a dry stream (*mi-na-se*, literally, "shoals that have no water in them"), or to the course of a river unseen beneath the earth's surface. But with the increasing prominence of the specific place called Minase, in Settsu Province, as a site of Imperial retreat, later poets tended to abandon this fixation on the name itself and substituted descriptions of putative elements of a more particular Minase scene—wind blowing across adjacent hills, or stag's cries, or temple bells resounding in an otherwise tranquil and seemingly empty space.[73] Also, by yet another route, chrysanthemums—which were so prominent in Ōigawa poesy—also found a place in Minase verse; and, in fact, that commonly held association was one that bound these two sites in a special relationship with one another which would cause them to appear as adjacent and coordinate subjects in various *waka* programs, as in the Saishōshitennōin.[74] Thus, in yet another way, the Ōigawa and Minase moments in the program emerge again as conjoined moments in a very long continuum across time—one that reaches back, in this case, at least as far as one of the very earliest poetry competitions on record—a *kiku awase*, or "chrysanthemum match" held at the court of Emperor Uda in the autumn of 891. On this particular occasion, competing teams presented fine examples of chrysanthemums expertly arranged in miniature landscapes presented for viewing on lacquered trays. These elaborate tray scenes (called *suhama*) were the topical prompts for their poems, and because each tray depicted a different famous place, each poem celebrated both that place and the central theme, the chrysanthemum and its great vitality, as well—and, in turn, offered prayers that that same everlasting vitality might be shared by the royal convener of the *utaawase* itself. The first of these trays depicted Minase: another depicting Ōigawa followed soon after.[75]

It is intriguing to think, again, of how the Saishōshitennōin program replicates these storied moments in *waka* history: for here, as at this *kiku awase* of old, miniature artificial landscapes were being manufactured and would be displayed with poems (which likewise, in their own way, would replicate selected famous scenes)—and all this was taking place because an Emperor had asked for it, as a result of which what then was done was done to honor that energizing and empowering authority, and to strive (at least rhetorically) for its perpetuation. The Saishōshitennōin poets seem to have been very much aware that this was their task; and, in carrying it out in their Minase poems, they also strove to bring all of the strains of its traditional poesy into play, as a means for once more contributing to the forces that might ensure their own latter-day sovereign's long life and ensure his success in subsequent endeavors.

Thus, for example, in the scenes which the poems offered by Teika and Ariie portray, the "buried Minase river" once more gives life to a garden (*niwa*) of chrysanthemums, the flowers of immortality, cultivated here by an off-stage sage-king who has obtained (through them) the means for evading death forever. (A garden or courtyard [*niwa*] is often described as the de-limited site in which a sage [*sen* or *hijiri*] performs the ascetic acts by which he guarantees his own immortality; and the consumption of fluid gathered from chrysanthemums growing within that space is often mentioned as one of those magical means in both Chinese and Japanese depictions of such sages.) So these poems are not only possible "scripts" for paintings but also for renewed expressions of hope for the "endlessness" of Gotoba's life span and of his transcendent authority.

Ariie:
yorozuyo no chigiri zo musubu Minasegawa
  sekiiruru niwa no kiku no shitamizu
Minase is a river that gives the promise of thousands of years of life:
  channeled to this garden, it flows beneath chrysanthemums.

Teika:
kono sato ni oisenu chiyo o Minasegawa
  sekiiruru niwa no kiku no shitamizu.
Here at Minase River, let me see you thrive, unaging, for a thousand ages:
  channeled to this garden, the river flows beneath chrysanthemums.[76]

In both poems, the river itself (or its name) is the guarantor of Gotoba's longevity. In Ariie's, its waters seal a vow that he will live for "innumerable ages" (*yorozuyo no chigiri zo musubu*); in Teika's, the river's participatory role in this conjuring is compounded by the contingent use of the first syllable of its name (*mi-*) as the verb "see," the object of which is "the thousands of ages (*chiyo*) through which the sage king will dwell, without every growing old (*oisenu*), in this village (*sato*) where he himself (with the river's aid) has caused these magical chrysanthemums to grow." (That which "sees" may be the river, as witness; the sage-king himself, "observing" his own immortality; or another observer—the speaker of the poem—who rejoices at the thought of this everlasting union of person and place.) It is also probably no coincidence that the second halves of both these poems are identical: some or all of the participants may have been in close contact about their respective preparations for the whole Saishōshitennōin project, and these two poets may have exchanged views about how best to handle this particular scene.

In any case, whether through joint consultation or no, both Ariie and Teika seem to have come up with similar responses to the Minase topical prompt: by reaching back into *waka*'s living history to frame their poems, they could once more add layers of time and signifying nuance to the Saishōshitennōin program. And, in this setting, they could scarcely have written poems about Minase without conveying gestures of reverence to Gotoba himself. He was no doubt pleased by their compliments—their prayers that he, in effect, might never grow old, nor ever die—but he still precluded them by choosing his own poem over theirs for inscription on one of the doorways in what would be a room within his own living quarters in the monastery. There—whenever he might chance to occupy that space—he could then look forward to enjoying his own representation of his own return to "his" Minase.

Explicit prayers for his longevity, like those in Ariie's and Teika's Minase poems, appear in one other particular phase of the program—in the treatment of the place called Shikama Market (*Shikama no ichi*), which was specified for assignment to Gotoba's dining area. There, in the room where the Retired Emperor would take sustenance, the scene depicted would perhaps have been rather quotidian, perhaps something of the kind that has come to be called *fūzoku ga*, scenes of daily life: for, if the poems composed for it served as cue, it would have shown a bustle of merchants, tradesmen, townsfolk, and peasants, buying and selling a variety of local goods. In several of the Shikama poems, this crowd is represented by the word *tami*, "the people," and their "great number" metonymically prompts

hopeful speculation about the great number of Gotoba's own years of life
to come:

Shunzei's Daughter:
itomanami Shikama no ichi ni tatsu tami mo
  shino ni kazu sou kimi ga yo no aki
The number of your people who crowd Shikama Market
  grows ever greater, leaving no space in which they may stand:
  so may the autumns of your life add up, unceasingly.

Teika:
kimi ga yo wa tare mo Shikama no ichijiruku
  toshi aru tami no amatsusora kana
It is clear to all that while you live it shall be thus, at it is in Shikama Market:
  the people shall enjoy the heavenly gift of rich harvests, year after year.

Tomochika:
kimi ga yo wa Shikama no ichi ni tatsu tami no
  kazu kagirinaku kuni zo sakafuru[77]
May your years be thus: as limitless as the numbers of the people who crowd
  Shikama market,
  in a realm that knows no end to prosperity.

All three of these sample poems feature thematically appropriate puns and
plays which underscore the gestures of honor to Gotoba. In Shunzei's
Daughter's poem, for example, *itomanami* (literally, "as there is no interval")
describes the shoulder-to-shoulder crowding in the market but also suggests
the wish that there shall be no interruption in the years of the ex-Emperor's
life. In both Teika's and Tomochika's, the first two syllables of the place-
name, "Shika-," are used in overlapping structures so that they also mean
"thus" (*shika*). The form of the verb *sakafu* ("prosper") used by Tomochika
is rather unusual; one would expect, instead, *sakaeru*, an inflected form of
sakau—but *sakafuru*) is not unprecedented.

But the chosen poem, Jien's, takes a somewhat different approach to the
topic, through play with the name of one of the commodities traditionally
associated with Shikama Market in poetry—an indigo dye (*ai*) used locally
since ancient times to make a dark blue cloth (called *kachi*).

inishie no ai yori mo koki miyo nare ya
  Shikama no ichi no iro o miru kana[78]
May your lifetime be still richer than the indigo of ancient times:
  we see now the color of the cloth they sell in Shikama Market.

The poem is a riddle that offers its own solution, for "the color of the cloth they sell in Shikama Market" is indeed *ai* (*ai-iro*). In earlier Shikama Market poesy, Shikama's *kachi* cloth, dyed in this color (*iro*) called *ai*, was more often than not the matériel for play on the sound of these names, with *ai* standing for passionate love (*ai*), *iro* for "erotic desire" as well as color, and *kachi* for "winning, exceeding, overwhelming," with further amplification of the figural complexity in variants which manipulate the sound of *aisome* ("to start to dye"/"to begin to fall in love").[79] Jien has almost—but not quite—divested this cluster of figures of its conventionalized erotic nuance: in his poem, *iro* still may suggest desire, but it is now his, and the people's, desire for Gotoba's long life, and their "love" (*ai*) is that of loyal subjects for their overlord, as well as the color of a cloth that they can see (*miru*)—perhaps on the surface of the painting upon which this very poem was eventually inscribed. If, indeed, Jien's second line is thus literally deictic, it can be read as directing its reader-viewer toward contemplation of the way that it, and the painting of which it became a part or partner, and the space they occupy, together with the other poem-and-painting pairs of the program, might act as a charm for Gotoba's physical, personal, and political benefit.[80] And, furthermore, if this is the significance of Jien's gesture, it is important to note that it is one made by replicating *and* altering a handful of gestures and usages of the past that were "native" to the topic of Shikama Market. Jien knew exactly what to do with the commodities he found available there, and he seems to have also sensed that the Emperor's dining room was a good place to offer this sort of toast to his health in verse. Indeed, what better way was there to show his "love" for this patron?

The Shikama poems remind us of several important features of *uta-makura meisho* poesy. We see here, as so often with other site-topics, how physical or material properties or products of specific places are transformed into template tropes that are then circulated and replicated widely and which may endure as fixed nodes of *waka*'s rhetorical vocabulary. We also see that the strategic deployment and reinvigoration of these energetic nodes is itself a mode of signification. The resuscitation of the old in the new Saishōshi-tennōin program signifies a propulsive drive toward the future. Celebration of the durable "old" is, in and of itself, an affirmation of a past that is treated as if contiguous with the present and therefore powerful as a determinant of what lies ahead. The allusive gesture, the weaving of the intertextual fabric and its display, are steps in the creation of a design that can be read as aesthetic exercise and enshrined as an objet d'art but which also, at the same time, and through those gestures and displays, embodies and energizes an action. The energy that lay at hand in allusive, intertextual *utamakura meisho* poesy was unleashed in the Saishōshitennōin both to build and to destroy:

the program propelled the special languages integrated there—the languages of poetry, painting, and spatial design—into actions that were recapitulations of actions past, designed and redesigned to cause change in the present and to ensure the future.

The design and use of intertextual energies in such complex signifying compositions was something that Teika, in particular, knew a great deal about; and he knew, among other things, how to find the properties that might release the energies needed for this program, not only in texts, sites, and precedents that were already configured for association with royal charisma and authority—like Ōigawa—but elsewhere, throughout the canons of text-shaped memory, wherever a richness rooted in the past might be mined once again for signification in the present. The allusive pantomimes then performed with these properties may not read as explicit gestures of fealty or prayers for longevity, but they nonetheless powerfully celebrate the claim to continuity with the past, and thus enrich and energize the "new" design in analogous ways. Teika's poem, chosen for inscription on the Ōyodo no ura scene, is a good example of this intertextual and intertemporal operation:

> Ōyodo no ura ni karihosu mirume dani
>   kasumi ni taete kaeru karigane[81]
> At Ōyodo Strand they are cutting and drying *mirume* seaweed,
>   but even the sight of returning wild geese is lost in the mist.

The seaside activity described—yet another quotidian scene—appears again and again in ancient poetry. Its pictorial representation might well occupy the foreground or lower quarter of an Ōyodo no ura painting, while geese might be shown disappearing into clouds of mist above, in the upper portion of the picture plane. Similarly, on the surface of the poem itself, Teika places an obvious focus for the reader's attention—an old and oft-repeated *kake-kotoba* pun on *mirume*, which is both the name of a type of edible algae (*Codium fragile*) and a phrase that means "the eye that sees" or simply sight (*miru me*). But this surface feature, appearing in conjunction with the name of the place itself, is a signal of the whole poem's allusive engagement with the contours of another particular textual site or moment—one occupied by an exchange of poems, between a romantically inclined man and a rather disinterested lady, in section 75 of the *Ise monogatari* (Tales of Ise):

> (The lady:)
> Ōyodo no hama ni ou chō miru kara ni
>   kokoro wa naginu katarawanedomo

Having seen you, like the "sea"-grass that grows on Ōyodo Beach,
  my heart is content, though we have not met.
(The man:)
Sode nurete ama no kari hosu watatsumi no
  miru o au ni te yamamu to ya suru[82]
Can you be satisfied to take "seeing"
  —like the "sea"-grass that fisherfolk harvest,
    wetting their sleeves—
  in exchange for "meeting?"

In these poems, the *miru* seaweed is present only as a part of the wordplay packages that these two protagonists (who are not fisherfolk, and do not dwell near the sea) toss at one another. In Teika's new poem, it retains the plasticity that makes it an apt implement for such play, and is still involved with that part of the poem that has to do with the act of "seeing," but it is also part of a program for a *mise-en-scène* that would yield a representation of an actual, and nameable, seaside place. Teika also replicates the structure of the earlier Ōyodo poems with an extended preface that embeds the word for seaweed, *mirume,* and then segues into an adjacent syntactical sphere in which *mirume* means "the eyes that see" (or, try to see) the flying geese. But whereas this kind of play, in the *Ise* poems, serves almost exclusively as a preface or guide phrase that propels the auditor or reader toward the main statements of those poems, Teika's analogous turn on *mirume* marks the word as an organic, native occupant of the constructed marine scene that is his poem's product or visual adjunct. These, then, are some of the ways that Teika's poem simultaneously displays its sameness and its difference vis-à-vis the earlier poems. Through these gestures, the Ōyodo no ura moment in the total program is specially marked as one enriched by its special relationship to a particular, older, classic text, at the same time showing how it has been made anew for the present project. The tie to *Ise* determined, in part, what Teika wrote here: but the energy captured and released through the process of thus looking back toward and into that text is energy now redirected into and for the new Saishōshitennōin text, strengthening its roots in the past while complicating and enriching its discourse for the present.

Similarly, of course, the presence in memory of moments in *Tale of Genji* both determines and enriches the moments in the Saishōshitennōin program that are planned as pauses along the imagined journey at the two sites among the forty-six in the program that are most closely associated with that text: Suma and Akashi. Teika's Suma poem, though not selected for inscription, is typical:

Suma no ama no narenishi sode mo shio tarenu

seki fukikoyuru aki no urakaze[83]

Tears are falling once again upon the sleeves of the fisherman who has grown
used to living here at Suma:
the autumn wind is blowing across the barrier.

In *Genji,* Suma is the site of the protagonist's life in exile, a place where tears
continually weight his sleeves, where unbearable loneliness is heightened by
the ravaging autumn winds that blow off the nearby sea. In the Saishōshitennōin Suma verses, this configuration remains in place, and, through
direct, explicit gestures to the *Genji* text, Suma is once more portrayed as a
site defined by grief, loss, and isolation: yet the very act of allusive engagement with this Suma intertext renders this new invocation of the site's
negative power as a positive, enriching force for the Saishōshitennōin program. That negativity is not effaced, or even reduced, but, by virtue of the
fact that it is there because it has been sought out in the past and thus
brought forward into the present exercise, it simultaneously takes on positive
value as well: once more, the past is validated for the purpose of releasing
its constructive energy into the endeavor at hand.

Then, just as in *Genji,* an Akashi interval follows upon the Suma period,
and with it comes some thematic amelioration of the Suma trials. Genji finds
comforting companionship, and love, of a sort, at Akashi—a gentler place,
marked for poetry by the tranquil moon that shines above the nearby sea.
This is the view of Akashi replicated in the Saishōshitennōin poems, of which
Teika's may serve again as an example:

Akashigata isa ochikochi mo shiratsuyu no
okabe no sato no nami no tsukikage[84]

It is hard to tell whether the Akashi shore is far or close
in the moonlit view from the village on the hill bathed in white dew.

There are many poems like this one in the full Saishōshitennōin set: ostensibly, they describe presences in or views of scenes constructed and configured in past poesy. They need not offer explicit prayers for or compliments
to the project's patron in order to fit in; rather, they offer the illusion of a
viewer or a person within a scene who stands where countless others have
stood, and, by the offering of that gesture alone, they place the moment of
present composition, or utterance, and the moment of the program as a
whole, in a literary continuum that is thus made to appear whole, un-
ruptured, and in order. Positive energy is released through the occupation
of this position, just as it is in the performance of an explicitly allusive gesture
to a poem of the past. The very act of composing poems on these topics,
these famous places, is ipso facto intertextual, and thereby contains within

itself a vast potential for the generation of positive energy; even when the mode of generation is retrospective, it serves to connect the experience of the past (however inaccurately or fictitiously "remembered," or misrepresented) to what lies at hand and to what lies ahead as well. Thus, the past is imposed upon the present and future as a defining discourse. Events in other spheres of action may bring about other results; but, for a brief time, and in a confined space, there prevails the momentary illusion that language thus deployed can control the world rather than be controlled by it.

It will be remembered that Teika sought to control the "mysterious" properties attributed to the sites of the far northeast, Michinoku, by allocating their representations to a relatively out-of-the-way quarter of the Saishō-shitennōin building. This perceived need to neutralize the powers latent in these sites, or to naturalize their exotic properties, parallels and is an extension of the approach taken by generations of court poets as they appropriated the names and features of these distant places and "tamed" them for domestic use in mainstream *waka*. With this precedent in view, the Saishōshi-tennōin poets treat the Michinoku *meisho* topics just as they do the other topics in the program: they craft new poems that transparently bear the marks of the old; they occupy rhetorical positions in which they claim to enjoy a new view of what others have seen before; and they seek out ways to recast conventional materials into new shapes that are particularly apt for the project at hand. Sometimes, as has been noted, the participating poets seem to depart deliberately, en masse, from precedent, perhaps in order to mark the product of their collective endeavor as something truly new, even if configured largely within the confines of the tried and true. In their poems on the topic of Abukumagawa (a Michinoku river), for example, all but one participant introduces plovers (*chidori, tomochidori*) to the river scene. Their presence cannot be accounted for through reference to earlier Abukumagawa poesy; rather, one supposes, there may have been collective agreement, arrived at on some other basis, that the Abukumagawa painting should feature these birds, huddling together on the frozen river, buffeted by the chill winds of a wintry night. Yet, the one poet who omits *chidori* in his Abukumagawa poem—Ietaka—is the one whose poem was chosen for inscription on the painting. In their place, as it were, another time-enriched figure surfaces:

kimi ga yo ni Abukumagawa no mumoregi mo
    kōri no shita ni haru o machikeri[85]
The buried tree beneath the waters of Abukuma River has encountered your

reign:
    beneath the ice it was waiting for the spring!

Jien and Shunzei's Daughter also found ways to work the phrase *kimi ga yo ni au* ("to encounter [be lucky enough to live at that same time as] your reign," and thus reactivate the most common of the conventional means whereby the name of Abukumagawa had been naturalized for use in verse about various kinds of encounters, romantic and otherwise. But Ietaka's deployment of the figure of the buried tree is as unprecedented as is the inclusion of the plovers in the poems offered by his peers. Perhaps it can be best explained as having surfaced through association, as Ietaka (and, perhaps, his peers) "remembered" a particular, earlier Abukumagawa verse—one also composed on an occasion that called for celebration of royal vitality and its endurance. The poem in question is one that is said to have been composed by one of the most famous of Ietaka's own Fujiwara forebears, Michinaga, when one of Gotoba's forebears, the Emperor Ichijō, paid a visit (*miyuki*) to the private residence of his consort, Jōtōmon'in, who was Michinaga's daughter:

> kimi ga yo ni Abukumagawa no soko kiyomi
>   seze o kasanete sumamu to zo omou[86]
> Since the bottom of Abukuma River, encountering your reign, is pure,
>   I would dwell there in that clarity for age upon age!

Michinaga's *seze* are, of course, both "shoals" and "many ages": his poem reveals his self-assurance, or arrogance, for it is an expression of his *own* desire to dwell at length in the "pure" age that has been blessed by the presence of this sovereign, who is his son-in-law. Ietaka, on the other hand, is more subtle, and more modest; and his poem is an adept rearrangement of an array of available matériels assembled to meet the challenge of the Saishōshitennōin project—in this case, assembled, in part, from a textual site that is part of his family heritage. But where Michinaga placed "shoals" in the Abukumagawa, as part of a figural package that draws together the stream and its pure, clean (*kiyoshi*) bottom or "foundation" (*soko*) and a verb that doubly signifies as "to be clear" and "to dwell" (*sumu*), Ietaka interpolates his *umoregi*—buried trees that have weathered a long winter, out of sight beneath a layer of ice, in anticipation of a coming spring. They, too, now encounter a revitalizing, charismatic force: *kimi*, Gotoba. Once more, they are dredged up out of memory to glisten in a new setting, the very making of which may generate its own revitalizing force for that ruler's cause. The Abukumagawa painting, which surely would have featured plovers, ice, and a ravaging wind, was clearly designed to be a winter scene: yet the poem chosen to be inscribed upon it looks ahead to spring, to renewal, to yet another beginning. And once more, as so often before, a buried tree is manipulated into this scheme, and is once more prevailed upon to release its positive, transforming energy upon what lies ahead.

Shiogama, the last of the *meisho* in the Michinoku phase of the sequence, is also the last in the linear sequence of the program as a whole. But, although located at this sequential terminus, the topic is treated as an opening, a beginning (just as, in many textual/visual programs that follow the course of the twelve months, or the seasons, the end is treated also as the start of something new). Jien's poem, chosen for inscription, announces not only the new beginning of a year, in spring, but also the beginning of a new day:

> hito towaba ikaga kataran
>> Shiogama no matsukaze yuruki haru no akebono[87]
> Should someone ask, how shall I describe it:
>> this spring dawn, its gentle wind in Shiogama's pines?

Should description fail, the contiguous painting may be of aid: in a viewing of this terminus of the Saishōshitennōin program, description of the imagined Shiogama scene will be doubly served by these adjacent texts—doubled, as is the meaning of *haru no akebono*, "a dawn in spring" *and* "spring's dawning." Description of what might be "seen" at Shiogama is also deferred, but through, alternative means in Teika's poem: whereas Jien wonders how to tell (*ikaga kataran*) of Shiogama's beauty, Teika forswears speaking in any detail (*iwaji*) of how it looks in springtime, in favor of a resonant utterance of its name.

> kasumi to mo hana to mo iwaji
>> haru no kage izuko wa aredo Shiogama no ura[88]
> I shall not speak of mist, nor of blossoms:
>> one can see these sights of spring everywhere—but then, there is the Shiogama Bay.

Teika's recourse, as a means of invoking Shiogama, is to resuscitate the language of the old Michinoku song that first brought the name of that place to the attention of court poets—the song which, no doubt, was part of what inspired Tōru to recreate a miniature Shiogama within the controlled environs of his garden:

> Michinoku wa izuko wa aredo
>> Shiogama no ura kogu fune no tsunade kanashi mo[89]
> Say what one may of places here and there in Michinoku,
>> how moving it is to watch a boat making its way across Shiogama Bay!

Now, another miniature Shiogama is to be made, under controlled conditions, upon the walls of the Saishōshitennōin: gazing upon its representation, the viewer will be able to imagine him- or herself standing where ancient travelers have stood, or, for that matter, where Tōru and his companions once stood, gazing in admiration at the simulacrum of an idealized Shiogama. To that Shiogama—to those Shiogamas—spring has come once more: in the act of return, renewal is accomplished, or, at the very least, hopes for renewal are raised once more.

Imagine Gotoba, scanning the complete set of the Saishōshitennōin poems offered for his consideration by all ten poets, including himself, or scanning the completed, mounted paintings with the poems he has selected inscribed upon them, representing a much larger creative enterprise. Here, at the figural end of the imagined geopolitical journey, the ersatz *miyuki*, in far-off Michinoku, he meets spring, and spring meets him. So long as the program of poems and paintings remained in place, that encounter and renewal could be reenacted in any season. Even after the paintings, and the building, were gone, the reenactment might still be carried out through a reading of the remaining poems, and, through them, the magical journey through an idealized realm could be performed repeatedly. Perhaps, even after the paintings and the buildings were gone, Gotoba did repeat that journey through what was then reduced to a textual space; and perhaps, as he did so, he felt revitalized, and in control once more. But his final, physical journey through the landscape he had once ruled, and which he and his comrades in poetry had re-created in the Saishōshitennōin, would be a journey into exile.

Epilogue: Recovering the Buried Tree

By the time of Buson's Matsushima encounter with that fragment of a buried tree from Natorigawa in the early eighteenth century, the arts of *haikai* (light verse) and, especially, the *hokku* (or *haiku*, the seventeen-syllable verse of the kind that might open a *haikai no renga* sequence) had long since flowered over and out of the *waka* tradition, of which that fragment was an unmistakable symbol and vehicle. Buson shirked its weight: others sought it out and put it to use. The story, as Buson tells it, may also be read as a parable about the relationship of *haikai* to *waka*: the ancient matter of poetic language was still present, still available for rediscovery and new encounters, but one might choose either to bear or to free oneself of its weight. In any given moment of *haikai* production, such figures as that of the buried tree might be very likely to rise to the surface, but might as easily remain out of view, or be suppressed—depending on the inclination of the poet or poets on hand.

To *haikai* poets like Buson and his friends, and to the many others in earlier and later generations who devoted so much of their creative energies to the production of *hokku* (often in extended, elaborate sequences, sometimes composed by single individuals but often by collectives of various numbers of poets), *waka* and its traditions formed a very prominent part of the multitextual substratum that underlay these more up-to-date productions. *Waka* was not the only element in this stratigraphy: "classical" Chinese texts, and "classical" Japanese texts of many kinds besides *waka,* as well as a great deal of extracanonical literary and cultural material—folk-songs and street-songs, colloquial proverbs and by-words, familiar quotations from all kinds of sources, and much else—also took their place in this textual substrata, this multilayered lode over which the *haikai* tradition situated itself, and on which it fed through its own allusive and intertextual operations. Still, *haikai's* genealogical ties to *waka* were its strongest, and not only because the very form of the seventeen-syllable *hokku* or *haiku* was so literally and obviously that of a fragment or shard of the *tanka,* corresponding to the "upper" three-fifths of the structure of the older vessel. The eclectic and virtuosic intertextual performances of *haikai* poets, which can be read as analogous, retrospective reenactments, in an altered scale and tenor, of the intertextual moves performed by their acknowledged forebears—the *waka* poets of so many earlier generations—take place in a far more wide-open arena than did those that they mirror, in the canons of *waka.* But, wherever the traces and benefits of that relatively greater degree of freedom of movement can be discerned, so can what is perhaps the most important aspect of the genealogical relationship of the two genres be discerned as well—the rootedness of the one in the other, the persistence and the nurturing of a ground in and over which experimentation and change ensues. So, while the ascendancy and institutionalization of the *haikai* tradition and the cultural (and commercial) success of the *hokku* (and of *haiku* poets) had the effect of relegating *waka,* the far more convention-bound institution, to the shadows, the practices and products of *haikai* poets also had the effect of making the *waka* tradition, as a collective "text," or residual corpus, look all the more like one of its own "buried trees." For there it lay in the receding but well-remembered and still accessible past, seemingly inert, at least partially if not entirely hidden from view, yet also present and far from truly dead, at least insofar as it continued to contribute to the creation of other forms of (textual) life. And, of course, new *waka* continued to be made even in the age of *haikai,* and while many poets adhered almost exclusively to one genre or another, still others moved freely, if deliberately, among the genres, producing texts of both kinds, with ample consciousness of both their differences and their hereditary ties.

This relationship between *waka* and *haikai* was represented by the invocation and inscription of the figure of the buried tree on at least one noteworthy occasion: when the poet and literary scholar Kitamura Kigin (1624–1705) created his first comprehensive handbook of and treatise on *haikai* composition, he gave it the name *Umoregi*. This was in 1655, when Kigin was just beginning to establish himself as a *haikai* master worthy of the mantle of the late Matsunaga Teitoku (1571–1653) and independent of his own teacher, Teitoku's disciple Yasuhara Teishitsu (1610–1673). The text probably circulated among Kigin's own disciples, undergoing some revisions over a lengthy period. When Kigin finally published *Umoregi* almost nineteen years later, in 1673, he did so as part of an effort to stem the rise of the rival Danrin *haikai* school, which eschewed the relative formalism and scholasticism that were the hallmarks of Teitoku and his followers (known as the Teimon school).[1] In this public version of *Umoregi*, Kigin articulated (through example) his view of the esthetic goals of *haikai* composition, linking those goals explicitly to those of the older traditions of *waka*: he presented *haikai* as a genre which, much like its immediate predecessor, *renga*, was deeply dependent upon the networks of association fixed in the *waka* tradition but was also distinguished by its bravura projection of *waka*'s lexical system into an altered realm of formal significance, through extended linked-verse series structured by those associations as they are made to shift and evolve over textual space and time.[2]

But what was perhaps of greatest interest and practical importance in *Umoregi*, so far as aspiring *haikai* poets were concerned, were the dozens of exemplary *haikai* verses he used to illustrate such general points. Like the authors of innumerable commentaries and handbooks on the composition of *waka*, Kigin gave special attention in *Umoregi* to the problems of composing *haikai* verses that allude directly, through partial quotation or paraphrase, to earlier verses (here, as elsewhere, termed *honka*, "foundation poems"). Likewise, in subsequent years, Kigin would become especially famous for his commentaries on literary classics, commentaries originally conceived and presented as lectures designed to help his students learn to understand and use the literary past in the shaping of their own new works.[3] In so doing, he aligned himself with what were by then countless generations of poets and scholars who had similarly sought to shape the new through study of and reference to the old. An essential element of Kigin's mission as *haikai* master was the teaching of, and the exemplary exercise of, this traditional art of weaving texts with texts.

Nowhere in *Umoregi* did Kigin explain or discuss his choice of title for the work; there is no articulation of the figure, nor is it used in any of the example texts. Apparently, the mere naming of it as such said enough: the word alone evoked a whole history of poetry up to that time, a history within which Kigin sought to place his own *haikai* art. Thus Kigin proclaimed that his *haikai*, like that of the other followers of Teitoku, was an art of the present linked formally, linguistically, and esthetically to the poetry of the past. And from Kigin's point of view that past was indeed a "buried tree," a vibrant fossil eternally awaiting and readily available for discovery and rediscovery so that it might once again flower forth with new vitality, a corpus concealed and distanced by accrued layers of time yet also familiar and close at hand, readily available for the makers of new poetic texts.[4]

Kigin needed only the word *umoregi* to signify the durable resources of the *waka* tradition. In the experience of some of his contemporaries, however, the durable *substance* of *umoregi* itself figured in encounters that became, in turn, occasions for new poem-making in the *waka* form. Whenever it appears in such contexts in the annals of these latter phases of *waka*'s history, *umoregi* seems to stand for much of what has gone on before—what has been said, written, and done—in that history, much as it did in the title of Kigin's treatise. At the same time, in these annals, we see how the age-old fetishization of *waka*-related objects, and places, has now become part of tourism and is absorbed into a burgeoning culture of commodity manufacture and exchange. Travel to what had once been the most remote of famous places had become much easier by the seventeenth century, and would become more so. Still, as the poet Mochizuki Chōkō (1619-1681) tells it in his personal anthology, he and his literary friends were deeply moved by the sight of the souvenirs that one of their number, a certain "Naoshige," brought back to Kyoto from "a trip to see the *utamakura*" of Michinoku. "He came back with plants of many kinds from several different places of great fame," Chōkō recalls. "Those who saw them were so deeply impressed that they felt they had to record their thoughts in poems that might then be attached to them; and, watching them, I felt compelled to join in." Among these souvenirs was a stalk of *hagi* (lespedeza) from Miyagino, *susuki* (miscanthus) from the grave of Sanekata, and, of course, *umoregi* from Natorigawa: to these emblems of the poetic experience of the past, reaffirmed and reclaimed through these acquisitions, Chōkō and his friends were appending their new verses. He says that their poems were "written and tied onto" the Michinoku treasures: thus, as on so many other occasions and in so many other contexts, writing on paper serves literally as the medium that binds its maker to the forces that reside in living or once-living things, and their energies fuse. For attachment to the Natorigawa *umoregi*, Chōkō wrote:

Natorigawa yo ni arawareshi umoregi o
   ukise ni shizumu hito ni misebaya.[5]
How I would like to show this buried tree from Natorigawa that has now come
   to the surface of this world
   to those who are sinking in shoals of grief!

For much of his life, Chōkō, who had studied with Teitoku in his youth and
received instruction from him in the "secret transmission" of the literary
classics, lived in relative seclusion in a retreat near Hirosawa Pond in the
western suburbs of Kyoto. In this poem, composed (as he tells it) within the
circle of his friends, he reaches out to offer the souvenir *umoregi* as a salve
to those who have no other access to such revivifying substances. In uttering
and inscribing the poem, Chōkō stands, as it were, on solid, dry ground,
while others wallow in the "shoals of grief" (*ukise* is also "floating shoals,"
since *uki-* may be an adjective, "sad," or a verb, "float"): a display of the
Natorigawa *umoregi* fetish to such sufferers, he says, will surely cheer
them—presumably because it is a thing of durable value, in contrast to the
passing pleasures of the "floating [sad] world" (*ukiyo*). The poem indirectly
invokes the origins of Natorigawa *umoregi* poesy in those "sad shoals," for
they are sites where worldly passions have been fostered and nurtured for
as long as poetic memory can recall; but, for Chōkō, the bit of a buried tree
that is now at hand is their perfect antidote. This is, then, an adroit transposition of the Natorigawa matériel, with its original eroticism effaced through
the process of transfer to the recluse's (ostensibly) calmer and relatively
detached world—one in which this bit of Natorigawa *umoregi* and the other
"grasses and trees" brought back from Michinoku nevertheless retain or have
even gained in significance, as emblems of an ideal but still accessible past.

   In Buson's *Shin hanatsumi* we read of two refashionings of Natorigawa
umoregi as instruments for writing (and for poem-making): the unnamed
daimyō (probably Date Yoshimura) had some of what his workmen had
found for him in the river made into a box that would hold fine paper and
an inkstone (*ryōshi, suzuri no hako*) and gave these as a gift to the household
of the Nijō poets; and Buson's friend Gantō also had the fragment from that
same lode which eventually came into his hands made into an inkstone lid
(*suzuri no futa*). Alongside these two episodes we find still others—evidence
that, in certain literary-minded circles, which were linked in turn to certain
daimyō and other aristocratic households, the manufacture and exchange of
such commodities was itself a kind of fetish. In his personal anthology, the
scholar and poet Murata Harumi (1746-1811) remembers having been
asked by the Wife of Lord Koshi (*Koshi no kimi no kita no kata*) to compose

a poem for inscription upon an inkstone lid made of *umoregi*, whereupon
he wrote:

> umoregi mo ima yori yo ni sakayubeki
>   kotoba no hana no haru ni ainaba[6]
> This buried tree will surely flourish from now on
>   if it encounters springs, like this one, in which words are in bloom.

Harumi characterizes the words (*koto no ha*) of the poems that will be
written out of this inkstone-box as the agents that will enable the buried tree
from which it has been made to experience a new and ever-renewing vitality.
Recovered from the watery site of its preservation, it now has the opportunity to "flower forth," realizing a long-hidden potential. By claiming that the
present ("this world," *ima [no] yo*) is a springtime for poetry—a season in
which words are in full flower (*kotoba no hana no haru*)—Harumi praises
his own times (and his own skill) and thanks his patroness for providing him
with just such an occasion as this for "new" poem-making in the manner of
the old and celebrated past; and he anoints her *umoregi* inkstone lid as the
medium through which the energies that the buried tree has held within
itself may be transmitted for use in an unending future. "So long as poetry
survives," he says, "this inkstone-lid, and the ancient, long-dead and now
reborn tree from which it has been made will prosper: but your request, and
my fulfillment thereof, are also deeds that will insure that survival."

On another occasion, Harumi's close associate Katō Chikage (also known
as Tachibana Chikage, 1735-1808) was called upon to perform a similar
exercise, and responded in kind—though, in this instance, the item that had
been fashioned from what was said to be Natorigawa *umoregi* was not a tool
for writing but an implement for the dressing and decoration of a woman's
hair—a comb. Asked for a poem that might be inscribed upon the comb
itself, Chikage wrote:

> miyabito no yoyo no kotoba ni Natorigawa
>   na wa arawareshi soko no umoregi[7]
> It gained its fame among the words of generations of courtiers,
>   and now it surfaces once again—a "buried tree" from Natorigawa's depths.

If these words were indeed chiseled into the brittle surface of the *umoregi*
comb, the result would have been an object that told the joint story of these
words and of the comb, both in text and in the supratextual dimension created
in the manufacture of that comb itself. As Chikage says, the name of the river
and of its treasured trees had indeed been appropriated by generations of
denizens of the Imperial court and its extended family (*miyabito*) for use in

their own literary undertakings: in their hands, these words had been made to appear again and again, as if rising out of the depths of memory, on the surface of texts. Every new use revealed and spoke of a history of prior uses, earlier exposures. The present moment of poem-making—Chikage's—is yet another in that series. And something else that is new—this comb with a poem on it—is being made, to be held in the hand, worked through the hair, or perhaps left there to help keep a coiffure in place. This comb is as utilitarian and special as are the words inscribed upon it; rendered from such ancient matériel, it is also as at once old and new as they. Will the poem be read each time the woman uses the comb? Or will the comb simply be placed in her hair, without special regard for what is written there? Does it matter? The words will remain in place, and available, so long as the comb is used. If fashions change and the comb is no longer useful, it will be put away, out of sight, as the *umoregi* of which it is made once was—to await rediscovery and careful, perhaps loving use in other hands.

We know that Natorigawa was not the only place in which lodes of *umoregi* were to be discovered. Legend has it that they were once found in the vicinity of the capital, near the rocky shoals of the Ōigawa, and that the early Heian-period image of the bodhisattva Jizō (Kṣitigarbha) known as the Umoregi Jizō, which has long been an object of worship at the Kōryūji monastery in nearby Uzumasa, was made from that lode. An unpublished monastery document, *Umoregi Jizō Bosatsu ki,* relates the tale: an Ōi villager found the image among the remains of a decayed *bodhi* tree long known for its miraculous powers. Installed in the Jūrin'in subtemple in the Kōryūji complex, the image survived a fire in 1150; in 1179, it was cleaned and restored under the guidance of the sculptor Inshō; it was twice stolen and returned in 1222-1224.[8]

The entire figure, including the body of the bodhisattva and the lotus flower upon which he stands, are made from a single piece of wood: the whole sculpture is just less than one meter in height. But the Umoregi Jizō is not made of *umoregi:* its raw material was *hinoki,* Japanese cypress, perhaps darkened by hundreds of years of exposure[9] (figure 14). In addition to the legend, there is perhaps another explanation as to how it came to be called Umoregi Jizō—through a conflation with the literal sense of the name Jizō (which means "stored in the earth" and is a literal translation of the Sanskrit name Kṣitigarbha). Thus, the image's appellation describes it doubly as an entity that has emerged after ages of concealment within the earth, where it gathered and preserved its strength, and now is at hand and ready to release its force and share its power with those who worship it.

14. The Kōryūji "Umoregi Jizō" image. Courtesy Kōryūji.

The Jūrin'in is no more: today, the Umoregi Jizō (still labeled as such) is on permanent public display, along with the monastery's other great sculptures, in Kōryūji's Hall of Sacred Treasures, the Reihōden. But for a period of some four years near the end of the eighteenth century, the Jūrin'in's Jizō Hall served as the temporary residence of the poet Ozawa Roan (1723-1801?), who had lost his own home in the great fire of the first month of Temmei 8 (1788)—which also destroyed the Imperial Palace, Nijō Castle, and much else in the city.[10] During this period, it seems, Roan became familiar with the legend of the Jizō's origins and used that story to launch a sequence of poems focusing on the image and its setting:

> Kono hozon o Umoregi no Jizō to nan ieru, niwa ni takaki bodaiju ari, sono naka yori arawaretamau to zo iu, sono ki ni hana sakeri, ōku no yamahachi muragarikite hinomosu hana ni mutsururu koe kyō yomu ni nitari.
>> Bodaiju no hana ni nakiyoru yamahachi wa
>> ima mo hannya o yomu ka to zo kiku[11]
>
> The main image here is called the Umoregi Jizō. There is a great bodhi tree in the courtyard, and they say the image was found inside it. The tree was in bloom, and throngs of wild honeybees had gathered in its branches; their constant buzzing, as they clung throughout the day to the blossoms, sounded like voices of priests chanting sūtras:
>> The wild honeybees that are crying amidst the blossoms of the *bodhi* tree
>> Sound as if they even now are chanting the *Heart Sūtra*!

In the version of the origin-tale with which Roan seems to have been familiar, the tree from which the image had been made was one that still grew in the temple grounds, and at this encounter—presumably in midsummer—it was in full flower. Roan mirrors the *umoregi*'s durable vitality, its potential for flowering forth anew, in the *bodhi* tree's flourishing yellow blooms. The conceit comparing the buzzing of bees to the chanting of priests (or the other way around) is an old one:[12] here it is perhaps also prompted by the fact that Kōryūji stands near a place called Hachioka, the Hill of Bees, and was once called Hachiokadera. But all this is perhaps so much stage-setting for Roan's further contemplations of the Jizō image itself. The first of these is formulated as an invocation of Jizō's assistance in promoting Roan's worldly career as professional poet:

> hozon ni tatematsuru to te:
>> hana sakanu mi zo taguinaki
>> umoregi no mikage mo yo ni wa idekeru mono'o[13]
> A poem composed as an offering to the image:
>> I am alone in my failure to flower forth,
>> though this buried tree's blessings are known throughout the world.

Roan poses as "one who has not blossomed," in contrast to the once-flourishing tree that is now the Jizō and to whom these words are addressed. He regards the image as a locus from which preservative, transformative, and life-giving powers flow outward into the world at large, and he wants to partake of them. The endeavor in which Roan hopes to "flower forth" is, of course, the production of verse; in the verses that follow immediately upon this prayer, in Roan's personal anthology, he pleads, further, that such an endeavor may also be received and aided by Jizō as a properly spiritual effort, a process leading toward transcendence:

> Shichigatsu nijūyokka Jizōson no mae ni arite omoiishi koto:
> > utsusemi no yo no koto no ha ni madowazu wa
> > > mutsu no chimata mo hitosuji no michi
> > hitosuji no michi shirube seyo koto no ha wa
> > > kono yo nagara no mutsu no chimata o
> > negigoto o ada ni kutasu na
> > > umoregi no mi no na ni ou o chigiri ni wa shite[14]
>
> Thoughts I had in the presence of the Holy Image of Jizō on the twenty-fourth day of the seventh month:
> > So long as I do not lose myself amidst the words that are the poems of this fleeting world,
> > > the Ways of the Six Realms will be as One Way.
> > Be my guide toward the One Way, oh words of Song:
> > > though you are of this world, you can guide me through the Ways of the Six Realms.
> > Do not scorn my prayers, nor let them decay:
> > > I shall take the fact that your name is *Umoregi* as your pledge.

The first of these poem-prayers is a pledge to Jizō: "I shall keep sight of the single goal of transcendence [*hitosuji no michi*], and if I do I know that these worldly efforts (these activities in "the six realms" of the nontranscendent, *mutsu no chimata*) will not deter me"; and the second then calls upon the poems (*koto no ha*) that are the products of those worldly efforts to point the traveler on his life's journey, to serve as guides through and then beyond this world, even though they remain manifestations of it.[15] Then, having thus pledged himself to these attitudes, Roan turns back to the Jizō image itself and calls upon it to guarantee these prayers. He ironically poses the possibility of his prayers' "decay" against the decaying process that has miraculously produced the *umoregi* from which the Jizō is believed to have been made: he insists that he will take that word, *umoregi*, in the image's name as a charm *against* decay—as a promise (*chigiri*) of residual, permanent, positive strength, ensuring that the poems Roan has made on this occasion, and on others as well, will continue, perpetually, to do their work for him. And, as Roan points out, this Jizō is an *umoregi* in both name (*na*) and form (*mi*), in repute and in substance: there is no difference between what it is called and what it is. He can therefore rely on this name, this word, to retain its meaning, and its power, just as he relies upon the image, the Jizō, and the powers that it both represents and releases into the world at large. Long stored in earth, like Jizō himself—and like the tree from which this image of him has been made—these powers are now here at hand. For Roan, they are a promise from the past to make the present, and future, possible, and to give them meaning.

But there are no such guarantees. Words, and meanings, are in constant change; signification is lost, gained, and shifts over time. Though seized upon by poets as a possible constant, the significance of the figure of the buried tree was always in flux; so was the significance of the allusive gesture, in and of itself.

In an imaginary tour of "the famous places of his domain" (*Ryōnai meisho waka*), a series of twenty-one verses, Date Yoshimura (1680-1751) wrote this, on the topic of Natorigawa:

> samidare ni mikasa masareru
> Natorigawa nami no mumoregi kuchi ya hatemashi.
> In constant summer rains, the flood-waters are gathering:
> will the buried trees in Natorigawa's waves now crumble and be gone?[16]

Gone, from this exercise, are the erotics of the earliest Natorigawa verse. The ancient lovers whose passions surfaced only in the river's shoals are nowhere to be seen; in their place is language that Yoshimura borrows from other canonical sites.[17] The buried trees upon which Yoshimura fixes his (imaginary) gaze in this poem are *figures,* but they are also *things.* For Yoshimura, the river's hidden trove of *umoregi* is one of the many prized properties of the lands he rules: the possibility of their final decay and disappearance are of concern not only because their substance itself is of value but also because they represent, and are, the past—his past, as lord of this domain and as a participant in *waka*'s history. Yoshimura and his predecessors and successors as Sendai Daimyō did undertake to preserve this past, by relocating and identifying anew the places in their realm that had been made famous through their repeated naming in verse; they also did undertake to control the flooding of the Natori River, and the discovery of the lode of *umoregi* that the Tenrin'in abbot told Buson about could well have come about quite accidentally, in the course of this large-scale civic enterprise. In verse, Yoshimura might fret about the rising waters; in reality, he could do something about them, and thereby both preserve and change the course of the river and the shape of his land.

In 1823, a samurai in the service of the Sendai fief named Yamashita Shūkichi was patroling the grounds of Aoba Castle, the Daimyō's headquarters, when he stumbled upon an outcropping of a substance that proved to be *umoregi* in the vicinity of a place called Serpent's Mouth Spring (Tatsu no kuchizawa). Prosperous though the domain was, samurai of Yamashita's rank (*ashigaru*) were always on the lookout for ways to supplement their income. With the Daimyō's blessing, Yamashita and a samurai colleague attempted to make some plates and bowls out of the *umoregi* they had chanced upon, and put them out for sale; but their manufacturing technique was found wanting and the project came to a quick end. Two years later, a Sendai townsman, Ishigaki Yūkichi, made another attempt at the production of *umoregi* dinnerware and tea ceremony pieces, from the same Aoba Castle lode, and this time the effort, which made use of new methods for rendering the brittle material of the transformed wood, was successful. Thus began a modern resurgence of *umoregi* craft (*umoregi zaiku*) which survives in Sendai as a small, tourist-oriented local industry to this day.[18]

Aoba Castle stood on a height overlooking the Hirose River; today, the grounds are occupied by parts of the campus of Tōhoku University, city parks, and museums. The lode of *umoregi* that Yamashita Shūkichi found at the foot of the castle there was not of the same type as that found in earlier times in the nearby Natori River. Natorigawa *umoregi* was formed when ancient trees of a type called metasequoia, ancestor of *keyaki,* fell and then lay submerged for thousands of years in the river's waters; the Aoba Castle lode, on the other hand, was simple bogwood, part of a larger deposit of common lignite. Sources for modern *umoregi* craft have been almost exclusively of this latter type: discoveries of true underwater *umoregi* are now extremely rare. But in 1899, a massive lode of this scarce substance was found in the Kitakami River, which flows to the north of and parallel to the Natori River in what was, by then, no longer the Sendai domain but the new Miyagi Prefecture. A Sendai townsman, one Yagi Kyūhei, acquired it and had a small house built for himself from it. Every wooden element in this showpiece house, from the ceiling panels and crossbeams to the floorboards of the verandas, was made from this single huge piece of *umoregi,* and the result was something of a cause célèbre in turn-of-the-century Sendai. In 1937, the land on which the Yagi house stood was acquired by the city for the construction of a new high school, and a site was sought for its relocation.

After a short period during which the future of the *umoregi* house seemed in doubt, the entire disassembled structure was transferred to the possession of the Zuiganji monastery in Matsushima, where it was eventually reassembled, as a suite of reception rooms in a wing off the monastery's main hall, in 1943.[19]

On a visit to Zuiganji in November 1995, I asked at the temple office if I might see these rooms. A curator of temple properties informed me that they were usually opened only for the reception of the monastery's most distinguished visitors; but he agreed to show them to me and the friends who had accompanied me. We followed him along the temple's rear galleries to a small attached building on a slope slightly above the other buildings of Zuiganji. There, with its spare furnishings under dust covers, was the *umoregi* room: its floor, ceiling, decorative lintels, *tokonoma* all intact. Had one not been told, one might mistake the material from which the room was made for nicely polished and aged but everyday *keyaki* rather than ancient *umoregi*. The room's beauty is understated, subtle, even sober. The curator, Horino Sōshun, then showed me to the shops near the temple where modern *umoregi* crafts—tea and incense caddies, earrings and tie pins, pendants and brooches, calligraphy-paper boxes and the like—are sold to tourists. On the way, we passed the gate of Tenrin'in, where Buson lodged when he came to Zuiganji, and where the piece of Natorigawa *umoregi* unexpectedly came into his hands. As we parted, Horino gave me the address of one of the two local craftsmen (two brothers) who are the only present practitioners of fine *umoregi* carving.

The next day I went to see this craftsman, Otake Takashi, who lives and works in an artists' collective on the outskirts of the Akiu spa town, on the Natori River—about one hour from the city of Sendai. In a corner of his shop lies what is left of that piece of *umoregi* discovered by Yamashita Shūkichi at the foot of Aoba Castle in 1823—now about three feet long and two feet wide, unpolished and otherwise unremarkable in appearance. The *umoregi* with which he and his brother work comes mostly from the Kitakami River area, and supplies of it are dwindling. Still, Otake was kind enough to chip off three small fragments from a large chunk of *umoregi* that lay in the center of his studio, and on which he was then working, and gave them to me. I gave one away before I left the country and kept the others; they were by no means too heavy to bear on my journey homeward.

Glossary of Names and Terms in Chinese and Japanese

Abe no Kiyoyuki 阿部清行
ai 藍
ai 愛
ajari 阿闍利
Akasaka (castle) 赤坂城
Akashi 明石
Akazome Emon 赤染衛門
aki ni arawaruru koi 秋顕恋
Akishino gessei shū 秋篠月清集
Amaterasu no omikami 天照大神
Anpō 安法
Anpō Hōshi shu 安法法師集
Antoku 安徳
Aoba (castle) 青葉城
Aritsune (Ōe 大江) 有経
Ariwara Narihira 在原業平
Ariwara Yukihira 在原行平
Ashigara no seki 足柄関
ashigaru 足軽
Ashikaga Yoshihisa 足利義尚
Asukai Masatsune 飛鳥井雅経

Asukai Masayo 飛鳥雅世
Atsunari (Prince) 敦成
bakufu 幕府
banka 挽歌
Bashō 芭蕉
bettō 別当
bugyōnin 奉行人
bundai 文台
Bunji rokunen nyōgo judai waka
　文治六年女御入内和歌
butsuzō 仏像
byōbu uta 屏風歌
Byōdōin 平等院
chigo 稚児
chikai 誓い
chōka 長歌
choku 勅
chokusenshū 勅選集
chōrō 長老
Chōshū eisō 長秋詠藻
Chōyō 重陽

235

Chūgū 中宮

Chūinshū 中院集

daii 大意

Daijōe 大嘗会

Daijōe byōbu 大嘗会屏風

Daijōsai 大嘗祭

Dairi 内裏

Dairi meisho hyakushu chū 内裏名所百首注

Dairi shiika awase 内裏詩歌合

Daisaiin no Shōshō 大斎院少将

Daisaiin saki no gyoshū 大斎院前御集

daiza 台座

Date Masamune 伊達政宗

DateYoshimura 伊達吉村

Dōin 道因

Dōjo 道助

Dōkō 道響

Dōmyō 道命

doroe byōbu 泥絵屏風

e 絵

Edo ha 江戸派

Eiga monogatari 栄華物語

Eiga no taigai 詠歌大概

Eigohyakushu waka 詠五百首和歌

eigu 影供

eigu utaawase 影供歌合

Eiun 永運

en 艶

eni 縁

Enjitsu 円実

Enkan 円観

Enshōji 円勝寺

Enshōji 延勝寺

eshi 絵師

Etchū no kami 越中守

fū 風

Fūga wakashū 風雅和歌集

Fujikawa hyakushu waka 藤川百首和歌

Fujiwara Akinaka 藤原顕仲

Fujiwara Akisue 藤原顕季

Fujiwara Akiuji 藤原顕氏

Fujiwara Ariie 藤原有家

Fujiwara Chikatsune 藤原親経

Fujiwara Hōshi 藤原褒子

Fujiwara Ienaga 藤原家長

Fujiwara Ietaka 藤原家隆

Fujiwara Kanefusa 藤原兼房

Fujiwara Kaneie 藤原兼家

Fujiwara Kenshō 藤原顕昭

Fujiwara Kintō 藤原公任

Fujiwara Kiyosuke 藤原清輔

Fujiwara Kiyotada 藤原清正

Fujiwara Korechika 藤原伊周

Fujiwara Koremasa 藤原伊尹

Fujiwara Korenaga 藤原伊長

Fujiwara Kuniyuki 藤原国行

Fujiwara Masatsune 藤原雅経

Fujiwara Michinaga 藤原道長

Fujiwara Michitsuna 藤原道綱

Fujiwara Mitsunori 藤原光範

Fujiwara (Nakamikado) Moriyori 藤原（中御門）盛頼

Fujiwara Motoie 藤原基家

Fujiwara Nagaie 藤原長家

Fujiwara Nagakane 藤原長兼

Fujiwara Nobukiyo 藤原信清

Fujiwara Norikane 藤原教兼

Fujiwara Norimune 藤原範宗

Fujiwara Sanekata 藤原実方

Fujiwara Shōshi 藤原影子

Fujiwara Shunzei (Toshiyori) 藤原俊成

Fujiwara Suemichi 藤原季道

Fujiwara Sukezane 藤原資実

Fujiwara Tadahira 藤原忠平

Fujiwara Tadayoshi 藤原忠良

Fujiwara Tameie 藤原為家

Fujiwara Tamesada 藤原為定

Fujiwara Tametsugu 藤原為継

Fujiwara Tameuji 藤原為氏

Fujiwara Teika 藤原定家

Fujiwara Tokihira 藤原時平

Fujiwara Toshinobu (Tokinobu, Takanobu) 藤原節信

Fujiwara Yasumitsu 藤原康光

Fujiwara Yasusue 藤原保季

Fujiwara Yoshisuke 藤原良輔

Fujiwara Yoshitsune 藤原良経

fukaki e 深き江

fukaki eni 深き縁

Fukakusa no sato 深草里

Fukuro zōshi 袋草紙

fūryū 風流

fusuma 襖

fūzoku ga 風俗画

fuzoku uta 風俗歌

gagaku 雅楽

gakuso 楽所

ganmon 願文

ga no uta 賀歌

Gantō 雁宕, i.e. Isaoka Shiryō-emon 砂岡四良衛問

ge 藝

gegyō 夏行

Genji monogatari 源氏物語

Genji monogatari kogetsushō 源氏物語湖月抄

Gensui 源水

Godaigo 後醍醐

Gohorikawa 後堀河

Goichijō 後一条

Gojō Higashi no Tōin 五條東洞院

gokō 御幸

Gokyōgoku Sessho ki 後京極摂政記

Gong ye zhang 公治長

Goreizei 後冷泉

Gosaga 後嵯峨

Gosanjō 後三条

Gosen wakashū 後選和歌集

Goshirakawa 後白河

Gosho 御所

Gosuzaku 後朱雀

Gotoba 後鳥羽

Gotoba-in gyoshū 後鳥羽院御集

Gotokudaiji Sanesada 後徳大寺実定

Goyōzei 後陽成

Gusai (Kyūsei) 救済

gyoganji 御願寺

Gyōi 行意

Gyokaku 魚鶴

gyōkō 行幸

Hachidaishū shō 八代集抄

Hachijōin Sanjō 八条院三条

Hachioka 蜂岡

Hachiokadera 蜂岡寺

haikai 俳諧 (誹諧)

Haku no haha 伯母

hanja 判者

hare 晴

hashira-e 柱絵

Hatsusegawa 初瀬川 (泊瀬川)

Heike monogatari 平家物語

Higuchi Ichiyō 樋口一葉

hijiri 聖

hikaika 誹諧歌

Hirano 平野

hirō 披露

Hirosawa shūshō 広沢輯藻

hiru no onza 昼御座

Hitomaro 人麻呂

Hitomi Sukesada 人見資貞

Hitomi Suketada 人見資忠

hō 袍

Hōgen 法眼

Hōjō 北条

Hōjōki 方丈記

Hōjūji 法住寺

Hokekyō 法華経

hokku 発句

Hongū 本宮

honka 本歌

honkadori 本歌取り

Horikawa 堀河

Horikawa hyakushu 堀河百首

Hosokawa Yūsai 細川幽斎

Hosshōji 法勝寺

Hyakurenshō 百練抄

hyakushu 百首

Hyakushu waka, natsu dokugin
  百首和歌、夏独吟

Hyōe no naishi 兵衛内侍

Ichijō 一条

Ichijō sesshō shū 一条摂政集

ichinichi issaikyō shosha kuyō 一日
  一切経書写供養

ide 堰、井出

in 院

Inshō 印性

Inshō 院尚

Ise monogatari 伊勢物語

Ishigaki Yūkichi 石垣勇吉

Isonokami sasamegoto 石神私淑言

Izumi Shikibu 和泉式部

Izumi Shikibu nikki 和泉式部日記

Izumi Shikibu shū 和泉式部集

Jakuren 寂連

ji 寺

Jie 滋恵

Jien 滋円

Jigen 滋源

Jijō sanjūrokunin utaawase 治承三
  十六人歌合

jisetsu 時節

Jizō 地蔵

jo 序

Jōkaku 上覚

Jōkyūki 承久記

Jōshōji 成勝寺

Jōtōmon'in 上東問院

jukkai 述懐

Juntoku 順徳

Jūrin'in 十輪院

kachi 葛

kachi 勝ち

Kagerō nikki 蜻蛉日記

kago 歌語

Kaikoku zakki 廻国雑記

kaikyū 懐旧

kakekotoba 掛詞

Kamakura 鎌倉

Kamo no Chōmei 鴨長明

Kamo no Mabuchi 賀茂真淵

Kan'in no sannomiya 閑院三宮

kanji rakuyō 関路落葉

kanjō 灌頂

Kannōji 感應寺

Kannon 観音

Kantō chōbuku 関東調伏

Kanzeon bosatsu fumon bon 観世
  音菩薩普門品

Karasumaru Mitsuhiro 烏丸光広

karon 歌論

Kasajima dōsojin 笠島道祖神

Kasuga 春日

Katō Chikage (Tachibana Chikage)
  加藤千蔭（橘千蔭）

kawabe no koi 河辺恋

kawa no ue no haru no tsuki, kajō
  shungetsu 河上春月

Kawara no in 河原院

Kawasaki 川崎

Keichū 契中

keiki 景気

keman 華鬘

Kengei 兼芸

Ken gozen 健御前

Kenpō meisho hyakushu 健保名所
  百首

Kenpō meisho sanbyakushu shō
健保名所三百首抄

Kenpō meisho shihyakushu shō
健保名所四百首抄

Kenreimon'in ukyō no daibu shū
健礼門院右京大夫集

Kenshunmon'in 健春門院

kibutsu 奇物

kibutsu chinshi 寄物陳思

kichū saibō 羈中歳暮

kigo, kigoteki 記語、記語的

Kii 紀伊

kikuawase 菊合

Kiku no sekku 菊の節句

Kindai shūka 近代秀歌

ki ni yosuru koi 寄木恋

Kinnaka (Ōe 大江) 公仲

Ki no Tsurayuki 紀貫之

Kinshi 忻子

Kin'yō wakashū 金葉和歌集

Kisen 喜選

kisho 貴所

Kitakami 北上

Kitamura Kigin 北村季吟

Kōfukuji 興福寺

kōhai 光背

kōhon 広本

Kohon setsuwa shū 古本説話集

Kojidan 古事談

Kojiki 古事記

kokeika 古渓花

Kokin waka rokujō 古今和歌六帖

Kokin wakashū 古今和歌集

Kōkō 光孝

Kokon chomonjū 古今著聞集

Kokubunji 国分寺

Kokubunniji 国分尼寺

kongen 坤元

Kon'in no migi no ōimochigimi
近院右大臣

Konkōmyō saishōōkyō 金光明最勝
王経

Konkōmyō Shitennō Gokokuji
金光明四天王護国寺

Konoe 近衛

Konoe Iezane 近衛家実

konomu 好む

Korai fūteishō 古来風体抄

Koreakira 惟明

Koretaka no miko 惟喬親王

Kōryūji 広隆寺

kōshi 講師

Koshi no kimi no kita no kata 越の
君の北の方

Kosobe no nyūdō 古曾部入道

Kōtaigō 皇太后

Kōtaigōgū no Daijin 皇太后宮大進

Kōtaigōgū no Daijin shū 皇太后宮
大進集

Kōtaishi 皇太子

kotobagaki 詞書

Kotojirishū 琴後集

koya 小屋

Koya 昆陽

Kōya 高野

Kōyasan senzui byōbu 高野山山水
屏風

Kōyōin 高陽院

Kōyō wakashū 黄葉和歌集

ku 句

kuchiki 朽ち木

kudai 句題

kugikakushi 釘かくし

Kujō Kanezane 九条兼実

Kujō Michiie 九条道家

Kumano 熊野

Kunaikyō 宮内卿

kuni 国

kuniburiuta 国俗歌

kutsu 朽つ

kyōgen 狂言

Kyōgoku no miyasundokoro 京極 御息所

kyōshū 郷愁

Kyūan hyakushu 久安百首

Kyūshū kadan 九州歌壇

makurakotoba 枕詞

Makura no sōshi 枕草子

Makura no sōshi shunshoshō 枕草 子春曙抄

Man'yōgana 万葉仮名

Man'yōshū 万葉集

mappō 末法

Masayo shū 雅世集

Matsudaira Sadanobu 松平定信

Matsuda Sadahide 松田貞秀

Matsumura Gekkei 松村月渓

Matsunaga Teitoku 松永貞徳

Matsushima 松島

meibutsu 名物

Meigetsuki 明月記

meisan 名産

meisho 名所

Mibu no Tadami 壬生忠見

Mibu no Tadamine 壬生忠岑

Michinoku 陸奥

Midō 御堂

Miidera 三井寺

mikotonori 勅

Minamoto Ienaga 源家長

Minamoto Michitomo 源通具

Minamoto Nakakuni 源仲国

Minamoto Sadanobu 源定信

Minamoto Sanetomo 源実朝

Minamoto Shigeyuki 源重之

Minamoto Tamenori 源為憲

Minamoto Tōru 源融

Minamoto Toshiyori (Shunrai) 源俊頼

Minamoto Yorimasa 源頼政

Minamoto Yoritomo 源頼朝

Minamoto Yoshiari 源能有

Minase 水無瀬

Minase koi jūgoshu utaawase 水無 瀬恋十五首歌合

miyuki 行幸、御幸

Mochihito 以仁

Mochizuki Chōkō 望月長孝

Montoku 文徳

Montoku jitsuroku 文徳実録

Mon'yōki 門葉記

Morinaga 護良

Mori Ōgai 森鴎外

Motoori Norinaga 本居宣長

mumoregi ni yosuru koi 寄埋木恋

Mumyōshō 無名抄

Murakami 村上

Murasaki Shikibu 紫式部

Murata Harumi 村田春海

Mutsu 陸奥

mutsu no chimata 六つの巷

Myōbu 命婦

Nachi 那智

Nagara 長柄

nagarau 流らふ

nagarau 長らふ/永らふ

nagauta 長歌、長唄

Nagisa no in 渚院

Naidaijinke hyakushu 内大臣家百首

Nakanoin Michikatsu 中院通勝

Nakashima Mitsukaze (Kōfū) 中島 光風

Nakatsukasa 中務

Naniwa 難波

Natorigawa 名取川

nenobi 齢延び

ne no hi 子の日

Nihon kōki 日本後記

Nihon shoki 日本書記

Nijō Yoshimoto 二条良基

Ninnaji 仁和寺
Ninshi 任子
niwa 庭
Nō 能
Nōin 能因
Nōin Hōshi shū 能因法師集
Nōin kongenki 能因坤元儀
Nōin utamakura 能因歌枕
no no miyuki 野の御幸
Norihira 憲平
nosuji 野筋
Ōe Kin'yori 大江公資
Ōe Masafusa 大江匡房
Ogura hyakunin isshu 小倉百人一首
Ogurayama 小倉山
Ōigawa 大井河
Ōigawa gyōkō waka koshō 大井河
　行幸和歌考証
ōkan 横巻
oko 嗚呼
Oku no hosomichi 奥の細道
Ōnakatomi Yorimoto 大中臣頼基
Ōnakatomi Yoshinobu 大中臣能宣
Onjōji 園城寺
Ono no Komachi 小野小町
Oshikōchi no Mitsune 凡河内躬桓
Ōtaka Gengo 大高源吾
Ōū kanseki monrōshi 奥羽観蹟聞
　老志
Ōutadokoro 大歌所
Ozawa Roan 小沢蘆庵
rakkei kuyō 落慶供養
Reihōden 霊宝殿
Reizei 冷泉
ribetsu 離別
Rikuzen 陸前
rokudō 六道
Rokujō eisō 六条詠草
Rokushōji 六勝寺
Roppyakuban utaawase 六百番歌合

rufubon 流布本
ryakubon 略本
Ryōnai meisho waka 領内名所和歌
ryōshi 料紙
Ryōzen 良遷
ryū 流
Ryūgen 隆源
Ryūgen kuden 隆源口伝
Sadahide shū 貞秀集
Saga 嵯峨
Saidaimon 西大門
Saigyō 西行
Saishōji 最勝寺
Saishōkō 最勝講
Saishōkōin 最勝光院
Saishōshitennōin 最勝四天王院
Saishōshitennōin meisho shōji waka
　最勝四天王院名所障子和歌
Saishōshitennōin waka 最勝四天
　王院和歌
Sakanoue no Korenori 坂上是則
Sakuma Dōgan 佐久間洞巌
Sanbōe 三寶絵
sanga 山河
Sanjōnishi Sanetaka 三条西実隆
Sanjō Shirakawa 三条白河
Sanju 散手
Sanju hajin raku 散手破陣楽
sanka 山河
Sankashū 山家集
san moji dai 三文字題
Sarashina nikki 更級日記
Sasaki Hirotsuna 佐々木廣綱
seidan 清談
Seigan chawa 清巖茶話
Seiryōden 清涼殿
Sei Shōnagon 清少内言
Seitaka 勢多伽
Seiwa 清話
Sekidera Komachi 関寺小町

sen 仙

Sendai 仙台

Sengohyakuban utaawase 千五百番歌合

Senshumon'in 宣秋門院

Sentō (palace) 仙洞

Sentō kudai gojūshu 仙洞句題五十首

Senzai wakashū 千載和歌集

Serikawa 芹川

Sesshō 摂政

Setsugyoku shū 雪玉集

seze 世世

Shakkyōka 釈教歌

Shaku'a 釈阿

Shariden 舎利殿

Shibun yōryō 紫文要領

Shichijōin 七条院

Shigeyuki shū 重之集

Shi ji 史記

Shikama no ichi 飾麻市

shikashū 私家集

Shika wakashū 詞花和歌集

shikishi 色紙

shi moji dai 四文字題

Shinchokusen wakashū 新勅撰和歌集

Shin'en 信円

Shin gosen wakashū 新後選和歌集

Shin hanatsumi 新花つみ

Shin kokin wakashū 新古今和歌集

Shinryū 晋流, i.e. Fujii Hanzaemon 藤井半左衛門

Shinsei 真静

Shin shoku kokin wakashū 新続古今和歌集

Shin shūi wakashū 新拾遺和歌集

Shiogama 塩釜

Shirakawa 白河、白川

Shirakawa no in 白川院

Shirakawa no seki 白河関

Shirakawa Sanjōbō 白川三条房

Shiroishi 白石

shisenshū 私選集

Shitennō 四天王

Shitennōji 四天王寺

Shōchi tokai hen 勝地吐懐編

shōgun 将軍

shōji 障子

shōji no ga 障子画

Shōkōmyōin 勝光明院

Shoku gosen wakashū 続後選和歌集

Shoku goshūi wakashū 続後拾遺和歌集

Shoku kokin wakashū 続古今和歌集

Shoku nihongi 続日本紀

Shoku senzai wakashū 続千載和歌集

Shōmu 聖武

Shōnan'inza 松南院座

Shoren'in 青蓮院

Shōtetsu 正徹

Shōtoku Taishi Shōmangyō kōsan zu 聖徳太子勝鬘経講讃図

shugyōja 修行者

Shūi gusō 拾遺愚草

Shūi wakashū 拾遺和歌集

shukke zatō kyōgen 出家座頭狂言

Shūko jūshu 集古十種

Shūmyōshū 衆妙集

Shunzeikyō kujūga no uta 俊成卿九十賀歌

Shunzeikyō no musume 俊成卿女

Sōa (Yahantei, Hayano Hajin) 宋阿（夜半亭、早野巴人）

Sōkonshū 草根集

sōmon 相聞

sōmonka 相聞歌

Son'en 尊円

Sone Yoshitada 曾禰好忠
Sonshōji 尊勝寺
Sonsō Kojū 巽窓潮十
sōshi 冊子
suki 好き、数奇
Suma 須磨
Sumiyoshi 住吉
Suruga 駿河
Susa no o no mikoto 素戔嗚尊
Sutoku 崇徳
Tachibana Kiyotomo 橘清友
Tachibana Michisada 橘道貞
Tachibana Narisue 橘成季
tachihaki senjō 帯刀先生
Taiheiki 太平記
Taikenmon'in 待賢門院
Taira 平
Taira Kanemori 平兼盛
Takakura 高倉
Takarai Kikaku 宝井其角
Taketori monogatari 竹取物語
Takiguchi Morifusa 滝口盛房
tami 民
tanken no tsuba 探剣の鍔
Tanpoku 澤北
tatsumi 辰巳、巽
Tatsu no kuchizawa 辰ノ口澤
tazu 鶴
Teimon 貞門
Teishin kō 貞信公
tenma 天魔
Tenma 天魔
Tennōji 天王寺
Tenrin'in 天麟院
Tenrinjōō 天輪聖王
tera 寺
Toba 鳥羽
tobira-e 扉絵
Tōdaiji 東大寺
Tōgū 春宮

Tōji senzui byōbu 東寺山水屏風
Tokiwa Tanpoku 常盤澤北
   (Tokiwa Tadanao 常盤貞治)
tōkoku fuzoku goshu 東国風俗五首
Torii no shōji 鳥居障子
Tosa nikki 土佐日記
Toshiyori zuinō 俊頼髄脳
Tsuchimikado 土御門
tsukasameshi 司召
tsukinami byōbu 月並屏風
Tsukuba shū 菟玖波集
Tsurugaoka Hachiman 鶴岡八幡
Uda 宇多
Uji 宇治
Ujishūi monogatari 宇治拾遺物語
Ukeragahana うけらがはな
Ukon no Taifu 右近大夫
umoregi 埋木
Umoregi Jizō 埋木地蔵
Umoregi Jizō Bosatsu ki 埋木地蔵
   菩薩記
umoregi zaiku 埋木細工
utakotoba 歌詞
utamakura 歌枕
utsushi 写し、移し、現し/顕し
Uzumasa 太秦
waka 和歌
Wakadokoro 和歌所
Waka dōmōshō 和歌童蒙抄
Waka iroha 和歌色葉
Wakamizu 若水
Waka no ura 和歌浦
Watanabe no Chōjitsu Tonō 渡邊
   長七唄
Watanobe no hashi 渡辺橋、渡部橋
Wen xuan 文選
Xianyang 咸陽
Yagi Kyūhei 八木九兵衛
Yamabe Akahito 山部赤人
Yamashita Shūkichi 山下週吉

Yasusuke-ō no haha 康資王母
Yodogawa 淀川
Yōen 永縁
yo no sue 世の末
Yosa Buson 輿謝蕪村
Yōzei 陽成
yū 優
Yuge 弓削
yūgen 幽玄

yūjo 遊女
Yūki 結城
Yūsei (Yūshō) 祐盛
Yūshi Naishinnō 祐子内親王
zattai 雑体
Zeami 世阿弥
zōka 雑歌
Zuiganji 瑞岸寺

Notes

The following abbreviations appear in the notes.

KM   Imagawa, ed., *Kundoku meigetsuki*
MINZ   Ishida and Satsukawa, eds., *Minamoto Ienaga nikki zenchūkai*
NKBT   *Nihon koten bungaku taikei*
NKBZ   *Nihon koten bungaku zenshū*
SKT   *Shinpen kokka taikan henshū iinkai*, ed., *Shinpen kokka taikan*
SNKBT   *Shin nihon koten bungaku taikei*

PROLOGUE: THE BURIED TREE

1 "Yamato uta ni meisho aru wa, nao neru ni makura aru ga gotoshi. Makura ni
   yorite yume atsushi. Meisho ni yorite kaku naru. Utamakura no shō, kedashi kore
   ga tame ka." Keichū, *Shōchi tokai hen (ikkan bon)*, in Hisamatsu, ed., *Keichū
   zenshū*, 11:23. The title *Shōchi tokai hen* may be translated roughly as "A miscellaneous compilation of comments on famous places." Keichū produced this
   work in two stages, publishing one volume, with preface, in 1692, and three
   additional volumes in 1696.
2 "Tatoeba, senzui o tsukuru ni, matsu o uubeki tokoro ni wa iwa o tate, ike o hori
   mizu o makasubeki chi ni wa yama o tsuki, chōbō o nasu ga gotoku, sono tokoro
   no na ni yorite uta no sugata o ba kazarubeshi. Kore ra imijiki kuden nari." Kamo
   no Chōmei, *Mumyōshō*, in Takahashi, ed., *Mumyōshō zenkai*, p. 236.

3 "Moshi uta no sugata to meisho to kakeawazu narinureba, koto tagitaru yō ni te, imijiki fuzei aredo, yaburete kikoyuru nari." Ibid.

4 For two brief discussions of the term *sugata*, see Brower and Miner, *Japanese Court Poetry,* p. 511; and Taniyama, "Sugata," in Inukai et al., eds., *Waka daijiten,* p. 544.

5 "Akikaze no uta, monosabkishiki sugata naru ni yori, Fukakusa no sato koto ni tayori ari. Tsukushite kakubekarazu." Takahashi, ed., *Mumyōshō zenkai,* p. 236. For an insightful discussion of this poem and of other aspects of Shunzei's art, see Shirane, "Lyricism and Intertextuality: An Approach to Shunzei's Poetics."

6 The work of the scholar Nakashima Mitsukaze (or Kōfū) is widely recognized for its contribution to the clarification of the early history of the term *utamakura.* See, for example, Katagiri, "Utamakura no seiritsu," in Katagiri, *Kokin wakashū no kenkyū,* pp. 110-111. For Nakashima's seminal study, "Utamakura gengi kōshō," see Nakashima, *Jōsei kagaku no kenkyū,* pp. 180-296.

7 As many scholars have noted, Sei Shōnagon's famous *Pillow Book* (*Makura no sōshi*) bears strong resemblance, in part, to such *utamakura* handbooks. There is still no consensus on the meaning of the title by which that work is known, but the text's rich interaction with the minutiae of poem-making clearly displays a linkage to the attitudes and conditions that gave rise to those texts called *utamakura.* For a fine study in English, see Morris, "Sei Shōnagon's Poetic Catalogues."

8 The multifaceted definition of *utamakura* given here is based in part upon those devised by contemporary Japanese scholars. For example, Komachiya Teruhiko defines the term as "a poetic word that bore a conventionalized aesthetic sense and performed a unique expressive function, borne out of a purification or abstraction from a geographical place's actual configuration, or through impressions formed vis-à-vis such geographical places on the basis of older poems, or through impressions or associations formed about certain place names through either auditory or visual means, or through the spatial possession of objects [from those places], or through other means." He adds that in the *Kokin wakashū* (compiled 905), one of the earliest works in which such words can be seen in use in this way, that usage is "by and large symbolic" (or "semiotic," i.e., *kigoteki*). See Komachiya, "*Kokinshū*-teki hyōgen no tokushitsu to sono tenkai," in Fujioka et al., eds., *Shinpojiam Nihon bungaku 2, Kokinshū,* p. 188. Sugitani Yoshirō endorses a definition similar to Komachiya's, adding that "poetic expressions made through the use of *meisho utamakura* (*utamakura* that are the names of famous places) are of two kinds, those that have to do with the sounds of that place-name, and those that have to do with the scenic or other properties of that place." See Sugitani, "Utamakura: *Kokin wakashū* no gihō," in *Issatsu no kōza* henshū bu, ed., *Issatsu no kōza: Kokin wakashū,* p. 622.

9 Ben-Porat, "The Poetics of Literary Allusion," pp. 107-108.

10 Preminger and Brogan, eds., *The New Princeton Encyclopedia of Poetry and Poetics,* pp. 38-39, 620-622.

11 Shirane, "Lyricism and Intertextuality," pp. 71, 76.

12 Ibid., pp. 72, 82.

13 For another more recent discussion of allusion in late Heian and early Kamakura-period *waka,* see Bialock, "Voice, Text, and the Question of Poetic Borrowing in Late Classical Japanese Poetry." Bialock makes interesting use of studies of allusion in other traditions, particularly the work of Gian Biagio Conte. In *The Rhetoric of Imitation,* Conte suggests that "allusion functions like the trope of classical rhetoric. A rhetorical trope is usually defined as the figure created by dislodging of a term from its old sense and its previous useage and by transferring to a new, improper, or 'strange' sense and usage. The gap between the letter and the sense in figuration is the same as the gap produced between the immediate, surface meaning of the word or phrase in the text and the thought evoked by the allusion. . . . In both allusion and the trope, the poetic dimension is created by the simultaneous presence of two different realities whose competition with one another produces a single more complex reality. Such literary allusion produces the simultaneous coexistence of both a denotative and a connotative semiotic" (p. 24). In another passage which bears resonance for the study of *waka,* Conte says that "'tradition' is a necessary precondition for both emulation and allusion. The tradition both conditions the later poet's work and helps him to formulate its distinctive qualities. A more rigorous definition of this tradition may perhaps be given by calling it a poetic langue, a system of literary conventions, motifs, ideas, and expressions, with its laws and constraints, that each 'speaker' (writer) will use in his or her own way" (p. 37).

14 The writing of the *hokku* sequence itself was initiated when, in the summer of 1777, Buson undertook a *haikai* poet's version of a traditional form of ascetic austerity, a period of retreat (*gegyō*) during the hot, damp weather: the task which Buson imposed upon himself for this period, in lieu of but perhaps tantamount to some other devotional practice, was the composition of ten *hokku* per day, to serve collectively as a memorial for his deceased mother. (The date of Buson's mother's death is unknown; 1777 may have marked the thirty-third or the fiftieth anniversary. See Takahashi Hiromichi, "'Shin hanatsumi' ni tsuite," p. 30.) In so doing, he would replicate but enlarge (by a factor of ten) the task undertaken by the poet Takarai Kikaku (1661–1707), one of Basho's most influential disciples and a key transgenerational link between him and Buson: in a similar hundred-day *gegyō* late in the seventeenth century, Kikaku composed *one* verse per day in his own mother's memory, and he published the results in 1690. (See Shimizu Takayuki, ed., *Yosa Buson shū,* p. 256.) But the result of Buson's parallel effort fell far short of the projected goal of one thousand verses. Some time in the fifth month, at the height of summer, distress over his daughter's failed marriage overcame him, and the *gegyō* was broken off after the composition of just one hundred and thirty-seven *hokku.* Apparently, Buson then (or perhaps later) filled the blank pages of the booklet (*sōshi*) in which he had begun to record the *gegyō* verses with meandering, free-form prose reminiscences of episodes in his earlier life, including several incidents from his northeastern travels. The retrospective mood of the memorial verses carried

over into the prose memoir; in two parallel but distinct modes, Buson reinscribed his past.

Seven years later, in the spring of 1784, when Gekkei found this booklet among his late master's unpublished papers, he remounted its pages in scroll format (ōkan), added seven illustrations in his own hand to the memoir section, and wrote an afterword in which he gave the text a title. Kikaku had published the collected results of his gegyō under the title Hanatsumi (Flower gathering) in 1690, and in recollection of it, Buson's was called Shin hanatsumi (A new flower gathering). Thus it became just one of many works, including both paintings and texts, which Buson's executors released to the public after his death, often with their own added colophons, in order to raise funds for his survivors. In spite of the somewhat special circumstances of its composition and publication, Shin hanatsumi is today one of Buson's best-known works, perhaps thanks in parts to such admiring readers as the modern poet Kawahigashi Hekigotō (1873-1937), who considered it to be representative of Buson "at his peak" (quoted by Shimizu in Yosa Buson shū, p. 256).

In his afterword Gekkei calls the text Zoku hanatsumi (Flower gathering: continued), but when it was finally published in 1797 it appeared as Shin hanatsumi. The poet Sonsō Kojū had published a work called Zoku hanatsumi in 1735, so the change may have been made to avoid confusion. There was apparently no title in Buson's draft, but it is thought that Gekkei came up with Zoku hanatsumi on the basis of his recollection that Buson had consciously patterned his gegyō after Kikaku's (Takahashi, "'Shin hanatsumi' ni tsuite," p. 30. See also Shimizu, Yosa Buson shū, pp. 256, 318). Translations of these titles follow Donald Keene's in World Within Walls: Japanese Literature of the Pre-Modern Era, 1600-1867, pp. 128, 354. Though some Japanese commentators do call the prose portion of Shin hanatsumi a jo, it is rather misleading to refer to it in English as "the preface to the collection," as does Keene, as it comes at the end of the text and comprises about one-third of its entire length.

Shin hanatsumi is a hybrid text, and its title compounds the pastiche. Like so many others that announce a "shin (new) something-or-other" (e.g., the Shin kokin wakashū), the title that Gekkei bestowed on this text suggests that it takes a retrospective stance, and that it seeks to borrow something of the aura of its namesake, but that it is nonetheless new, a thing of its own times even if framed or shaped by some relationship to one or several models or predecessors. But the contour and texture of the relationship of Shin hanatsumi to Kikaku's Hanatsumi is typically haikai-esque: the linkage exists in principal, destined by the circumstances of its making, and is enshrined in the explicitness of the posthumous title, but otherwise it manifests itself only in glancing, passing gestures of indirection. Only one of the poems in the hokku sequence makes what can be identified as an explicit allusion to a poem by Kikaku's, but this recollective or parodistic moment immediately passes, yielding to other hokku moments that are shaped in other ways. The prose memoir actually begins with matters pertaining to Kikaku, specifically, and an account, from Buson's point of view, of the recent history of the manuscript of Kikaku's collected works, and Buson's involvement with them. One might see both the *hokku* that echoes Kikaku's (the eighth in the completed portion of the sequence) and the opening section of the memoir, and perhaps other parts of the *Shin hanatsumi* text as well, as recollective moments (of different kinds) that form through free association, clustering spontaneously around the occasion, the recollective character of which has been defined by its doubly memorial stance.

15 Yosa Buson, *Shin hanatsumi,* in Shimizu Takayuki, ed., *Yosa Buson shū,* pp. 299–301.

16 Shimizu, *Yosa Buson shū,* p. 299.

17 Ibid. The standard *shaku* varied somewhat in the Tokugawa period, but the piece of *umoregi* given Buson would seem to have been roughly twelve inches long.

18 In his youth, Yoshimura spent much of his time in Kyoto, in close association with various noble (*kuge*) families, who retained strong claims on the orthdox traditions of court poetry. Meanwhile, during a surge in interest in local archae-ology in Sendai, Yoshimura's adoptive father, Tsunamura (1659–1719), ordered the Confucian scholar Sakuma Dōgan to compile a historical survey of the two northern provinces over which he held sway, with emphasis on the literary history of sites located therein. The survey, entitled *Ōu kanseki monrōshi* (A survey of Mutsu and Dewa Provinces based on observation of artifacts and consultation with the ancients), was completed in 1719, just a few weeks after Yoshimura succeeded Tsunamura as Daimyō. The heir continued to show an interest in local literary lore, compiling, among his various poetic compositions, several groups of poems on the *meisho* (famous places) of Mutsu and Dewa, while both male and female members of the Date family continued to study *waka* under the guidance of Kyoto masters. (Takahashi Tomio, "Oku yukashi," p. 153; Kikuchi Katsunosuke, *Miyagi ken kyōdoshi nenpyō,* pp. 117, 121, 132; *Miyagi kenshi* henshū iinkai, ed., *Miyagi kenshi*: 14 *[Bungei geinō]*, pp. 96–98; and Matsuno Yōichi, private corre-spondence, 2 May 1992.)

19 Kojima Noriyuki and Arai Eizō, ed., *Kokin wakashū* (SNKBT 5), p. 200.

20 For more on these stories of medieval eccentric antiquarianism—in which the above-mentioned Nōin figures as a prominent collector of this kind of literary detritus—see chapter 3.

21 Tanpoku (Tokiwa Tadanao, d. 1744), a native of Shimotsuke Province, was a physician noted for his promotion of education among the common classes. Both he and Shinryū (Fujii Hanzaemon, 1680–1761), a resident of the town of Sukagawa, were disciples of Kikaku. (Matsuo Yasuaki et al., eds., *Buson jiten,* pp. 348–351.)

22 "Etaki mono wa shiite uru ga yoshi. Mitaki mono wa tsutomete miru ga yoshi. Mata kasanete mirubeku ubeki ori mo koso to, tōkan ni sugosubekarazu. Kasanete hoi toguru koto wa kiwamete kataki mono nari" (Shimizu, ed., *Yosa Buson shū,* p. 313).

23 Gantō (Isaoka Shiryōemon, d. 1773) was a native of the castle town of Yūki in Shimōsa. He was a friend of Buson's from the time that both were youthful

students of *haikai* under Sōa (i.e., "Yahantei," Hayano Hajin). (Matsuo et al., eds., *Buson jiten,* p. 341). It was shortly after the death of Sōa, in the summer of 1742, that Buson abandoned his work on the posthumous papers of Kikaku and set off from Edo for the northeast, where Gantō served as his chief host and Tanpoku as his companion on several excursions from Ganto's home in Yūki to various towns and sites in the adjacent regions (Shimizu, *Yosa Buson shū,* p. 296).

24 For the purposes of this study, the canon is defined as the range of works included in the *Shinpen kokka taikan* (New edition of the great collection of Japanese poetry), compiled by a committee of hundreds of scholars (and published by Kadokawa Shoten) who collectively strive for exhaustive, inclusive, and authoritative treatment of bona fide versions of those hundreds of texts in which poems are found and of which the tradition is thought to consist. As of 1996, ten volumes of this collection have appeared, and they include all the *chokusenshū* (in volume one) as well as many anthologies compiled privately rather than under public auspices (i.e., the so-called *shisenshū*); the "personal" anthologies devoted (primarily) to the works of individual poets (*shikashū*); the texts of *utaawase* (poetry competitions) and other collective and topically or numerically structured compositional exercises (*hyakushu* and the like); and poems found in other texts, such as diaries and fictional narratives (*nikki, monogatari*) and in treatises on poetry (*karon*). Texts included (so far) date in origin from the eighth through the early nineteenth centuries. There is, of course, much duplication, because a given poem may appear in more than one or in many of these texts. I have seen no count of the total number of poems included, and have not attempted to count them myself, but their number must run to the tens or hundreds of thousands, if not more. And if this canon does not represent every *waka* ever written down, it can be thought of as representing that body of poetry that has formed and has been read as the basis and substance of the *waka* tradition as a whole. But a study of what is and what is not included in such a collection, which professes to represent the whole of a tradition and to document the content of a canon, could be quite informative.

CHAPTER ONE. *UTAMAKURA,* ALLUSION, AND INTERTEXTUALITY

1 The term *sōmon* (or *sōmonka*) is one of the three major classifying terms borrowed from Chinese anthologizing practice (specifically, from *Wen xuan*) for use in the organization of the *Man'yōshū:* poems are placed under this rubric in nine out of its twenty chapters. (The two other major classifications are *zōka,* "miscellaneous songs," and *banka,* "funerary songs.") *Sōmonka* have been called relationship poems or simply love poems because so many of them are expressions of the longing of one person for another, and, although the term is also applied to soliloquies, most *sōmon* appear in pairs. Some scholars see in these pairs a pattern that eventually lends itself to the development of fictional and semifictional narratives, many parts of which are often built around the dynamics of such exchanges. Poem exchanges are, for example, at the core of many of the short narratives that make up the various sections of such early works as *Ise monogatari*

and *Yamato monogatari* (ca. 950) and the pattern remains prominent, in embedded form, in *Genji monogatari* (ca. 1000-1100) as well. And such exchanges are also a major element of the structure of such works as *Kagerō nikki*, *Izumi Shikibu nikki*, and *Towazugatari*, and many other "diaries" of the Heian and Kamakura periods.

2 *Shūi gusō* #2503 in Kubota, ed., [*Yaku chū*] *Fujiwara Teika zenkashū* 1:415. Kubota follows Reizei Tameomi's practice (as editor of *Fujiwara Teika zenkashū*, published in 1940) in numbering the poems in the collection; thus, in this *sōmonka* section, the poem in each pair that is ostensibly Teika's own is given one number, and the poem paired with it, as Teika's correspondent's verse, is given the same number, enclosed in parentheses.

3 *Kokin wakashū* #650, in Kojima and Arai, ed., *Kokin wakashū*, SNKBT 5, p. 200.

4 I use the word *poesy* here to refer to the corpus (and to various corpora) of texts composed by poets who were conscious of their poem-making as activity taking place within the context of a tradition—the *waka* tradition.

5 The word translated here and throughout this study as "buried tree" is written in pre-modern texts both as *umoregi* and *mumoregi*. Throughout the following discussion, both forms will be used, as dictated by the form found in the text cited in each instance. The word is a compound of the combining form (*ren'yōkei*) of the intransitive verb *umor[u]*, which means to lie in concealment beneath a surface (under ground or water, for example), and the word *ki*, "tree" (which frequently becomes -*gi* in such compounds). In literary texts written or copied after the Heian period (794-1185), words incorporating forms of the verb *umor[u]* were often read *mmor[u]*; the literal rendition of this pronunciation in phonetic script (with the phonetic character *mu* as the first syllable) thereafter brought about the derivative form *mumor[u]*. (Ōno, Satake and Maeda, ed., *Iwanami Kogo jiten*, p. 1258.)

6 Helen Craig McCullough has suggested "River of Scandal" as an apt translation of the name of the river, given its consistent usage in the thematic context established through the appearance of this particular poem in the *Kokinshū*. See McCullough, *Kokin wakashū, The First Imperial Anthology of Japanese Poetry*, p. 141, note to poem #628. In my paraphrases I generally prefer to reproduce the name as it appears, rather than translate it, but in some cases it may be useful to do both as a way of indicating the double valence of the name.

The etymology and orthographic history of the place-name Natori is rather obscure. There is some evidence that an earlier name for the district through which the river flows (Natori-gun) was Nitori, written in a way suggesting that the area was a source of cinnabar; but this same name may also have been pronounced Natori. Both names appear in *Shoku nihongi* (compiled in 797) in entries describing eighth-century events in the area, but it is not entirely clear whether the two names refer to two separate localities or just one. (See *Kadokawa Nihon chimei daijiten* henshū iinkai, ed., *Kadokawa Nihon chimei daijiten 4: Miyagi-ken*, p. 397.) To complicate the issue, the discovery in 1980 at an archaeological site in Sendai-shi of a ceramic vessel with the place-name Natori written on it seems to date the now-standard orthography to the first half of the seventh century. (See Aoki, Inaoka, Sasayama, and Shirafuji, ed., *Shoku nihongi* [SNKBT 1], p. 430, supplementary note 6.26.)

7 For a thorough study of the early uses of place-names in Japanese poetry, leading up to the emergence of the concept of *utamakura,* see the first two parts ("La Poésie des sites et de l'itinéraire dans le *Man'yō-shū*" and "La rhétorique des noms de lieux à l'époque classique") of Pigeot, *Michiyuki-bun: Poétique de l'itinéraire dans la littérature du Japon ancien,* pp. 15-168. Pigeot's presentation serves as the basis for her analysis of a medieval genre of travel accounts, the *michiyuki-bun,* but it is also an excellent digest of Japanese scholarship on early literary place-name usage.

8 "Yo ni utamakura to iite, tokoro no na kakitaru mono ari," from Hashimoto, ed., *Toshiyori zuinō,* in Hashimoto et al., eds., *Karon shū* (NKBZ 50), p. 115.

9 For the episode in *Kojidan,* see Kuroita, ed., *Shintei zōho kokushi taikei,* 18:34.

10 When Bashō visited Kasajima during his journey to the northeast in 1689—the journey recorded in his *Oku no hosomichi* (The narrow road to the Northeast)— he particularly recalled Saigyō's poem in memory of Sanekata (*Shin kokin wakashū* #793) and asked to see the miscanthus that had been planted on Sanekata's grave in reference to Saigyo's mention of that plant in his poem. Then Bashō, in turn, wrote his own poem—a *haiku,* rather than a *tanka*—in which he plays on the presence of the word *kasa* (umbrella) in the place-name Kasajima. For an English version of the entire passage, including Saigyō's poem, see McCullough, ed., *Classical Japanese Prose: An Anthology,* pp. 531-532.

11 For an account in English of the powers ascribed to names, including place-names, in early Japanese culture, see chapter six, "The *Kotodama* of Names," in Plutschow, *Chaos and Cosmos: Ritual in Early and Medieval Japanese Literature,* pp. 75-87.

12 *Gosen wakashū* #960, in Katagiri, ed., *Gosen wakashū,* SNKBT 6, pp. 282-283.

13 *Miotsukushi* were deployed for the purpose of guiding ships through such hazardous estuaries as that at Naniwa, which is at the mouth of the Yodo River. Though they were a feature of other locations, the association of *miotsukushi* with Naniwa in particular is very strong—and is much strengthened by the prominence, in the *waka* tradition, of this particular poem by Motoyoshi. The translation "channel buoy" is used by Edward G. Seidensticker in his rendering of the title of a chapter in *The Tale of Genji*—"Miotsukushi"—which takes its name from a poem presented in the text as one prompted, in part, by recollection of Motoyoshi's poem on the part of the fictional character (Hikaru Genji) on the occasion of his own passage through the Naniwa area.

"Channel buoy" is also the translation used for *miotsukushi* by such translators as McCullough and Steven D. Carter. Carter's translation of Motoyoshi's poem is: "Like a channel buoy/bobbing off Naniwa strand,/my name is tossed about./But still I will come to you—/though it be death to proceed" (see Carter, *Traditional Japanese Poetry: An Anthology,* p. 211). This translation reflects a commentary tradition which holds that the first syllable of the place-name Naniwa may also be read as having a contingent function in the clause "ima hata onaji na," meaning "whatever happens now, my name/reputation (*na*) will be what it is" (that is, it is already ruined, and nothing can change that now).

14 *Motoyoshi Shinnō shū* #51, 52, in SKT 3: *Shikashū hen*, p. 151.

15 Kristeva, *Revolution in Poetic Language*, pp. 59-60. Lynne Huffer explains cogently that "the Kristevan text is conceived as a kind of process where 'meaning' (*signifiance*) is produced not through the intentionality of a coherent subject, the author, but rather as a result of the forces, drives, and modalities that bring writing into existence. The text thus becomes its own process or production rather than a container for self-expression or a mimetic tool of referential reflection." See Huffer, "Julia Kristeva (1941-)," in Sartori and Zimmerman, ed., *French Women Writers: A Bio-Bibliographical Source Book*, p. 245. The following discussion of intertextuality and allusion is based on a number of texts, including Kristeva, *Revolution in Poetic Language*, Ben-Porat, "The Poetics of Literary Allusion"; Laurent Jenny, "The Strategy of Form"; Alter, "Allusion," in *The Pleasures of Reading [in an Ideological Age]*, pp. 111-140; Worton and Still, eds., *Intertextuality: Theories and Practices*.

16 See Hashimoto, Ariyoshi, and Fujihira, ed., *Karon shū* (NKBZ 50), pp. 482 and 510 for Motoyoshi's poem and pp. 481 and 509 for the *Kokinshū* poem. For a translation of the complete *Kindai shūka*, see Brower and Earl Miner, trans., *Fujiwara Teika's Superior Poems of Our Time*. The fact that Teika's father, Shunzei, reproduced and discussed Motoyoshi's poem as a model in his own treatise, the *Korai fūteishō* (1155), might also be of some additional significance. (See Hashimoto et al., eds., *Karonshū*, p. 403.)

17 Alter, *The Pleasure of Reading*, p. 112; Ben-Porat, "The Poetics of Literary Allusion," pp. 107-108.

18 Alter, *The Pleasure of Reading*, p. 112.

19 Brower, *Alexander Pope: The Poetry of Allusion*, pp. viii, 1.

20 Greene, *The Light in Troy*, p. 15.

21 Greene, *The Light in Troy*, pp. 16, 18, 19.

22 Lacan, "The Agency of the Letter in the Unconscious, or Reason Since Freud," p. 153.

23 Lacan, "The Agency of the Letter," pp. 155, 157.

24 I refer here to the standard works in English on Japanese poetry: Brower and Miner, *Japanese Court Poetry*; Miner, *An Introduction to Japanese Court Poetry*; and McCullough, *Brocade by Night: "Kokin wakashū" and the Court Style in Japanese Classical Poetry*.

25 *Izumi Shikibu shū* #726, SKT 3:260. For further discussion of this poem, see chapter 2.

26 The earliest and perhaps still the best account in English is in *Japanese Court Poetry*, where Brower and Miner also discuss Maynard Mack's characterization of allusion (in the works of Pope) as productive of a "metaphor of tone," and then proceed to apply this language to their account of Japanese praxis. (See *Japanese Court Poetry*, pp. 14-15, 290-291.)

27 Mark Morris points toward some answers to these questions in "*Waka* and Form, *Waka* and History." For counterarguments, see Miner, "Waka: Features of Its Constitution and Development." There are also some excellent studies of allusion and of what might be called intertextuality in the field of Chinese poetry: see, for example, Lattimore, "Allusion and T'ang Poetry," and Owen, *Remembrance: The Experience of the Past in Classical Chinese Literature* and "Place: Meditation on the Past at Chin-ling."

28 See, for example, Earl Miner's essay on "the development of a systematic poetics" in Miner, Odagiri, and Morrell, ed., *The Princeton Companion to Classical Japanese Literature*, pp. 3–17; and Helen McCullough's more specific discussion of the use of the terms in Ki no Tsurayuki's preface to the *Kokin wakashū*, in *Brocade by Night*, pp. 326–337.

29 In addition to some of the works already cited, there is, for example, Huey's *Kyōgoku Tamekane: Poetry and Politics in Late Kamakura Japan*, the fourth and fifth chapters of which are devoted to detailed analyses of the style of the poetry of Tamekane (1254–1332) and a few of his contemporaries.

30 See, for example, Carter, *Waiting for the Wind: Thirty-Six Poets of Japan's Late Medieval Age*, p. 311. For a fuller development of this perspective, see Carter, "*Waka* in the Age of *Renga*."

31 See, for example, passages in Teika's *Kindai shūka* and *Eiga no taigai* (NKBZ 50:471, 493).

32 For example, in *Kindai shūka* Teika specifically recommends that "old words" are best taken from the first three Imperial anthologies—the *Kokin wakashū, Gosen wakashū,* and *Shūi wakashū.* (Brower and Miner, *Fujiwara Teika's Superior Poets of Our Time*, p. 18.) Elsewhere, he and Shunzei both recommend (through practice or through explicit statement) the *Man'yōshū* and certain other classic texts—*The Tale of Genji* and *The Tales of Ise,* for example—as appropriate sources for *honka* (foundation poems) or as fulcrums of allusion, and they specifically recommend *against* allusion to relatively recent poems or poems that are unlikely to be recognized. Allusions to Chinese poems and other texts are also acceptable, if handled properly.

33 In one sense, the Saishōshitennōin project may have been rather successful: Ariyoshi Tamotsu suggests, without going into much detail, that this project heralded a resurgence of *meisho* poetics that continued thereafter for several decades. (See Ariyoshi, *Shin kokin wakashū no kenkyū: kihan to kōsei*, p. 257, 278.) What he must have in mind is the prominence of famous place-name usage in various poem programs and sequences of the mid-thirteenth century, such as the *Kenpō meisho hyakushu* (Sequences of one hundred poems composed on famous-place topoi in the Kenpō era) composed under Emperor Juntoku's auspices in 1215, which will be discussed at several points below.

34 The term *Yamato uta* is a predecessor to the term *waka*; if anything, it carries a stronger implication that the Japanese poem is specifically Japanese (rather than Chinese, or anything else), in part because the words *Yamato* and *uta* are Japanese rather than Chinese words. The term *Yamato kotoba* is also used to mean

"the words of the Japanese language," as distinct from those of other languages; but, in both cases, a name for a particular region, Yamato, which happened to be geographically central, and which (partly for that reason) became the political center as well, is being used to represent the whole of a nation that was once composed of many culturally distinct regions (with distinctive languages, musics, customs, rituals, etc.).

35 See Kurano, ed., *Kojiki* (NKBT 1), p. 89.

36 I have used the standard five-line lineation for romanized transcription of the thirty-one syllable Japanese poem here in order to emphasize the syllabic (metrical) structure, but elsewhere I prefer to use a more condensed two-part transcription wherever possible, as a way of focusing on a poem's overall syntactic structure rather than its metrics per se.

37 *Man'yōshū* #919 in Takagi, Gomi, and Ōno, ed., *Man'yōshū* 2 (NKBT 5), p. 137.

38 More will be said about these poems and about the ideology of Imperial pilgrimage and presence in the land in chapter 4.

39 See Kuwata, *Hosokawa Yūsai*, p. 46; SKT 9:17 (*Shūmyōshū* #600) and 9:52, (*Kōyō wakashū* #1625).

40 "Seventeenth-century nostalgia was a physical rather than a mental complaint, an illness with explicit symptoms and often lethal consequences. First medically diagnosed and coined (from the Greek *nosos* = return to native land, and *algos* = suffering or grief) in 1688 by Johannes Hofer, nostalgia was already common; once away from their native land, some people languished, wasted away, and even perished. . . . Swiss mercenaries throughout Europe were nostalgia's first victims. Simply to hear a familiar herder's tune made them deeply homesick for beloved alpine scenes. . . . No picture so vividly evoked the Alps as an alpine melody. Such music haunted the bearer with 'an image of the past which is at once definite and unattainable.'" Lowenthal, *The Past Is a Foreign Country*, p. 10. The quotation is from Zwingmann, "'Heimweh' or 'Nostalgic Reaction': A Conceptual Analysis and Interpretation of a Medico-Psychological Phenomenon," cited by Lowenthal from Fred Davis, "Nostalgia, Identity and the Current Nostalgia Wave," p. 415; for the same passage, Lowenthal also cites Jean Starobinski's extremely stimulating essay "The Idea of Nostalgia."

41 Jameson, "Walter Benjamin, or Nostalgia," pp. 53, 68.

42 Norinaga developed his notion of *mono no aware o shiru* most fully in two parallel works, *Shibun yōryō* (a treatise on the aesthetic principles of *The Tale of Genji*) and *Isonokami sasamegoto* (a treatise on the aesthetic principles of Japanese poetry). See Hino, ed., *Motoori Norinaga shū*. The best study of the development of these ideas in English is Thomas J. Harper's unpublished Ph.D. dissertation, "Motoori Norinaga's Criticism of the *Genji monogatari*: A Study the Background and Critical Content of his *Genji monogatari tama no ogushi*"; see especially chapter 7 and appendix I.

43 Strachey, ed., *The Standard Edition of the Complete Psychological Works of Sigmund Freud*, 8:121–122.

44 The passage comes out slightly differently in the version "translated with the

author's [i.e., Groos'] permission": "When not too mechanical, as sometimes when dressing we put on everything in its right relation but without attention, recognition is pre-eminently pleasurable. Even the mere coefficient of recognition is accompanied with a mild satisfaction such as Faust experienced when after a foreign sojourn he found himself once more in his study. . . . The act of recognition being so pleasurable, we would naturally expect man to make use of its for its own sake—that is, experimentally. Aristotle, indeed, grounds appreciation of art in pleasurable recognition, and, while not going to that length, we must admit that the idea deserves consideration." See Groos, *The Play of Man*, p. 123.

45 Morris, "Sei Shōnagon's Poetic Catalogues."

46 The original passage quoted by Morris ("Sei Shōnagon's Poetic Catalogues," p. 18) is in the section "Names and Propositions" in Mill, *The System of Logic*, 1:36. Morris also cites Claude Lévi-Strauss as the definitive debunker of Mill's argument, and the key passage to which he refers is from Lévi-Strauss' *The Savage Mind*: "We need to establish that proper names are an integral part of systems we have been treating as codes: as means of fixing significations by transposing them into terms of other significations. Would this be possible if it were true, as logicians and some linguists have maintained, that proper names are, in Mill's phrase, 'meaningless,' lacking in signification?" (p. 172).

47 Mill, "Names and Propositions," p. 35.

48 Mill says, "Proper names are attached to the objects themselves, and are not dependent on the continuance of any attribute of the object" ("Names and Propositions," p. 36). But one might say that Japanese poets willfully insist on the continuance of the attributes of the names with which they play.

49 "*Natorigawa: Ikanaru na o toritaru naran to kikamahoshi*." In section 62 of *Makura no sōshi* in the NKBT edition (Ikeda and Kishigami, eds.), p. 102. Some commentators feel certain that Shōnagon is specifically alluding in this quip to Mibu no Tadamine's Natorigawa poem in *Kokin wakashū* (#628), on which see the discussion in chapter 2.

50 Seidensticker, trans., *The Tale of Genji*, p. 452. For the passage in Japanese, see Abe, Akiyama, and Imai, eds., *Genji monogatari* 3 (NKBZ 14): 240.

51 Seidensticker, trans. *The Tale of Genji*, p. 453; Abe et al., eds., *Genji monogatari*, 3:242.

52 Stevens, "An Ordinary Evening in New Haven," in *The Collected Poems of Wallace Stevens*, pp. 465-487. See also Bloom, *Wallace Stevens: The Poems of Our Climate*, pp. 305-337.

53 *The Collected Poems of Wallace Stevens*, p. 473.

54 Ibid., p. 471.

55 For further discussion and illustration of this point, see chapter 2.

56 The translation of the prose is from McCullough, trans., "A Tosa Journal," in *Classical Japanese Prose: An Anthology*, p. 81; the translation of the poem is my own. There are many good modern editions of *Tosa nikki*: one is Hagitani, ed., *Tosa nikki*, which also includes an edition of Tsurayuki's collected poetic works (*Tsurayuki shū*). For this passage, see p. 80.

57 From McCullough, trans., in *Classical Japanese Prose*, pp. 82–83. The lineation of the translation of the poem has been revised here. In Hagitani, ed., *Tosa nikki*, see p. 81.

58 My own translation; see Hagitani, ed., *Tosa nikki*, pp. 99–100.

59 The assessment is made in Tsurayuki's critical disquisition in the preface to the *Kokinshū* (SNKBT 5:13) on the best-known poets of the preceding generation. See also McCullough, trans., *Kokin wakashū*, p. 7. In the *Kokinshū* (where it appears as poem #53), and in *Ise monogatari* (section 82), Narihira's *yo no naka ni* poem appears with the word *nakariseba* instead of *sakazareba*, yielding something more like "If there were no cherry blossoms at all in this world." But all versions place the composition to Narihira's visit to the Nagisa villa in the retinue of its owner, Prince Koretaka 844–897, who had inherited the residence (on a hill overlooking the Yodo River) from his father, the Emperor Montoku. The poem is characteristic of those of the era in its roundabout rhetoric, which is designed to praise the cherries (they *do* exist in the world, and no one, including the poet, would have it otherwise); and it also features an intentional ambiguity: *haru no kokoro* can mean both "the heart of [an anthropomorphized] spring" and "that which people feel in their hearts in spring."

60 Parts of these paraphrases are adapted from McCullough's translations in *Classical Japanese Prose*, pp. 98–99.

CHAPTER TWO. STORIES OF THE TREE, STORIES OF THE RIVER

1 Like other lignites (such as bogwood,) the fossilized trees (*umoregi*) of Japan are of relatively recent formation: they are usually dated to the Neocene segments of the Tertiary era, some five million years ago. They are generally of the genus Sequoia, and have been found most frequently in the area of Sendai and in the Izu Peninsula; less extensive deposits have also been discovered in Fukui, Kyoto, and the area of Mount Fuji. See Aoki Jun'ichi, "Umoregi," in *Encyclopedia Japonica* (*Dai Nihon hyakka jiten*) 2:686, and Takeuchi Nobuko, "Umoregi saiku," in Endō, Kodama, and Miyamoto, ed., *Nihon no meisan jiten*, p. 96.

2 The principles that are said to govern the arrangement of poems in most classical anthologies are best explained in the seminal work of Konishi Jin'ichi: see his article "Association and Progression" (translated by Brower and Miner). The operations of "association and progression" are also emphasized in Brower and Miner's discussions of the major anthologies in *Japanese Court Poetry*, a work much influenced by (and dedicated to) Konishi (see, for example, their explication of "association and progression" in the *Shin kokin wakashū*, pp. 319–329). Miner has elaborated further on these ideas in later works, often with a broadly comparative approach: see, for example, his essay "Some Issues for Study of Integrated Collections" in Fraistat, ed., *Poems in Their Place*, pp. 18–43.

3 The best available English translations of these songs, with their prose contextualizations, are in Edwin Cranston's *A Waka Anthology, Volume One: The Gem-Glistening Cup*, pp. 7–130.

4 For Donald Keene's complete translation see J. Thomas Rimer's *Modern Japanese Fiction and Its Traditions*, pp. 275-305.

5 For a complete translation, see McCullough, trans., *Tales of Ise: Lyrical Episodes from Tenth-Century Japan*.

6 For more examples of poems classified in this manner in books 11 and 12 of the *Man'yōshū*, see Cranston, *A Waka Anthology*, pp. 688-694 and 702-704.

7 *Man'yōshū* #2723, NKBT 6:229.

8 The structure [noun] + *o* (i.e., *wo*) + [verb stem] + *mi* is found frequently in early (i.e., pre-Heian) song-poems, where it is used as a way of explaining why certain conditions give rise to certain other circumstances (states of being, action, inaction, etc.), as in *se o hayami* ("the water flows swiftly over the shallows, [so it is difficult to cross the stream]"). We have seen it in Akahito's "Waka no ura" poem (*Man'yōshū* #919) as well. Helen McCullough associates its presence there with the influence of "[Chinese] Six Dynasties reasoning," a rhetorical mode much favored by the circle of poets of which Akahito was a member (the so-called *Kyūshū kadan*). See McCullough, *Brocade by Night*, p. 109. But the appearance of such clauses in anonymous poems in various sections of the *Man'yōshū*, and elsewhere, may suggest that the genealogy of this rhetorical mode may not be exclusively Chinese.

9 The use of *umoregi no* as a *makurakotoba* per se does not seem to be very widespread. In his study of *makurakotoba*, Fukui Kyūzō cites only this and one other *Man'yōshū* poem (#1385, discussed below), and a passage in Ki no Tsurayuki's *kana* preface to the *Kokin wakashū* (also discussed below) as examples of such usage. (See Fukui and Yamagishi, eds., *Makurakotoba no kenkyū to shakugi*, p. 237.) There may, of course, have been other occurrences in texts which simply do not survive, which would support this treatment; but further consideration of the use of the figure in other structures (as is attempted here) may help to illuminate the function and significance of these words in these settings, where, at least traditionally, the usage has been treated as *makurakotoba* and left at that, without further explanation.

10 See, for example, Kubota, *Man'yōshū hyōshaku* 7:245; Kōnosu, *Man'yōshū zenshaku* 3:584; and Omodaka, *Man'yōshū chūshaku* 11:415. Almost all commentators paraphrase the function of the clause with the modern Japanese *umoregi no yō ni*, "like a buried tree," but I think this oversimplifies its role in the poem. It is perhaps easier for contemporary minds to grasp the meaning of a simile than to understand other kinds of relationships between words in the poems of distant times and places which are certainly as intimate as simile but which cannot be resolved as the virtually complete identification of the characteristics of one entity with those of another. I am inclined to follow Konishi Jin'ichi in treating both *joshi* and *makurakotoba* as types of "guide phrase" (for which he has coined the term *dōshi*.) See Konishi, *A History of Japanese Literature, vol. 1: The Archaic and Ancient Ages*, pp. 234-236, etc. Cranston usefully refers to both as "preposited structures" in the commentary in *A Waka Anthology*.

11 The title of these works may be translated as "A beginner's guide to *waka*

composition" and "The ABC's of *waka.*" Norikane treats the figure as one of two to be handled as winter images (the other is *hahakigi,* "broom tree"), in a section on the proper treatment (seasonal and general) of various other trees and plants, and he explains exactly what it is (suggesting that this is apparently not self-evident): "A *mumoregi* is a decayed tree that lies beneath the waters of a stream in a mountain valley" (*mumoregi to wa kusaretaru ki no yama no tanimizu no shita nado in fushitaru o iu nari*). Jōkaku echoes this and adds "[The figure] is used in this poem to refer obliquely to feelings of love that are deeply buried" (*shita ni omoi shizumitaru kokoro ni yosete yomeri*). For *Waka dōmōshō,* see Kyūsojin, ed., *Nihon kagaku taikei, bekkan* 1:269; for *Waka iroha,* see Sasaki, ed., *Nihon kagaku taikei* 3:181.

12 *Man'yōshū* #1385, NKBT 5:261.

13 The word *yuge* may be a contraction of *yumike,* "bow carving" or "bow carver." (Ōno et al., *Iwanami kogo jiten*: 1329.) It should be noted that in early Japan bows were not only weapons for the hunt or battle but were also implements of ritual: their strings might be "twanged" to summon deities or to drive demons away.

What was once called "the Yuge River plain" was later called the "Yamato River plain" and is now called "the Hasegawa plain," in Yao City, Ōsaka Prefecture. (NKBT 5:261, note to poem #1385; see also the entry on "Yuge" in *Kadokawa Nihon chimei daijiten 27: Ōsaka-fu,* pp. 1244-1245, for a discussion of the association of this place-name with the ancient clan name "Yuge," which may indeed be traced to the clan's hereditary involvement in bow-making and which is attached in turn to the ceremonial names of some members of the powerful Mononobe clan.)

This is the only poem in the *Man'yōshū* in which the phrase *makana mochi* appears, yet it is nonetheless traditionally treated as a *makurakotoba*; and the name of the Yuge River, toward which it here leads, is itself not mentioned in any other *Man'yōshū* poem, nor, for that matter, in any subsequent major collection.

14 Watase Masatada reads the *no* in *umoregi no* as an indicator that *umoregi* is the subject of the verb *arawaru* and thus argues that the figure is not simply part of a guide-phrase (*joshi*) beginning from *makana mochi* (which reading would throw all the semantic labor of the poem onto its last eight syllables). He writes, "If one reads the text up to this point as a *joshi,* the poem ceases to be a metaphorical poem (*hiyuka*)." In Itō and Inaoka, eds., *Man'yōshū zenchū* 7:361. About one-third of the poems in book seven of the *Man'yōshū,* in which this poem is included, are poems classed as *hiyuka* and organized under a series of such headings as "poems that refer to birds," "poems that refer to rivers," "poems that refer to rain," etc. For a study of these classifications which focuses on their emulation of certain analogous Chinese practices, see Yiu, "The Category of Metaphorical Poems (*hiyuka*) in the *Man'yōshū*: Its Characteristics and Chinese Origins."

15 Kubota Utsubo imagined this scenario in an early postwar commentary: "A man

and a woman who live in the vicinity of the Yuge river plain are taking great care to keep their relationship a secret. Hearing of the discovery of a fossilized tree, the woman compares it to her self and directs the poem to the man in the form of a statement of her fears" (Kubota, *Man'yōshū hyōshaku* 5:257). Note that Kubota takes it for granted that *umoregi* were to be found in the vicinity, that Yuge was a bow-making place, and that the poem-speaker is female, but the basis for these assumptions is not clear. Clearly, any such pretext can only be reconstructed by reading back from the poem, and any such pretext may well be fallacious and misleading. It is entirely possible, and well worth considering, that the only pretext for the poem was a context that cannot be reconstructed but that somehow made poem-making possible and appropriate.

16 As Mark Morris has said, "A poetic which employs elaborate mechanisms such as *utamakura, kakekotoba*, or *makura kotoba* revels by choice in setting up a disjunction or tension between word and syntax—the paradigmatic and the syntagmatic. It opposes charged bits of vocabulary to the contrary 'natural' flow of the syntactic horizon. We could speculate that you almost have to use such strategems in order to squeeze a satisfying production out of thirty-one syllables." (From Morris, "Sei Shōnagon's Poetic Catalogues," p. 38.) My point, which is derived in part from Morris' insight, is that the occurrence of both of the figures in *Man'yōshū* #1385, for example, is a conscious complication of its mode of statement, and that this complication is much of what makes it a poem.

17 For important studies of this process of the conventionalization of figural language in *waka*, see Suzuki, "Kodai waka ni okeru shinbutsu taiō kōzō: Man'yō kara ōchō waka e" and "*Kokin*-teki hyōgen no keisei."

18 *Sendai-shi shi* henshū iinkai, ed., *Sendai-shi shi 1: honpen* 1:299–300.

19 There is often this kind of close association between "famous local products" and the fame and function of particular places and place-names in the poetic tradition (*meisho utamakura*): see, for example, the discussion of "Shikama Market" (Shikama no ichi) in chapter 4. In the case of Natorigawa *umoregi*, it may be that the fame of such poems as *Kokin wakashū* 650 is in large part responsible for the fame of the commodity.

20 SNKBT 5:200. See also the discussions of this poem in the prologue and in Chapter 1.

21 SNKBT 5:194.

22 There is one version of a *Kokin wakashū* poem (*sumikechi no uta* #1108, one among those "crossed out" in some variant editions) which names and plays with Natorigawa in a manner quite similar to *Kokin wakashū* #650 and #628. This poem apparently appeared in some early (and now lost) texts of the anthology in a position quite close to #650 (that is, just after #652) and thus within the continuing sequence of poems about concealed love. But, whereas in some versions this poem reads: "Inugami no Tokonoyama naru Natorigawa/isa to kotae-yo waga na morasu na" (Oh, Natorigawa at Tokonoyama of Inugami/tell them, "No, nothing of the kind!" and do not let them know my name!), in others it reads, "Inugami no Tokonoyama naru Isayagawa/isa to," which has, in place of

Natorigawa, the name of a river that can serve as a preposited aural guide to *isa* ("No!"), and thus changes the poem from one that seems to assemble an assortment of names related only by their possible association with the subject of sexual passion to one that turns on an obvious "syntactic doubling." "Inugami no Tokonoyama" ("Inugami's 'Bed Mountain'") is a known place in Ōmi Province; but this version of #1108 is the only poem (except for some later ones that imitate it) that associates an Ōmi Natorigawa with these other Ōmi sites; there is, in fact, no known Ōmi Natorigawa. An appended note in *Kokin wakashū* says that, according to some sources, the poem was addressed by an (unnamed) Emperor to an *uneme* (a low-ranking female court attendant selected from the provinces to wait upon the Emperor). The poem also bears a strong resemblance to an anonymous poem in *Man'yōshū* book 11 (#2719), which plays with Isayagawa, not Natorigawa. (See SNKBT 5:336-337.) This assembled evidence would seem to suggest—although it cannot be proven—that the earliest versions of this poem did not mention Natorigawa but that that name was substituted for Isayagawa at some point in the poem's transmission from one source to another. Given these uncertainties, this poem will not be given further attention in this discussion.

23 According to *Engi shiki,* a handbook of legal codes roughly contemporaneous with the *Kokin wakashū*, Michinoku was at least twenty-five days' and sometimes as much as fifty days' journey from Heian-kyō, the capital and seat of elite society and culture. (See SNKBT 5, appendix, pp. 32-33.) In Tadamine's poem, the words "Michinoku ni ari to iu" are reminders of this remoteness: the river and the province through which it flows are equally exotic, from the viewpoint of the capital-based poet, but this remoteness may be part of what makes their invocation as effective as they are in the poem's figural scheme.

24 SKT 3:38 (*Tadamine shū* #67). I say the poem is implicitly *dai shirazu* in the *Kokin wakashū* because, as elsewhere in the anthology, the *kotobagaki "dai shirazu"* which appears before poem 647 applies to that poem and all those that follow it up to the next poem with a different *kotobagaki,* in this case poem #654.

25 It is believed that Tadamine may have assembled a collection of his own works as part of the process of preparing sources from which poems could be selected for inclusion in the *Kokinshū,* but the extant versions of *Tadamine shū* appear to have been assembled by other, later hands. Fujioka Tadami, "*Tadamine shū*" in Inukai et al., eds., *Waka daijiten,* p. 630.

26 Konishi, ed., "*Fuzoku no uta*" in Konishi and Tsuchihashi, eds., *Kodai kayō shū* (NKBT 3), p. 446.

27 Suzuki Hideo views much of the process that gave what came to be called *meisho utamakura* their place in court poetry as part of a still larger political process which led to the near-destruction of local and regional identity. See Suzuki, "Utamakura no honsei." The court's appropriation and neutralization of *kuniburiuta* may also have been motivated by a desire to co-opt and neutralize the local spirits (*kunitama*) to whom the songs were originally directed. (Kobayashi Shigemi, "Kuniburiuta," in Inukai et al., eds., *Waka daijiten,* p. 264.)

28 *Kokin waka rokujō* #1746, SKT 2:217. Cranston defines *hayashikotoba* as "mean-

ingless words and phrases in *kayō* [songs], sung as refrains or for their rhythm" (Cranston, *A Waka Anthology,* p. 782). For an example, see his translation of *Nihon shoki* song #10 (p. 71).

29 Two examples of cross-genre transference of this textual node may be of interest here. The protagonist of the *kyōgen* Natorigawa—one of many extant libretti in the subgenre called *shukke zatō kyōgen,* which are burlesques featuring the antics of buffoonish Buddhist clerics—is a monk who is so forgetful that he even has trouble remembering his name. He "loses" his name, he thinks, in the torrents of Natorigawa, but a local man comes to his aid and helps him "retrieve his name" (*natori*) from the waters. At one point the monk exclaims, "I have nothing at all to do with love, so it's really irritating to see my name carried off in this stream" (*koi o suru ni wa aranedo, ukina o nagasu haradachi ya*)—a line which spoofs both the monk's supposed asceticism and the river's poetic associations with amorous pursuits. See Furukawa, ed., *Kyōgen shū: chū* (Nihon koten zensho 63), p. 201.

  In the Edo *nagauta* "Natorigawa"—a song in the vast repertoire of dramatic ballads usually performed with *shamisen* accompaniment—the libretto reads, in part, "My love is hopeless, a *shamisen* without strings; I cannot sleep but weep all night . . . together, you and I are just like Natorigawa; ah, our love is a Natorigawa indeed!" (*Wa ga koiji wa, ito naki, shami yo nan no ne mo sede nakiakasu . . . yakku futari to futari ga Natorigawa, ōsore futari to futari ga Natorigawa.*" (Takano Tatsuyuki, ed., *Nihon kayō shūsei* 9:45–46.) This is a tissue of *waka* figures and phrases, in which Natorigawa is merely a variable, but a prominent one, for it marks this song about a frustrated and probably scandalous love as just slightly different—but different enough to be distinct—from all the others of its kind in the same genre.

  Both the *kyōgen* and the *nagauta*—undated works in genres identified with the Muromachi and Tokugawa eras, respectively—may be thought of as perform-ative texts designed for informed but not necessarily exclusively elite audiences, and to that extent may be seen as examples of texts in which the manipulation of such names as Natorigawa is grounded in an awareness of their intertextual genealogy which may or may not be concise or comprehensive but which none-theless senses the word's historical texture; that is, whether or not the audience recognizes the allusion to poetic precedent in all its complexity, it can be expected to recognize the name and to hear it ring with an inherently referential richness and resonance.

30 SNKBT 5:9. "Unnoticed" is Helen McCullough's translation of *hito shirenu koto* in McCullough, *Kokin wakashū,* p. 5.

31 See, for example, McCullough, *Brocade by Night,* chapter 5, for a thorough analysis of the *Kokin wakashū* prefaces.

32 Much of the prose of the *kana* preface falls into the alternating five- and seven-syllable cadence of *waka,* and *waka* rhetoric, including many *makurakotoba,* is employed with much bravado. In her comparison of the rhetoric of the *kana jo* and with that of the *mana jo* ("Chinese preface") of the *Kokinshū,* McCullough

observes that Tsurayuki "naturalizes" the figurative language of the former through the use of such images as that of the buried tree. See McCullough, *Brocade by Night*, p. 321.

33 McCullough, tr., *Kokin wakashū*, p. 3. The passage has been shown to have been modeled on the "Major Preface" of the *Shi jing*, "a short, anonymous composition believed to date from the first century A.D.": "to maintain correct standards concerning good and ill, to move heaven and earth, to stir the spirits and gods, nothing is better than poetry. The former Kings used it to ensure correct relations between husband and wife, to encourage filial piety, to foster upright conduct, to render moral instruction attractive, and to improve social customs." McCullough, *Brocade by Night*, p. 304. See also Wixted, "The *Kokinshū* Prefaces: Another Perspective."

34 See chapter 1. Scholars place Izumi Shikibu's birth somewhere between 974 and 979, and she is thought to have died in about 1035.

35 *Izumi Shikibu shū* #726, SKT 3:260. The poem also appears in *Shinchokusen wakashū* (the ninth Imperially commissioned anthology, compiled in 1232-1234 by Fujiwara Teika at the command of Retired Emperor Gohorikawa) as a *dai shirazu* (topic unknown) poem, #1200, in the second chapter of "miscellaneous" poems (SKT 1:283.)

36 Murasaki Shikibu was born in 970. Widowed in 1001, she began her service in the salon of Emperor Ichijō's consort Fujiwara Shōshi in 1005 or 1006 and remained with her at court until around 1014—during which time, it is believed, she wrote both *Genji monogatari* and the diary known as *Murasaki Shikibu nikki*. After a brief hiatus, she subsequently returned to the retinue of Shōshi, perhaps in the winter of 1018—by which time the now Retired Empress had taken the devotional name "Jōtōmon'in"—but almost nothing is known of her activities or movements thereafter. Murasaki Shikibu does write about having read letters from Izumi Shikibu (who served at least briefly in Shōshi's retinue, beginning in 1009), and she makes some critical comments on her poems—but she does not give any indication that the two women actually ever met, even though they may well have done so.

37 *Murasaki Shikibu shū* #102, SKT 3:247. The poem also appears in *Gyokuyō wakashū*, a fourteenth-century Imperial anthology, in the first book of spring poems, #65, with a more detailed *kotobagaki*: "In that period when Jōtōmon'in was Empress-Consort, [Murasaki Shikibu] wrote this poem to send along with a spray of red plum blossoms from her private residence" (*Jōtōmon'in Chūgū to mōshihaberikeru toki, sato yori mume o orite mairasu to te*). (SKT 1:422.) Empress Shōshi, later known as Jōtōmon'in (988-1074), was elevated to the rank of Chūgū in 1000 and retained that title until 1012, when she was given the higher rank of Kōtaigō. Richard Bowring is in error, in his translation of *Murasaki Shikibu shū*, in interpreting *mairasu* as a verb for Murasaki Shikibu's return to the palace; it means "sending something to the palace." Bowring, *Murasaki Shikibu: Her Diary and Poetic Memoirs*, p. 103.

38 *Horikawa hyakushū* #1522, SKT 4:246. The poem subsequently appeared in

Shika wakashū, a mid-twelfth-century Imperial anthology, as poem #342 in the first book of "miscellaneous" poems. (SNBKT 9:326). In *kaikyū* poems, the composer adopts the posture of one who stands on the threshold of old age and looks back on the past contemplatively—bewailing his age, longing for lost, outlived companions, lamenting the physical devastations of the passage of time, comparing the present unfavorably with the past, etc. Though previously identified and addressed in various compositional contexts, the topic *kaikyū* comes into particular prominence in the *Horikawa hyakushu,* where it is one of twenty miscellaneous topics, and is treated for the first time as a labeled topical section within an imperial anthology in *Shin kokin wakashū* (1205). (Takizawa Sadao, "*Kaikyū,*" in Inukai et al., eds., *Waka daijiten,* p. 147.) Masafusa is one of three poets among the *Horikawa hyakushu* sixteen who use the verb "decay" or "rot" (*kutsu*) in their *kaikyū* poems.

39 See, for example, Kudō Shigenori, ed., SNKBT 4:246.

40 McCullough, trans., *Kokin wakashū,* p. 192. The figure of the rotten tree (*kuchi-ki*) carries associations of uselessness (i.e., the futility of trying to make something of that which is already beyond use) that may be traced to a passage in Confucius' *Analects* ("A piece of rotten wood cannot be carved, nor can a wall of dried dung be trowelled," in book five, "Gong ye zhang." See D. C. Lau, trans., *Confucius: The Analects,* p. 77).

Almost nothing is known about Kengei; he is the author of three poems in *Kokin wakashū.* The women "laughed when they looked at him," we may assume, because of his aged appearance—but monkish solemnity itself is often the object of derision (usually from young women) in *waka* scenarios, episodes in narrative fiction, drama, and other genres.

41 McCullough, trans., *Kokin wakashū,* p. 56.

42 *Chōshū eisō* #111, SKT 3:621. *Chōshū eisō* is Shunzei's anthology of his own works. The poem also appears in *Fūga wakashū,* a mid-fourteenth-century Imperial anthology, as poem #1469 in the first book of miscellaneous poems (SKT 1:583.)

43 See Hisamatsu Sen'ichi, ed., "*Chōshu eisō*" in Hisamatsu et al., eds., *Heian Kamakura shikashū* (NKBT 80), p. 276 (note on poem 111). Comparison may be made to a *chōka* Shunzei composed in 1150 for the *Kyūan hyakushu* (and labeled *tanka* in accordance with a convention stemming from an editorial error in early versions of the *Kokinshū,* in which the *chōka* in book 19 were mistakenly labeled *tanka*). This poem, #100 in *Chōshu eisō,* makes bravado use of various conventional figures, including *umoregi no* as a pre-posited modifier for the verb clause *shizumeru koto*—"the condition of being 'submerged,'" or out of sight) and a large number of place-names and their clichéd associations in registering this kind of complaint, which is itself a highly conventionalized pose.

44 *Goshūi wakashū* #972 and *Shigeyuki shu* #182 (Nishi Honganji bon), SKT 1:133 and 3:136. In the early Heian period, the *tsukasameshi* was held in the first month of the year; hence the association with spring. (After the twelfth century it was usually held in autumn.) In *Goshūishū* the poem is grouped with others (in the

second chapter of "miscellaneous" poems) that express frustration at being over-looked or ill-served at the time of the *tsukasameshi*. There is also a very similar poem—possibly a variant—elsewhere in *Shigeyuki shū* (#87; SKT 3:134): "haru-goto ni wasurarenikeru mumoregi wa/tokimeku hana o yoso ni koso mire" (The buried tree that has been forgotten spring after spring/gazes from afar at flowers that are in the height of bloom).

45 *Kin'yō wakashū* #525, in Kawamura and Kashiwagi, eds., *Kin'yō wakashū*, SNKBT 9:149. In *Kin'yōshū* #523, Minamoto Sadanobu (late eleventh-early twelfth century) also says he is a "tree buried at the bottom of a ravine" (*tani no mumoregi*) which has never had its day of glory, while the younger visitors to his "mountain retreat" (*yamazato*, not necessarily a very rustic dwelling), with whom he has agreed to compose poems in celebration of the blossoming flowers, are the flourishing "mountain cherry blossoms of Yoshino": "Yamazato ni hitobito makarite, hana no uta yomikeru ni yomeru: minahito wa Yoshino no yama no sakurabana/orishiranu mi ya tani no mumoregi." Both Akinaka's and Sadanobu's poems are grouped with others of their kind (*jukkai*, "expressing frustration") in the first chapter of "miscellaneous" poems in *Kin'yōshū* (ibid., pp. 148-149). Thus, the figure is displayed as one possible and apparently admirable tool for treating the *jukkai* topos—a determination on the part of the anthology editors that is no doubt shaped by their familiarity with earlier poems of "complaint" by Izumi Shikibu, Masafusa, and others.

The phrase *hana no miyako* ("the city of flowers"; "the flowery capital") used by both Shigeyuki and Akinaka was a well-fixed collocation long before their time; it occurs for the first time in *chokusenshū* poems in the anthology that precedes the *Kin'yōshū* (i.e., the *Goshūi wakashū*, where it is used in four poems), but the *locus classicus* appears to be a poem in the "Suma" chapter of *The Tale of Genji*: it is addressed to Genji by Myōbu, a woman of the court, when he is on the point of leaving the capital in disgrace to take up residence in relatively remote Suma, and is in turn a response to a poem in which Genji himself wonders when he will return to see "the spring blossoms of the city" (*haru no miyako no hana*) once again. (See NKBZ 13:175 and Edward G. Seidensticker, trans., *The Tale Genji*, p. 229.)

46 *Shoku senzai wakashū* #874, SKT 1:499.

47 The *Kyūan hyakushu* was originally conceived ca. 1143, under the sponsorship of Retired Emperor Sutoku, but the fourteen contributors' collected poems were not submitted to him until 1150. (Taniyama Shigeru, "*Kyūan hyakushu*" in Inukai et al., eds., *Waka daijiten*, pp. 223-224.)

48 *Kyūan hyakushu* #419, SKT 4:286.

49 The jarring effect of *choku naraba* is not unprecedented: the phrase also appears at the beginning of a poem in *Shūi wakashū* (#531). That earlier usage—in a poem which, according to some sources (e.g., *Ōkagami*) was composed by Tsura-yuki's daughter—reportedly was questioned and criticized by Saigyō as an incur-sion of "the ordinary" into the realm of poetic language (*utakotoba naraneba*). See Komachiya, ed., *Shūi wakashū* (SNKBT 7), p. 151, note on poem 531. But

Suemichi is probably deliberately imitating that questionable usage and perhaps is thereby legitimizing what might otherwise be seen as a repeated offense.

50 This poet's personal name is unknown, and the appellation by which she is identified (Shunzeikyō no musume) is somewhat misleading: she was actually the daughter of Shunzei's daughter, "Hachijōin Sanjō" (Teika's sister), but was raised by her grandparents and was sponsored in her long career at court by Shunzei rather than by her own father, Fujiwara (Nakamikado) Moriyori, who fell into political disgrace after the Shishi no Tani conspiracy of 1177. Though one among a handful of female members of Gotoba's (and, later, Juntoku's) literary coterie, Shunzei's Daughter stands out as one of the most accomplished and respected members of the whole group, and seems frequently to have participated on an equal footing with her male counterparts in their creative undertakings, even when she was the sole female contributor or one of just two or three women to be included in otherwise all-male activities. In the Saishōshitennōin project of 1207 (discussed in chapter 4), she was the only female participant among a total of ten poets. For a detailed study of her works, see Morimoto, Shunzeikyō no musume no kenkyū.

51 Sentō kudai gojūshu #76, SKT 4:627.

52 McCullough, trans., The Tale of the Heike, p. 157. See also Takagi et al., eds., Heike monogatari 1 (NKBT 32), p. 316.

53 For more on the Jōkyū (or Shōkyū) war and its consequences, see Mass, The Development of Kamakura Rule, pp. 3–58; and Brownlee, "Crisis as Reinforcement of the Imperial Institution," pp. 59–77, and "The Shōkyū War and the Political Rise of the Warriors," pp. 193–201. William McCullough has translated another version of Jōkyūki (which does not include the poem in the account of Seitaka's arrest): see his "Shōkyūki," especially pp. 215–450. McCullough has also translated yet another literary chronicle of the same events in "The Azuma kagami Account of the Shōkyū War." See also chapter 4 for an account of related events.

54 Matsubayashi, ed., Jōkyūki, pp. 140–141.

55 Actually, Dōjo managed to live on to the age of 54; he died in the spring of 1249. (Sakamoto Masahito, "Dōjo," in Kokushi daijiten henshū iinkai, ed., Kokushi daijiten 10, p. 108.)

56 It might be observed that "parting" (ribetsu) is itself a standard topical category in the waka tradition, to which, for example, a separate section is devoted in Kokin wakashū and in many other anthologies and topically-structured compositions. In a sense, this episode in Jōkyūki allies itself with and partakes of this tradition, which had already been thoroughly incorporated into the conventions of prose narrative (as in, for example, the first part of the "Suma" chapter of Genji monogatari); here, however, the intertextual fabric is further complicated by the intensity of the homoerotic relationship (understood in the narrative rather than explicitly described there) between the Prince and the boy, which replaces the intensity of the heterosexual or asexual relationships that provide the context for the majority of ribetsu scenarios.

Similarly, the *Heike monogatari* account of Yorimasa's death is contextualized by a tradition of narrating the delivery of death poems (especially in and after battles) that reaches back to to the earliest Japanese narratives—the *Kojiki, Nihon shoki,* and *Shoku nihongi,* and beyond them to the classical Chinese histories, such as the *Shi ji.*

57 *Sekidera Komachi,* in NKBT 41:290. See also Brazell, trans., "Komachi at Seki-dera," in Keene, ed., *Twenty Plays of the Nō Theatre,* p. 70.

58 Ijichi, ed., *Tsukuba shū shō* in NKBT 39, p. 123. Gusai's name is also read "Kyūsei."

59 Ibid., p. 138.

60 Ibid.

61 Ariyoshi, *Saigyō,* pp. 46–62, 244–245.

62 It is generally believed that Saigyō himself compiled the earliest version of *Sankashū,* in which case he may be thought of as the author of both this particular "Natorigawa crossing" story and the story of himself as traveler.

63 *Sankashū* #1130, in Ariyoshi, *Saigyō,* p. 53; see also Kazamaki, ed., *Sankashū,* in NKBT 29, p. 199.

64 See McCullough, *Brocade by Night,* pp. 331–332, for a discussion of the *momiji/nishiki* trope (*mitate*); the *Kokin wakashū* poems that exemplify the convention, in McCullough's analysis, are #283, 291, 294, 296, 314, and 420. The poetic viewing of the reflection (*kage*) of flowers or foliage in the bottom (*soko*) of a river or pond is itself a fixed posture: see, for example, *Kokin wakashū* 124 and 304 and *Shūi wakashū* 25 and 87.

65 *Shin kokin wakashū* #553, in Tanaka and Akase, eds., *Shin kokin wakashū,* SNKBT 11, p. 553. Katagiri cites this poem as one of the rare examples of Natorigawa poesy that "sets aside [metaphorical treatment of] human affairs to describe the natural scene (*jinji o hanarete shizen'ei to shite yomareta sukunai rei*)." Katagiri, *Utamakura utakotoba jiten,* p. 306. Shigeyuki did eventually travel to Michinoku in 995, in the company of the banished Sanekata, and he died in the northeast ca. 1000; but this poem is known to be from a much earlier period, during which Shigeyuki was head of the Crown Prince's personal bodyguard (*tachihaki senjō*). Norihira Shinnō, later Emperor Reizei, was named Crown Prince (*Kōtaishi, Tōgū*) about two months after his birth in 950 and took the throne (upon the death of his father, Murakami) for just two years, 967–969. The *hyakushu* that includes this poem is one of the oldest surviving one-hundred-poem sequences in the canon. (Kawamura Teruo, "Shigeyuki," in Inukai et al., eds., *Waka daijiten,* p. 440.)

66 In *Shigeyuki shū,* which includes the whole *hyakushu,* this poem (#275) appears with the word *yasose* ("many [literally, eighty] shoals") in place of *yanase.* (SKT 3:137.) While it is easy to imagine the replacement of the *hiragana* character *so* by *na,* or vice-versa, at various stages of transcription, there is no way to tell which version is "correct." Yet the difference deeply alters the effect of the poem. *Yasose* is, stylistically, quasi-archaic: it is one of a category of words which, from Man'yō times on, were used in poetry to describe collectively a very large number of

objects—here, the river's many (poetically famous) shoals. *Yanase*, on the other hand, may be either singular or plural, but in any case describes, quite specifically, a man-made shoal, a device conventionally described in *waka* as the source and cause of the intensification of the noise produced by the flowing water of a stream, or a place where objects flowing in a stream may be trapped and held motionless. The very sound of both words, *yasose* and *yanase* (but especially the latter) seems to echo the Natorigawa *fuzoku uta/Kokin waka rokujō* #1746 song discussed above ("ya nase to mo yase to mo," "nanase tomo yase to mo"; but, whereas *ya nase*, etc., are numberings of *se* in the early song, *yanase* is a concretized, specific item in the *Shin kokin wakashū* version. Such imagistic specificity may have appealed to the compilers (Emperor Gotoba, Fujiwara Teika, et al.), but they may not have been deaf to the aural interplay between Shigeyuki's "newer" poem and the older song.

Another Natorigawa poem in the "ten love poems" section of the same *hyakushu* shows Shigeyuki taking up another position vis-à-vis these conventional materials: in this instance he treats the site as one in which, yet again, a crisis in a romantic adventure may occur—or, one might say, as a place in which some originating adventure, such as that which might have set the stage, supposedly, for the *fuzoku uta/Kokin waka rokujō* poem ("Natorigawa seze ka wataru") is still in process. In this poem, "Natorigawa watarite tsukuru oshimada o/moru ni tsuketsutsu yogare nomi suru" (The more they leak, the more do I neglect to tend the fields on the islet I used to reach by crossing Natorigawa), *moru* suggests "the leaking of rumors (about the love affair)," and *yogare* (literally, "skipping a night") stands for the idea of "the neglecting of a woman by a man"—that is, his failure to visit her for one or more successive nights after having been more attentive for some time previously. Clearly, Shigeyuki is here endeavoring to extend and embellish one or another of the ongoing stories of Natorigawa love while also, by this means, fulfilling one of the specific tasks of the *hyakushu* project.

67 *Nōin Hōshi shū* #126, SKT 3:337. *Nōin Hōshi shū* is one of several collections of Nōin's oeuvres, and is one of those thought to have been compiled by someone other than the poet himself.

68 See Mezaki, "Nōin no den ni okeru ni, san no mondai," in Mezaki, *Heian bunkashi ron*, pp. 320–353; see also the discussions of other episodes in Nōin's travels in chapter 3.

69 This is the same town as that which provided the base for Buson's *Shin* northeastern sojourn, as described in *Shin hanatsumi*. (See prologue.)

70 McCullough, trans., *The Taiheiki*, p. 36.

71 Gotō, Kamada, and Okami, eds., *Taiheiki* 1, NKBT 34, p. 65.

72 Mochizuki, ed., *Bukkyō daijiten*, 1:299.

73 Gotō, *Taiheiki no kenkyū*, pp. 10–11.

74 Modern commentators sometimes refer to poems composed at a remove from the sites they name and purport to take as setting (in contrast to those poems made in what can be documented as "real" experience in a named sites), as *kijō*

no uta ("desk-top" or academic) poems. The term and the distinction are mildly though not innocuously pejorative.

75 "Kōtaigōgū" refers to Emperor Goshirakawa's consort Kinshi; it is the appellation by which she was known prior to her elevation to Empress (Chūgū) in 1172.

76 Morimoto Motoko, "Wakamizu," in Inukai et al., eds., *Waka daijiten*, p. 1096.

77 *Kōtaigōgū no Daijin shū* #6, SKT 7:174.

78 See Katagiri, *Utamakura utakotoba jiten*, pp. 459–460; see also Kamens, "Dragon-girl, Maidenflower, Buddha," especially pp. 416–424.

79 Taniyama, ed., *Roppyakuban utaawase (shō)*, in NKBT 74, p. 453.

80 Ibid.

81 *Sengohyakuban utaawase* round 1,227, poems 2452–2453 and commentary, SKT 5:492. (Hidari no uta wa, Natorigawa seze no mumoregi arawarete ika ni sen to ka aimosomeken, kono uta no kami san ku o torite, ima no uta no koshi yori shimo san ku ni okarete haberumeri, hajime no ni ku bakari atarashiku haberu ka na. Migi no uta wa, waga koi o hito shirurame shikitae no makura nomi koso shiraba shirame, to haberu uta ni tsukite, nerareneba makura mo utoki toko no ue ni to wa yomiokarete, ware shirigao ni moru namida ka na to haberu shimo no ku okashiku habereba, izuko furushi to mōsubekarazu, furuuta no, makura bakari zo shiraba shiruran to haberu kotoba ni tsukite, makura mo utoki to nasaretaru bakari nareba, atarashiki uta nareba, shō to sadamemōshihaberinu.)

82 See chapter 1. Again, on two apparently unrelated occasions both Yoshitsune and Teika (who knew one another's work quite well) combined elements of these two particular foundation poems in one of their own new poems.

83 *Sengohyakuban utaawase* round 1,337, SKT 5:504. Yoshitsune's poem was, "Nagekazu yo ima hata onaji/Natorigawa seze no umoregi kuchihatenu to mo" (It has made no complaint—and neither shall I—for it can make no difference now, if I should perish, rotting away like the buried trees in Natorigawa's shoals), and Yasusue's, "Ima kon to chigiri wa taete/nakanaka ni tanomenu tsuki zo yogare-zarekeri" (Your pledge—"I'll come"—is broken now, but, on the other hand, the unreliable moon makes an appearance each night without fail.) The problem with Koreakira's poem was that he used two verbs, *tanomu* and *chigiru*, that were thought to be too similar in meaning. The fault was compounded by the fact that both *tanomu* and *tanomi* as well as *chigiri* had been used by a contestant in round 1,334. "I must say that the effect of this is unpleasant to the hearer," Kenshō complained, "and this makes me fear that the contest will invite censure as both insipid and frivolous" (tada kikinikushi to bakari mōshihaberinu, utaawase wa wazurawashiku hakanaki toga o motomehaberu nari). Kenshō admitted that forms of both *chigiru* and *tanomu* occur in a poem included in the *Kin'yō wakashū* (#470; SNKBT 9:134), but set this precedent aside in awarding the round to Yoshitsune.

Eventually, Jakuren's *Roppyakuban utaawase* Natorigawa poem and Yoshitsune's *Sengohyakuban utaawase* Natorigawa poem would appear together, as poems 1118–1119, in the second book of love poems in *Shin kokin wakashū*. In their anthologized settings, such mini-groupings offer a brief exemplum for treatment of such conventional materials—illustrations of their use in diverse settings and in response to various topical challenges—while at the same time performing other roles (as building-blocks of a quasi-narrative, for example) in the unfolding sequence of the anthology.

84 *Minase koi jūgoshu utaawase* #121, SKT 5:413.

85 *Man'yōshū* #1108, NKBT 2:207. The Hatsusegawa is a river in old Yamato Province, now Nara Prefecture. *Mio* are navigable river channels, where water generally flows without interruption and hazards are few; *ide* are man-made channels, used to divert river water to rice fields.

86 *Minase koi jūgoshu utaawase* #122 and commentary, SKT 5:413.

87 *Shūi gusō* #2073, *Shoku gosen wakashū* #135, in Kubota, ed., *[Yakuchū] Fujiwara Teika zen kashū* 1:337 and SKT 1:291.

88 *Fuboku wakashō* #3245, SKT 2:542; see also Hagitani, ed., *Heianchō utaawase taisei* 3, p. 861.

89 But such does not seem to have been the case when, some two hundred years later, Fujiwara Tametsugu (1206?-1265) introduced another summer figure, the floodwaters of "fifth-month rains" (*samidare*) into a Natorigawa poem: "Natorigawa seze ni ari chō mumoregi mo/fuchi ni zo shizumu samidare no koro (Even the buried trees, which, they say, lie in every shoal in Natorigawa/are buried in pools at the time of fifth-month rains). (*Shin gosen wakashū* #212, SKT 1:392.) When composing a hundred-poem sequence in 1319, Fujiwara Tamesada (1293-1360, not an immediate relation) must have had this poem in mind (if not in hand) when he wrote, "Natorigawa seze no mumoregi ukishizumi/arawarete yuku samidare no koro" (The buried trees in the Natorigawa shoals float up, then sink/appear, then vanish, at the time of fifth-month rains). (*Shin shūi wakashū* #265, SKT 1:656.) And, in turn, Asukai Masayo (1390-1452), compiler of the last *chokusenshū*, the *Shin shoku kokin wakashū*) must have had these poems and their relationship to the rest of Natorigawa poesy (including Shigeyuki's *Shin kokin wakashū* 553—the *yanase* version) in view when, addressing the topic *samidare*, he wrote "hare yaranu satsuki no ame no Natorigawa/yanase no nami zo oto masariyuku" (At Natorigawa, amidst fifth-month rains that will not clear/the roar of waves breaking in the sluices is louder than ever). (*Masayo shū* #522, SKT 8:16.)

90 Akase Tomoko, "Kaisetsu," in Satake, ed., *Dairi meisho hyakushu chū*, p. 177. In addition, a letter written by Teika to Ietaka during this interval, in which he discusses in detail the good and bad points of a few of the poems that both men were preparing to submit for the completed *hyakushu*, shows how seriously both men viewed the undertaking. See Kubota, ed., *Meisho hyakushu uta no toki Karyū kyō to naidan no koto* in Hisamatsu, ed., *Karon shū 1* (Chūsei no bungaku), pp. 287-301. For a brief discussion of parts of the letter, see Kubota, *Fujiwara Teika*, pp. 203-206.

91 Later medieval and early modern poets and scholars of poetry held the contributions of the four aforementioned poets—Juntoku, Teika, Ietaka, and Shunzei's Daughter—in highest regard: they studied them in such digests as the *Kenpō*

meisho sanbyakushu shō (including the three hundred poems by Juntoku, Teika, and Ietaka) and the *Kenpō meisho shihyakushu shō* (which added Shunzei's Daughter's poems, for a total of four hundred selections.) *Dairi meisho hyakushu chū* (see preceding note) is a Muromachi or early Tokugawa-era example of a *Kenpō meisho sanbyakushu shō*, a three-hundred-poem digest. Such digests may have been read both as source-books illustrative of the individual styles of the three or four representative poets *and* as an exemplum of the collective treatment of *meisho* topics in an era recognized as a kind of golden age of place-name poesy.

92 *Kenpō meisho hyakushu* #951, SKT 4:346.

93 For a brief discussion of conventional uses of the figure of the sleeve, see Katagiri, *Utamakura utakotoba jiten*, pp. 235–236.

94 *Kenpō meisho hyakushu* #949, SKT 4:346.

95 *Kokin wakashū* #557, SNKBT 5:175. For another translation and a comment on the jewel imagery in this and the poem sent to Komachi by the gentleman, Abe no Kiyoyuki, see McCullough, trans., *Kokin wakashū*, p. 127.

96 *Kenpō meisho hyakushu* #955, SKT 4:346.

97 *Kenpō meisho hyakushu* #954, 958, 960, SKT 4:346.

98 *Shoku gosen wakashū* #1168–1169, SKT 1:312.

99 *Chūinshū* #35–36, SKT 7:456.

100 The earliest appearance of Ashigara no seki (located by most commentators in the mountains of old Sagami province, on the road to Suruga) in a *chokusenshū* poem is *Gosen wakashū* #1361 (SKT 1:63), by the tenth-century poet Shinsei. See Himematsu no kai, ed., *Heian waka utamakura chimei sakuin*, p. 23, and Katagiri, *Utamakura utakotoba jiten*, pp. 15–16.

101 On the poetic use of the word *nageki*, see Katagiri, *Utamakura utakotoba jiten*, pp. 300–301.

102 For a brief discussion of these events, see Huey, *Kyōgoku Tamekane*, pp. 19–21.

103 *Sadahide shū* #69, SKT 7:754.

104 Hurvitz, trans., *Scripture of the Lotus Blossom of the Fine Dharma*, p. 311. The Japanese reading of the Chinese *Lotus Sūtra* text is taken from Sakamoto and Iwamoto, ed. and trans., *Hokekyō (chū)*, p. 244. The passage comes from near the beginning of the twenty-fourth chapter of the *Lotus*, the full title of which is *Kanzeon bosatsu fumon bon*.

105 For a study of the integration of secular *waka* figures and rhetoric into Buddhist devotional verse (*Shakkyōka*), and discussions of the dynamics of reading such hybrid texts, see Kamens, *The Buddhist Poetry of the Great Kamo Priestess*. On Japanese Lotus Sūtra poetry in particular, see also Yamada Shōzen, "Poetry and Meaning: Medieval Poets and the *Lotus Sūtra*" in Tanabe and Tanabe, eds., *The Lotus Sūtra in Japanese Culture*, pp. 95–117.

106 Shōtetsu has been called "the last great poet of the classical *uta* form" (Carter, *Traditional Japanese Poetry*, p. 282; see also Carter's introduction to Carter, ed., *Conversations with Shōtetsu*, especially pp. 3–39). But of course *waka*'s history does not end with him.

107 The topics are written with three or four Chinese characters each, although a
    Japanese transcription of the way they would be read would require more char-
    acters; see examples below.

108 *Sōkonshū* #7427, SKT 8:204.

109 *Sōkonshū* #7815, SKT 8:204.

110 *Sōkonshū* #8427, SKT 8:219.

111 In *Seigan chawa* (Tea talk by the verdant cliff), one of the collections of
    Shōtetsu's recorded "conversations" about the art of *waka,* he specifically advises
    that caution be used in emulating the *Kenpō meisho hyakushu*: "Those in the
    beginning stages of poetic training should not compose poems on the topics used
    for the *Kenpō meisho hyakushu.* Famous places have certain expressions that
    have been used with them since ancient times, and poems composed today also
    generally conform to the tradition. They have only a slight touch of originality.
    It seems that beginners have a fondness for writing poems on famous places.
    This is because they think them easy. I, too, will write a poem on a famous place
    when I cannot write any other kind. By using a famous place in your poem, you
    can fill up two or three lines and thus save that much effort . . . I have been
    writing poetry for some forty years now, but I have yet to compose a set of poems
    on the topics for those hundred-poem sequences." (Carter, trans., *Conversations
    with Shōtetsu,* p. 137). If this last statement is accurate, Shōtetsu must have made
    the three poems cited here sometime after he made this boast in *Seigan chawa,*
    the recording of which some scholars date as late as 1448. (Ibid., p. 41). But—
    maybe Shōtetsu forgot.

112 *Setsugyoku shū* #3870, SKT 8:666.

113 Kubota, *[Yakuchū] Fujiwara Teika zenkashū,* 2:126.

114 *Shūi gusō* #3577, ibid., p. 128.

115 Yanase, "*Fujikawa hyakushu*" in Inukai et al., *Waka daijiten,* p. 861.

116 *Setsugyoku shū* #4052, SKT 8:670.

117 *Shūi gusō* #1198 in Kubota, *[Yakuchū] Fujiwara Teika zenkashū,* 1:18: "kokonoe
    no hana no utena o sadamezu wa/keburi no shita ya sumika naramashi" (Had he
    [Amida] not guaranteed the existence of the nine-stage lotus throne/my future
    dwelling would surely be one obscured by hellish smoke.) For the portion of the
    hyakushu devoted to fifteen love poems "which refer to famous places" (*koi
    nijūgo shu: meisho ni yosu*), Teika offered a Natorigawa-plus-sleeve poem (*Shūi
    gusō* #1162; ibid., p. 178): "arawarete sode no ue yuku Natorigawa/ima wa wa ga
    mi ni seku kata mo nashi" (My love for you has been exposed, and now I find I
    have no way/to stem the flow of the Natorigawa that pours across my sleeve).

118 In almost any other poem this *seze* might well be read *yoyo*—a Japanese
    (*kun'yomi*) rather than Sino-Japanese (*on'yomi*) reading; but the weight of pre-
    cedent brought to bear in this poem insures the reading *seze,* in harmony with
    the other elements of Natorigawa poesy that are brought to the poem as a whole.
    Or, one might say, the transference of these elements of secular poesy to the
    quasi-devotional sphere also transforms the meaning of the words that embody
    that transfer, even though their sound (*seze*) remains unchanged.

119 *Michikatsu shū* #1217, SKT 8:802.

120 *Kaikoku zakki,* in Tsukamoto, ed., *Nikki kikō shū* (Yūhōdō bunko 96), p. 147.

121 Dōkō's lifespan coincided almost exactly with that of the great *renga* poet Sōgi (1421–1502), and in fact *Kaikoku zakki* was for a long time mistakenly attributed to Sōgi.

CHAPTER THREE. FETISHES AND CURIOS

1 Higuchi, *Gotoba-in,* p. 54.

2 Higuchi cites the research of Furutani Minoru as the source for the numbering of twenty-seven Kumano pilgrimages (*miyuki*) by Gotoba. A chronology of the life of Gotoba compiled by Okano Hirohiko and included in Maruya Saiichi's *Gotoba-in* lists thirty-one pilgrimages, as do several other sources. Commentary in one modern edition of Ienaga's diary suggests that the stop at Nagara described there occurred during the pilgrimage of Kennin 3.3 or 7 (1203). See MINZ, p. 116.

3 There had been a bridge nearby with this name, Watanobe no hashi, since antiquity. According to Motoori Norinaga (*Kojiki den,* section 35), its site was that occupied in later times by the Tenjin Bridge. MINZ, p. 116, note 8.

4 MINZ, p. 115.

5 *Kokin wakashū* #826, SNKBT 5:248.

6 McCullough, trans., *Kokin wakashū,* p. 180.

7 *Kokin wakashū* #890, SNKBT 5:269.

8 Katagiri, *Utamakura utakotoba jiten,* p. 295. For the passages in the historical chronicles, see Kuroita, ed., *[Shintei zōho] Kokushi taikei* 3:114 (*Nihon kōki*) and 56 (*Montoku jitsuroku*).

9 Matsumura and Yamanaka, ed., *Eiga monogatari* 2 (NKBT 76), pp. 498–499.

10 *Kokin wakashū* #1051, SNKBT 5:319.

11 Compare, for example, *Kokin wakashū* #900–909.

12 SNKBT 5:11. Translations adapted from McCullough, trans., *Kokin wakashū,* pp. 5–6.

13 SKT 1:136. Also so presented in her personal anthology, *Akazome Emon shū* #528, SKT 3:324. Tennōji is the Shitennōji monastic complex in modern Osaka. The *kotobagaki* for a number of other Nagara Bridge poems in several collections describe journeys to Tennōji as the occasions on which various poets passed through Nagara; see, for example, Minamoto Shunrai's poem in *Senzai wakashū* (#1030: SNKBT 10:308.) The temple is said to have been founded by Shōtoku Taishi in the mid-sixth century, in miraculous circumstances described in several traditional sources. By the Heian period Shitennōji was a major Tendai center; then, as Pure Land faith intensified during tenth and eleventh centurites, the temple's magnificent Great Western Gate (Saidaimon) came to be identified as the entrance to Amida's Western paradise, and so the temple achieved new status as a pilgrimage destination for royal and aristocratic devotees. (Ōhashi, Toshio "Jōdokyō no tenkai," in chapter 4, "Heian Bukkyō no minshuteki tenkai" of Nakamura et al., eds., *Ajia Bukkyō shi, Nihon hen II: Heian Bukkyō [Kizoku to Bukkyō]* 2:250–253.)

14 SNKBT 10:308-309. Dōmyō was one of the sons of Fujiwara no Michitsuna. A disciple of the distinguished monk Jie, he held the ecclesiastical title "Ajari" and eventually occupied the position of Bettō (chief administrative officer) of Tennōji. This poem and *Senzai wakashū* #1030 and #1032 form a small but distinct "Nagara Bridge" group within the sixteenth (miscellaneous) book of the anthology.

15 *Senzai wakashū* #1032, SNKBT 10:309. Although the date of Dōin's death is not known, there are records of his activities through the year 1179.

16 SNKBT 7:132. A somewhat earlier example of a "Nagara no hashibashira" poem composed in association with the production of a screen painting is to be found in *Goshūi wakashū* #426 (SKT 1:118). The occasion was the sixtieth birthday of the Regent (Sesshō) Fujiwara Kaneie, in 988. For inscription with or as commentary on the "Nagara Bridge" scene—one of twelve scenes on what was apparently a pair of six-fold screens—Taira Kanemori (d. 990) wrote: "Kuchi mo senu Nagara no hashi no hashibashira/hisashiki koto no mie mo suru ka na" (This pillar of the Nagara Bridge, which has not rotted away (like the rest): long may I gaze upon it, as I do now!), in obvious reference to the elderly, "long-surviving" Kaneie. According to Kanemori's personal anthology, the other *meisho* represented on this screen were Yoshinoyama, Shirara no hama, Naniwa, Suma, Mizu no mimaki, Shikazuka no watari, Musashino, Futamura no yama, Magaki no shima, Asaka no numa, and Suenomatsuyama. (SKT 3:117). All are used in one way or another to convey wishes for Kaneie's continued good health and long life. He died two years later, as did Kanemori.

17 *Goshūi wakashū* #1071 and *Kintō shū* #438, SKT 1:136 and 3:309.

18 *Shin kokin wakashū* #1596, SNKBT 11:466.

19 The attribution to Tadamine, however, appears to be erroneous: the poem in question appears in the *rufubon* version of *Tadami shū*—the private collection of the works of Tadami, Tadamine's son—as a response to a poem received from a prostitute (*yūjo*) as Tadami passed through Nagara on his way to the hot springs in Iyo; and in the Nishi Honganji version of *Tadami shū* it appears as the prostitute's response to a poem she received from Tadami.

20 *Jijō sanjūrokunin utaawase* #25, SKT 5:227.

21 Fujiwara Masatsune, also known as Asukai Masatsune (1170-1221), was a major figure in Gotoba's literary coterie and served as one of the editors of the *Shin kokinshū*. For his contributions to the Saishōshitennōin project, see chapter 4.

22 MINZ, pp. 115-117.

23 MINZ, p. 117.

24 Masatsune's diction may be compared to Narihira's in *Kokin wakashū* #879 "*kore so kono tsumoreba hito no oi to naru mono . . .* " (. . . *this,* this [moon] which, each time it appears, brings old age closer); and the similar *kore ya kono . . .* in the famous poem attributed to Semimaru in *Gosen wakashū* (#1089): "kore ya kono yuku mo kaeru mo wakaretsutsu/shiru mo shiranu mo Ausaka no seki" (This, this is where they come and go, taking leave of one another again and again/and where friends and strangers alike may meet—*this* is Ausaka Barrier, "the Barrier on the Hill of Meeting), which is one of the most important of the foundation

texts for *Ausaka no seki* poesy. (SNKBT 6:323). Poems that explain miraculous discoveries and other unexpected, auspicious events as if part of a divine, universal plan to please an emperor are numerous; see the following chapter for some specific examples.

It has been noted that at least two other poems that begin with the phrase "kore so kono . . ." are to be found in Masatsune's personal collection (*Asukai shū* #12 and #474), suggesting that perhaps this was a phrase he particularly favored; but the poem attributed to him here by Ienaga is not found in the collection. (See *Minamoto Ienaga nikki* kenkyūkai, ed., *Minamoto Ienaga nikki: kōi, kenkyū, sōsakuin,* p. 251.)

25 MINZ, pp. 117-118.

26 MINZ, p. 119.

27 A "Poetry Office" was instituted at various times, by various Emperors, to assist in the collection of compositions presented at various courtly occasions and in the preparation of Imperial anthologies. A number of courtiers would be assigned as staff members of the office (*yoriudo*), and the anthology editors (*sensha*) would then be named from among their number. Since the process of selection and anthology arrangement was in many cases carried out in the private homes of the editors, there was often no need to assign any specific physical space in the palace itself for the "Office"'s use. But Gotoba did establish a physical Wakadokoro for the *Shinkokinshū* editing process, and its layout is described in detail, and with a diagram, in Teika's diary *Meigetsuki* (in the entry for Kennin 1.7.27 [1201]. See KM 1:264. (See figure 6.)

28 The date of this event has been used by scholars of the period to identify the excursion to Kumano during which the fragment of the bridge pillar was found as one of those that took place in the previous year. See note 1 to this chapter. As noted below, there is also an account of this Uji excursion in Teika's diary, *Meigetsuki.*

29 MINZ, p. 119.

30 *Kokin wakashū* #983, SNKBT 5:295.

31 The complexity of this poem has long made it the subject of controversy. Perhaps its least well understood element is the play on the name of the direction *tatsumi.* Uji does lie to the southeast of the capital city, but when Kisen says "thus do I live" (*shika zo sumu*) he makes a kind of hidden, graphic play on *tatsumi,* which can also be written with a character (also read *kyō*) that can also mean "modesty" or "humility." In ancient Chinese symbolic texts this character was associated with a hexagram that represents "gentility." As noted below, however, *shika zo sumu* was often read as "deer live there" (the word for "deer," *shika,* being a homonym for a word for "thus . . ."). Compared to these elements, Kisen's pun on "Uji-yama," involving the embedded sound of the word *ushi,* meaning "sad, gloomy, lamentable," is relatively transparent. Kojima and Arai (in SNKBT 5) take all this to mean that Kisen insists that he has merely gone to live at Uji unpretentiously, in quiet reclusion, but "the world" takes his act as a significant, symbolic act of rejection of its woeful ways.

In *Mumyōshō* (section 39), Chōmei reports that while no house was still standing (ca. 1211) at the site of Kisen's hermitage on Ujiyama, its foundations (*dō no ishizue*) were still clearly visible, and he strongly recommends that the place be visited as a pilgrimage site, along with the graves of Sarumaru and Kuronushi (who figure prominently in Tsurayuki's pantheon of the ancients in the *Kokinshū* preface) and the supposed site of Tsurayuki's house (Takahashi, ed., *Mumyōshō zenkai*, p. 117.) Chōmei seems to have left no record of ever having gone there himself, but some of his contemporaries certainly did; and when one of them, the poet Jakuren (1139?–1202) went there and was told that what he was looking at were the remains (*ato*) of Kisen's hut, he wrote a verse which, not surprisingly, explicitly reuses and resituates the "remains" of Kisen's poem ("*Waga io wa . . .*") amidst other resonant elements of Uji poesy: "arashi fuku mukashi no io no ato taete/ tsuki nomi zo sumu Uji no yamamoto" (The ancient remains have all been blown away in the storm winds/ and only the moon dwells [or: shines] here at the foot of Uji Mountain.) (*Jakuren Hōshi shū* #160; SKT 4:41.) Once again, one set of presences has been replaced by others; the moon is now the sole inhabitant of this otherwise deserted place, yet something of Kisen's still lingers, and his words still echo here. The poem thus implies that though Kisen's hut may be gone, the poems made therein and thereabouts remain as "visible" as the "foundations" of the building do, and that their "traces" (*ato*) may still serve as the foundations for new poems. And, of course, they could do so even for poets who were not "on the spot" when, for whatever reasons, they were moved to write poems using these "remains"; see, for example, Gotoba's poem in the miscellaneous section of a sequence of five-hundred (*Eigohyakushu waka*): "Izuku ka mo mukashi no io no ato naran/ yo o Ujiyama no aki no yūgure" (Where are the remains of the ancient hut?/[They are hard to discern as] this autumn night descends on Ujiyama, "the mountain of grief.") (*Gotoba-in gyoshū* #1057, SKT 4:135.)

32 Ienaga literally says that Yoshitsune seemed willing to go and cut greens growing on the banks of the river himself in order to provide delicacies for Gotoba's consumption.

33 MINZ, p. 119. The poem is also to be found in Yoshitsune's personal anthology, *Akishino gessei shū* (#1146) among others he composed during the Uji excursion (see SKT 3:648).

34 *Gotoba-in gyoshū* #1648, SKT 4:144.

35 *Gotoba-in gyoshū* #1649, SKT 4:144.

36 Kubota, ed., *[Yakuchū] Fujiwara Teika zenkashū* 1:421.

37 SNKBT 5:211.

38 Translation adapted from McCullough, trans., *Kokin wakashū*, p. 153.

39 *Gotoba-in gyoshū* #1651, SKT 4:144.

40 MINZ, p. 119.

41 KM 2:121.

42 MINZ, p. 120, n. 2. See also the entry in *Meigetsuki* for Genkyū 1.7.16. (KM 2:122) At an *utaawase*, or on similar occasions, the task of the *kōshi* was to chant

the poems offered by his team (or sometimes by both teams) after they had first been pronounced by their composers and then were written down in the "minutes" of the gathering.

43 The *eigu utaawase* tradition overlaps with other forms of *eigu,* the presentation of offerings—often including poems—before the portraits of exalted figures in various scholarly and literary traditions. The practice in fact seems to be an amalgam of similar rites conducted by scholarly cults in honor of Confucius and in certain Buddhist sects in honor of their patriarchs. See Katano, "'Hitomaro eigu' no hensen to sono wakashiteki igi," in Katano, *Nihon bungei to kaiga no sōkansei no kenkyū,* pp. 153-180, and Yamada, "Hitomaro eigu no seiritsu to tenkai."

   The Hitomaro portrait displayed on this occasion was itself said to have had a somewhat miraculous origin, according to an account in *Kokon chomonjū* (section 204), a collection of tales compiled by Tachibana Narisue in 1254: an eleventh-century court poet, Fujiwara Kanefusa, had seen Hitomaro in a dream and then had commissioned a painter to render his image according to what he had seen. Emperor Shirakawa acquired the portrait and installed it in the treasure hall of the Shōkōmyōin, an Imperial family chapel in the precincts of the Toba Detached Palace; one of the outstanding poets of his court, Fujiwara Akisue, had asked that it be given to his family, but instead he was allowed to make a copy, and this was handed down through several generations. Meanwhile, the original Kanefusa painting was destroyed by fire when it was lent to Emperor Goreizei's consort, the lady known in retirement as the Ono Empress; a text of the *Kokin wakashū* said to have been Tsurayuki's own was reported lost in the same fire. Thus, the copy of the portrait owned by Akisue's descendants became the sole authoritative image, and it was this copy that came into use in the *eigu* conducted at court during the reign of Gosaga, in the mid-thirteenth century. See Nishio and Kobayashi, ed., *Kokon chomonjū* (Shinchō Nihon koten shūsei 60), 2:262-263.

44 *Eigu utaawase* #211, SKT 5:622.

45 *Eigu utaawase* #212, SKT 5:622.

46 Katagiri cites poems found in two tenth-century anthologies, *Ichijō sesshō shū* (Fujiwara Koremasa's personal anthology) and *Goshūi wakashū* (specifically, poem #529, by Fujiwara Korechika) as early examples of this play. Katagiri, *Utamakura utakotoba jiten,* pp. 1-2.

47 "Yasoujikawa no tsukikage o/nagara no hashi no ue ni miru ka na." Tameie's quotation differs slightly from the versions of the poem found in Ienaga's diary and in Yoshitsune's collected works.

48 SKT 5:622.

49 Miki, Asami, Nakamura and Koura, ed., *Uji shūi monogatari, Kohon setsuwa shū,* SNKBT 42:88, 427. For a complete translation of the *Uji shūi monogatari* version of the story, see D. E. Mills, trans., *A Collection of Tales from Uji: A Study and Translation of Uji shūi monogatari,* p. 202.

50 There is some confusion about the name of this protagonist, but most scholars

agree that Ryūgen (dates unknown) is meant to figure in the story, in part because he fits the role of *utayomi*: he was descended from distinguished poets, participated in the *Horikawa hyakushu* program, and his poems are included in several *chokusenshū*, beginning with *Kin'yō wakashū*. (He is also believed to be the author of a short, undated poet's handbook, known as *Ryūgen kuden*, which demonstrates the use of particular items of poetic vocabulary (*kago*) through selected examples, with some explanatory commentary. See Sasaki, ed., *Kagaku taikei* 1:108–117). Furthermore, his grandmother was "Haku no haha"'s sister, and so it seems plausible, to some readers, that word of the gift given to Yōen might have reached Ryūgen quickly, through family connections.

Technically, the term *utayomi* means "one who participates in *waka*-composing occasions" such as *utaawase*, and this would certainly apply to Yōen (and to Ryūgen, who also appears in the story.) But the term is often used in ways that seem somewhat derogatory, carrying connotations of the dilettante and dabbler; the term *kajin*, on the other hand, usually denotes a more serious, accomplished poet.

51 See Yamanaka, "Minamoto no Tōru," in Yamanaka, *Heian jinbutsushi*, especially pp. 34–42.

52 *Kokin wakashū* #1088–1089, SNKBT 5:330. Translations adapted from McCullough, trans., *Kokin wakashū*, p. 243.

53 See Sakakura, Ōtsu, Tsukishima, Abe, and Imai, eds., *Taketori monogatari, Ise monogatari, Yamato monogatari* (NKBT 9), p. 158.

54 Translation adapted from McCullough, trans., *The Tales of Ise*, p. 124. In *Shoku Goshūi wakashū*, a *chokusenshū* compiled in the early fourteenth century, this poem is presented as having been composed when Ariwara no Narihira (825–880) "went to [Tōru's] house and saw how he had made a model of the place called 'Shiogama,'" (#975; SKT 1:545). The attribution may be traceable to a long-standing confusion arising from Narihira's apparent presence as protagonist in some (but by no means all) of the sections of *Ise monogatari* and his authorship of some (but by no means all) of the poems included therein.

55 *Kokin wakashū* #852, SNKBT 5:256.

56 *Kokin wakashū* #848, SNKBT 5:255.

57 For a study of Anpō (dates unknown) and his circle see Inukai, "Kawara no in no kajintachi: Anpō Hōshi o jiku to shite." As Inukai notes (p. 68), the mansion/monastery itself had, by Anpō's time, already taken on the character of an *utamakura* site (*utamakurateki seikaku*). Bernard Frank has also discussed the design of the *Kawara no in* garden as an exercise in *fūryū* and has investigated the history of the mansion in the generations after Tōru's death. See Frank, "Rapports sur les conférences: Histoire et philologie Japonaises."

58 *Anpō Hōshi shū* #13–14, SKT 3:158.

59 These are actually very closely related usages of a single verb, which shares the root *utsu-* with the adjectival *utsushi* that means "real," i.e., "physically present in such a way as to be visually apprehensible." Thus the verb that can mean "copy" or "move" means "to transfer something from one place to another so as to be

visually apprehensible in that new place." (Ōno Susumu et al., eds., *Iwanami kogo jiten*, p. 173.)

60 Royall Tyler has also described this double aspect of the garden in a discussion of Zeami's Nō play, "Tōru." See Tyler, "A Critique of 'Absolute Phenomenalism.'"

61 Sakakura et al., eds., *Ise monogatari* in NKBT 9:158.

62 SKT 3:158.

63 Hashimoto et al., eds., *Karon shū*, p. 262.

64 Ibid. According to Toshiyori, Nōin explained to his companion, the distinguished poet Fujiwara Kanefusa (1004-1069), that the tree was one of those that Ise had planted on a particular New Year's first "Day of the Rat" (*Ne no hi*)," that is, the first day of the first month of each New Year that was said to be governed by that particular zodiacal sign. The custom of plucking and transplanting such seedlings, and then binding their branches together with poem sheets on which were written prayers for long life on this particular day itself embodied a pun: the name of the day, *Ne no hi* overlaps aurally with the intent of the custom, *nenobi* (stretching out the span of life) and with the word for the seedlings' roots (*ne*). Thus, *Ne no hi* was invariably an occasion that called for poem-making, and poem-making on this occasion invariably called for the manipulation of these and related puns.

65 The title "Ukon no taifu" given Fujiwara Kuniyuki (dates unknown) here apparently is indicative of the fact that he had distinguished himself as a court musician. (Ibid., p. 262, n.8.)

66 Toshiyori only quotes the latter part of this famous poem, anthologized as *Goshūi wakashū* #518/ *Nōin hōshi shū* #101 (SKT 1:121/ 3:337.) For further discussion of the poem and the controversy surrounding it, see below.

67 Hashimoto et al., eds., *Karonshū*, pp. 262-263.

68 Ozawa, Gotō, Shimazu and Higuchi, ed., *Fukuro zōshi chūshaku* 1:266.

69 After he took vows (ca. 1013, at the age of about 26), Nōin abandoned his career as a professional court scholar and took up a life of relative retirement at a place called Kosobe, in what is now part of Ōsaka Prefecture. He was known as "the Kosobe monk" (*Kosobe no nyūdō*).

70 Kin'yori (d. 1040) was apparently a close friend of Nōin's; the exchange of a number of visits and poems between them is recorded in Nōin's personal anthology, *Nōin hōshi shū*.

71 Ozawa et al., eds., *Fukuro zōshi chūshaku* 1:266.

72 Ozawa et al., eds., *Fukuro zōshi chūshaku* 1:271. The term translated here as "pure aesthetic conversation" is *seidan*, "conversation unconcerned with worldly matters, devoted to the discussion of art and culture" (*zoku seken no koto ni kankei shinai fūryū na dangi*. (Ibid., notes, p. 275). The ancient Chinese Seven Sages of the Bamboo Grove are the exemplary practitioners of *seidan* (Chinese *qing tan*.)

73 Ozawa et al., eds., *Fukuro zōshi chūshaku* 1:266-267.

74 Nishio and Kobayashi, ed., *Kokon chomonjū* 1:224-225.

75 Nothing is said here, however, about the mode or medium of "presentation" or

"publication." It is unclear just how the teller of the tale imagines the poem to have been initially "broadcast" (*hirō*) or otherwise made known to the poem-consuming public. The earliest anthologies in which it appears are Nōin's own personal anthology, *Nōin Hōshi shū,* compiled ca. 1045–1049, and *Goshūi wakashū,* the compilation of which was completed in 1086. The circumstances of any prior circulation of the poem are not known.

76 In an article first published in 1959, Mezaki Tokue used the *kotobagaki* in the *Nōin Hōshi shū* as reliable documentation and confirmation of the poet's travels to several parts of Japan, including the Northeast. One of the extant versions of the *Nōin hōshi shū* is believed to have been compiled by Nōin himself, a fact which of course lends support to Mezaki's argument. The *Nōin Hōshi shū kotobagaki* preface to this particular poem says "In the spring of the second year [of the Manju era, i.e., 1025] I decided to take myself off to Michinoku for a while, and when I took lodging at Shirakawa Barrier [I wrote . . .] (*ninen no haru Michinokuni ni akarasama ni kudaru to te, Shirakawa no seki ni yadorite*). (SKT 3:337.) [The *Goshūi wakashū kotobagaki,* on the other hand, says, "When he went to Michinoku, and was at the Shirakawa Barrier, he wrote . . ." (*Michinokuni ni makarikudarikeru ni, Shirakawa no seki nite yomihaberikeru*). (SKT 1:121.)]

Mezaki also suggested that much of Nōin's travel was undertaken in connection with his involvement in the procuring of horses from provincial breeders and their conveyance for use in the court stables, and that such activities may have been somewhat secretive: there may therefore have been good reason, he argues, for the fact that few of his contemporaries knew of two Nōin's "real" trips to the Northeast, but that that gap in knowledge may be responsible for the rise of the "traditional view" that Nōin's '*Miyako o ba* . . ." poem was "fabricated out of his imagination" (*kakū sōzo no saku to suru densetsu*). See Mezaki, "Nōin no den ni okeru ni, san no mondai," especially pp. 344–345. On the basis of such argumentation, the traditional dogma, that Nōin *wasn't* there, has been replaced in the minds of some by another dogma, which holds that he *was* .

77 Several poets of the generation prior to Nōin's referred to the Shirakawa in Michinoku in poems they composed at the "Shirakawa Palace" (*Shirakawa no in*), a royal residence in the eastern suburbs of the capital. Examples may be found in the private anthologies of Ōnakatomi Yoshinobu (#177, in SKT 3:124), and Fujiwara Sanekata (#177, in SKT 3:223); see also *Goshūi wakashū* #93, by Fujiwara Nagaie [1005–1064]), a contemporary of Nōin's (SKT 1:111.) All rather playfully juxtapose the one "Shirakawa" with the other; the same is true of a poem found in two places in *Kintō shū* (#36 and #509), with different accounts of the circumstances of composition but in both cases involving exchanges between Kintō, who had a villa at Shirakawa, and Izumi Shikibu. See Ii, Tsūmoto and Shindō, ed., *Kintō shū zen'yaku* (*Shikashū zen'yaku sōsho* 7), pp. 81–84, 387–388.) It is perhaps of some significance that in this exchange, which seems to have taken place in the third month of 1004, when Izumi Shikibu's husband Tachibana Michisada was appointed Governor of Michinoku, and left the capital for the province (to be followed shortly thereafter by Shikibu herself), the poems

from both sides use the end of spring (that is, its "departure") and its rising mists as metaphors for travel and separation.

78 Bashō's well-known description of his visit to Shirakawa Barrier in *Oku no hoso-michi* includes references not only to Nōin's poem but to several others that treat it as *honka*, including three poems from the *Senzai wakashū* (#365, 142, and 543) by Minamoto Yorimasa, Fujiwara Suemichi and Inshō. It is particularly interest-ing to note that Suemichi's poem is a deliberate mixing-up of the *Michinoku* Shirakawa with the *miyako* Shirakawa, and that both Yorimasa's and Inshō's poems were composed at *utaawase* in the capital, on travel topics, i.e., *kanji rakuyō* ("autumn leaves scatter in the road to the Barrier") for Yorimasa's poem, and *kichū saibō* (in the midst of a journey, the year draws to a close) for Inshō's. In each case, the poet has availed himself of the northeastern Shirakawa and its associations—now deeply marked by what Nōin (and his predecessors and other successors) have previously done with them—in order to meet the specific com-positional challenges that are presented to them in these settings.

79 *Shūi wakashū* #339, SNKBT 7:339.

80 There is no holograph of the text of *Nōin utamakura,* and the full extent of its original contents is unknown. Two versions, obviously somewhat fragmentary, have been in circulation for several centuries: they are known as the *kōhon* (full text) and the *ryakubon* (abbreviated text). But passages that cannot be found in either of these are quoted in several medieval works, indicating that still other versions were in circulation at one time or another. (Hirano Yukiko, "*Nōin uta-makura,*" in Inukai et al., eds., *Waka daijiten,* p. 795. For a full discussion of these textual problems, see Sasaki's introduction to *Nōin utamakura* in *Nihon kagaku taikei* 1:32–44.)

81 Sasaki, ed., *Nōin utamakura [kōhon],* in *Nihon kagaku taikei* 1:75, 96.

82 Many scholars have been interested in the apparent relationship between content and structure of the lists in *Nōin utamakura* and those in Sei Shōnagon's *Makura no sōshi*. Her *Seki wa* list (*dan* 111 in NKBT 19:169) and Nōin's are indeed quite similar, but hers is longer and contains several otherwise unknown names, whereas Nōin's are all well-documented *meisho*. The relationship between the two works is complicated by the fact that Nōin is believed to be the redactor of one of the more preeminent of the many versions of *Makura no sōshi*. For a discussion of this issue, see Morris, "Sei Shōnagon's Poetic Catalogues," pp. 32–33.

83 Only one of Nōin's lists of *meisho* of the sixty-six provinces contains more entries than that for Michinoku, and that is the list for Yamashiro, the province in which the capital city itself was located, for which eighty-six items are listed. Yamato and Settsu, two provinces immediately adjacent to Yamashiro, come in next, with forty-three and thirty-five, and Ōmi, another adjacent province, is next, with twenty-six. These tabulations are made from the lists as they appear in the *kōhon* version, the standard modern edition of which (in *Nihon kagaku taikei*) is based on a printed version first published in 1693. As noted above, it seems likely that the lists therein are not exactly as Nōin first composed them. Furthermore, some

medieval works cite the title of another book of lists, *Nōin kongengi* which seems to have dealt only with *meisho*. (*Kongen* is an erudite Chinese word for "the earth," so *Kongengi* would seem to be an appropriate title for a work concerned chiefly with toponyms.) Some scholars believe this *Kongengi* to have been identical with the province-by-province listing of *meisho* in *Nōin utamakura*, while others think that *Kongengi* was an entirely different work. (See Hirano, "*Nōin utamakura*," in Inukai et al., eds., *Waka daijiten*, p. 795.)

84 *Nihon kagaku taikei* 1:78. One might include in this group of entries those in which Nōin makes note of some of those usages which today we would call *makurakotoba* (though he does not use the term)—for example, "*Yama: ashibiki to iu, shinateru ya to iu*," which simply indicates that the word *yama* (mountain) may be preceded by either of these phrases. (In this particular instance, Nōin goes on to say that "Sosa no o no mikoto [a.k.a. Susa no o no mikoto] was the first to do this, when he said, *Ashibiki no yama e iraji* (I will not go to those mountains). See *Nihon kagaku taikei* 1:73.)

85 *Nihon kagaku taikei* 1:79.

86 *Nihon kagaku taikei* 1:74. Ide is now in Tamamizu-chō, Tsuzuki-gun, near the southern border of Kyōto Prefecture. There is a long-standing controversy in *karon* as to whether *kaeru* and *kawazu* are and always have been one and the same or whether *kawazu* designates a particular kind of frog, or sub-species, such as that which today is often called *kajika*, a "singing frog" (*polypedates buergari*). In *Mumyōshō*, Kamo no Chōmei records a friend's statement to the effect that the *only* frogs that may properly be called *kawazu* are those to be found at Ide. (Takahashi, ed., *Mumyōshō zenkai*, p. 66.)

87 SNKBT 5:53. The poem appears with the designations "topic unknown" and "author unknown," but in some texts there is an additional note indicating that some sources attribute it to Tachibana Kiyotomo (d. 789), whose family did in fact have residences in the Ide area. The poem appears in *Kokin wakashū* as the last in a sequence in the second book of spring poems on *yamabuki* (*kerria japonica*, sometimes called "Japanese rose" or "Japan globeflower"), and it is also the *locus classicus* for the very strong association of that flower with this site. (It is perhaps worth noting here that Ide does not appear in the list of *meisho* for Yamashiro, the province in which it is located, in Nōin's province-by-province listing. For that matter, there is no separate "yamabuki" entry, either.)

88 *Shigeyuki shū* #89, SKT 3:135.

89 *Nōin Hōshi shū* #185, SKT 3:338. Nōin's toying with the name of the "flower without ears" (*miminagusa*) is reminiscent of the games played with it in *Makura no sōshi* (Nōin bon) *dan* 131 (NKBZ 11:266-267).

90 There is at least one other instance of the use of the phrase in an anthologized poem: it is by a contemporary of Shigeyuki's, Daisaiin no Shōshō, and occurs in one of her responses in a series of exchanges with her mistress, Daisaiin Senshi (see *Daisaiin saki no gyoshū* #321, SKT 3:286.) Most of the poems included in this work seem to have been composed between 984 and 986. The denizens of the Saiin were trained to be adroit users of the *waka* lexicon; so, even though no

earlier use of the "flooded seedling-field" phrase can be found, it seems unlikely that it originated with Shōshō, but, rather, that she was deliberately deploying words which had a ring of familiarity, to produce a particularly resonant effect.

91 Toshinobu's dates are unknown, and there is no agreement about his name: it is read, variously, as Toshinobu, Tokinobu or Takanobu. In 1044 he was named "Provisional Governor of Kawachi (*Kawachi no gon no kami*). Two of his poems are in *Goshūi wakashū*, and another is in *Kin'yō wakashū*.

92 Ozawa et al., eds., *Fukuro zōshi chūshaku* 1:263.

93 Although there is some uncertainty, *Mumyōshō* is believed to have been written sometime after the eleventh month of 1211; *Hōjōki* was written in the third month of the following year. For a very interesting treatment of Chōmei's prose oeuvres, see Thomas Blenman Hare, "Reading Kamo no Chōmei," especially pp. 18-187 and 227 on *Mumyōshō*. For a complete translation of *Mumyōshō* see Hilda Katō, "The *Mumyōshō* of Kamo no Chōmei and its Significance in Japanese Literature."

94 Both Onjōji and the site of the Ausaka Barrier lie within the boundaries of the modern city of Ōtsu, Shiga Prefecture. For early examples of poems on this spring (*Ausaka no seki no shimizu*) see *Shūishū* #170 and *Kokin rokujō* #72 (both by Tsurayuki); poems on "The Rock-spring on Ausaka Mountain" (*Ausakayama no iwashimizu*) (e.g., *Kokin wakashū* #1004, by Tadamine) appear to be closely related.

95 Takahashi, ed., *Mumyōshō zenkai*, p. 70.

96 Takahashi, ed., *Mumyōshō zenkai*, p. 71.

97 Katagiri, *Utamakura utakotoba jiten*, p. 449.

98 Takahashi, ed., *Mumyōshō zenkai*, pp. 65-67.

99 See prologue.

100 The Xian-yang Palace was the residence of the Qin Emperor Huang-di, who unified China in 231 B.C. The "decorative nail-head cover" (*kugikakushi*) is a small metal disk that would have been used in the finishing of exposed exterior timbers. The "dagger-guard" (*tanken no tsuba*) is the round part of the short sword between the blade and the handle: the sword is gripped just above the *tsuba*, which, along with the handle, would remain in view when the blade itself was concealed within its holster. Buson uses a form of the word *suku* (i.e., *monozukite*) to convey the idea that the owner of this *tsuba* "regarded it with a connoisseur's avidity."

101 Shimizu, ed., *Yosa Buson shū*, p. 298.

102 Ibid.

103 Ibid., p. 47. Buson recorded the full text of both *kotobagaki* and *hokku* in a letter sent to Takai Kitō (1741-1789) in the winter of 1782 and in another addressed to Shōfū and Ikkei, two Ōsaka-based poets, and dated Tenmei 3.8.4 (i.e., fourth day of the eighth month of Tenmei 3 [1783]. For texts of these letters, see Ōtani Tokuzō, Okada Rihei and Shimai Kiyoshi, ed., *Buson shū: zen* (Koten haibungaku taikei 12), pp. 389 and 519.

104 From the letter to Shōfū and Ikkei. Buson goes on to discuss what sort of painting might best accompany the poem. See Ōtani et al., eds., *Buson shū*, p. 519.

105 See, for example, *Kokin wakashū* #284 and #320 (both anonymous), as well as *Shin kokin wakashū* #158 (by Ietaka).

106 Tokiwa Tanpoku (Tokiwa Tadanao of Karasuyama, Nasu-gun, Shimotsuke province) was a disciple of Kikaku (as was Buson) and also a physician noted for his efforts to promote public education. He died in 1744. Ōtaka Gengo (1672–1703) was also known as Tadao and was also a disciple of Kikaku as well as a noted devotee of tea, but his fame rests on his role as one of the "Forty-seven Rōnin" of Akō who avenged the murder of their master in the notorious vendetta case dramatized in the popular play *Kanadehon Chūshingura*.

107 Shimizu, ed., *Yosa Buson shū*, pp. 298–299.

108 Ibid., p. 313. See also prologue, note 22, for the Japanese text.

CHAPTER FOUR. THE SAISHŌSHITENNŌIN POEMS AND PAINTINGS

1 Matsubayashi, ed., *Jōkyūki*, p. 53. The passage in question occurs only in the *kokatsujibon* version of *Jōkyūki*.

2 The Kamakura Shogunate was established following the conclusion of the Genpei War of 1180–1185, which ended with the death of the child-Emperor Antoku and the virtually total rout of the Taira clan forces by those of the Minamoto and their allies. Minamoto Yoritomo then began the process of establishing a military government, based at Kamakura, which appropriated some, though not all, of the perquisites and prerogatives previously held by the Emperors, Retired Emperors (*In*) and their direct designees. The Imperial institution remained in place, in Kyoto, and for several decades a complex sorting-out of lines of authority between Kyoto and Kamakura continued, much to Gotoba's dissatisfaction, and leading eventually to the crisis of the Jōkyū War of 1221. For an account of this period and these developments, see Mass, *The Development of Kamakura Rule*, especially chapter one, "The Jōkyū War and Its Aftermath."

3 Many Japanese scholars hold the view that the most important corpus of early place-name poetry that served as precursor to the crystallization of the concept of [*meisho*] *utamakura* (at about the time of the compilation of the *Kokin wakashū*) is that composed for inscription on or inspired by the viewing of screen paintings (*byōbue*) presented to Emperors and other royal and aristocratic individuals on their important anniversaries or to set the scene for the observance of such ancient court rituals as the *Daijōe*, the feast accompanying the first New Year's rite of prayer for good harvest celebrated by each Emperor at the beginning of his new reign. *Daijōe byōbu*—and the poems that came with or on them—were originally presented as tribute from selected provinces: they depicted scenes of those provinces, and, almost without exception, made frank avowals of hope for the Emperor's long life and reign and of allegiance to him. Most of the surviving *byōbue-uta* or screen-poems of the late ninth and early tenth centuries are also of this congratulatory type, concerned with the expression of prayers for long life and avowals of loyalty often cloaked in imagery derived from or closely related to the subjects of and figures in the corresponding screens. Some of the *Daijōe byōbu* and other *byōbue* poems are direct adulations of the

ruler or other presentee: others more indirectly celebrate them by focusing on images of vitality, endurance, and renewal in natural landscapes. But in both cases, images associated with particular places are employed—sometimes literally, sometimes figuratively—to exalt the personage to whom such presentations were made. Thus there is the suggestion that it is not only the poet who exalts the personage but the land and landscape who do so, too. The best available study of the *Daijōe byōbu* screens—based largely on the extant poems, and on descriptions found in some contemporary records—is Akiyama Terukazu's "Daijōe yuki suki byōbu," which appears as chapter 2 of part 1 of his *Heian jidai sezokuga no kenkyū*, pp. 67–91. See also Yagi, *Daijōe waka no sekai*. For a study in English of the Daijōsai, the accession rite of which the Daijōe was a part, see Robert S. Ellwood, *The Feast of Kingship*.

4 In contrast to the *Daijōe* poems and poems composed on various occasions for inscription on *byōbu*, or as a response to the viewing thereof, poems composed on the occasions of *miyuki* have never been treated as forming a significantly coherent group of works within the *waka* corpus. But notable examples do appear in works as early as the *Kojiki, Nihon shoki*, and the *Man'yōshū*. Some of the best known examples in the latter are by Yamabe Akahito (see the discussion, below, of his MYS #917–919.) For a discussion of this type of occasional poetry and its relationship to the cult of rulership, see Gary L. Ebersole, *Ritual Poetry and the Politics of Death in Early Japan*, pp. 23–54.

5 An even richer repository of *byōbu uta* composed on such occasions can be found in books 1 through 4 of *Tsurayuki shū*. The latter contains poems composed for several dozen occasions of *byōbu* presentation, and its *kotobagaki* offer detailed descriptions of the topics featured in each painting program. (See Hagitani, ed., *Tsurayuki shū* in Hagitani, ed., *Tosa nikki*, pp. 137–213, or SKT 3:58–67.) Like Teika, some three centuries later, Tsurayuki seems often to have been supervisor in such projects; in many cases, however, it is not clear whether the poems or paintings were programmed first; perhaps, often, production of both was simultaneous. For a study of Tsurayuki's screen-painting poems, see Watanabe, "Ki no Tsurayuki no isō."

6 For texts of the poems composed for Ninshi's presentation *byōbu* (*Bunji rokunen nyōgo judai waka*), see SKT 5:887–894. With three topics selected for the representation of each month, the poets composed on thirty-six individual topics. (An additional and apparently less formal screen [*doroe byōbu*] was also prepared, depicting one winter and one summer scene.) Place-name poetics did not figure very large in this particular *tsukinamie* program, but it was not wholly absent, either: the panel for the first month included a depiction of "courtiers gathering young shoots in a pine grove on the First Day of the Rat" (*nobe no matsubara ni ne no hi shitaru tokoro*. Ibid., p. 888). In response to this topic, three of the poets (Kanezane, Yoshitsune, and Shunzei) composed verses that explicitly mention Kasugano—a site long associated with New Year's *ne no hi* observances, in part because of the suggestive appearance of its written name, usually represented with two characters, that mean "spring sun" or "spring day" (and which

might also be read *haru no hi*). In Teika's poem this association is subtly but still unmistakably evoked, through graphic play: he writes, *komatsubara haru no hikage*—"in pine groves lit by spring sunshine," where the embedded *haru no hi..* again suggests Kasuga. In a similar manipulation of poetic convention, five of the eight poems composed in conjunction with the depiction of one of the tenth-month topics, "crane" (*tazu*) specifically mention "the beach at Naniwa" (Naniwagata), and thus exercise a site-and-bird association that can be traced as far back as the *Man'yōshū* (poem #1164, which also appears as *Kokin rokujō* #1963) and on into the *chokusenshū*, beginning with *Kokin wakashū* #913).

7 There is no complete collection of the poems composed for Shunzei's birthday celebration screen (*Shunzeikyō kujūga no uta*), but accounts of the occasion and some of the poems composed for it can be found in the diaries of Minamoto Ienaga (see MNZ 122–148), Yoshitsune (*Gokyōgoku Sessho ki*, in Shintei zōho shiseki shūran kankōkai, ed., *Shintei zōho shiseki shūran* 3, pp. 83–85) and in *Kenreimon'in ukyō no daibu shū* (SKT 3:119, poems #256–258). Unfortunately, the portion of Teika's own diary covering the period of the celebration is not extant. (See also Kubota, *Fujiwara Teika*, pp. 171–172.) Three of the twelve poems chosen for inscription on the screen (according to Ienaga) interpolate place-names as part of the scheme chosen for addressing the twelve seasonal topics: Yoshitsune describes "mists over Ama no Kaguyama" in his poem on *kasumi* (the first topic for the spring panel), Gotoba sets his poem on "young grasses" (*wakakusa,* the second topic for spring) at Kasugano, and Tango, addressing "plovers" (*chidori,* the first winter topic), places both those birds and calling geese (*karine*) in a poem set at Ashiya no sato. In the Saishōshitennōin poems, *wakakusa* is also a main feature associated with Kasugano, but Ashiya no sato is treated as a summer rather than a winter site, with a different set of characteristic features, and Ama no Kaguyama is not treated at all. Nonetheless, because of its prominence among the text-and-image productions of Gotoba's coterie, Katano Tatsurō lists the Shunzei birthday-screen project, as well as Ninshi's presentation-screen project, as the most important precursors of the Saishōshitennōin program. He also treats these three projects together as "the finale of Heian-style *byōbuuta.*" See Katano, "Heianteki byōbuuta no shūen," in Katano, *Nihon bungaku to kaiga no sōkansei no kenkyū*, pp. 212–216.

8 Most of the details in the following account are adapted from Fukuyama Toshio, "Saishōshitennōin to sono shōjie," in Fukuyama, *Nihon kenchiku shi no kenkyū*, pp. 513–535. Fukuyama's sources include *Meigetsuki, Fujiwara Ienaga nikki,* and *Mon'yōki* (the diary of Gotoba's son Son'en).

9 Ibid., pp. 515–516.

10 In the mid-eighth century, when the Imperial house formally and fully embraced Buddhism for the first time and began to employ Buddhism's new powers to buttress its own, Emperor Shōmu ordered the construction of a monastery in each province of the nation, each named Konkōmyō Shitennō Gokokuji, "monastery for the protection of the nation by the Four Deva Kings of the *Konkōmyō* Sūtra." These are the temples known familiarly as the Kokubunji. Copies of the

Konkōmyō Saishōōkyō sūtra, invoking that divine protection, were to be stored within these monasteries, and its contents studied and disseminated to all the people of the land. This was all undertaken in light of passages in the sūtra itself, wherein the Four Deva Kings guarantee the safety and prosperity of all states whose sovereigns revere the sūtra and spread its teachings. (On the Kokubunji and Kokubunniji—convents established at the same time, for the same purpose— see Inoue Kaoru, "Kokka Bukkyō no tenkai," in Nakamura et al., eds., *Ajia Bukkyōshi, Nihon hen I: Asuka, Nara Bukkyō*, pp. 188-198.) Also, for several centuries, annual formal readings of this sūtra, invoking the protection of the Four Kings in the name of the Emperor, were held under Imperial auspices at various sites—at the Imperial Palace itself, in the Kokubunji, and at other temples all over the country, including the Yakushiji in Nara. The royal sponsors thus displayed themselves as virtuous kings, worthy successors to the role of Cakra-vartin ("Wheel-turning Noble King," *Tenrinjōō*) and qualified to expect the protection of the Four Deva Kings. Minamoto Tamenori's *Sanbōe* (984) includes accounts of the founding of and procedures for the Gosaie, an annual first-month feast during which the *Konkōmyō saishōōkyō* was read both at court and in the Kokubunji, and the Saishōe, held at Yakushiji in the third month of each year. (For translations, see Kamens, *The Three Jewels*, pp. 251-253, 286-287.)

11 These six earlier royal temples, all built by Gotoba's royal ancestors (the Emperors Shirakawa, Horikawa, Toba, Sutoku and Konoe and by Toba's consort, Empress Taiken'monin, respectively), are known collectively as the Rokushōji. The sites of all six can still be found in the Okazaki section of Kyoto. See Mochizuki, *Bukkyō daijiten* 5:5065-5066, and Takagi, "Insei jidai no Bukkyō," section 1 in chapter 4, "Heian Bukkyō no minshūteki tenkai," in Nakamura et al., *Ajia Bukkyōshi, Nihon hen I: Asuka, Nara Bukkyō*.

12 Fukuyama, "Saishōshitennōin," p. 517; see also MINZ, pp. 295-297, and Higuchi, *Gotoba-in*, p. 233. Ienaga reports that a courtier named "Saki no Dainagon [Fujiwara] Nobukiyo" was put in charge of the plans for the construction of the building as a whole, while "[Minamoto] Nakakuni no Ason" was in charge of the preparation of the Buddha images (*butsuzō*). In the relevant diary entries, Ienaga usually refers to the Saishōshitennōin as "*Midō*" (His Majesty's Hall [for worship]); Teika does likewise in most of the relevant passages in *Meigetsuki*.

13 Fukuyama, "Saishōshitennōin," p. 517, quoting *Meigetsuki* for Jōgen 1.2.2. See KM 2:273.

14 MINZ, p. 296.

15 Fukuyama, "Saishōshitennōin," pp. 518-519, quoting *Meigetsuki* for Jōgen 1.2.20. See KM 2:287. See also Ariyoshi, "Saishōshitennōin shōji waka," in Ariyoshi, *Shinkokin wakashū no kenkyū*, p. 260.

16 The only other mention of the Chinese part of the program appears in *Meigetsuki*, Jōgen 1.7.20, where Teika reports that the topics (*dai*) for the poems have been announced and that each *shi* poet was expected to submit twenty poems. (See KM 2:303.)

17 The assumed difference between the *wa* and *kan* ("Japanese" and "Chinese")

elements of the text of the program should perhaps not be overly exaggerated (any more than, say, the difference between paintings that happen to be described respectively as *kara-e* and *yamato-e* ["Chinese paintings" and "Japanese paintings."] It is difficult to identify a point at which "Chinese poems" written by Japanese poets may have ceased to seem utterly "other" (if they ever were) but rather simply *an* other mode of Japanese textual expression. One wonders if, in some respects, *kanshi* composed for and deployed in such settings as the Saishō-shitennōin program were not in fact at least potentially viewable or readable as a kind of text that was virtually as "Japanese" as were the adjacent *waka*, and which differed from them only in the style of calligraphy used for their inscription, as well as the obviously different visual impact of the density of Chinese characters used exclusively in that inscription, in contrast to the inscriptions of *waka* in presumably all-*kana* or mixed *kana/kanji* orthographies.

18 *Meigetsuki*, Jōgen 1.4.21; KM 2:282. For a reading of this section of the diary, see Kubota, *Fujiwara Teika*, pp. 185-186. The art historian Chino Kaori has suggested to me (in conversation) that the most famous of all extant late-Heian and early-Kamakura period Japanese landscape screen paintings—the *Tōji senzui byōbu* and the *Koyasan senzui byōbu*—may be quite comparable in style and general format to the paintings that would have been executed for the Saishō-shitennōin program. In addition, the "four-seasons/*meisho*" painting mounted on the sliding panels of the doorways known as the *Torii no shōji* in the "day sitting room" (*hiru no onza*) of the Seiryōden in the Kyoto Imperial Palace (Gosho) when it was reconstructed in the second year of the Kansei Era (1790) may offer a useful visual analogy. See Shimada, *Kinsei fukko Seiryōden no kenkyū*, pp. 33-38. Records of paintings executed at the time of an even later palace reconstruction, in the second year of the Ansei era (1855), show that many of the *meisho* that figure in the Saishōshitennōin program were still serving as primary decorative subjects on *fusuma* in various sectors of the Gosho. See Fujioka, *Kyōto Gosho*, pp. 260-273. For models of Heian-period rooms in buildings of the *shinden* style which may be comparable to the interior spaces in the Retired Emperor's living quarters of the Saishōshitennōin, see Ike Kōzō, "Sumai," in Kyōto-shi, ed., *Yomigaeru Kyōto*, pp. 122-129.

19 KM 2:282.

20 Chino has noted some departures from convention in the poems composed for the program which may or may not have been reflected in one way or another in the accompanying paintings. She observes, for example, that while most of the poems on Kasugano—the first *meisho* in the sequence—emphasize "picking new herbs" and "snow," which are standard Kasugano features, six out of the ten poems also mention plum blossoms, which are not. All ten Miwayama poems mention the cuckoo (*hototogisu*), though that bird is not conventionally associated with that site. The prominence of chrysanthemums in nine out of the ten Minase poems and of plovers (*[tomo]chidori*) in all but one of the Abukumagawa poems (see below) is likewise unorthodox. To this extent, then—if not more so—the designers of the program (and, perhaps especially, Teika) seem to have been

willing to depart from or alter custom, perhaps in search of an air of freshness in a program that otherwise dealt mostly in the tried and true. Chino also suggests that such contemporaneous compilations of notes on *meisho* and their accustomed associations as can be found in the *waka* handbook *Waka iroha*, which was compiled by the monk Jōkaku and submitted to Gotoba during the early stages of the *Shinkokinshū* production process, may well have served Teika and his associates as a guide to the current standards in *meisho* topical treatment—and may even have served as one of the standards with which, at points, they chose to differ. See Chino, "Meishoe no seiritsu to tenkai," p. 119. For Jōkaku's notes on *meisho* (i.e., *tokoro no na*) usage, see Sasaki, ed., *Waka iroha*, in *Nihon kagaku taikei* 3:158-174; see also table 1 for notes on Jōkaku's lists of the most frequently used features of those Saishōshitennōin *meisho* (i.e., all but six or seven) that are listed in *Waka iroha*.

21 Kubota, *Fujiwara Teika*, p. 185; KM 2:287.

22 Since no full description of the completed program exists, the exact number of *shōji* eventually used for the completed program is unknown.

23 KM 2:287.

24 Traditional sources say that the first *Saishōkō* were held under imperial auspices during the reign of Ichijō, in the fifth month of 1002 or 1010. Prelates from four prominent monasteries—Tōdaiji, Kōfukuji, Enryakuji, and Onjōji—were selected to perform the readings in the Imperial Palace. It was reported that the Four Deva Kings made themselves physically manifest during a *Saishōkō* held in the reign of Gosuzaku (1036-1045), after which seats were always prepared for them at subsequent observances. (See Mochizuki, *Bukkyō daijiten* 2:1413.) These traditions attest to the durability of the Shitennō cult in imperial household ritual, and suggest again that in his activities *circa* 1207 Gotoba was simply building anew upon established practices—and that those practices may still have been thought of as least potentially efficacious.

25 KM 2:288. Koya was linked with Nagara through its proximity to the ancient city of Naniwa, in Settsu Province ("Tsu no kuni.") In its earliest appearances (in poems anthologized in *Shūi wakashū*) the name "Koya" is manipulated for its sonic evocation of synonymous words ("little hut," "this one," etc.). The replacement sites, Waka no ura and Fukiage, are also linked by their mutual proximity along the coast of Kii Province.

26 See chapter 3 for the account of the origins of this "poetry desk." It is conceivable that Nagara Bridge was dropped as a topic because someone—perhaps Gotoba—thought that its associations with "rot" and "decay" would be inauspicious. Conversely, the favor of inclusion was shown toward such relatively uncommon *meisho* as "Nonaka no shimizu," a spring that could be celebrated for its "unceasing" flow of sweet water throughout the ages.

27 Virtually nothing is known about any of these painters or the significance of their various titles and appellations except with regard to Sonchi, who is the recognized founder of an atelier of painters known as the Shōnan'inza of Kōfukuji, Nara. Sonchi's origins, and the dates of his birth and death, are unknown, and the

earliest mention of his name is in the *Meigetsuki* entry (Jōgen 1.5.14; KM 2:292) that reports the Saishōshitennōin project assignments. Later, both he and Kaneyasu, one of the other Saishōshitennōin painters, as well as Ariie—a Saishōshitennōin poet—and two other painters contributed wall paintings for the decoration of a nine-story pagoda at Hosshōji in 1213, and in recognition of his participation Sonchi was awarded the rank of Hōgen, one of the highest honors for which a court painter (*eshi*) was eligible. Lists of Sonchi's works in medieval catalogs include paintings on both secular and religious topics, but the only extant work recognized as his is a depiction of Prince Shōtoku delivering his lecture on the Śrīmālā Sūtra (*Shōtoku Taishi Shōmangyō kōsan zu*). This is believed to be the same painting as that for which Sonchi received a commission in 1222 from the Hōryūji monastery, for mounting in its Shariden (Hall of Relics). On Sonchi, see also Hamada Takashi, "Sonchi," in *Kokushi daijiten* iinkai, ed., *Kokushi daijiten* 8:679, and Morisue, *Chūsei no shaji to geijutsu,* pp. 326-331.

28 The *hare/ge* distinction was also commonly applied to various poem topics and occasions. In table 1, the *hare* and *ge* designations for the work of these four painters have been applied as *hare/ge* designations for the *meisho* topics themselves; but, it should be noted, this designation is speculative, and, in any case, does not seem to have been a major determining factor in the composition of the poems themselves. The designation may simply have been a convenience for organizing the work of the painters, but it may have been based on a recognition of differing styles of which the respective painters were masters, or a way of insuring that there was indeed some variation in the style and content of the paintings that would be mounted in the various parts of the building.

29 *Meigetsuki* Jōgen 1.5.14; KM 2:292.

30 *Meigetsuki* Jōgen 1.5.16; KM 2:293. See also Kubota, *Fujiwara Teika,* p. 187.

31 Chino, "Meishoe no seiritsu," pp. 119-120.

32 Fukuyama ("Saishōshitennōin," p. 521) suggests that the change had something to do with the desire for quasi-natural continuity with the adjacent *meisho* scenes.

33 KM 2:297.

34 For a study of these poems and the occasion in English, see E. B. Ceadel, "The Ōi River Poems and Preface." See also Inoue Fumio, "Ōigawa gyōkō waka koshō," in Muromatsu, ed., *Kokubun chūshaku zensho* 12 (not paginated.) Tsurayuki's preface is also reproduced in book 14 of the literary tale collection *Kokon chomonjū.* See Nishio and Kobayashi, ed., *Kokon chomonjū* 2:147-148.

35 Fukuyama, "Saishōshitennōin," pp. 521-522. The Saishōkōin was destroyed in a fire in 1226, but Fukuyama notes that, upon hearing this news, Teika wrote admiringly (in *Meigetsuki*) of what he remembered about its furnishings. Fukuyama takes this as strong evidence that Teika was familiar with the Saishōkōin paintings, and that they therefore were likely candidates as models for the Saishōshitennōin program.

36 Fukuyama, "Saishōshitennōin," p. 522; *Meigetsuki* Jōgen 1.6.10, 12; KM 2:297-298.

37 Fukuyama, "Saishōshitennōin," p. 522; *Meigetsuki,* Jōgen 1.9.24; KM 2:309–310.

38 *Meigetsuki,* Jōgen 1.10.24; KM 2:313.

39 This passage in Gotoba's poetic memoirs (*Gotoba-in gokuden*) is often cited as evidence of the strained relations between the two men. See Robert H. Brower, "Ex-Emperor Go-Toba's Secret Teachings: Go-Toba no In Gokuden," pp. 3–70, esp. pp. 13–22, for an account of their relationship, and pp. 39–40 for a translation of Gotoba's comments on the Ikuta no mori controversy.

40 Fukuyama, "Saishōshitennōin," p. 523. Fukuyama also notes that a mask for the character Sanju (featured in the *gagaku* dance "Sanju hajin raku") now in the possession of the Tōdaiji, in Nara, bears an inscription which indicates that it was made and used at the Saishōshitennōin dedication ceremony, and that an early nineteenth-century catalog of rare antiquities (*Shūko jūshu*) contained a drawing of a ceremonial apron (*hō*) with an inscription that also identified it as having been used in the same *kuyō.*

41 KM 3:40.

42 See Takakusu and Watanabe, ed., *Taishō shinshū daizokyō, zushō* vol. 12, p. 164.

43 Fukuyama, "Saishōshitennōin," p. 527. For *Hyakurenshō,* see Kuroita ed., *[Shintei zōho] Kokushi taikei* 11:154.

44 Fukuyama, "Saishōshitennōin," p. 527. For *Rokudaishōjiki,* see Hanawa, ed., *Gunsho ruijū* 2:412.

45 Fukuyama, "Saishōshitennōin," p. 527 and KM 6:76.

46 Fukuyama, "Saishōshitennōin," p. 528 and *Taishō daizōkyō, zushō* 12:245.

47 Fukuyama, "Saishōshitennōin," pp. 528–533.

48 Though poems are of course as susceptible to loss as anything else, there was a long-standing belief among practitioners of the the *waka* tradition that its works were more resistant to time's exigencies than other creations—of both many and nature—might be. Tsurayuki weaves this notion throughout his *Kokin wakashū kana* preface, and concludes: "Time may pass and circumstances may change, pleasures and sorrows may succeed one another, but these poems will endure. If this collection survives—if the length of its life is like a long green willow branch, if it is no more scattered and lost than are the needles of a pine tree, if it goes on and on like a vine, if it lingers like a bird's track, then those who understand the nature of poetry, and who have grasped the essence of things, will not fail to look up to the past as to the moon in the vast heavens, nor will they withhold their affectionate regard from our own times." (McCullough, trans., p. 8). The reiteration of this sentiment—often, in language that deliberately imitates Tsurayuki's—in many prefaces to later *chokusenshū* and in many *waka* treatises is a mark of the tenacity of this self-serving belief.

49 Emperor's or Empress's visitations of varying duration in various locales distinct from their normal abodes—including, for example, brief stays in relatives' or in-law's mansions, day-trips for the viewing of scenery at its seasonal best, and extended religious pilgrimages to remote sites—were all termed *miyuki* (also *gyōkō* or *gokō.* The first term was used in respect to excursions by reigning Emperors and Empresses; the latter, in respect to excursions by retired and/or

cloistered rulers and their consorts.) In thinking about the significance of *miyuki* —a subject which, in and of itself, has received very little attention from Japanese scholars—I have been influenced by Clifford Geertz's essay "Centers, Kings, and Charisma: Reflections on the Symbolics of Power" in Geertz, *Local Knowledge,* pp. 121-146. Geertz writes that "Royal progresses . . . locate the society's center and affirm its connection with transcendent things by stamping a territory with ritual signs of dominance. When kings journey around the countryside, making appearances, attending fêtes, conferring honors, exchanging gifts, or defying rivals, they mark it, like some wolf or tiger spreading his scent through his territory, as almost physically part of them. . . . The royal occupation gets portrayed as being a good deal more than merely hedged with divinity" (p. 125). And the essay concludes with this suggestive claim: "It is not, after all, standing outside the social order in some excited state of self-regard that makes a political leader numinous but a deep, intimate involvement—affirming or abhorring, defensive or destructive—in the master fictions by which that order lives" (p. 146). Although the status and ritual significance of the Japanese Emperor in medieval times was by no means the same as that of the rulers discussed as examples by Geertz, his observations about royal movements through geopolitical space seem very pertinent to an assessment of the meaning of *miyuki.*

50 During the Chōyō feast (*Chōyō no en*), which was patterned on Chinese precedent, courtiers would pass wine cups in which chrysanthemums were floating, in the belief that drinking *sake* imbued with their vapors would prolong life, and poems on the theme of vitality and longevity would be composed in both Chinese and Japanese. The association of chrysanthemums with longevity is also an ancient Chinese importation. For details on the Chōyō feast, see Yamanaka, *Heian-chō no nenjū gyōji,* pp. 238-245.

51 *Tadamine shū* #91, SKT 3:40.

52 *Yorimoto shū* #25, SKT 3:77. The poem's turn (*kakekotoba*) on the word *kiku* has it function both as the verb "hear[d]" and as the noun "chrysanthemum." Transparent as this play may be, the word's double function in two overlapping syntactic schemes also emphasizes the link between the temporal *foci* of the two halves of the poem (*kyō/kinō*, today/yesterday).

53 *Korenori shū* #42, SKT 3:54.

54 *Shoku kokin wakashū* #161, SKT 1:351. Korenori's "*kono kawa no* . . ." follows as #1662 under the same *kotobagaki* in an Ōigawa mini-sequence in the second of the three miscellaneous chapters of *Shoku kokin wakashū,* a mid-thirteenth-century *chokusenshū.* The third poem in the group is attributed to Uda's granddaughter Nakatsukasa (b. 910/912?): "Ōigawa soko ni mo miyuru Kameyama no/miyuru kage wa ikuyo henuran" (Through how many reigns has Kameyama's reflection/shown so clearly on the bottom of the Ōi river—and for how many more will it be there?). Though obviously composed on another occasion, Nakatsukasa's poem adopts the mood and means of the 907 Ōigawa verses, and of other similar verses composed on similar occasions elsewhere and at other times. It adds, as one of its particular fillips, the figure of Kameyama, "Tortoise Moun-

tain," which rises directly above the Ōigawa's north bank, and which bears a name name evocative of great numbers of years, or of agelessness. The poem does not appear in extant versions of *Nakatsukasa shū*, and it lacks its own *kotobagaki* in *Shoku kokin wakashū*, so nothing can be said about the circumstances of its own composition.

55 *Yorimoto shū* #28, SKT 3:77.

56 One likely means for capturing the scenic moment and preserving it for posterity's observation would be in painting. More than one scholar has pointed out that the 907 Ōigawa *miyuki* poems could easily have served as the textual basis or as inscriptions for a *byōbu* or *shōji* painting of the site and/or of this specific *miyuki*. Furthermore, the congratulatory and felicitous modes and means employed in these poems do bear strong resemblance to the modes and means employed in poems that we know to have been composed in conjunction with pictorial projects.

57 *Korenori shū* #17, SKT 3:54.

58 *Shūi wakashū* #1128, SNKBT 7:323. The poem is also reproduced in several tale collections, including *Yamato monogatari* (dan 19); and it is the poem selected to represent Tadahira (under the name Teishinkō) and his work in Teika's *Ogura hyakunin isshu* (The Ogura one hundred poems by one hundred poets.) Ogura-yama is a peak on the north bank of Ōigawa: the full title of Teika's "One hundred poems . . ." anthology contains the place-name because he is believed to have compiled it for use in a program of inscriptions—and possibly paintings—on the walls of a home he built in the vicinity of the mountain.

59 See Komachiya, notes to *Shūi wakashū* #1128 in SNKBT 7:323.

60 *Saishōshitennōin waka* #231, SKT 5:900. The *Saishōshitennōin waka* will here be identified by the abbreviation SW. Numbering is as in the edition in SKT 5, pp. 896-905. There is also a printed version in *Gunsho ruijū*, but the SKT text, based on a manuscript copy in the Takamatsu no Miya collection (collated with another in the Naikaku Bunko), and prepared by Gotō Shigerō, is far more reliable. There is also a text known as *Saishōshitennōin meisho shōji waka* (re-produced in *Gunsho ruijū*) which purports to present poems composed when Gotoba visited the monastery with a group of courtiers "on the tenth day of the tenth month in the first year of the Jōkyū era" (1219). Fourteen of the thirty-five *meisho* topics in this sequence are the same as those of the 1207 program; but scholarly consensus has judged the text a forgery. See Fukuyama, "Saishōshi-tennōin," pp. 533-534 and Katano, "*Saishōshitennōin meisho shōji waka* wa isho ka," in Katano, *Nihon bungei to kaiga no sōkansei no kenkyū*, pp. 230-255. Katano also discusses the 1207 program in a chapter on "lyrical landscape poetry and its pictorial character" in another chapter of the same book: see pp. 100-104.

61 SW #236, SKT 5:900.

62 *Gosen wakashū* #1075, SNKBT 6:318. Some versions have *Serikawa no nobe no furumichi*—"the old paths around the fields of Serikawa."

63 According to Katagiri (in notes to *Gosen wakashū* #1075, SNKBT 6:318), Saga had enjoyed hunting in the Serikawa area, but his successors Seiwa and Yōzei were more strictly observant of religious prohibitions against the killing of ani-

mals, so the Serikawa hunting grounds were neglected during their reigns. Kōkō then revived the hunt, and Yukihira's poem is apparently a celebration of that return to the royal practices of the past. Katagiri also notes that "Saga no yama" refers not only to "the mountains in the Saga district," through which the Serikawa flows, but also to the Emperor Saga, a figurative "mountain" whose daunting precedents are now being revived out of awe and admiration (not to mention a desire to enjoy the hunt.)

I have been frustrated in my attempts to find useful studies of the processes by which many Emperors acquired public appellations (as distinct from their private, and rarely used, personal names) that are identical with place-names (Saga, Uda, Daigo, etc.). It is usually assumed that such naming derives from associations between each royal individual and the location of one or another of their private residences—often, residences they occupied after leaving the throne. But this pattern is not evinced consistently in the appellations of Emperors in the Heian period or, for that matter, at other times. The history of such appellation and its relationship to place-naming in general invites further study.

64 SW #238, SKT 5:900.

65 SNKBT 5:96.

66 SNKBT 5:107.

67 SW #103, SKT 5:898.

68 Takagi, Gomi, and Ōno, ed., Man'yōshū 2, NKBT 5:137.

69 For another translation of these poems, see Cranston, A Waka Anthology, pp. 308–309.

70 SW #104, SKT 5:898.

71 These include three utaawase held in the sixth, eighth and ninth months of 1202, and the participants included several of the Saishōshitennōin poets—Teika, Ietaka, Masatsune, Ariie, and, of course, Gotoba himself, as well as Shunzei. See SKT 5:408–416 for texts of the poems composed on these occasions—many of which, in turn, made their way into subsequent anthologies.

72 SW #132, SKT 5:898.

73 See Katagiri, Utamakura utakotoba jiten, pp. 387–388.

74 The Ōigawa and Minase scenes apparently were not "adjacent" or "coordinate" in terms of their spatial positioning in the Saishōshitennōin rooms, but, as shall become clear, the features emphasized in the representations of both sites serve to link them "across" that space from their respective, disparate positions therein.

75 For texts of the 891 kiku awase poems, see SKT 5:21–22 or Hagitani, ed., Heianchō utaawase taisei 1, pp. 13–21.

76 SW #135–136, SKT 5:898.

77 SW #164, 166, and 169, SKT 5:899.

78 SW #162, SKT 5:899.

79 See, for example, Shika wakashū #234 (SNKBT 9:290). Compare also Shunzei's poem, "on love at first meeting" (hajimete au koi) "Tanomazu wa Shikama no kachi no iro o miyo/aisomete koso fukaku naru nare" (If you don't believe me, look, then, at the color of Shikama kachi cloth:/they say that it grows deeper once

the dying has begun [as does my love for you, now that it has begun].) *Chōshū eisō* #509, in SKT 3:630.

80 There is another possibility to consider: *iro*, here, may not have only its conventionally double poetic meaning of "color" and "erotic desire" but may also suggest the Buddhist term for "form" or outward physical dimension, *rūpa*, usually translated as *shiki* or *iro*. Thus, the second half of the poem may mean that "in our view of the configuration of Shikama Market [in this painting] we can see how rich your lifetime is and will be."

81 SW #326, SKT 5:902.

82 Ōtsu and Tsukishima, eds., *Ise monogatari*, in NKBT 9:154.

83 SW #146, SKT 5:899. Kubota (in [*Yakuchū*] *Fujiwara Teika zenkashū* 1, p. 501, supplemental note 1832) indicates that the poem works allusively with a prose passage that describes Genji's emotional state as autumn comes to Suma, at which time he formulates his own view of his condition with language borrowed from a poem attributed to Ariwara no Narihira, his famous predecessor as exile in the same locale. For a translation of the relevant passage—frequently noted for its intertextual richness—see Seidensticker, trans., *The Tale of Genji*, pp. 235-236.

84 SW #156, SKT 5:899. Here the foundation for the allusive interplay is a poem which Genji sends to the Akashi Lady in anticipation of their first meeting: "Ochikochi mo shiranu kumoi ni nagamewabi/kasumeshi yado no kozue o zo tou" (Weary of gazing at clouds that seemed both far and near/I shall now seek out the treetops near that house that has been shrouded in the mist.) In Abe, Akiyama, and Imai, eds., *Genji monogatari* 2, NKBZ 13, p. 238. In Teika's poem, the first two syllables of the word *shiratsuyu* ("white dew") provide an incomplete replication of the phrase *ochikochi mo shiranu*, "I can't tell far from near . . . ." The "village on the hill" (*okabe no sato*) is equivalent to the house (*yado*) toward which Genji says his gaze is drawn; but the first two syllables of the word *okabe* also suggest the verb *oku*, which is used to describe the presence of "dew" on those surfaces upon which it falls and rests.

85 SW #417, SKT 5:904.

86 *Shika wakashū* #161, SNKBT 9:266. The commentator for this modern edition, Gotō Shigenori, specifies that the occasion of the *miyuki* was the celebration of the fiftieth day after the birth of the royal couple's child, Prince Atsunari (the future Emperor Goichijō), in 1008. He also notes that Michinaga offered a very similar verse for consideration at a poetry contest at the palace in 986, during the first year of Ichijō's reign.

87 SW #452, SKT 5:905.

88 SW 456, SKT 5:905. Kubota notes a similarity to Teika's famous poem, composed in 1186: "Miwataseba hana mo momiji mo nakarikeri/ura no tomoya no aki no yūgure" (As I gaze out over the scene, there are neither cherry blossoms nor colored leaves;/autumn evening at a hut by a bay). Textual sites of his own creation are prominent in Teika's memory, too.

89 *Kokin wakashū* #1088, SNKBT 5:330. A *tsunade* is a rope attached to a small

boat so that it can be pulled by another larger boat or by horses or laborers on land.

EPILOGUE. RECOVERING THE BURIED TREE

1 For texts of the various versions of *Umoregi* (also called *Haikai umoregi*) and discussion of its composition and publication history, see Ogata, ed., *Kigin hairon shū* (Koten bunko 151), pp. 3–8, 11–19, 29–104, 127–179.

2 Among various distinctions to be made between the two forms of verse in question here—*waka* and *haikai*—is that of length: *waka*, for the most part, are thirty-one syllable poems which break up into "lines" of five syllables, then seven, then five, and then two more of seven syllables, while *haikai* are just seventeen syllables long and correspond to the first three lines of the *waka*, i.e., five, seven, and five syllables. *Haikai* were often composed in linked series of varying length, as in *renga*, the genre which stands, genealogically, between *waka* and *haikai*. What are known as *haiku* are verses that fit the various formal requirements for the opening verse (*hokku*) of a *haikai* sequence.

3 Among these works are *Hachidaishū shō*, on the first eight Imperial *waka* anthologies; *Genji monogatari kogetsushō*, on *The Tale of Genji*; *Makura no sōshi shunshoshō*, on Sei Shōnagon's *Pillow Book*.

4 It is also possible that Kigin used the title "Umoregi" to invoke the idea of obscurity—his own, as a relatively unrecognized *haikai* master in 1655. Similarly, the word *Umoregi* stands alone as a trope for obscurity (rather than for other aspects of its poetic usage) in the titles of two Meiji-period literary works. Mori Ōgai (1862–1922) used *Umoregi* in place of a literal rendering of the German title of his translation of Ossip Schubin's *Die geschichte eines Genies*, the title character of which is an obscure composer; and Higuchi Ichiyō (1872–1896) used the same title for a story of a porcelain maker who insists on traditional quality at the expense of commercial success, and, as a result, lives in "obscurity" and utter frustration. Both uses are analogous to Kigin's in that they stand for and unleash associations that may govern the perceptions, expectations, and understandings of the reader who moves beyond these titles into the body of the texts that appear under them, or then reflects back upon the title from the perspective of the body of the text. Robert Danly notes that the title of the Ichiyō story "suggests the idiom '*isshō o umoregi ni owaru*,' to lead an obscure life or end one's days in obscurity." See Danly, *In the Shade Of Spring Leaves*, p. 301 n. 1 and pp. 75–78, for a discussion of the story "Umoregi." Ōgai's "Umoregi" appeared in ten installments in the periodical *Shigarami zōshi* from April 1890 through May 1891 and is reprinted in Yoshida, ed., *Mori Ōgai zenshū*, vol. 8, pp. 28–81. Ichiyō's "Umoregi" appeared in three installments in *Miyako no hana* in November and December 1892 and is reprinted in Shioda, Wada, and Higuchi, ed., *Higuchi Ichiyō zenshū*, vol. 1, pp. 150–178.

5 *Hirosawa shūsō* #933, SKT 9:206.

6 *Kotojirishū* #1123, SKT 9:564. Harumi was one of the primary figures in the emergence of the so-called Edo-ha group of neoclassical poets. The Edo-ha

movement stemmed from the teachings of the philologist Kamo no Mabuchi (1697–1769), who redirected scholarly attention to the *Man'yōshū* and advocated its contents as the model for a Japanese poesy predating the eras of heavier Chinese influence; but, in fact, the Edo-ha poets were quite eclectic in the modeling of their poems on the styles of several eras, and were particularly drawn to the *Shin kokinshū* as an aesthetic and formal exemplar. (On Harumi and the Edo-ha movement, see Tsujimori, "Murata Harumi no Edo-ha kafū," in Tsujimori, *Kinsei kōki kadan no kajintachi*, pp. 69–80.) The lady from whom Harumi received this commission may very well have been the wife of Matsudaira Sadanobu (1758–1829). According to Matsuno Yōichi (private correspondence, September 1993), the appellation "Koshi no kimi" is probably derived from the courtesy title "Etchū no kami," one of several held by Sadanobu during his lifetime. Murata Harumi, Katō Chikage (see below), and other poet-scholars were mainstays of Sadanobu's literary salon in Edo.

7 *Ukeragahana* #1317, SKT 9:518. On Chikage's role in the emergence of the Edo-ha movement, see Tsujimori, "Tachibana Chikage no keishō to Edo-ha no juritsu," in Tsujimori, *Kinsei kōki kadan no kajintachi*, pp. 56–68.

8 Yanaibara and Kiyotaki, *Koji junrei Kyōto, 13: Kōryūji*, plate 52 and p. 131. The image is designated an "important cultural property" (*jūyō bunkazai*).

9 Mochizuki, ed., *Kōryūji*, plates 46–47 and p. 24.

10 On Roan, an idiosyncratic figure who followed neither the neoclassical teachings traced to Mabuchi nor the strict courtly style advocated by the traditional Kyoto-based schools, but advocated rather a "poetry of everyday words" (*tadakotouta*), see Kagawa, "Ozawa Roan," in Hisamatsu and Sanekata, ed., *Kinsei no kajin* (*Nihon kajin kōza* 5), pp. 153–186; on his Uzumasa period in particular, see pp. 155–162.

11 *Rokujō eisō* #1777, SKT 9:443–444. See also Hisamatsu Sen'ichi and Ikeda Toshio, eds., "Ozawa Roan," in Takagi Ichinosuke and Hisamatsu Sen'ichi, ed., *Kinsei wakashū* (NKBT 93):316.

12 See, for example, *Sanbōe* tale 2.12 ("A Woman of Yamato Province"), in Kamens, trans., *The Three Jewels*, p. 220, where the chanting of seven supernatural monks on a rooftop is compared to "a crowd of droning bees."

13 *Rokujō eisō* #1778, SKT 9:444.

14 *Rokujō eisō* #1779–1781, SKT 9:444.

15 The idea that poetic production, though a secular endeavor, may nonetheless serve as a means toward Buddhist enlightenment or transcendence is rooted in Heian and Kamakura-period *waka* theory and practice; Roan is replicating this time-honored poet's pose. His use in this context of the phrase *mutsu no chimata* is of particular interest. The earliest attested use of this phrase (an equivalent of the more common terms *rokudō* or *mutsu no michi*, "six Ways," or types of unenlightened existence) is in a poem in the sixth chapter of *Taiheiki*. On his way past Tennōji (in Osaka) to fight in the battle of Akasaka Castle (in 1322), the aged warrior Hitomi Sukesada leaves a verse posted on the left pillar of a stone *torii*, expressing his hope of winning glory in the forthcoming fight: "Hana sakanu oigi

no sakura kuchinu tomo/sono na wa koke no shita ni kakureji" (Though withered and flowerless the ancient cherry tree/beneath the moss its name will not be hidden). And, on the opposite pillar, his son Hitomi Suketada writes: "Mate shibashi ko o omou yami ni mayouran/ mutsu no chimata no michi shirube sen" (Wait a bit! I shall guide you on the Six Roads/lest in the darkness of parental love you lose the way). (NKBT 34:204 and McCullough, trans., *The Taiheiki*, p. 170.) Roan's use of both the *hana sakanu . . .* and *mutsu no chimata* figures in the Uzumasa Jizō series seems to echo their juxtaposition in the *Taiheiki* passage.

16 The *Ryōnai meisho waka* series is reproduced in *Miyagi-ken shi* hensan iinkai, ed., *Miyagi-ken shi 14: bungei geinō*, pp. 98-99. See also prologue, note 18.

17 The *locus classicus* for the use in poetry of the phrase *mikasa masar[u]* (the volume of water increases) is in a verse in the personal anthology of the tenth-century poet Sone Yoshitada (*Yoshitada shū* #8); and the phrase *samidare ni mikasa masar[u]* can be found in a poem by Yūsei (or Yūshō) Hōshi (1118-1200) in *Shoku kokin wakashū* (#242). See NKBT 80:44 and SKT 1:323.

18 Ishigaki, *Sendai umoregi zaiku no yūrai*, p. 4.

19 Ishigaki, *Sendai umoregi zaiku no yūrai*, pp. 8-10.

Selected Bibliography

Abe Akio, Akiyama Ken, and Imai Gen'ei, eds. *Genji monogatari*. 6 vols. (NKBZ 12-17.) Tokyo: Shōgakukan, 1970-76.

Akiyama Terukazu. "Daijōe yuki suki byōbu," in Akiyama, *Heian jidai sezokuga no kenkyū*. Tokyo: Yoshikawa Kōbunkan, 1964, pp. 67-91.

Alter, Robert. *The Pleasures of Reading: in an Ideological Age*. New York: Simon and Schuster, 1989.

Aoki Jun'ichi. "Umoregi," in *Encyclopedia Japonica* (*Dai Nihon hyakka jiten*) vol. 2. Sōga Tetsuo, gen. ed. Tokyo: Shōgakukan, 1968, p. 686.

Aoki Kazuo, Inaoka Kōji, Sasayama Haruo, and Shirafuji Noriyuki, eds. *Shoku nihongi*. (SNKBT 1.) Tokyo: Iwanami Shoten, 1989.

Ariyoshi Tamotsu. *Saigyō: hana no shita ni haru shinan*. (Ōchō no kajin 8.) Tokyo: Shūeisha, 1985.

————. *Shin kokin wakashū no kenkyū: kihan to kōsei*. Tokyo: Sanseidō, 1968.

Asanuma Keiji. "Honkadori ni tsuite: tekisutoron no kanten kara," in Nihon bungaku kenkyū shiryō kankōkai, ed., *Saigyō, Teika*. Tokyo: Yūseidō, 1984, pp. 256-270.

Ben-Porat, Ziva. "The Poetics of Literary Allusion," in *PTL* 1 (1976):107-108.

Bialock, David T. "Voice, Text, and the Question of Poetic Borrowing in Late Classical Japanese Poetry," in *Harvard Journal of Asiatic Studies*, 54:1 (June 1994), pp. 181-231.

Bloom, Harold. *A Map of Misreading*. New York: Oxford University Press, 1975.

————. *Wallace Stevens: The Poems of Our Climate*. Ithaca and London: Cornell University Press, 1976.

Bowring, Richard, trans. *Murasaki Shikibu: Her Diary and Poetic Memoirs*. Princeton: Princeton University Press, 1982.

Brazell, Karen, trans. "Komachi at Sekidera," in Donald Keene, ed., *Twenty Plays of the Nō Theatre*. New York: Columbia University Press, 1970, pp. 66-78.

Brower, Reuben Arthur. *Alexander Pope: The Poetry of Allusion*. Oxford: Clarendon Press, 1959.

Brower, Robert H. "Ex-Emperor Go-Toba's Secret Teachings: Go-Toba no In Gokuden," in *Harvard Journal of Asiatic Studies*, 32 (1972), pp. 3-70.

————. "Waka," in *Kodansha Encyclopedia of Japan*, volume 8. Tokyo: Kodansha International, 1983, pp. 201-217.

Brower, Robert H., and Earl Miner. *Japanese Court Poetry*. Stanford: Stanford University Press, 1961.

Brower, Robert H., and Earl Miner, trans. *Fujiwara Teika's Superior Poems of Our Time*. Stanford: Stanford University Press, 1967.

Brownlee, John. "Crisis as Reinforcement of the Imperial Institution: The Case of the Jōkyū Incident, 1221," in *Monumenta Nipponica*, vol. 24 no. 1-2 (1969), pp. 59-77.

————. "The Shōkyū War and the Political Rise of the Warriors," in *Monumenta Nipponica*, vol. 30 no. 2 (1975), pp. 193-201.

Carter, Steven D. "*Waka* in the Age of *Renga*," in *Monumenta Nipponica*, vol. 36 no. 4 (Winter, 1981), pp. 425-444.

Carter, Steven D., ed. *Conversations with Shōtetsu (Shōtetsu monogatari)*. Robert H. Brower, trans. Michigan Monograph Series in Japanese Studies Number 7. Ann Arbor: Center for Japanese Studies, University of Michigan, 1992.

Carter, Steven D., ed. and trans. *Traditional Japanese Poetry: An Anthology*. Stanford: Stanford University Press, 1991.

————. *Waiting for the Wind: Thirty-six Poets of Japan's Late Medieval Age*. New York: Columbia University Press, 1989.

Ceadel, E. B. "The Ōi River Poems and Preface," in *Asia Major,* new series III, 1953, pp. 65-106.

Chino Kaori. "Meishoe no seiritsu to tenkai," in Takeda Tsuneo, ed., *Nihon byōbue shūsei 10: Keibutsuga, Meisho keibutsu*. Tokyo: Kōdansha, 1980, pp. 115-121.

Conte, Gian Biagio. *The Rhetoric of Imitation: Genre and Poetic Memory in Virgil and Other Latin Poets*. Translated and edited by Charles Segal. Ithaca and London: Cornell University Press, 1986.

Cranston, Edwin A., ed. and trans. *A Waka Anthology: Volume One; The Gem-Glistening Cup*. Stanford: Stanford University Press, 1994.

Cranston, Edwin A., trans. *The Izumi Shikibu Diary: A Romance of the Heian Court*. Cambridge: Harvard University Press, 1969.

Danly, Robert Lyons. *In the Shade Of Spring Leaves: The Life and Writings of Higuchi Ichiyō, a Woman of Letters in Meiji Japan*. New Haven and London: Yale University Press, 1981.

Ebersole, Gary L. *Ritual Poetry and the Politics of Death in Early Japan*. Princeton: Princeton University Press, 1989.

Ellwood, Robert S. *The Feast of Kingship: Accession Ceremonies in Ancient Japan.* Tokyo: Sophia University, 1973.

Frank, Bernard. "Rapports sur les conférences: histoire et philologie Japonaises," in *Notice sur la IVe Section (Sciences et philologiques), Annuaire 1976-77.* Paris: Ecole Pratique des Hautes Etudes, Sorbonne, 1977, vol. 109, pp. 1035-1055; and *Annuaire 1977-78* (1979), vol. 110, pp. 1167-1185.

Freud, Sigmund. *The Standard Edition of the Complete Psychological Works of Sigmund Freud,* James Strachey, general editor. Vol. 8: *Jokes and Their Relation to the Unconscious.* London: The Hogarth Press and the Institute of Psycho-Analysis, 1960.

Fujihira Haruo. *Shinkokin to sono zengo.* Tokyo: Kasama Shoin, 1983.

Fujioka Michio. *Kyōto Gosho.* Tokyo: Shokokusha, 1956.

Fujioka Tadaharu. *Ki no Tsurayuki.* (Ōcho no kajin 4). Tokyo: Shūeisha, 1985.

Fujita Yuriko. "Daijōe byōbuuta no seikaku o megutte," in *Kokugo to kokubungaku,* vol. 55, no. 1 (April 1978), pp. 47-60.

Fukui Kyūzō and Yamagishi Tokuhei, eds. [Shintei zōho] *Makurakotoba no kenkyū to shakugi.* Tokyo: Yūseidō, 1960.

Fukuyama Toshio. *Nihon kenchiku shi no kenkyū.* Kyoto: Kuwana Bunseidō, 1943.

Furuhashi Nobuyoshi. *Kodai waka no hassei.* Tokyo: Tokyo Daigaku Shuppankai, 1988.

Furukawa Hisashi, ed. *Kyōgen shū: chū.* (Nihon koten zensho 63.) Tokyo: Asahi Shinbunsha, 1954.

Geertz, Clifford. *Local Knowledge: Further Essays in Interpretive Anthropology.* New York: Basic Books, 1983.

Gotō Tanji. *Taiheiki no kenkyū.* Kyoto: Daigakudō Shoten, 1938; rpt. 1973.

Gotō Tanji, Kamada Kisaburō, and Okami Masao, eds. *Taiheiki.* 3 vols. (NKBT 34-36). Tokyo: Iwanami Shoten, 1960-62.

Greene, Thomas M. *The Light in Troy: Imitation and Discovery in Renaissance Poetry.* New Haven and London: Yale University Press, 1982.

Groos, Karl. *The Play of Man.* Elizabeth L. Baldwin, trans. New York and London: D. Appleton and Company, 1919.

Hagitani Boku, ed. *Heianchō utaawase taisei.* 10 vols. Rpt. Kyoto: Dōhōsha, 1979.

————. *Tosa nikki* (Nihon koten zensho 35.) Tokyo: Asahi Shinbunsha, 1950.

Hanawa Hokiichi, ed. *Gunsho ruijū.* 19 vols. Tokyo: Keizai Zasshisha, 1898-1902.

Hare, Thomas Blenman. "Reading Kamo no Chōmei," in *Harvard Journal of Asiatic Studies,* 49, no. 1 (June 1989), pp. 163-228.

Harper, Thomas J. "Motoori Norinaga's Criticism of the *Genji monogatari:* A Study of the Background and Critical Content of His *Genji monogatari tama no ogushi.*" Ph.D. dissertation, University of Michigan, 1971.

Hashimoto Fumio, Ariyoshi Tamotsu, and Fujihira Haruo, eds. *Karon shū.* (NKBZ 50). Tokyo: Shōgakukan, 1975.

Higuchi Yoshimaro. *Gotoba-in: ware koso wa, niishimamori yo* (Ōchō no kajin 10.) Tokyo: Shūeisha, 1985.

Himematsu no kai, ed. *Heian waka utamakura chimei sakuin.* Kyoto: Daigakudō Shoten, 1972.

Hino Tatsuo, ed., *Motoori Norinaga shū*. (Shinchō Nihon koten shūsei 64.) Tokyo: Shinchōsha, 1983.

Hisamatsu Sen'ichi, ed. *Chōshu eisō*, in Hisamatsu et al., eds., *Heian Kamakura shikashū* (NKBT 80). Tokyo: Iwanami Shoten, 1964.

————. *Keichū zenshū*, vol. 11 [*Meisho kenkyū* 1]. Tokyo: Iwanami Shoten, 1973.

Hisamatsu Sen'ichi and Ikeda Toshio, eds. "Ozawa Roan," in Takagi Ichinosuke and Hisamatsu Sen'ichi, eds., *Kinsei wakashū* (NKBT 93.) Tokyo: Iwanami Shoten, 1966.

Hollander, John. *The Figure of Echo: A Mode of Allusion in Milton and After*. Berkeley, Los Angeles, London: University of California Press, 1981.

Huey, Robert N. *Kyōgoku Tamekane: Poetry and Politics in Late Kamakura Japan*. Stanford: Stanford University Press, 1989.

Huffer, Lynne. "Julia Kristeva (1941-)" in Eva Martin Sartori and Dorothy Winne Zimmerman, eds., *French Women Writers: A Bio-Bibliographical Source Book*. Westport, Conn.: Greenwood Press, 1991.

Hurvitz, Leon, trans. *Scripture of the Lotus Blossom of the Fine Dharma (The Lotus Sūtra)*. New York: Columbia University Press, 1976.

Ii Haruki, Tsūmoto Nobuhiro, and Shindō Kyōzō, eds. *Kintō shū zen'yaku*. (Shikashū zen'yaku sōsho 7.) Tokyo: Kazama Shobō, 1989.

Ijichi Tetsuo, ed. *Tsukuba shū shō* in *Renga shū* (NKBT 39.) Tokyo: Iwanami Shoten, 1960.

Ikeda Kikan and Kishigami Shinji, eds. *Makura no sōshi* (NKBT 19). Tokyo: Iwanami Shoten, 1958.

Imagawa Fumio, ed. *Kundoku Meigetsuki*. 6 vols. Tokyo: Kawade Shobō Shinsha, 1977-79.

Inoue Fumio. *Ōigawa gyōkō waka koshō*, rpt. in Muromatsu Iwao, ed., *Kokubun chūshaku zensho* 12. Tokyo: Kokugakuin Daigaku Shuppanbu, 1912.

Inoue Minoru. "'Aware' to 'mono no aware,'" in Inoue, *Nihon bungaku no genri*. Tokyo: Kazama Shobō, 1983, pp. 18-38.

Inukai Kiyoshi. "Kawara no in no kajintachi: Anpō Hōshi o jiku to shite." *Kokugo to kokubungaku*, vol. 44, no. 10 (October 1967), pp. 68-78.

Inukai Kiyoshi, Inoue Muneo, Ōkubo Tadashi, Ono Hiroshi, Tanaka Yutaka, Hashimoto Fumio, and Fujihira Haruo, eds., *Waka daijiten*. Tokyo: Meiji Shoin, 1986.

Ishida Yoshisada and Satsukawa Shuji, eds. *Minamoto Ienaga nikki zenchūkai*. Tokyo: Yūseidō, 1968.

Ishigaki Hiroshi. *Sendai umoregi zaiku no yūrai*. Private publication, Sendai:1971.

Issatsu no kōza henshū iinkai, ed. *Issatsu no kōza Nihon no koten bungaku 4: Kokin wakashū*. Tokyo: Yūseidō, 1987.

Itō Haku and Inaoka Kōji, ed. *Man'yōshū zenchū*. 20 vols. Tokyo: Yūhikaku, 1983-88.

Jameson, Frederic. "Walter Benjamin, or Nostalgia," in *Salmagundi*, no. 10-11 (Fall-Winter 1969-70), pp. 52-68.

Jenny, Laurent. "The Strategy of Form," in Tzvetan Todorov, ed., *French Literary Theory Today: A Reader* (translated by R. Carter). Cambridge: Cambridge University Press and Paris: Editions de la Maison des Sciences de l'Homme, 1982, pp. 34-63.

Kadokawa Nihon chimei daijiten henshū iinkai, ed. *Kadokawa Nihon chimei daijiten*. 47 vols. Tokyo: Kadokawa Shoten, 1978-90.

Kagawa Keishō. "Ozawa Roan," in Hisamatsu Sen'ichi and Sanekata Kiyoshi, eds., *Kinsei no kajin* (Nihon kajin kōza 5). Tokyo: Kōbundō, 1969, pp. 153-186.

Kamens, Edward. "Dragon-girl, Maidenflower, Buddha: The Transformation of a *Waka* Topos, 'The Five Obstructions,'" in *Harvard Journal of Asiatic Studies*, 54, no. 2 (December 1993), pp. 389-344.

————. *The Buddhist Poetry of the Great Kamo Priestess: Daisaiin Senshi* (Michigan Monographs Series in Japanese, Number 5.) Ann Arbor: Center for Japanese Studies, University of Michigan, 1990.

————. *The Three Jewels: A Study and Translation of Minamoto Tamenori's Sanbōe.* (Michigan Monographs Series in Japanese Studies, Number 2.) Ann Arbor: Center for Japanese Studies, University of Michigan, 1988.

Kanazawa Norio. "Utamakura ishiki no henbō to sono teichaku katei," in Watanabe Nobuo, ed., *Miyagi no kenkyū* 5: *Kinsei hen* III. Ōsaka: Seibundō, 1983, pp. 7-62.

Katagiri Yōichi, ed. *Gosen wakashū*. (SNKBT 6.) Tokyo: Iwanami Shoten, 1990.

————. "Utamakura no seiritsu," in Katagiri, *Kokin wakashū no kenkyū*. Tokyo: Meiji Shoin, 1991.

————. *Utamakura utakotoba jiten*. (Kadokawa Shōjiten 35.) Tokyo: Kadokawa Shoten, 1983.

Katano Tatsurō. *Nihon bungei to kaiga no sōkansei no kenkyū*. Tokyo: Kasama Shoin, 1975.

Katō, Hilda. "The *Mumyōshō* of Kamo no Chōmei and its Significance in Japanese Literature," in *Monumenta Nipponica*, vol. 23, no. 3-4 (1968), pp. 321-430.

Kawahira Hitoshi. "Honkadori to honzetsudori: 'moto' no kōzō," in *Waka bungaku ronshū 8: Shinkokin to sono jidai*. Tokyo: Kasama Shobō, 1991, pp. 197-230.

Kawamura Teruo. "Kago, utamakura no seiritsu," in *Kokubungaku kaishaku to kyōza no kenkyū*, vol. 34, no. 15 (November 1989), pp. 80-93.

————. "Utamakura: kisetsu no kyōrai o megutte," in Waka Bungaku Kai, ed., *Waka bungaku no sekai 10: Ronshū waka to retorikku*. Tokyo: Kasama Shoin, 1986.

Kawamura Teruo and Kashiwagi Yoshio, eds. *Kin'yō wakashū* (in SNKBT 9). Tokyo: Iwanami Shoten, 1989.

Kazamaki Keijirō, ed. *Sankashū* (in NKBT 29). Tokyo: Iwanami Shoten, 1961.

Keene, Donald, trans. "The Tale of the Bamboo Cutter," in J. Thomas Rimer, *Modern Japanese Fiction and Its Traditions*. Princeton: Princeton University Press, 1978, pp. 275-305.

————. *World Within Walls: Japanese Literature of the Pre-Modern Era 1600-1867*. New York: Grove Press, 1976.

Kikuchi Katsunosuke. *Miyagi-ken kyōdoshi nenpyō*. Sendai: Hōbundō, 1972.

Kojima Noriyuki and Arai Eizō, eds. *Kokin wakashū*. (SNKBT 5.) Tokyo: Iwanami Shoten, 1989.

Kokushi daijiten henshū iinkai, ed. *Kokushi daijiten*. 14 vols. Tokyo: Yoshikawa Kō-bunkan, 1979-93.

Komachiya Teruhiko. "*Kokinshū* no utamakura: waka hyōgen ron josetsu." *Nihon bungaku* 15, no. 8 (August 1966), pp. 24-32.

————. "*Kokin*-teki bigaku no keisei katei: Tsurayuki no utamakura-teki hyōgen o tōshite," in *Bungaku, gogaku* no. 52 (June 1969), pp. 12-18.

————. "*Kokinshū*-teki hyōgen no tokushitsu to sono tenkai," in Fujioka Tadaharu et al., eds., *Shinpojiam Nihon bungaku 2, Kokinshū*. Tokyo: Gakuseisha, 1976, pp. 179-194.

————. "Minamoto Shigeyuki no eika no tokushitsu: sono tabi to utamakura hyōgen o megutte," in *Tokyo Gakugei Daigaku Kiyō*, dai ni bumon, no. 25 (1974), pp. 213-221.

Komachiya Teruhiko, ed. *Shūi wakashū* (SNKBT 7). Tokyo: Iwanami Shoten, 1990.

Konishi Jin'ichi. *A History of Japanese Literature, vol. 1: The Archaic and Ancient Ages*. Aileen Gatten and Nicholas Teele, trans.; Earl Miner, ed. Princeton: Princeton University Press, 1984.

————. "Association and Progression: Principles of Integration in Anthologies and Sequences of Japanese Court Poetry, A.D. 900-350," Robert H. Brower and Earl Miner, trans., in *Harvard Journal of Asiatic Studies*, 21 (1958), pp. 67-127.

Konishi Jin'ichi, ed. "*Fuzoku no uta*," in Konishi and Tsuchihashi Yutaka, eds., *Kodai kayō shū* (NKBT 3). Tokyo: Iwanami Shoten, 1957.

Kōnosu Morihiro. *Man'yōshū zenshaku* (rpt.) 6 vols. Tokyo: Shūei Shobō, 1987.

Kristeva, Julia. *Revolution in Poetic Language*. Margaret Waller, trans., with an introduction by Leon S. Roudiez. New York: Columbia University Press, 1984.

Kubota Jun. *Fujiwara Teika: ransei ni hana ari* (Ōchō no kajin 9.) Tokyo: Shūeisha, 1984.

————. "Meisho waka ni tsuite," in Waka Bungaku Kai, ed., *Waka bungaku no sekai*, vol. 2. Tokyo: Kasama Shoin, 1974, pp. 137-158.

————. *[Yakuchū] Fujiwara Teika zenkashū*. 2 vols. Tokyo: Kawade Shobō Shin-sha, 1985.

Kubota Jun, ed. *Meisho hyakushu uta no toki Karyū kyō to naidan no koto* in Hisamatsu Sen'ichi, ed., *Karon shū 1: Chūsei no bungaku*. Tokyo: Miyai Shoten, 1971, pp. 287-301.

Kubota Utsubo. *Man'yōshū hyōshaku* (New ed.) 11 vols. Tokyo: Tokyodō Shuppan, 1984-85.

Kurano Kenji, ed. *Kojiki* (NKBT 1.) Tokyo: Iwanami Shoten, 1958.

Kuroita Katsumi, ed. *[Shintei zōho] Kokushi taikei*. 38 vols. Tokyo: Kokushi taikei Kankōkai, 1929-62.

Kuwata Tadachika. *Hosokawa Yūsai*. Tokyo: Ōbunsha, 1985.

Kyōto-shi, ed. *Yomigaeru Kyōto: Heian kento sennihyakunen kinen*. Kyōto: Kyōto-shi, 1994.

Kyūsojin Hitaku, ed. *Nihon kagaku taikei, bekkan*. 6 vols. Tokyo: Kazama Shobō, 1959-84.

Lacan, Jacques. "The Agency of the Letter in the Unconscious, or Reason Since

Freud," in *Ecrits. A Selection*. (Translated from the French by Alan Sheridan.) New York: W. W. Norton, 1977, pp. 146–178.

Lattimore, David. "Allusion and T'ang Poetry," in *Perspectives on the T'ang*. (Arthur F. Wright and Denis Twitchett, eds.) New Haven and London: Yale University Press, 1973, pp. 405–439.

Lau, D. C., trans. *Confucius: The Analects (Lun yü)*. Harmondsworth: Penguin Books, 1979.

Lévi-Strauss, Claude. *The Savage Mind*. Chicago: University of Chicago Press, 1966.

Lowenthal, David. *The Past Is a Foreign Country*. Cambridge and New York: Cambridge University Press, 1985.

Maruya Saiichi. *Gotoba-in* (Nihon shijin sen 10.) Tokyo: Chikuma Shobō, 1973.

Mass, Jeffrey P. *The Development of Kamakura Rule, 1180–1250: A History with Documents*. Stanford: Stanford University Press, 1979.

Matsubayashi Yasuaki, ed. *Jōkyūki* (Shinsen nihon koten bunko 1.) Tokyo: Gendai Shichōsha, 1974.

Matsumura Hiroji and Yamanaka Yutaka, eds. *Eiga monogatari*. 2 vols. (NKBT 75–76.) Tokyo: Iwanami Shoten, 1964–65.

Matsuo Yasuaki et al., eds. *Buson jiten*. Tokyo: Ōfūsha, 1990.

McCullough, Helen Craig. *Brocade By Night: "Kokin wakashū" and the Court Style in Japanese Classical Poetry*. Stanford: Stanford University Press, 1985.

McCullough, Helen Craig, ed. *Classical Japanese Prose: An Anthology*. Stanford: Stanford University Press, 1990.

McCullough, Helen Craig, trans. *Kokin wakashū: The First Imperial Anthology of Japanese Poetry*. Stanford: Stanford University Press, 1985.

————. *Tales of Ise; Lyrical Episodes from Tenth-Century Japan*. Stanford: Stanford University Press, 1967.

————. *The Taiheiki: A Chronicle of Medieval Japan*. New York: Columbia University Press, 1959.

————. *The Tale of the Heike*. Stanford: Stanford University Press, 1988.

McCullough, William, trans. "The *Azuma kagami* Account of the Shōkyū War," in *Monumenta Nipponica*, vol. 23, nos. 1–2 (1968), pp. 102–155.

————. "*Shōkyūki*: An Account of the Shōkyū War of 1221," in *Monumenta Nipponica*, vol. 19, nos. 1 and 3 (1964), pp. 103–215 and 420–455.

Mezaki Tokue. "Nōin no den ni okeru ni, san no mondai," in Mezaki, *Heian bunkashi ron*. Tokyo: Ōfūsha, 1968, pp. 320–353.

Miki Sumito, Asami Kazuhiko, Nakamura Yoshio, and Koura Kazuaki, eds. *Uji shūi monogatari, Kohon setsuwa shū*. (SNKBT 42.) Tokyo: Iwanami Shoten, 1990.

Mill, John Stuart. *The System of Logic*. Fifth edition. London: Parker, Son and Bourn, 1862.

Mills, D. E., trans. *A Collection of Tales from Uji: A Study and Translation of Uji shūi monogatari*. Cambridge: Cambridge University Press, 1970.

Minamoto Ienaga nikki kenkyūkai, ed. *Minamoto Ienaga nikki: kōi, kenkyū, sōsakuin*. Tokyo: Kazama Shobō, 1985.

Minegishi Yoshiaki. *Utaawase no kenkyū*. Tokyo: Sanseidō, 1969.

Miner, Earl. *An Introduction to Japanese Court Poetry*. Stanford: Stanford University Press, 1968.

―――. *Comparative Poetics: An Intercultural Essay on Theories of Literature*. Princeton: Princeton University Press, 1990.

―――. "Some Issues for Study of Integrated Collections" in Neil Fraistat, ed., *Poems in Their Place: The Intertextuality and Order of Poetic Collections*. Chapel Hill and London: University of North Carolina Press, 1986, pp. 18-43.

―――. "*Waka:* Features of its Constitution and Development," in *Harvard Journal of Asiatic Studies*, 50, 2 (December 1990), pp. 669-706.

Miner, Earl, Hiroko Odagiri, and Robert E. Morrell, eds. *The Princeton Companion to Classical Japanese Literature*. Princeton: Princeton University Press, 1985.

Miyagi-ken shi henshū iinkai, ed. *Miyagi-ken shi*: vol. 14, Bungei geinō. Sendai: *Miyagi-ken shi* Kankōkai, 1958.

Mochizuki Shinjō, ed. *Kōryūji*. Kyoto: Yamamoto Koshū Shashin Kōgeibu, 1963.

Mochizuki Shinkō, ed. *Bukkyō daijiten*. 10 vols. (Revised ed.) Tokyo: Sekai Seiten Kankō Kyōkai, 1958-63.

Morimoto Motoko. *Shunzeikyō no musume no kenkyū*. Tokyo: Ōfūsha, 1976.

Morisue Yoshiaki. *Chūsei no shaji to geijutsu*. Tokyo: Unebi Shobō, 1941.

Morris, Mark. "Sei Shōnagon's Poetic Catalogues," in *Harvard Journal of Asiatic Studies*, 40, no. 1 (June 1980), pp. 5-54.

―――. "*Waka* and Form, *Waka* and History." *Harvard Journal of Asiatic Studies*, 46, no. 2 (December 1986), pp. 551-610.

Nakamura Hajime et al., eds. *Ajia Bukkyō shi, Nihon hen*. 9 vols. Tokyo: Kōsei Shuppansha, 1972-76.

Nakashima Michikaze (Kōfū). "Utamakura gengi kōshō," in Nakashima, *Jōsei kagaku no kenkyū*. Tokyo: Chikuma Shobō, 1945, pp. 180-296.

Nishimura Tōru. "Fuzoku uta kara utamakura e" in Wakamori Tarō, ed., *Kodai bungei to minzoku: Minzoku bungaku kōza* 4. Tokyo: Kōbundō, 1960, pp. 249-278.

―――. *Uta to minzokugaku*. (Minzoku mingei sōsho.) Tokyo: Iwasaki Bijutsusha, 1966.

Nishio Kōichi and Kobayashi Yasuharu, eds. *Kokon chomonjū*. 2 vols. (Shinchō Nihon koten shūsei 59-60). Tokyo: Shinchōsha, 1983.

Ogata Tsutomu, ed. *Kigin hairon shū* (Koten bunko 151). Tokyo: Koten Bunko, 1960.

Ōgihata Tadao. "Michinoku no utamakura," in Itō Nobuo and Takahashi Tomio, ed, *Kodai no nihon* 8. Tokyo: Kadokawa Shoten, 1970, pp. 276-291.

Okumura Tsuneya. *Utamakura*. Tokyo: Heibonsha, 1977.

Omodaka Hisataka. *Man'yōshū chūshaku*. 22 vols. Tokyo: Chūō Kōronsha, 1957-77.

Ōno Susumu, Satake Akihiro and Maeda Kingorō, eds. *Iwanami Kogo jiten*. Tokyo: Iwanami Shoten, 1974.

Ōtani Tokuzō, Okada Rihei and Shimai Kiyoshi, eds. *Buson shū: zen*. (Koten haibungaku taikei 12.) Tokyo: Shūeisha, 1972.

Owen, Stephen. "Place: Meditation on the Past at Chin-ling," in *Harvard Journal of Asiatic Studies*, 50, no. 2 (December 1990), pp. 417-457.

————. *Remembrance: The Experience of the Past in Classical Chinese Literature*. Cambridge and London: Harvard University Press, 1986.

Ozawa Masao. *Kokinshū no sekai*. Tokyo: Hanawa Shobō, 1961.

Ozawa Masao, Gotō Shigerō, Shimazu Tadao, and Higuchi Yoshimaro, eds. *Fukuro zōshi chūshaku*. 2 vols. Tokyo: Hanawa Shobō, 1974-76.

Pigeot, Jacqueline. *Michiyuki-bun: Poétique de l'itinéraire dans la littérature du Japon ancien*. Paris: Editions G.-P. Maisonneuve et Larose, 1982.

Plutschow, H. E. *Chaos and Cosmos: Ritual in Early and Medieval Japanese Literature*. Leiden: E. J. Brill, 1990.

Preminger, Alex, and T. V. Brogan, eds. *The New Princeton Encyclopedia of Poetry and Poetics*. Princeton: Princeton University Press, 1993.

Sakakura Atsuyoshi, Ōtsu Yūichi, Tsukishima Hiroshi, Abe Toshiko, and Imai Gen'ei, eds. *Taketori monogatari, Ise monogatari, Yamato monogatari*. (NKBT 9.) Tokyo: Iwanami Shoten, 1957.

Sakamoto Yukio and Iwamoto Yutaka, eds. and trans. *Hokekyō*. 3 vols. (Iwanami Bunko 33-304-1, 2, and 3). Tokyo: Iwanami Shoten, 1962-67.

Sakuma Dōgan. *Ōu kanseki monrōshi*, rpt. in Suzuki Shōzō, ed., *Sendai sōsho* vols. 15-16. Sendai: Hōbundō, 1972.

Sakurai Mitsuru. *Man'yōbito no sekai: minzoku to bunka*. Tokyo: Yūzankaku, 1992.

Sasaki Nobutsuna, ed. *Nihon kagaku taikei*. 10 vols. Tokyo: Kazama Shobō, 1956-63.

Sasaki Tadasato. *Utamakura no sekai*. Tokyo: Ōfūsha, 1979.

Satake Akihiro, ed. *Dairi meisho hyakushu chū: Sochiku bunko zō*. (Kyoto Daigaku Kokugo Kokubun Shiryō Sōsho.) Kyoto: Rinsen Shoten, 1982.

Seidensticker, Edward G., trans. *The Tale of Genji*. New York: Alfred A. Knopf, 1976.

Sendai-shi shi henshū iinkai, ed. *Sendai-shi shi 1: honpen 1*. Sendai: Sendai Shiyakusho, 1954.

Shimada Takehiko. *Kinsei fukko Seiryōden no kenkyū*. Tokyo: Shibunkaku Shuppan, 1987).

Shimizu Takayuki, ed. *Yosa Buson shū* (Shinchō Nihon koten shūsei 32.) Tokyo: Shinchōsha, 1979.

Shimura Shirō. *Heianchō sanbungaku utamakura chimei sakuin*. Mitaka: Oka Shobō, 1990.

Shinpen kokka taikan henshū iinkai, ed. *Shinpen kokka taikan*. Tokyo: Kadokawa Shoten, 1980-.

Shintei zōho shiseki shūran kankōkai, ed. *Shintei zōho shiseki shūran*. 43 vols. Kyoto: Rinsen Shoten, 1967-68.

Shioda Ryōhei, Wada Yoshie, and Higuchi Etsu, eds. *Higuchi Ichiyō zenshū*. 4 vols. Tokyo: Chikuma Shobō, 1974-94.

Shirane, Haruo. "Lyricism and Intertextuality: An Approach to Shunzei's Poetics," in *Harvard Journal of Asiatic Studies*, 50, no. 1 (June 1990), pp. 71-85.

Sonoda, Kōyū. *Waka no ura: rekishi to bungaku*. Osaka: Izumi Shoin, 1993.

Starobinski, Jean. "The Idea of Nostalgia," in *Diogenes* no. 54 (Summer 1966), pp. 81-103.

Stevens, Wallace. *The Collected Poems of Wallace Stevens*. New York: Alfred A. Knopf, 1955.

Sugitani Yoshirō. "Utamakura: *Kokin wakashū* no gihō," in *Issatsu no kōza* henshū bu, ed., *Issatsu no kōza: Kokin wakashū*. Nihon no koten bungaku 4. Tokyo: Yūseidō, 1987, pp. 622-626.

Suzuki Hideo. "Kodai waka ni okeru shinbutsu taiō kōzō: Man'yō kara ōchō waka e," in Nihon bungaku kenkyū shiryō kankōkai, ed. *Kokin wakashū* (Nihon bungaku kenkyū shiryō sōsho.) Tokyo: Yūseidō, 1976, pp. 237-255.

————. "*Kokin*-teki hyōgen no keisei," in *Bungaku*, vol. 42, no. 5 (May, 1974), pp. 63-77.

————. "Utamakura no honsei," in *Ōta Yoshimaro Sensei koki kinen ronshū* kankōkai, ed., *Ōta Yoshimaro Sensei koki kinen kokugo kokubungaku ronsō*. Tokyo: Gunsho, 1988, pp. 275-291.

Tajiri Yoshinobu. "Meisho to sono uta," in Waka Bungaku Kai, ed., *Waka bungaku no sekai 5*. (Kasama sensho 80.) Tokyo: Kasama Shoin, 1977, pp. 73-94.

Takagi Ichinosuke, Gomi Tomohide, and Ōno Susumu, eds. *Man'yōshū*. 3 vols. (NKBT 4-6) Tokyo: Iwanami Shoten, 1957-62.

Takagi Ichinosuke, Ozawa Masao, Atsumi Kaoru, and Kindaichi Haruhiko, eds. *Heike monogatari*. 2 vols. (NKBT 32-3.) Tokyo: Iwanami Shoten, 1959.

Takahashi Hiromichi. "*Shin hanatsumi* ni tsuite," in *Bungaku kenkyū*, vol. 74 (December, 1991), pp. 30-38.

Takahashi Kazuhiko, ed. *Mumyōshō zenkai*. Tokyo: Sōbunsha, 1987.

Takahashi Tomio. "Oku yukashi," in Takahashi, *Michinoku: fudo to kokoro*. Tokyo: Shakai Shisōsha, 1967.

Takahashi Yoshio. *Tōkoku no utamakura*. Tokyo: Ōfūsha, 1991.

————. *Utamakura no kenkyū*. Tokyo: Musashino Shoin, 1992.

Takakusu Junjirō and Ono Gemmyō, eds. *Taishō shinshū daizōkyō, zuzō*. 13 vols. Rpt. Tokyo: Taishō Shinshu Daizōkyō Kankōkai, 1975-78.

Takano Tatsuyuki, ed. *Nihon kayō shūsei*. 12 vols. Tokyo: Shunjūsha, 1928-29.

Takeuchi Nobuko. "Umoregi zaiku," in Endō Moto'o, Kodama Kōta, and Miyamoto Tsuneichi, eds., *Nihon no meisan jiten*. Tokyo: Tōyō Keizai Shinpōsha, 1977, p. 96.

Tanaka Yutaka and Akase Shingo, eds. *Shin kokin wakashū* (SNKBT 11.) Tokyo: Iwanami Shoten, 1992.

Taniyama Shigeru, ed. *Roppyakuban utaawase (shō)* (in NKBT 74). Tokyo: Iwanami Shoten, 1965.

Tokuhara Shigemi. "Byōbuuta ni okeru shizen," in Katagiri Yōichi, ed, *Ōchō waka no sekai: shizen kanjō to biishiki*. Tokyo: Sekai Shisōsha, 1984, pp. 43-59.

————. "Byōbuuta no gutaisō," in *Kokugo to kokubungaku*, vol. 55, no. 6 (June 1978), pp. 24-36.

Tsujimori Shūei. *Kinsei kōki kadan no kajintachi*. Tokyo: Ōfūsha, 1977.

Tsukamoto Tetsuzō, ed. *Nikki kikō shū* (Yūhōdō bunko 96.) Tokyo: Yūhōdō Shoten, 1935.

Tyler, Royall. "A Critique of 'Absolute Phenomenalism,'" in *Japanese Journal of Religious Studies*, 9, no. 4 (December 1982), pp. 267-268.

Usuda Shōgo. "Saigyō no tabi to utamakura," in Nihon bungaku kenkyū shiryō kankōkai, ed., *Saigyō, Teika*. Tokyo: Yūseidō, 1984, pp. 101-120.

Watanabe Hideo. "Ki no Tsurayuki no isō: byōbue to byōbuuta o megutte," in *Kokubungaku kenkyū* no. 54 (October 1974), pp. 19-30.

Wixted, John Timothy. "The *Kokinshū* Prefaces: Another Perspective," in *Harvard Journal of Asiatic Studies*, 43, no. 1 (June 1983): 215-238.

Worton, Michael, and Judith Still, eds. *Intertextuality: Theories and Practices*. Manchester and New York: Manchester University Press, 1990.

Yagi Ichio. *Daijōe waka no sekai*. Ise-shi: Kōgakukan Daigaku Shuppanbu, 1986.

————. *Utamakura no shinkyū*. 2 vols. Osaka: Izumi Shoin, 1985-6.

Yamada Shōzen, "Hitomaro eigū no seiritsu to tenkai," in *Taishō Daigaku Kenkyū Kiyō* no. 51 (March, 1966), pp. 83-124.

————. "Poetry and Meaning: Medieval Poets and the *Lotus Sūtra*," in George J. Tanabe, Jr., and Willa Jane Tanabe, eds., *The Lotus Sūtra in Japanese Culture*. Honolulu: University of Hawaii Press, 1989, pp. 95-117.

Yamada Yoshio, Yamada Tadao, Yamada Hideo, and Yamada Toshio, eds. *Konjaku monogatari shū*. 5 vols. (NKBT 22-26.) Tokyo: Iwanami Shoten, 1959-63.

Yamanaka, Yutaka. *Heian jinbutsushi*. Tokyo: Tokyo Daigaku Shuppankai, 1974.

————. *Heianchō no nenjū gyōji*. Tokyo: Hanawa Shobō, 1972.

Yanaibara Isaku and Kiyotaki Eikō. *Koji junrei Kyōto, 13: Kōryūji*. Kyoto: Dankōsha, 1977.

Yiu, Angela. "The Category of Metaphorical Poems (*hiyuka*) in the *Man'yōshū*: Its Characteristics and Chinese Origins," in *Journal of the Association of Teachers of Japanese*, vol. 24, no. 1 (April 1990), pp. 7-33.

Yoshida Seiichi, ed. *Mori Ōgai zenshū*. 10 vols. Tokyo: Chikuma Shobō, 1971.

Japanese Poems Cited

Poems are listed alphabetically by their first two *ku*, followed by the poet's name in parentheses and page(s) on which the poem appears.

Akashigata isa ochikochi mo (Teika): 217
akihagi no furue ni sakeru (Mitsune): 81
amata aranu na o shi mo oshimi (anonymous): 66
arashi fuku mukashi no io no (Jakuren): 276 (n31)
arawarete sode no ue yuku (Teika): 272 (n117)
ari to mo mienu koke no shitamizu (Gusai): 90
ari to te mo awanu tameshi no (Jakuren): 97
ashihiki no yamaoroshi fukite (Gotoba): 134
ashima yori miyuru Nagara no (Kiyotada): 124
au koto o Nagara no hashi no (Korenori): 118
ause araba itowade yoshiya (Michikatsu): 113
Bodaiju no hana ni nakiyoru (Roan): 230
chiji no aki no hikari o kakete (Shunzei's Daughter): 209
chiyo hetaru matsu ni wa aredo (Tsurayuki?): 61
e ni fukaku toshi furu matsu wa (Yorimoto): 201
e ni fukaku toshi wa henikeru (Tadahira): 201
fukakarishi chikai no mama no (Sanetaka): 112
furihatete shirarenu tani no (Shunzei's Daughter): 86
hana sakanu mi zo taguinaki (Roan): 230

Index

Poets in the list of Japanese poems cited are not listed in this index unless they and/or their works are discussed at some length in the text.